Finding the Truth in the Courtroom

Finding the Truth in the Courtroom

Dealing with Deception, Lies, and Memories

EDITED BY HENRY OTGAAR

AND

MARK L. HOWE

OXFORD
UNIVERSITY PRESS

Oxford University Press is a department of the University of Oxford. It furthers
the University's objective of excellence in research, scholarship, and education
by publishing worldwide. Oxford is a registered trade mark of Oxford University
Press in the UK and certain other countries.

Published in the United States of America by Oxford University Press
198 Madison Avenue, New York, NY 10016, United States of America.

Library of Congress Cataloging-in-Publication Data
Names: Otgaar, Henry, editor. | Howe, Mark L., editor.
Title: Finding the truth in the courtroom: dealing with deception, lies,
and memories / Edited by Henry Otgaar & Mark L. Howe.
Description: New York : Oxford University Press, 2018. | Includes index. |
Identifiers: LCCN 2017015391 (print) | LCCN 2017016862 (ebook) |
ISBN 9780190612023 (UPDF) | ISBN 9780190669119 (EPUB) |
ISBN 9780190612016 (hardcover : alk. paper)
Subjects: LCSH: Evidence, Circumstantial. | Admissible evidence. |
Forensic psychology. | Deception. | Memory.
Classification: LCC K5490 (ebook) | LCC K5490 .F56 2017 (print) |
DDC 347/.064—dc23
LC record available at https://lccn.loc.gov/2017015391

9 8 7 6 5 4 3 2 1

Printed by Sheridan Books, Inc., United States of America

CONTENTS

ABOUT THE EDITORS

Henry Otgaar works as Assistant Professor at the Forensic Psychology section, Faculty of Psychology and Neuroscience, Maastricht University. His research expertise revolves around issues such as the development of memory; false memory; the link among trauma, memory, and psychopathology; and memory in the legal area. He has published numerous peer-reviewed articles, book chapters, and books on memory (e.g., *What Is Adaptive About Adaptive Memory?*, OUP 2014). He has received many (inter)national awards for his research such as the Edmond Hustinx Science Award and the Early Career Excellence Award. He also works as an expert witness for *the Maastricht Forensic Institute* and is an associate editor for *Memory* and a co-editor for *In-Mind*.

Mark L. Howe holds a Chair in Cognitive Science at City, University of London. His over 35 years of research on memory has addressed questions concerning memory development, memory illusions, the adaptive functions of memory, links between reasoning and memory, memory in traumatized and maltreated children, as well as memory and the law. He has published numerous peer-reviewed articles, book chapters, and books on memory development (e.g., *The Nature of Early Memory*, OUP 2011) and memory and the law (e.g., *Memory and Miscarriages of Justice*, 2018). In addition to editing a variety of books (e.g., *Stress, Trauma, and Children's Memory Development*, OUP 2008; *What Is Adaptive About Adaptive Memory?*, OUP 2014), he is the Associate Editor of *Developmental Review* and an Editor-in-Chief for *Memory*.

CONTRIBUTORS

Samantha J. Andrews
Department of Psychology
University of Cambridge
Cambridge, England, UK

Shari R. Berkowitz
Criminal Justice Administration
California State University,
    Dominguez Hills
Carson, California, USA

Irena Bošković
Section Forensic Psychology
Faculty of Psychology and
    Neuroscience
Maastricht University
Maastricht, the Netherlands

Laure Brimbal
The Graduate Center
John Jay College of Criminal Justice
City University of New York
New York, New York, USA

Mitchell L. Eisen
Department of Psychology
California State University,
    Los Angeles
Los Angeles, California, USA

Fiona Gabbert
Department of Psychology
Goldsmiths University of London
London, England, UK

Deborah Goldfarb
Department of Psychology
University of California, Davis
Davis, California, USA

Alejandra Gonzalez
Department of Psychology
University of California, Davis
Davis, California, USA

Gail S. Goodman
Department of Psychology
University of California, Davis
Davis, California, USA

Pär Anders Granhag
Department of Psychology
University of Gothenburg
Gothenburg, Sweden

Maria Hartwig
Department of Psychology
John Jay College of Criminal Justice
City University of New York
New York, New York, USA

Hayden M. Henderson
Department of Psychology
University of Cambridge
Cambridge, England, UK

Lorraine Hope
Department of Psychology
University of Portsmouth
Portsmouth, England, UK

Mark L. Howe
Section Forensic Psychology
Faculty of Psychology and
    Neuroscience
Maastricht University
Maastricht, the Netherlands;
Department of Psychology
City, University of London
London, England, UK

Marko Jelicic
Section Forensic Psychology
Faculty of Psychology and
    Neuroscience
Maastricht University
Maastricht, the Netherlands

Rakel P. Larson
Psychology Field Group
Pitzer College
Claremont, California, USA

Elizabeth F. Loftus
Department of Psychology and Social
    Behavior
Department of Criminology, Law, and
    Society
University of California, Irvine
Irvine, California, USA

Timothy J. Luke
Department of Psychology
John Jay College of Criminal Justice
City University of New York
New York, New York, USA

Ewout H. Meijer
Section Forensic Psychology
Faculty of Psychology and
    Neuroscience
Maastricht University
Maastricht, the Netherlands

Harald Merckelbach
Section Forensic Psychology
Faculty of Psychology and
    Neuroscience
Maastricht University
Maastricht, the Netherlands

Thomas Merten
Vivantes Netzwerk für Gesundheit
Klinikum im Friedrichshain
Department of Neurology
Berlin, Germany

Henry Otgaar
Section Forensic Psychology
Faculty of Psychology and
    Neuroscience
Maastricht University
Maastricht, the Netherlands;
Department of Psychology
City, University of London
London, England, UK

Vincent van de Ven
Faculty of Psychology and
    Neuroscience
Maastricht University
Maastricht, the Netherlands

Bruno Verschuere
Faculty of Social and Behavioural
    Sciences
Clinical Psychology
University of Amsterdam
Amsterdam, the Netherlands

Aldert Vrij
Psychology Department
University of Portsmouth
Portsmouth, England, UK

Finding the Truth in the Courtroom

1

Deception and Memory in the Courtroom

An Overview

HENRY OTGAAR AND MARK L. HOWE

Rudolf Hess has been regarded as one of the most controversial Nazi politicians during the Second World War. When Rudolf Hess had to appear in court during the Nuremberg trials that started in 1945, he almost immediately claimed to suffer from amnesia. When he was allowed to provide a statement in front of this special court, he declared that he *feigned* his memory loss. Bill Cosby has been considered as one of the most influential African American comedians. At this moment, he is facing multiple charges of sexual abuse. Specifically, more than 20 women claim to have *remembered* being abused by Bill Cosby.

What these cases tell us is that memory-based testimonies are in the foreground of many criminal trials. The point here is that considerable weight is being given to testimonies by legal professionals such as police, lawyers, and judges. This dependence on memory-based testimony is heightened when there exists little or no forensic technical evidence to back up claims from witnesses or suspects. Why this can be problematic is because witnesses, victims, and guilty suspects might use deceptive strategies to withhold the truth. Furthermore, when witnesses, victims, and suspects have to retrieve what ostensibly occurred during an event, their recollections are reconstructions of the event and during such reconstructive processes, memory errors might slip into the memory narrative, errors that even the persons themselves are unaware of. Although scholars have discussed at great length research on deception detection (e.g., Vrij, 2008) or the frailties of memory (e.g., Loftus, 2005), to date, there is no work that has linked these two concepts—deception and memory—together. The absence of such a link is peculiar because the acts of lying and remembering happen frequently in the legal arena, even within the same legal case. Hence, what is critically important is to have a clear idea about recent work on the combination of deception and memory and the relevance of this work for the courtroom. This book will do just that and will showcase the latest work on diverse areas in deception detection (e.g., psychophysiology of deception detection, (non)verbal indicators of deception) and the latest work on the fallibility of memory (e.g., false memory, suggestibility). This introductory chapter provides a brief synopsis of the different chapters that this book contains. Following this, it takes this one step further by discussing how deception might impact memory. Finally, this chapter explains why expert testimony on issues such as deception and memory are especially relevant in recent legal cases. It stresses the relevance of this expert testimony by showing that incorrect ideas about deception and memory are particularly prevalent in the courtroom.

MEMORY IN THE COURTROOM

The importance of memory in court becomes immediately apparent when looking at the statistics of wrongful convictions and which factors contributed to these miscarriages of justice. For example, the Innocence Project in the United States has documented that approximately 29% of 347 wrongful convictions were based on memory aberrations such as false memories (Innocence Project, 2016). Recent statistics from the Netherlands suggest that up to 15% of convictions might be wrongful ones and that in this percentage, false memories such as erroneous eyewitness statements have played a major contributing role (Derksen, 2016). These statistics evidently show that memory errors can permeate testimonies, leading to disastrous consequences such as wrongful convictions. It is therefore imperative to have a sound understanding of the functioning of memory and its relevance in court.

In chapter 2, Berkowitz and Loftus provide an overview of the contaminating effect that misinformation can have in legal cases. They describe cases in which they were involved showing the perils of misinformation on the functioning of memory. In their chapter they clearly show how relatively easy it is for misinformation to foster the creation of false memories. They illustrate this with both empirical work and case examples. A related issue is the concept of suggestibility, which is discussed in great detail in chapter 3 by Gabbert and Hope. They show how memory can be distorted in the investigative and legal process and discuss several factors that can effect memory distortion, including levels of stress and degree of intoxication.

An especially pertinent question relates to whether children's or adults' memory is more likely to be distorted. Chapter 4 focuses on this issue, and Otgaar and Howe note that the common assumption is that children's memory is more likely to be distorted than adults'. In their chapter, they show that this assumption is not just wrong, but that also it does not square with recent theoretical advances concerning the development of false memories. Otgaar and Howe argue first that children can provide highly accurate accounts of events even if they are highly traumatic events, and second, that in certain situations adults, not children, are more likely to produce false memories even when those memories are generated through external, suggestive pressure.

A theme that is increasingly attracting empirical and media attention is the neurobiological basis of false memories. In particular, in this line of research, a recurring issue is whether the neuroscience of false memories might be an interesting avenue for determining the veracity of memory-based testimony in legal cases. In chapter 5, van de Ven, Otgaar, and Howe describe which neurobiological correlates underlie false memories and whether these correlates might be helpful for legal cases concerning the reliability of testimony.

In chapters 6 and 7, the book changes focus and looks at a specific population, children, that requires special attention when involved in legal cases. In chapter 6, Henderson and Andrews concentrate on empirically validated ways to interview children. Next, chapter 7 focuses on three factors that are especially relevant when children have to testify in legal cases. Specifically, Goldfarb, Goodman, Larson, Gonzales, and Eisen discuss that in each case involving child witnesses, it is important to analyze the person, the topic, and context, particularly when those cases involve children recounting experiences of sexual abuse.

LYING AND MALINGERING IN THE COURTROOM

Besides the focus on memory in this book, attention is also devoted to the impact of deception in the legal arena. When talking about deception in the legal arena, one can refer to a number of different and diverse aspects of deception. The current book follows the definition by Vrij (2008, p. 15), who stated that deception is "a successful or unsuccessful attempt, without forewarning, to create in another a belief that the communicator considers untrue." Following this broad definition, in this book several aspects of deception are presented. For example, one often assumes that deception plays a key role when, for example, perpetrators intentionally fabricate a statement. However, symptoms of illnesses are sometimes exaggerated or completely fabricated in order to reduce the likelihood of imprisonment, an act of lying also referred to as *malingering*. Furthermore, some victims of sexual abuse falsely deny having been victimized because they might feel ashamed or because they are forced to do so. This book looks at deception from these several different positions.

It does this starting with chapter 8, in which Vrij discusses the latest work on nonverbal detection of deception. Vrij stresses that although it is assumed that lying is accompanied by certain nonverbal behaviors, systematic research has demonstrated that nonverbal cues to deceit are unreliable. He makes the argument that the analysis of speech content is more promising to detect deception and describes several new interview protocols that can be used in this regard.

In chapter 9, Luke, Hartwig, Brimbal, and Granhag discuss which interviewing protocols have recently been devised to improve deception detection. Specifically, they focus on a questioning technique called the Strategic Use of Evidence that refers to a framework to interview suspects. This technique is centered on a theoretical rationale of how suspects handle the challenge of being interviewed. This technique concentrates on affecting the strategies that innocent and guilty suspects use during an interview; when such strategies are influenced, this can improve the detection of deceit in guilty suspects.

In chapter 10, Meijer and Verschuere discuss how deception can be detected by using psychophysiology. They describe the limitations of the often used poly-graph as a tool to detect deception and introduce a more promising technique, the Concealed Information Test. Unlike the polygraph, the Concealed Information Test detects deception by tapping into memory processes. They make the case that this test can be used to detect memory or knowledge concerning the crime that had been committed.

In chapter 11, Jelicic, Merckelbach, and Bošković introduce a special form of deception and discuss the concept of malingering. Specifically, they describe which myths people have concerning feigning, including the erroneous idea that feigning can be detected via a clinical interview, the incorrect assumption that feigning is rare, or the flawed notion that feigners are ill. By referring to actual cases and empirical work, they argue that in forensic mental evaluations, symp-tom validity tests should be standard practice. Chapter 12 deals with diverse ways to detect false symptom claims by using various symptom validity tests. Merten discusses several symptom validity tests that have the potential to be used in legal settings and illustrates these with several case vignettes.

THE IMPACT OF DECEPTION ON MEMORY

The current book contains chapters dealing with the relevance of memory and deception in legal proceedings. By focusing on these themes separately, their combined effects remain unexplored. That is, in many cases, when perpetrators or victims lie about what ostensibly occurred, they later do come forward with the truth. A well-known example is the case of Ted Bundy. The notorious serial killer, Ted Bundy, who was charged and convicted with kidnappings, rapes, and murders in the United States during the 1970s initially denied any involvement in these offenses throughout his trials, ones that lasted over a decade. But, before his execution in the late 1980s, Bundy decided to confess to several of the murders he was convicted of (see Carlisle, 2014 for an overview). A relevant issue here is how Bundy's denials for those many years affected his memory for the actual details of the crimes. The more general question here is how deception affects memory. By asking this question, the two subthemes—deception and memory—become more interrelated.

A recent review showed that memory is affected in different ways by decep-tion, depending on the type of lie that is being told (Otgaar & Baker, in press). That is, there are different types of deception, including, for example, lies that do not require many cognitive resources, such as a false denial (e.g., I was not abused). Another example of such a rather simple form of deception is feigning amnesia (e.g., I cannot remember that I did that). These forms of deception are so simple because they do not need much cognitive effort to execute them. However, there are also other forms of deception that draw on more cognitive capacity. For example, perpetrators sometimes come up with a fabricated account of what allegedly happened. Interestingly, research suggests that memory is differentially influenced by these different forms of lying.

To see how these different forms of lying influence memory differently, first consider the research on false denials. This work suggests that false denials lead to forgetting effects. For example, Otgaar, Howe, Memon, and Wang (2014) asked participants (children and adults) about their memory concerning presented and nonpresented details of a video they had watched earlier (e.g., "What did the man steal?"). Next, a subgroup of participants had to (falsely) deny having seen each detail in response to these questions (e.g., "The man did not steal anything"). After a 1-week interval, participants were presented with a source memory test in which they were questioned whether they had seen certain details in the video and whether they had talked about these details during the first session with the interviewer. False denials did not affect memory for the details of the video. Interestingly, however, false denials did impair memory for having talked about certain details in the first interview (i.e., participants later falsely denied having *discussed* a previously denied detail). The researchers coined this effect: *denial-induced forgetting* (DIF).

In two subsequent experiments (Otgaar, Howe, Smeets, & Wang, 2016), the DIF effect was further examined with pictures rather than video (Experiment 1) and with the addition of an *external* denial group (i.e., someone else indicating that the participant's memory is incorrect by denying the existence of a previously present detail; Experiments 1 & 2). In both experiments, the authors again found DIF: The false deniers showed impaired memory for having discussed details in the initial interview, while in fact these details were mentioned in that interview. Overall, this research on the mnemonic effects of false denials seems to imply that doing so leads to impaired memory by increasing forgetting. Such forgetting effects have also appeared in studies on feigning amnesia. These studies using crime-relevant stimuli have shown that feigning amnesia leads to impaired memory in the form of enhanced rates of omission errors at the follow-up interview [i.e., failure to report critical details (Christianson & Bylin, 1999; van Oorsouw & Merckelbach, 2004)].

In terms of fabrication, work on self-generated lies (i.e., forced confabulations) has revealed that such confabulations can lead to false memories. That is, the majority of studies investigating the effects of (self-generated) fabrications on memory have used what is commonly referred to as the *forced confabulation paradigm* (Ackil & Zaragoza, 1998, 2011; Frost, LaCroix, & Sanborn, 2003; Hanba & Zaragoza, 2007; Zaragoza, Payment, Ackil, Drivdahl, & Beck, 2001). In this paradigm, participants (children or adults) are presented with certain stimuli or are subjected to a particular event and, after an interval, are forced to falsely describe an object/event (including those that were absent during the exposure phase). Specifically, participants assigned to the forced confabulation group are instructed to provide answers to all posed questions (some answerable and others unanswerable) even if they do not know the exact answer (i.e., forced guess), whereas those assigned to other groups are either instructed not to guess (e.g., Otgaar et al., 2014) or only guess when they would like to (e.g., Gombos, Pezdek,

& Haymond, 2012). For example, in response to the question of where a child was bleeding after falling off a chair (when in reality there was no blood visible), participants in the forced confabulation group have to provide some detail such as (falsely) stating that the child was bleeding on his head (Ackil & Zaragoza, 2011). This act of forced confabulation is similar to many forensic contexts in which a rememberer is coerced to speculate how events occurred. In both circumstances, there is not necessarily any malicious intent on the rememberer's behalf. A typical finding that has emerged is that participants who are forced to confabulate a detail (e.g., state that they saw a cat in the picture, while in reality no cat was present) will state, after a delay, that they recollect seeing that particular detail. Based on these types of studies, deception and memory seem to be more linked than previously thought. Theoretically, these studies suggest that forms of deception that involve many cognitive resources will result in commission errors (i.e., false memories) whereas more simple forms of deception (e.g., false denial) that do not require much cognitive effort will lead to omission errors (i.e., forgetting).

WHY DO WE NEED THIS BOOK?

A legitimate question is why the current book might be helpful for professionals working in the legal arena (e.g., forensic psychologists, therapists, judges, lawyers, police). The authors' take on this matter is that at this moment in time, scientific knowledge on issues such as deception and memory is lacking in the courtroom. Because knowledge about these issues is so poor in the legal community, naïve and often erroneous ideas regarding deception and memory currently dominate the legal arena—ideas that might result in disastrous consequences such as miscarriages of justice (see Howe, Knott, & Conway, 2018). Hence, this book might serve to inform not only the general public, but more specifically, legal professionals who are dealing with cases in which deception and memory play a role. By doing so, the book can provide critical knowledge about the science behind deception and memory and has the potential to debunk many myths on these issues.

A particularly poignant example in the area of deception detection is the incorrect idea that we can detect lying by looking at a person's body language. This naïve belief has been perpetrated in the media and on television by shows such as *Lie to Me*. Here, one of the main characters is a so-called body language scientist who can purportedly tell whether someone is lying or telling the truth when looking at certain microexpressions. In chapter 8, Vrij discusses how unreliable such signs actually are. Another example is the flawed use of Voice Stress Analyzers or the Scientific Content Analysis (SCAN) used by many law enforcement agencies to show whether someone is deceptive or not (see Bogaard, Meijer, Vrij, & Merckelbach, 2016 for a critical note on SCAN).[1] This issue relates to the limitations of the polygraph, which are discussed in chapter 10.

Other worrisome ideas are even expressed by politicians. President Donald Trump has repeatedly said that interrogation tactics such as torture might actually work in eliciting reliable information from suspects.[2] The contrary is true.

Indeed, the use of such tactics might actually increase the likelihood for the creation of false confessions. This is why experts were asked to write a chapter in which the use of proper interview protocols that have received empirical validation are reviewed, ones that have the potential to elicit reliable information (i.e., chapter 9).

Finally, in the area of memory, we also encounter several incorrect ideas about the functioning of memory. One is the pervasive myth of repression or the idea that entire traumatic memories can be blocked out of consciousness. Although scientific evidence for this idea is absent, the idea is still embraced among many psychologists (e.g., Patihis, Ho, Tingen, Lilienfeld, & Loftus, 2014). Furthermore, scholars have even recently suggested that the possibility to implant false memories is far more difficult than memory researchers have always argued (Brewin & Andrews, 2017). However, recent commentaries and even a review paper have criticized such a view and have demonstrated that about 30% of participants are susceptible to suggestive pressure and producing false memories, a percentage that can be considered alarmingly high in legal settings (see Scoboria, Wade, Lindsay, Azad, Strange, Ost, & Hyman, 2017).

As the authors have said, it is problematic that such flawed ideas about deception and memory are still common among the general public, some scientists, and those involved in the judiciary. Such flawed ideas can be particularly harmful when they pop up in legal cases and can lead to wrongful convictions. One way to remedy such flawed ideas is to provide legal professionals with up-to-date information concerning the science underlying deception and memory and to show the importance of this scientific work in the courtroom. The aim of this book is to provide such information and to inform the general public, clinical, and legal communities about what the up-to-date scientific work can tell us about the relevance of deception and memory in the courtroom.

NOTES

1. See for example: https://www.nij.gov/journals/259/pages/voice-stress-analysis.aspx
2. See for example: http://www.factcheck.org/2016/07/trump-torture/

REFERENCES

Ackil, J. K., & Zaragoza, M. S. (1998). Memorial consequences of forced confabulation: Age differences in susceptibility to false memories. *Developmental Psychology, 34*, 1358–1372. doi: 10.1037/0012-1649.34.6.1358

Ackil, J. K., & Zaragoza, M. S. (2011). Forced fabrication versus interviewer suggestions: Differences in false memory depend on how memory is assessed. *Applied Cognitive Psychology, 25*, 933–942. doi:10.1002/acp.1785

Bogaard, G., Meijer, E. H., Vrij, A., & Merckelbach, H. (2016). Scientific Content Analysis (SCAN) cannot distinguish between truthful and fabricated statements of a negative event. *Frontiers in Psychology, 7*, 243.

Brewin, C. R., & Andrews, B. (2017). Creating memories for false autobiographical events in childhood: A systematic review. *Applied Cognitive Psychology*, *31*(1), 2–23.

Carlisle, A. (2014). *I'm not guilty: The case of Ted Bundy*. Genius Books Publishing: Encino, CA.

Christianson. S. A., & Bylin, S. (1999). Does simulating amnesia mediate genuine forgetting for a crime event? *Applied Cognitive Psychology*, *13*, 495–511. doi: 10.1002/(SICI)1099-0720(199912)13:6<495: AID-ACP615>3.0.CO;2-0

Derksen, T. (2016). *Onschuldig Vast*. ISVW Uitgevers.

Frost, P., LaCroix, D., & Sanborn, N. (2003). Increasing false recognition rates with confirmatory feedback: A phenomenological analysis. *The American Journal of Psychology*, *116*, 515–525. doi: 10.2307/1423658.

Gombos, V., Pezdek, K., & Haymond, K. (2012). Forced confabulation affects memory sensitivity as well as response bias. *Memory and Cognition*, *40*, 127–134. doi: 10.3758/s13421-011-0129-5

Hanba, J. M., & Zaragoza, M. S. (2007). Interviewer feedback in repeated interviews involving forced confabulation. *Applied Cognitive Psychology*, *21*, 433–455. doi: 10.1002/acp.1286

Howe, M. L., Knott, L. M., & Conway, M. A. (2018). *Memory and miscarriages of justice*. Abingdon, UK: Routledge.

Innocence Project. (2016). DNA Exonerations in the United States. Retrieved from http://www.innocenceproject.org/dna-exonerations-in-the-united-states/

Loftus, E. F. (2005). Planting misinformation in the human mind: A 30-year investigation of the malleability of memory. *Learning & Memory*, *12*, 361–366.

Otgaar, H., & Baker, A. (in press). When lying changes memory for the truth. Memory.

Otgaar, H., Howe, M. L., Memon, A., & Wang, J. (2014). The development of differential mnemonic of false denials and forced confabulations. *Behavioral Sciences & Law*, *32*, 718–731. doi: 10.1002/bsl.2148

Otgaar, H., Howe, M. L., Smeets, T., & Wang, J. (2016). Denial-induced forgetting: False denials undermine memory, but external denials undermine belief. *Journal of Applied Research in Memory and Cognition*, *5*, 168–175. doi: 10.1016/j.jarmac.2016.04.002

Patihis, L., Ho, L. Y., Tingen, I. W., Lilienfeld, S. O., & Loftus, E. F. (2014). Are the "memory wars" over? A scientist-practitioner gap in beliefs about repressed memory. *Psychological Science*, *25*, 519–530.

Scoboria, A., Wade, K. A., Lindsay, D. S., Azad, T., Strange, D., Ost, J., & Hyman, I. E. (2017). A mega-analysis of memory reports from eight peer-reviewed false memory implantation studies. *Memory*, *25*, 146–163.

Van Oorsouw, K., & Merckelbach, H. (2004). Feigning amnesia undermines memory for a mock crime. *Applied Cognitive Psychology*, *18*, 505–518. doi: 10.1002/acp.999

Vrij, A. (2008). *Detecting lies and deceit: Pitfalls and opportunities*. Chicester, UK: John Wiley and Sons.

Zaragoza, M. S., Payment, K. E., Ackil, J. K., Drivdahl, S. B., & Beck, M. (2001). Interviewing witnesses: Forced confabulation and confirmatory feedback increases false memories. *Psychological Science*, *12*, 473–477. doi: 10.1111/1467-9280.00388

PART I

Memory in the Courtroom

2

Misinformation in the Courtroom

SHARI R. BERKOWITZ AND ELIZABETH F. LOFTUS

For decades, experts in memory have been testifying in court about the factors that affect the accuracy of eyewitness accounts, and both of us have had this opportunity a number of times. But recently we found ourselves in the unusual situation of consulting on the same case. Here's how that happened.

In the early nineties, a defendant, Tom,[1] was convicted of capital murder on the basis of an eyewitness's identification. Tom was sentenced to death. In his attempts to overturn his conviction, Tom sought to appeal, in part, on the grounds that his attorney was ineffective for failing to call an eyewitness-memory expert at the original trial. The defendant's postconviction attorney contacted one of us (SB) to evaluate the eyewitness memory factors that were present in Tom's case. Of particular interest was whether there were factors in the case that could have affected the eyewitness's memory and subsequent identification. SB reviewed the lengthy case file and wrote a report detailing the science of eyewitness memory research relevant to the case. A portion of SB's report highlighted certain factors that could have impaired the eyewitness's memory for the face of the perpetrator, including that the eyewitness's identification of Tom was cross-racial and that the eyewitness saw a weapon during the crime.

Tom's attorney was heartened to see that there were a number of problematic factors that could be responsible for a potential false eyewitness identification. The attorney realized, however, that a recent curious opinion by the United States Court of Appeals for the Fifth Circuit (5th Circuit) might make SB's report inadmissible. In *Day v. Quarterman* (2009), the 5th Circuit concluded that for a defendant to succeed in an ineffective assistance of counsel claim for not calling an expert witness (in this case an eyewitness-memory expert), the defendant must "name the [expert] witness, demonstrate that the [expert] witness was available to testify and would have done so" in a way favorable to the defendant (p. 538). A literal interpretation of that sentence might imply that the eyewitness-memory expert, SB, needed to be available to testify in the early 1990s—when she was 11 years old. Thus, to accommodate this potential hiccup, the attorney contacted the second author (EL) to provide a declaration in the case. EL fulfilled the attorney's request—after all, by the early 1990s, she had been testifying as an eyewitness memory expert for more than 20 years.

As expert witnesses in eyewitness memory, memory distortion, and false memory, we regularly receive phone calls and emails from attorneys, and families of the accused seeking our assistance. Many of these calls are in regard to what we might call a classic eyewitness memory case—an eyewitness has identified a stranger (the defendant) as a rapist, a robber, or a murderer. In such a case, we are tasked with assessing the myriad factors that could have affected the eyewitness's memory and subsequent identification of the defendant. For instance, conditions related to the eyewitness's opportunity to view the crime or the perpetrator could affect his/her ability to perceive and remember the details of the crime or the face of the perpetrator (for a review, see Loftus, 2010). In addition, certain lineup procedures may impair an eyewitness's memory and identification of the suspect (Wells & Olson, 2003). Although the specific eyewitness memory factors vary from case to case, one crucial factor that can distort and contaminate an eyewitness's memory is misinformation.[2] This chapter provides a review of the scientific research on misinformation and highlights the sources of misinformation that eyewitness-memory experts come across in criminal investigations and trials. The chapter concludes with recommendations for legal professionals who may encounter misinformation in the context of a legal case.

THE SCIENCE OF MISINFORMATION

In a legal case, misinformation consists of any faulty information that an eyewitness receives after the crime takes place. Whether this misinformation is about the color of the getaway car, the demands the robber made to the bank teller, or the identity of the perpetrator, misinformation can alter what an eyewitness remembers about the crime and/or the perpetrator. To understand the processes and implications of misinformation on eyewitness memory, researchers commonly run participants through the following paradigm: an eyewitness views a simulated crime, later the eyewitness is provided with misinformation about the crime (this may be through leading questions, photographs, etc.), and eventually the eyewitness is given a memory test. Coined the "misinformation effect," the results of such research routinely reveal that a substantial proportion of participants accept the misinformation and incorporate it into their memory (Frenda, Nichols, & Loftus, 2011; Zaragoza, Belli, & Payment, 2006).

In an early study, Loftus, Miller, and Burns (1978) demonstrated that misinformation could dramatically alter an eyewitness's memory. In one experiment, some of the participants watched a slide show in which a red Datsun approached a stop sign, turned right, and knocked down a pedestrian who was crossing at the crosswalk. Participants then answered several questions about their memory of the accident. Critically, some participants were asked if another car had passed the red Datsun while it was stopped at the *yield sign*. Twenty minutes later, participants were asked to identify which of two images they had seen in the slideshow at the beginning of the experiment—a red Datsun stopped at a stop sign (correct answer) or a red Datsun stopped at a yield sign (misinformation answer). After a single question containing a subtle piece of misinformation, 59% of participants accepted the misinformation into memory and indicated that the red Datsun was stopped at a different street sign. Later studies showed the power of misinformation with a variety of other materials. From seeing barns that never existed (Loftus, 1975) to seeing a thief take a ring from a victim when no jewelry was ever taken (Drivdahl & Zaragoza, 2001), misinformation studies consistently illustrate how easily memory for important details can be contaminated.

Over the past four decades, research on the misinformation effect demonstrates that a bit of misinformation can substantially alter what we remember. Building on this research, memory researchers have gone on to demonstrate the misinformation effect in various samples, including infants, young children, the elderly, and even gorillas, and pigeons (Harper & Garry, 2000; Poole & Lindsay, 2001; Rovee-Collier, Borza, Adler, & Boller, 1993; Schwartz, Meissner, Hoffman, Evans, & Frazier, 2004; Wylie et al., 2014).

More recently, researchers have tested the misinformation effect on a handful of people with an exceptional autobiographical memory, also known as *highly superior autobiographical memory* (HSAM) (Parker, Cahill, & McGaugh, 2006; Patihis et al., 2013). These HSAM individuals have served as a remarkable sample for memory researchers because HSAMs have been shown to correctly remember details from their past with 97% accuracy (LePort et al., 2012). But would the memories of these special participants be susceptible to misinformation? To answer this question, Patihis and colleagues (2013) ran HSAM participants through several false memory paradigms, including the misinformation paradigm. Surprisingly, HSAM participants were somewhat more likely statistically to adopt the misinformation into their memories than were control participants. These HSAM findings suggest that perhaps no one is immune from the dangers of the reconstructive nature of human memory.

Although all humans may be susceptible to misinformation, researchers have identified certain conditions under which people may be more likely to fall prey to misinformation effects. For instance, the passage of time increases the chance that eyewitnesses will adopt misinformation and that their memories will be altered (see Loftus, 2005 for a review). Two specific periods of time are particularly likely to affect the eyewitness's ability to detect misinformation and integrate it into their memory. One is the amount of time that takes place between when the eyewitness viewed the crime and when the misinformation is introduced to the eyewitness. The other is the amount of time between when the eyewitness receives the misinformation and participates in a memory recall task (e.g., a lineup or interview). Research demonstrates that the longer the period of time is between these events, the more likely that an eyewitness will adopt the misinformation.

Besides situational factors that might elevate the misinformation effect, there are also internal factors that can moderate this effect. An eyewitness's intelligence may affect the likelihood that they accept misinformation. While some misinformation studies have tested relatively intelligent samples (e.g., college students),

Zhu et al. (2010) found that even among a large sample of Chinese college students, misinformation is more likely to be accepted by those with low intelligence and poor perceptual abilities. Moreover, certain temporary psychological states may also increase the likelihood that eyewitnesses will be swayed by the misinformation. Individuals who are sleep deprived (Frenda, Patihis, Loftus, Lewis, & Fenn, 2014), individuals who merely think they are intoxicated (Assefi & Garry, 2003), and individuals who have been hypnotized (Scoboria, Mazzoni, Kirsch, & Milling, 2002) are even more vulnerable to the misinformation effect than rested, knowingly sober, or unhypnotized individuals.

What is more, the misinformation effect does not discriminate against the types of memory that it contaminates. In other words, even our memories for important or newsworthy events are not immune from distortion. Although emotional events are generally better remembered than neutral events (Levine & Pizarro, 2004), our memories for well-rehearsed and emotional events can be mistaken. For instance, research on "flashbulb memories" reveals that people sometimes hold onto their memories for very surprising, highly emotional and consequential events (e.g., memories of 9/11 or the JFK assassination) with a lot of confidence and detail (Brown & Kulik, 1977). Yet even such highly confident memories for emotional events can be inaccurate (Neisser & Harsch, 1992; Talarico & Rubin, 2003). Of relevance here, Levine and Bluck (2004) studied whether people could falsely remember events that never happened during one of the most infamous criminal trials in U.S. history—the O.J. Simpson murder case. Approximately 2 months after the verdict, participants were asked how they felt about the verdict and how clearly they remembered certain events having happened at the trial. Some of these events actually happened—"O.J. Simpson mouthed the words 'thank you' to the jury," and some of these events were plausible, but fictional—"Judge Ito told audience members they would have to leave if there were any further disruptions." On average, participants reported that they remembered the fictional events somewhat clearly. Interestingly, those participants who were happier about the verdict were more likely to misremember events that never happened at the criminal trial. Taken together, these results suggest that even powerful and distinctive events in the news—events we are sure we remember accurately—can be misremembered.

Misinformation can distort an eyewitness's memory for salient and emotional details, but it can also distort an eyewitness's memory for a person's face. In one study, researchers documented that misinformation provided during a highly stressful experience drastically altered eyewitnesses' memories for a critical person's identity (Morgan, Southwick, Steffian, Hazlett, & Loftus, 2013). The participants in this study were highly trained members of the U.S. military who attended Survival School training. While specific details about this training are classified, the training is designed to assist military personnel should they ever be captured as a prisoner of war (see Morgan et al., 2000 for more on Survival School). As such, the military participants attempted to evade the enemy over 4 days and were then captured and held for 3 days in a mock prisoner of war camp. During the first day of their confinement, military participants were interrogated individually for 30 highly stressful minutes. In the course of the highly stressful interrogation, military participants were instructed to keep eye contact with their interrogator while maintaining a height less than their interrogator (by bending their knees). If the military participants failed to maintain eye contact or a height less than the interrogator, or if the military participants refused to answer questions during the interrogation, the interrogator was permitted to "physically confront" the participants. This physical confrontation may have required the participants to sit or stand in a stress position, and also may have included slapping, punching, and slamming the participants into a wall. Given these severe interrogation tactics, it is possible that the level of stress and potential violence these military participants experienced may certainly be comparable to the experiences of actual crime victims.

Following the interrogation, while in isolation, some of the military participants were given misinformation in the form of a photograph that suggested their interrogator was Mr. X when in actuality the interrogator was Mr. Y (misinformation participants); some of the military participants did not receive this information (control participants). Upon release from the mock prisoner of war camp, all military participants were asked to identify their interrogator from a nine-person target-absent photo lineup—the actual interrogator was not present. Although the military participants were warned that the interrogator might not be in the lineup, 53% of control participants and 91% of misinformation participants falsely identified an innocent interrogator from the lineup; a difference that was statistically significant. What is particularly concerning, however, is that misinformation participants who had viewed a photo of Mr. X were far more likely than control participants (84% vs. 15%, respectively) to falsely identify Mr. X as their interrogator. These data have dangerous implications showing that misinformation in the form a photograph can strongly influence an eyewitness's memory of a perpetrator.

While misinformation in the form of a photograph can alter our memories for faces, and even the past (Frenda, Knowles, Saletan, & Loftus, 2013; Sacchi, Agnoli, & Loftus, 2007; Wade, Garry, Read, & Lindsay, 2002), new research illustrates that eyewitnesses can even be led to misremember the face they selected from a lineup. Cochran, Greenspan, Bogart, and Loftus (2016) showed participants a slideshow in which a man stole a radio from a car. Later, participants attempted to identify the thief from a six-person target-absent photo lineup. After a delay, participants were instructed that they would see the photograph of the man they had picked out earlier from the lineup. For some of these participants, however, the photograph was actually of a different man than they had originally selected—a misinformation photograph. Eventually, all participants were then instructed to make a selection from the same six-person target-absent photo lineup. Of those participants who failed to notice that they were given the misinformation photograph, over half of them switched their identification at the final lineup; the majority selected the misinformation photograph—a phenomenon the researchers coined "memory blindness." Thus, misinformation can be particularly powerful when we are blind to our memories being manipulated.

Although misinformation from an external source like an experimenter or co-witness can impair memory (Meade & Roediger, 2002; see Jack, Zydervelt, & Zajac, 2014 for an interesting discussion of whether it matters if the misinformation comes from an experimenter or cowitness), so, too, can misinformation from an internal source—the eyewitness. In a number of studies, researchers have examined what happens when eyewitnesses are forced to fabricate stories about what they had seen (Ackil & Zaragoza, 1998; Chrobak & Zaragoza, 2013; Pickel, 2004).

In one clever study, researchers assessed the "forced fabrication effect" on eyewitness memory (Chrobak & Zaragoza, 2008). Participants viewed a video in which two brothers had several adventures at a summer camp. In one of these adventures, the brothers sneaked away from the camp in the evening to use a canoe. The video then cut to the following morning where the camp director was seen scolding one of the brothers. Two days later, the participants were interviewed and forced to answer every question the interviewer asked, even if it meant making up answers. Some of the participants were forced to answer questions about where the brothers went that night, what they did, and whom they were with. Even though the participants had no knowledge of what happened that evening and insisted that they could not provide accurate answers, participants eventually fabricated stories that the brothers had stolen from the camp, visited the girls' camp, spied on the camp nurse, etc. A week later, participants completed a recognition test about what had happened in the video. Approximately 8 weeks later, participants were instructed to pretend they were eyewitnesses in the court of law and report everything they could possibly remember about the video. Alarmingly, after the 8-week delay, nearly half of the participants who were forced to fabricate about the canoe event adopted their fabrications into their memories. This result suggests that when an eyewitness (or suspect) is pressured to answer questions they do not know the answers to, their fabricated answers can in time become (false) memories.

Over the past three decades, researchers have found that misinformation can substantially alter memory as well as create false memories. With a rich false memory paradigm (a conceptual cousin of the misinformation paradigm), researchers have led participants to develop memories for wholly false events (Wade, Garry, Read, & Lindsay, 2002; for a review see Loftus, 2004). In other words, people can develop entire false beliefs and memories for events they never actually experienced. Misinformation about a childhood event that never happened has been introduced through various techniques in various combinations, including: repeated interviews (Loftus & Pickrell, 1995; Shaw & Porter, 2015), guided imagination (Goff & Roediger, 1998; Mazzoni & Memon, 2003), doctored photographs and videos (Nash & Wade, 2009), false advertisements (Braun, Ellis, & Loftus, 2002), false newspaper articles (Otgaar, Candel, Merckelbach, & Wade, 2009), and false feedback (Bernstein, Laney, Morris, & Loftus, 2005). Misinformation, coupled with suggestion, has led a substantial proportion of participants to falsely believe or remember that as children they had their ear licked inappropriately by the Pluto character at Disneyland (Berkowitz, Laney, Morris, Garry, & Loftus, 2008), they had nearly drowned and had to be rescued by a lifeguard (Heaps & Nash, 2001), and that they had witnessed their friend's demonic possession (Mazzoni, Loftus, & Kirsch, 2001). These rich false childhood beliefs and memories have been shown to influence participants' later thoughts, decisions, and behaviors (Bernstein & Loftus, 2009b). From altering a participant's willingness to pay for an item (e.g., a Pluto stuffed animal) to changing a participant's interest in ingesting a particular item (e.g., alcohol) (Clifasefi, Bernstein, Mantonakis, & Loftus, 2013), false beliefs and memories can have consequences.

Misinformation can also have disastrous consequences when it rears its head in legal cases. Innocent people have been accused of horrific crimes they never committed (Loftus & Ketcham, 1991), and have been wrongfully convicted on the basis of a sole eyewitness's identification (Garrett, 2011). Today, more than 350 innocent men and women have been exonerated by DNA evidence proving that they did not commit the crimes for which they were convicted (innocenceproject. org). These cases reveal that eyewitness error, which can occur as the result of misinformation, is one of the leading causes of wrongful conviction and has played a role in approximately 70% of the DNA exonerations (Garrett, 2011). It is important to note that these mistaken eyewitness memories and identifications are not necessarily the product of deceit or lies by the eyewitness. Instead, given the fallible nature of human memory and the potential for misinformation to seep into an investigation, it is likely that a number of these mistaken identification cases involve well-meaning eyewitnesses who came to genuinely believe that the person they identified was the actual perpetrator. While the consequences of memory errors can be devastating for those who are wrongfully convicted, these mistakes can also profoundly affect the eyewitnesses who made the false identifications (Thompson-Cannino, Cotton, & Torneo, 2009).

One of the more frightening effects of misinformation, however, is that in addition to altering eyewitness memory, it can also corrupt other evidence. Imagine what would happen if an eyewitness identifies Person A from a lineup, but later learns that Person C confessed to the crime. How would this information, particularly if the information is erroneous, affect the eyewitness's memory and identification? The answer is important for the pursuit of justice because this misinformation about Person C's confession can actually alter an eyewitness's memory (Hasel & Kassin, 2009). In one study, participants saw a thief steal a laptop from a laboratory. Participants then attempted to identify the thief from a six-person target-absent photo-lineup. Two days later, the participants returned to the lab to help with the investigation, and some of them were given misinformation. They were told that a different lineup member confessed to the theft and they read the thief's handwritten confession. Participants then had the chance to change their selection from the lineup. Startlingly, 61% of the participants who received misinformation that a different lineup member confessed switched their identification to the confessor. Moreover, these participants went on to describe why it was that the confessor better matched their memory of the thief. Therefore, when evidence is not kept independent from eyewitnesses, other evidence (potentially misinformation) can further contaminate their memories.

Perhaps if we could distinguish true memories from false memories we could be less worried about the rampant effects of misinformation on eyewitness memory, but as other authors of this book have noted, we are remarkably poor at detecting both deliberate deception as well as unintentional deception caused by memory illusions. Furthermore, there is reason to believe that eyewitnesses' modified memories have become their genuine memories rather than an outright fabrication (see Loftus, 2005 for a review). Thus, although we have learned a great deal about the reconstructive nature of human memory, there is currently no way to determine, without independent corroboration, whether a memory is true or false (Bernstein & Loftus, 2009a). In fact, false memories look and feel a lot like true memories—they can be described with confidence, emotion, and in detail (Laney & Loftus, 2008). Moreover, brain-imaging studies suggest that brain activation for true memories and false memories is remarkably similar (Stark, Okado, & Loftus, 2010). Therefore, eyewitness-memory experts cannot and should not draw conclusions about whether the eyewitness's memories in a particular case are correct or incorrect. Instead, the role of eyewitness-memory experts is to explain to the court how it is that certain factors, like misinformation, may influence an eyewitness's memory.

UNCOVERING MISINFORMATION IN THE COURTROOM

We now turn our attention to how eyewitness-memory experts are tasked with uncovering misinformation that can trickle into an investigation and impact what happens in the courtroom. As eyewitness-memory experts, attorneys sometimes retain us to assess the factors present in a case that can influence an eyewitness's memory and identification. Certain eyewitness memory factors are relatively easy to identify in a criminal case. For example, a police report typically notes if a victim saw a knife during a crime. With this information, eyewitness-memory experts are quickly clued to the potential for "weapon focus," which impairs an eyewitness's memory for the face of the perpetrator (Hope & Wright, 2007; Steblay, 1992). Likewise, a police report typically notes the ethnicity of both the eyewitness and the perpetrator. If the eyewitness is a different race than the perpetrator, this constitutes a cross-racial identification. Studies have consistently demonstrated that there is a cross-race identification problem such that people are better at identifying strangers' faces of the same race than strangers' faces of a different race (Meissner & Brigham, 2001). But in our experiences it is unlikely that misinformation an eyewitness receives is as easily identifiable in a police report as weapon focus or cross-race identification. After all, in criminal and civil cases, a police officer may fail to document the misinformation that was provided to an eyewitness. This may occur for a multitude of reasons including because an eyewitness may never know that he or she was even exposed to it, and because a police officer may be unaware that he or she disclosed any misinformation to the eyewitness. Therefore, the task of the eyewitness-memory expert may include uncovering the sources of misinformation that an eyewitness may have been exposed to during the course of an investigation and trial.

Fortunately, the scientific research on misinformation provides eyewitness-memory experts with many clues as to when the misinformation may have been introduced to an eyewitness. For example, eyewitness-memory researchers have identified three stages of eyewitness memory (Loftus, 1996). The first, *the acquisition stage*, accounts for when the crime or event is taking place. At this point, the eyewitness may encode bits and pieces of the event into memory. The second, *the retention stage*, refers to the period of time that passes between the crime or event and the eventual recollection of the memory. Depending on the crime or event, the retention interval could last hours, days, weeks, etc. The third and final stage, *the retrieval stage*, occurs when an eyewitness tries to recall information about the crime or event from their memory. Much of the misinformation an eyewitness receives may enter during the retention stage (Loftus, 2005) or even the retrieval stage (Cochran, Greenspan, Bogart, & Loftus, 2016).

Furthermore, through research and our personal experiences as expert witnesses on eyewitness memory (see Loftus, 2013; Loftus & Ketcham, 1991), we have come across several examples of misinformation that have been present in actual legal cases. To best illustrate how to search for misinformation in a case, the following text highlights specific sources of misinformation that have transpired in three cases for which we have consulted or testified. While these examples are not meant to be exhaustive, they do reflect some of the various forms of misinformation that can enter the courtroom.

Misinformation in the Form of Social Media

One afternoon, Carol heard gunshots fired into her neighbor's home.[3] Fortunately, no one was injured. After the shooting, Carol called 911. She explained that she did not know who the perpetrators were, but that they were two black males. Carol described the shooter as a light skinned black male, approximately 5'10", and the other perpetrator a dark-skinned black male, maybe 5'11". Following the shooting, Carol conducted her own investigation into the identities of the perpetrators by inquiring about the shooting with her neighborhood security personnel. One local security guard gave Carol the nickname of a possible suspect, "Corky." From there, Carol found Corky's real name, "Cornell Allen," and searched his Facebook and Instagram accounts. When she saw Cornell's photos, she claimed to have immediately recognized him as the shooter. At 5'5", however, Cornell was far shorter than Carol's description of the suspects and even Carol herself. A couple of weeks later, Carol visited the police department with dozens of photos of Cornell that she had printed off from his social media accounts. Instead of any formal identification procedure, the detective then showed Carol the same photos of Cornell that she had just given to him. She confirmed that she was 100% sure that Cornell was the shooter. A few months later, Carol participated in three photo lineups. The first of these two photo lineups pertained to Cornell. Carol was first shown a target-absent photo lineup, in which Cornell was absent. Nonetheless, Carol incorrectly identified one of the fillers as Cornell and indicated that she was certain it was him. A few hours later, Carol viewed a target-present photo lineup, and this time identified Cornell, again indicating that she was 100% sure. With nothing more than Carol's identification, Cornell was arrested. Although Cornell insisted that he was innocent and provided the full name of the person he had heard was the shooter—James Smith—Cornell was put on trial for multiple charges related to weapons violations and felonious assault.

Jack Greene, Cornell's public defender, hired SB to explain to the court the potential effects that the postevent information and possible misinformation could have had on Carol's identification (e.g., obtaining Cornell's name from the security guard, viewing Cornell's social media photos, etc.). SB testified to the court about the reconstructive nature of eyewitness memory as well as the scientific literature about the effects of misinformation on memory. In particular, drawing on some of the research mentioned earlier, SB explained to the court how the photographs Carol viewed could have altered her original memory for the shooter. Furthermore, and perhaps most important, Jack showed the court the photo of Cornell and the photo of the presumed shooter, James Smith. The two individuals bore a striking resemblance to each other. Ultimately, Cornell was found not guilty.

Misinformation in the Form of a Dream

In 2001, Kent Heitholt, left his office at a Missouri newspaper in the early morning hours and was brutally killed. For the next 2 years, the crime went unsolved. A newspaper article came out detailing what was known about the crime and the fact that the murderer remained free. A man named Charles Erickson read this article. Realizing that he had no memories for the night of the murder (he was intoxicated and may have blacked out), Charles began to wonder what he and his friend Ryan Ferguson had done the evening of the murder. A couple months later, Charles reported that he now had dreamlike memories of his and Ryan's involvement in the murder. Ryan tried to convince Charles that they had nothing to do with the murder; they were together the night of the murder, he agreed, but they had merely gotten drinks at a bar—that was it. By the time the Columbia police interrogated Charles, Charles struggled to provide details that the murderer would know. Yet to "assist" Charles in remembering more accurate details of the crime, the police took Charles to the scene of the crime to "refresh his memory" and fed him information in the interrogation about how Heitholt was strangled with his belt. Ultimately, Charles confessed and implicated Ryan in the murder. Although Ryan insisted he was innocent, Ryan was put on trial for murder. Along with some shaky eyewitness evidence putting Ryan at the scene of the crime (the eyewitness later recanted his testimony), Charles testified at Ryan's trial in detail about their involvement in the murder.

EL was hired by Ryan's attorney(s) to explain to the court the potential effects that misinformation and suggestion can have on eyewitness memory. In this case, there were many—media coverage about the crime, information supplied during interrogations, etc. EL further testified to the dangers of leading questions and contamination on memory (as in the interrogation Charles endured), and the science of rich false memories. Yet with no physical evidence connecting Ryan to the murder, Ryan was convicted of second-degree murder and sentenced to 40 years in prison. Charles, who pled guilty, was sentenced to 25 years in prison.

It was not until 2013 that the Missouri Court of Appeals vacated Ryan's conviction. After being locked up for nearly 10 years for a crime he did not commit, Ryan is now free and has published a book about his success at maintaining a healthy body while in prison (Ferguson, 2015). Ryan was also successful in a civil rights lawsuit. He was recently awarded $11 million; $1 million for each year he was in prison, and an additional $1 million to cover his legal fees (Keller, 2017).

Misinformation in the Form of Therapy

One day, a young man named Chris began to suspect that his older family friend, John, had sexually abused him as a child even though Chris had no memories of the abuse.[4] Chris explained that his suspicions arose from "weird" dreams and "flashes" in which he could see himself as a child with John. Chris went to see a therapist about these dreams, and over time, recovered memories that John had sexually abused him 20 years earlier. Based on Chris's newly discovered memories, John was arrested and faced trial for various charges connected to assault, and endangering and corrupting a minor.

John's attorney contacted SB to learn more about the scientific basis for recovered memories (for a review, see Berkowitz & Loftus, 2013). Upon her review of the case documents, SB explained to the attorney that she needed more information about the specific therapeutic process that Chris underwent to examine if the therapist used suggestive techniques that could have influenced Chris's apparent memories. To assess the potential for misinformation in this case it would have been helpful to have the following: the name, therapeutic orientation, CV, and educational background of the therapist; the publications the therapist authored; the conferences the therapist attended; the professional associations the therapist belonged to; the therapeutic techniques the therapist used with Chris; readings, books, or homework the therapist gave to Chris; and information about Chris's dreams and flashes (e.g., who he spoke to, what preceded these experiences, etc.). John's attorney submitted a discovery request for this information. After the court advised that it was inclined to order the State to obtain the information that SB requested, the State withdrew its charges against John.

Although these three cases provide just a glimpse into the role of eyewitness-memory experts in the courtroom, they do demonstrate the various sources by which eyewitnesses can be exposed to misinformation during the course of an investigation. In actual cases, misinformation may come from one or several sources, including attorneys, cowitnesses, family, friends, hypnotists, investigators, news media, photographs, police officers, social media, teachers, therapists, etc. In fact, misinformation need not be verbal. A creative set of experiments by Gurney, Pine, and Wiseman (2013) found that officers who provided misleading gestures (e.g., pointed to a wrist to imply a victim was wearing a watch instead of a ring) altered what eyewitnesses remembered from an earlier video. These nonverbal suggestions can also come in the form of a misleading confirmation of an eyewitness's identification. We have heard of cases in which eyewitnesses have received high-fives, pats on the back, and thumbs up from officers after making identifications. In one recent case that SB consulted on, the local police department honored two eyewitnesses for being outstanding citizens, thanking them for their ability to identify the defendant, and in turn, keep the streets safe. Notably, this recognition took place prior to the defendant's trial, and obviously could have long-term effects on the eyewitnesses' confidence. Post-identification feedback, such as the examples described above, inflates eyewitnesses' confidence in their identification, and also increases their confidence in how good their view was, how much attention they paid to the crime, their willingness to testify, etc. (Wells & Bradfield, 1998). Taken together, our experiences reveal that even if it is accidental, misinformation can easily be introduced into the courtroom.

Given the potential for misinformation to contaminate an eyewitness's memory (and potentially other evidence), it is crucial that legal professionals understand the all-too-human malleable nature of memory. Put simply, the courts must consider memory's reconstructive nature when weighing the effects of misinformation on memory, and in turn, the probative value of the eyewitness's testimony. As research has amply demonstrated over several decades by now, memory does not work like a DVR player. Contrary to what lay people may believe, the act of remembering a traumatic event (e.g., a crime) is not like a video recording (Loftus, 1996): Specific details, even for traumatic events, are not imprinted or burned into an eyewitness's brain. Instead, the human memory system is far more complex; memory is reconstructive and easily blends the actual, the imagined, and the suggested. That is why misinformation may permanently alter the eyewitness's original memory (see Zaragoza et al., 2006 for a review of the theoretical framework of misinformation).

One consequence of the widespread nature of misinformation is that once it is introduced into the court, it is hard to contain it. Like a virus, misinformation in the courtroom can be contagious and in some cases, life-threatening. Attorneys do have opportunities, however, to introduce the science of misinformation into the courtroom. For example, attorneys can consult with eyewitness-memory experts and attempt to introduce their testimony; some states are warming up to the idea of admitting eyewitness-memory experts (*Commonwealth of Pennsylvania v. Walker*, 2014; Utah *v. Clopten*, 2009). In January 2016, the Illinois Supreme Court reversed a defendant's conviction on the grounds that a trial court abused its discretion when excluding the defendant's request for an eyewitness-memory expert (*People of Illinois v. Lerma*, 2016). But not all states allow expert witnesses to testify to the science of eyewitness memory (*State of Louisiana v. Young*, 2010). Common reasons to preclude such experts from testifying at trial include that the expert invades the province of the jury, or that the science is already common sense to the jury. The latter notion is particularly disturbing given that 35 years of research has found that members of the legal community generally misunderstand several of the factors that can influence an eyewitness's identification (Benton, Ross, Bradshaw, Thomas, & Bradshaw, 2006; Deffenbacher & Loftus,

1982; Simons & Chabris, 2011; Wise, Pawlenko, Safer, & Meyer, 2009; Wise & Safer, 2010; Wise, Safer, & Maro, 2011).

If attorneys are prevented from introducing eyewitness-memory expert testimony, attorneys can pursue other strategies to introduce the science of misinformation in the courtroom. Prior to a trial, a defense attorney should file a motion to suppress the eyewitness's identification. Regardless of the success of this motion, the attorney may be able to glean whether the eyewitness in the case was exposed to misinformation. A suppression hearing may be one of the only opportunities for the attorney to learn about the potential misinformation in the case prior to trial. Before the trial begins, an attorney may also be able to examine what potential jurors know and understand about the science of eyewitness memory through strategic questions during jury selection. For example, during voir dire, an attorney may be permitted to assess potential jurors' experiences with misinformation and their understanding of memory. Next, the attorney may be able to educate the jury during opening statements. Whether it is through an informative statistic or a relatable analogy, the jury may be exposed to the science of misinformation. While the trial is underway, attorneys can cross-examine eyewitnesses in an effort to reveal any inconsistent statements, or highlight the eyewitnesses own memory mistakes. In closing arguments, an attorney may argue that the eyewitnesses are reliable/unreliable despite or as a result of the misinformation the eyewitnesses received throughout the investigation. Finally, an attorney may request that a jury instruction be given to the jury to educate them about the detailed intricacies of the science of eyewitness memory and misinformation.

Initial research, however, suggests that even recent efforts by some states to improve jury instructions (e.g., *State of New Jersey v. Henderson*, 2011) may fail to properly teach jurors how to discriminate the quality of the eyewitness's testimony (Papailiou, Yokum, & Robertson, 2015). Furthermore, to ensure that attorneys can best understand and represent the science of misinformation in the courtroom, research suggests that members of the legal profession may need a review course on the intricacies of eyewitness memory (Wise, Sartori, Magnussen, & Safer, 2014).

Yet despite the existence of these legal safeguards, it is clear that they are not failsafe. Although we have no data on how often such safeguards prevent wrongful convictions, we have some data on how often these safeguards failed to prevent known cases of wrongful conviction. University of Virginia law professor Brandon Garrett (2011) conducted an exhaustive review of the first 250 DNA exonerations. He found that 76% of these cases (190) involved an innocent person who was wrongfully convicted, at least in part, because of eyewitness error. His analysis of 161 of these 190 cases revealed that some of the DNA exonerees had relied on some of the very safeguards that are designed to protect the innocent. For instance, some innocent defendants had the benefit of a jury instruction. In one case, the jury was warned, "an individual can make a mistake as to identification even when the individual is trying to tell the truth" (pp. 85–86). Moreover, three innocent defendants were permitted to have an eyewitness-memory expert testify at their trial. Nonetheless, all of these individuals were wrongfully convicted.

These real-life legal cases indicate that the courts may not be properly designed to sort out misinformation from true information. In a 2012 decision, the United States Supreme Court may have only made it more challenging for judges to weigh the consequences of misinformation (*Perry v. New Hampshire*, 2012; see Berkowitz & Javaid, 2013). Rejecting decades of eyewitness memory science, an eight-member majority of the Court ruled that suggestive identification procedures violate a defendant's due process rights only if the suggestion was orchestrated by law enforcement. In other words, misinformation and suggestion introduced by the police may serve as grounds for an identification to be suppressed, but not misinformation and suggestion from non-state actors (e.g., cowitnesses). Therefore, given the limited mechanisms that exist in the legal system to challenge eyewitness identifications (McMurtrie, 2005), and the ubiquitous nature of misinformation, courts may be hard-pressed to detect accurate from inaccurate eyewitnesses.

CONCLUSION

Nearly 40 years ago, renowned eyewitness-memory researcher Gary Wells (1978) proposed that eyewitness-memory experts distinguish between factors that are specific to the crime or the eyewitness and outside of the control of the criminal justice system (estimator variables) from factors that are under the control of the criminal justice system (system variables). Estimator variables may include high stress, weapon focus, or cross-racial identifications, while system variables may include the construction of the lineup or the lineup instructions given to an eyewitness. This distinction is imperative, as we cannot ensure robbers only rob victims of the same race and do not use weapons, but we can ensure that law enforcement officers use proper interview and lineup procedures with eyewitnesses.

In 2014, the National Academy of Sciences reviewed the science of eyewitness memory and called for the collaboration of researchers, law enforcement, and the courts. The committee found that "A range of best practices has been validated by scientific methods and research and represents a starting place for efforts to improve eyewitness identification procedures" (National Research Council, 2014, p. 2). The committee offered several recommendations that could be of help to legal professionals and the courts in identifying and assessing the impact of misinformation. Some of these recommendations are specific to law enforcement and include: training all law enforcement officers on the science of eyewitness memory, the use of double-blind identification procedures to prevent eyewitnesses from receiving suggestions from law enforcement, the use of a standard lineup instruction, recording an eyewitness's initial confidence at the time of their identification, and video recording all identification procedures. Other recommendations are specific to judges and include: holding a pretrial review of an eyewitness's testimony, informing the jury about all prior identification procedures the eyewitness participated in, permitting eyewitness-memory experts to testify, and providing the jury with clear and concise instructions about the science.

In an effort to further help legal professionals eliminate misinformation, we offer our own additional recommendations: We call upon eyewitness memory scholars to further investigate the conditions under which eyewitnesses may resist misinformation (see Blank & Launay, 2014) and to continue pursuit of best practices for investigative interviewing (Gabbert, Hope, Fisher, & Jamieson, 2012). We also encourage investigators and police officers to videotape all eyewitness interviews as well as all suspect interrogations (see Nirider, Tepfer, & Drizin, 2012), and to document whether eyewitnesses were exposed to any potential sources of misinformation. For instance, has the eyewitness talked to other people? Has the eyewitness reviewed news media or social media about the case? Such a record may further assist the court in evaluating the value of the eyewitness's testimony. While we hope that attorneys, cowitnesses, forensic interviewers, investigators, and police officers will try to avoid introducing misinformation into the memories of eyewitnesses, we need to be vigilant to the potential for it to happen anyhow, and be alert to the potential for misinformation, however subtle, to also contaminate the courtroom.

NOTES

1. Given that this case is currently under review by the United States Court of Appeals for the Fifth Circuit, some of the case details have been abbreviated and the identifying information has been changed.
2. Although this chapter focuses exclusively on the effects of misinformation on an eyewitness's memory, misinformation can also contaminate the memories of other individuals in the courtroom—suspects, attorneys, police officers, jurors, and judges.
3. To protect the identities of the individuals involved in this case, some of the case details have been abbreviated and the identifying information has been changed. Per the request of the defendant (Cornell Allen) and the public defender (Jack Greene), however, we have included their actual names in the text.
4. To protect the identities of the individuals involved in this case, some of the case details have been abbreviated and the identifying information has been changed.

REFERENCES

Ackil, J. K., & Zaragoza, M. S. (1998). Memorial consequences of forced confabulation: Age differences in susceptibility to misinformation. *Developmental Psychology, 34*, 1358–1372. doi: 10.1037/0012-1649.34.6.1358

Assefi, S. L., & Garry, M. (2003). Absolut memory distortions: Alcohol placebos influence the misinformation effect. *Psychological Science, 14*, 77–80. doi: 10.1111/1467-9280.01422

Benton, T. R., Ross, D. F., Bradshaw, E., Thomas, W. N., & Bradshaw, G. S. (2006). Eyewitness memory is still not common sense: Comparing jurors, judges, and law enforcement to eyewitness experts. *Applied Cognitive Psychology, 20*, 115–129. doi: 10.1002/acp.1171

Berkowitz, S. R., & Javaid, N. L. (2013). It's not you, it's the law: Eyewitness memory scholars' disappointment with *Perry v. New Hampshire*. *Psychology, Public Policy, and Law, 19*, 369–379. doi: 10.1037/a0032840

Berkowitz, S. R., Laney, C., Morris, E. K., Garry, M., & Loftus, E. F. (2008). Pluto behaving badly: False beliefs and their consequences. *American Journal of Psychology, 121*, 645–662. doi: 10.2307/20445490

Berkowitz, S. R., & Loftus. E. F. (2013). A skeptical view of repressed memory evidence. *California Litigation, 26*, 18–23.

Bernstein, D. M., Laney, C., Morris, E. K., & Loftus, E. F. (2005). False memories about food can lead to food avoidance. *Social Cognition, 23*, 10–33. doi: 10.1521/soco.23.1.11.59195

Bernstein, D. M., & Loftus. E. F. (2009a). How to tell if a particular memory is true or false. *Perspectives on Psychological Science, 4*, 370–374. doi: 10.1111/j.1745-6924.2009.01140.x

Bernstein, D. M., & Loftus, E. F. (2009b). The consequences of false memories for food preferences and choices. *Perspectives on Psychological Science, 4*, 135–139. doi: 10.1111/j.1745-6924.2009.01113.x

Blank, H., & Launay, C. (2014). How to protect eyewitness memory against the misinformation effect: A meta-analysis of post-warning studies. *Journal of Applied Research in Memory and Cognition, 3*, 77–88. doi: 10.1016/j.jarmac.2014.03.005

Braun, K. A., Ellis, R., & Loftus, E. F. (2002). Make my memory: How advertising can change our memories of the past. *Psychology and Marketing, 19*, 1–23. doi: 10.1002/mar.1000

Brown, R., & Kulik, J. (1977). Flashbulb memories. *Cognition, 5*, 73–99. doi: 10.1016/0010-0277(77)90018-X

Chrobak, Q. M., & Zaragoza, M. S. (2008). Inventing stories: Forcing witnesses to fabricate entire fictitious events leads to freely reported false memories. *Psychonomic Bulletin & Review, 15*, 1190–1195. doi: 10.3758/PBR.15.6.1190

Chrobak, Q. M., & Zaragoza, M. S. (2013). When forced fabrications become truth: Causal explanations and false memory development. *Journal of Experimental Psychology: General, 142*, 827–844. doi: 10.1037/a0030093

Clifasefi, S. L., Bernstein, D. M., Mantonakis, A., & Loftus, E. F. (2013). "Queasy does it": False alcohol beliefs and memories may lead to diminished alcohol preferences. *Acta Psychologica, 143*, 14–19. doi: 10.1016/j.actpsy.2013.01.017

Cochran, K. J., Greenspan, R. L., Bogart, D. F., & Loftus, E. F. (2016). Memory blindness: Altered memory reports lead to distortion in eyewitness memory. *Memory & Cognition, 44*, 717–726. doi: 10.3758/s13421-016-0594-y

Commonwealth of Pennsylvania v. Walker, 92 A.3d 766 (2014).

Day v. Quarterman, 566 F.3d 527 (2009).

Deffenbacher, K. A., & Loftus, E. F. (1982). Do jurors share a common sense understanding concerning eyewitness behavior? *Law and Human Behavior, 6*, 15–30. doi: 10.1007/BF01049310

Drivdahl, S. B., & Zaragoza, M. S. (2001). The role of perceptual elaboration and individual differences in the creation of false memories for suggested events. *Applied Cognitive Psychology, 15*, 265–281. doi: 10.1002/acp.701

Ferguson, R. (2015). *Stronger, faster, smarter: A guide to your most powerful body*. New York: Penguin Books.

Frenda, S. J., Knowles, E. D., Saletan, W., & Loftus, E. F. (2013). False memories of fabricated political events. *Journal of Experimental Social Psychology, 49,* 280–286. doi: 10.1016/j.jesp.2012.10.013

Frenda, S. J., Nichols, R., M., & Loftus, E. F. (2011). Current issues and advances in misinformation research. *Current Directions in Psychological Science, 20,* 20–23. doi: 10.1177/0963721410396620

Frenda, S. J., Patihis, L., Loftus, E. F., Lewis, H., & Fenn, K. M. (2014). Sleep deprivation and false memories. *Psychological Science, 25,* 1674–1681. doi: 10.1177/0956797614534694

Gabbert, F., Hope, L., Fisher, R. P., & Jamieson, K. (2012). Protecting against susceptibility to misinformation with the use of a self-administered interview. *Applied Cognitive Psychology, 26,* 568–575. doi: 10.1002/acp.2828

Garrett, B. L. (2011). *Convicting the innocent: Where criminal prosecutions go wrong.* Cambridge, MA: Harvard University Press. doi: 10.4159/harvard.9780674060982

Goff, L. M., & Roediger III, H. L. (1998). Imagination inflation for action events: Repeated imaginings lead to illusory recollections. *Memory and Cognition, 26,* 20–33. doi: 10.3758/BF03211367

Gurney, D. J., Pine, K. J., & Wiseman, R. (2013). The gestural misinformation effect: Skewing eyewitness testimony through gesture. *American Journal of Psychology, 126,* 301–314. doi: 10.5406/amerjpsyc.126.3.0301

Harper, D. N., & Garry, M. (2000). Postevent cues bias recognition performance in pigeons. *Animal Learning & Behavior, 28,* 59–67. doi: 10.3758/BF03199772

Hasel, L. E., & Kassin, S. M. (2009). On the presumption of evidentiary independence: Can confessions corrupt eyewitness identifications? *Psychological Science, 20,* 122–126. doi:10.1111/j.1467-9280.2008.02262.x

Heaps, C. M., & Nash, M. (2001). Comparing recollective experience in true and false autobiographical memories. *Journal of Experimental Psychology: Learning, Memory, and Cognition, 27,* 920–930. doi: 10.1037///0278-7393.27.4.920

Hope, L., & Wright, D. (2007). Beyond unusual? Examining the role of attention in the weapon focus effect. *Applied Cogntiive Psychology, 21,* 951–961. doi: 10.1002/acp.1307

Jack, F., Zydervelt, S., & Zajac, R. (2014). Are co-witnesses special? Comparing the influence of co-witness and interviewer misinformation on eyewitness reports. *Memory, 22,* 243–255. doi: 10.1080/09658211.2013.778291

Keller, R. (2017). Ryan Ferguson awarded $11 million in civil rights lawsuit. Columbia Daily Tribune. Retrieved from http://www.columbiatribune.com/news/20170710/ryan-ferguson-awarded-11-million-in-civil-rights-lawsuit

Laney, C., & Loftus. E. F. (2008). Emotional content of true and false memories. *Memory, 16,* 500–516. doi: 10.1080/09658210802065939

Leport, A. K. R., Mattfeld, A. T., Dickinson-Anson, H., Fallon, J. H., Stark, C. E. L., Kruggel, F., Cahill, L., & McGaugh, J. L. (2012). Behavioral and neuroanatomical investigation of Highly Superior Autobiographical Memory (HSAM). *Neurobiology of Learning and Memory, 98,* 78–92. doi: 10.1016/j.nlm.2012.05.002

Levine, L. J., & Bluck, S. (2004). Painting with broad strokes: Happiness and the malleability of event memory. *Cognition & Emotion, 18,* 559–574. doi: 10.1080/02699930341000446

Levine, L. J., & Pizzaro, D. A. (2004). Emotion and memory research: A grumpy overview. *Social Cognition, 22,* 530–554. doi: 0.1521/soco.22.5.530.50767

Loftus, E. F. (1975). Leading questions and the eyewitness report. *Cognitive Psychology*, 7, 560–572. doi: 10.1016/0010-0285(75)90023-7

Loftus, E. F. (1996). *Eyewitness testimony*. Cambridge, MA: Harvard University Press.

Loftus, E. F. (2004). Memories of things unseen. *Current Directions in Psychological Science*, 13, 145–147. doi: 10.1111/j.0963-7214.2004.00294.x

Loftus, E. F. (2005). Planting misinformation in the human mind: A 30-year investigation of the malleability of memory. *Learning & Memory*, 12, 361–366. doi: 10.1101/lm.94705

Loftus, E. F. (2013). Eyewitness testimony in the Lockerbie bombing case. *Memory*, 21, 584–590. doi: 10.1080/09658211.2013.774417

Loftus, E. F., & Ketcham, K. (1991). *Witness for the defense: The accused, the eyewitness, and the expert who put memory on trial*. New York: St. Martin's Press.

Loftus, E. F., Miller, D. G., & Burns, H. J. (1978). Semantic integration of verbal information into a visual memory. *Journal of Experimental Psychology: Human Learning and Memory*, 4, 19–31. doi: 10.1037/0278-7393.4.1.19

Loftus, E. F., & Pickrell, J. E. (1995). The formation of false memories. *Psychiatric Annals*, 25, 720–725.

Loftus, G. R. (2010). What can a perception-memory expert tell a jury? *Psychonomics Bulletin and Review*, 17, 143–148. doi: 10.3758/PBR.17.2.143

Mazzoni, G. A. L., Loftus, E. F., & Kirsch, I. (2001). Changing beliefs about implausible autobiographical events: A little plausibility goes a long way. *Journal of Experimental Psychology: Applied*, 7, 51–59. doi: 10.1037///1076-898X.7.1.51

Mazzoni, G., & Memon, A. (2003). Imagination can create false autobiographical memories. *Psychological Science*, 14, 186–188. doi: 10.1046/j.1432-1327.1999.00020.x

McMurtrie, J. (2005). The role of social sciences in preventing wrongful convictions. *The American Criminal Law Review*, 42, 1271–1287.

Meade, M. L., & Roediger, H. L., III. (2002). Explorations in the social contagion of memory. *Memory & Cognition*, 30, 995–1009. doi: 10.3758/BF03194318

Meissner, C. A., & Brigham, J. C. (2001). Thirty years of investigating the own-race bias in memory for faces: A meta-analytic review. *Psychology, Public Policy, & Law*, 7, 3–35. doi: 10.1037//1076-8971.7.1.3

Morgan, C. A., III, Southwick, S., Steffian, G., Hazlett, G. A., & Loftus, E. F. (2013). Misinformation can influence memory for repeatedly experienced, highly stressful events. *International Journal of Law & Psychiatry*, 36, 11–17. doi: 10.1016/j.ijlp.2012.11.002

Morgan C. A., III, Wang, S., Mason, J., Southwick, S. M., Fox, P., Hazlett, G., Charney, D. S., & Greenfield, G. (2000). Hormone profiles in humans experiencing military survival training. *Biological Psychiatry*, 47, 891–901. doi: 10.1016/S0006-3223(99)00307-8

Nash, R. A., & Wade, K. A. (2009). Innocent but proven guilty: Eliciting internalized false confessions using doctored video evidence. *Applied Cognitive Psychology*, 23, 624–637. doi: 10.1002/acp.1500

National Research Council. (2014). *Identifying the culprit: Assessing eyewitness identification*. Washington, DC: The National Academies Press.

Neisser, U., & Harsch, N. (1992). Phantom flashbulbs: False recollections of hearing the news about Challenger. In E. Winograd & U. Neisser (Eds.), *Affect and accuracy in recall: Studies of "flashbulb" memories* (Vol. 4, pp. 9–31). New York: Cambridge University Press.

Nirider, L. H., Tepfer, J. A., & Drizin, S. A. (2012). Combatting contamination in confession cases. *The University of Chicago Law Review*, 79, 837–862.

Otgaar, H., Candel, I., Merckelbach, H., & Wade, K. A. (2009). Abducted by a UFO: Prevalence information affects young children's false memories for an implausible event. *Applied Cognitive Psychology, 23*, 115–125. doi: 10.1002/acp.1445

Papailiou, A. P., Yokum, D. V., & Robertson, C. T. (2015). The novel New Jersey eyewitness instruction induces skepticism but not sensitivity. *Plos One, 10*, 1–16. doi: 10.1371/journal.pone.0142695

Parker, E. S., Cahill, L., & McGaugh, J. L. (2006). A case of unusual autobiographical remembering. *Neurocase, 12*, 35–49. doi: 10.1080/13554790500473680

Patihis, L., Frenda, S. J., LePort, A. K. R., Petersen, N., Nichols, R. M., Stark, C. E. L., McGaugh, J. L., & Loftus, E. F. (2013). False memories in highly superior autobiographical memory individuals. *Proceedings of the National Academy of Sciences, 110*, 20947–20952, doi: 10.1073/pnas.1314373110

People of Illinois v. Lerma, 47 N.E.3d 985 (2016).

Perry v. New Hampshire, 132 S. Ct. 716 (2012).

Pickel, K. L. (2004). When a lie becomes the truth: The effects of self-generated misinformation on eyewitness memory. *Memory, 12*, 14–26. doi: 10.1080/09658210244000072

Poole, D. A., & Lindsay, D. S. (2001). Children's eyewitness reports after exposure to misinformation from parents. *Journal of Experimental Psychology: Applied, 7*, 27–50. doi: 10.1037//1076-898X.7.1.27

Rovee-Collier, C., Borza, M. A., Adler, S. A., & Boller, K. (1993). Infants' eyewitness testimony: Effects of postevent information on a prior memory representation. *Memory & Cognition, 2*, 267–279. doi: 10.3758/BF03202738

Sacchi, D. L. M., Agnoli, F., & Loftus, E. F. (2007). Changing history: Doctored photographs affect memory for past public events. *Applied Cognitive Psychology, 21*, 1005–1022. doi: 10.1002/acp.1394

Schwartz, B. L., Meissner, C. M., Hoffman, M. L., Evans, S., & Frazier, L. D. (2004). Event memory and misinformation effects in a gorilla (*Gorilla gorilla gorilla*). *Animal Cognition, 7*, 93–100. doi: 10.1007/s10071-003-0194-7

Scoboria, A., Mazzoni, G., Kirsch, I., & Milling, L. S. (2002). Immediate and persisting effects of misleading questions and hypnosis on memory reports. *Journal of Experimental Psychology: Applied, 8*, 26–32. doi: 10.1037//1076-898X.8.1.26

Shaw, J., & Porter, S. (2015). Constructing rich false memories of committing crime. *Psychological Science, 26*, 291–301. doi: 10.1177/0956797614562862

Simons, D. J., & Chabris, C. F. (2011). What people believe about how memory works: A representative survey of the U.S. population. *Plos One, 6*, 1–7. doi: 10.1371/journal.pone.0022757

Stark, C. E. L., Okado, Y., & Loftus. E. F. (2010). Imaging the reconstruction of true and false memories using sensory reactivation and the misinformation paradigms. *Learning and Memory, 17*, 485–488. doi: 10.1101/lm.1845710

State of Louisiana v. Young, 2009-KK-1177 (2010).

State of New Jersey v. Henderson, 27 A. 3d 872 (2011).

State of Utah v. Clopten, UT 84, 223 P. 3d 1103 (2009).

Steblay, N. M. (1992). A meta-analytic review of the weapon focus effect. *Law and Human Behavior, 16*, 413–424. doi: 10.1007/BF02352267

Talarico, J. M., & Rubin, D. C. (2003). Confidence, not consistency, characterizes flashbulb memories. *Psychological Science, 14*, 455–461. doi: 10.1111/1467-9280.02453

Thompson-Cannino, J., Cotton, R., & Torneo, E. (2009). *Picking Cotton: Our memoir of injustice and redemption*. New York: St. Martin's Press.

Wade, K. A., Garry, M., Read, J. D., & Lindsay, D. S. (2002). A picture is worth a thousand lies: Using false photographs to create false childhood memories. *Psychonomic Bulletin and Review, 9*, 597–603. doi: 10.3758/BF03196318

Wells, G. L. (1978). Applied eyewitness-testimony research: System variables and estimator variables. *Journal of Personality and Social Psychology, 36*, 1546–1557. doi: 10.1037/0022-3514.36.12.1546

Wells, G. L., & Bradfield, A. L. (1998). "Good, you identified the suspect": Feedback to eyewitnesses distorts their reports of the witnessing experience. *Journal of Applied Psychology, 83*, 360–376. doi: 10.1037/0021-9010.83.3.360

Wells, G. L., & Olson, E. A. (2003). Eyewitness testimony. *The Annual Review of Psychology, 54*, 277–295. doi: 10.1146/annurev.psych.54.101601.145028

Wise, R. A., Pawlenko, N. B., Safer, M. A., & Meyer, D. (2009). What US prosecutors and defence attorneys know and believe about eyewitness testimony. *Applied Cognitive Psychology, 23*, 1266–1281. doi: 10.1002/acp.1530

Wise, R. A., & Safer, M. A. (2010). A comparison of what U.S. judges and students know and believe about eyewitness testimony. *Journal of Applied Social Psychology, 40*, 1400–1422. doi: 10.1111/j.1559-1816.2010.00623.x

Wise, R. A., Safer, M. A., & Maro, C. M. (2011). What U.S. law enforcement officers know and believe about eyewitness factors, eyewitness interviews and identification procedures. *Applied Cognitive Psychology, 25*, 488–500. doi: 10.1002/acp.1717

Wise, R. A., Sartori, G., Magnussen, S., & Safer, M. A. (2014). An examination of the causes and solutions to eyewitness error. *Frontiers in Psychiatry, 5*, 1–8. doi: 10.3389/fpsyt.2014.00102

Wylie, L. E., Patihis, L., McCuller, L. L., Davis, D., Brank, E. M., Loftus, E. F., & Bornstein, B. H. (2014). Misinformation effects in older versus younger adults: A meta-analysis and review. In Toglia, M. P. Ross, D. F., Pozzulo, J. & Pica, E. (Eds.) *The elderly eyewitness in court*. (pp. 38–66). New York: Psychology Press.

Zaragoza, M. S., Belli, R. F., & Payment, K. E. (2006). Misinformation effects and the suggestibility of eyewitness memory. In Garry, M., & Hayne, H. (Eds.) *Do justice and let the sky fall: Elizabeth F. Loftus and her contributions to science, law, and academic freedom*. (pp. 35–63). Hillsdale, NJ: Lawrence Erlbaum Associates.

Zhu, B., Chen, C., Loftus, E. F., Lin, C., He. Q., Chen, C., Li, H., Xue, G., Lu, Z., & Dong, Q. (2010). Individual differences in false memory from misinformation: Cognitive factors. *Memory, 18*, 543–555. doi: 10.1080/09658211.2010.487051

3

Suggestibility in the Courtroom

*How Memory Can Be Distorted During the Investigative
and Legal Process*

FIONA GABBERT AND LORRAINE HOPE

More than a century of scientific research demonstrates that human memory is suggestible. Due to the largely reconstructive nature of human memory, recollections can be altered, deleted, and created by events, interventions, or phenomena that occur during and after the time of encoding, during the period of storage, and during attempts at retrieval. Distortions can range from relatively minor errors (such as a small mistaken detail) through to entirely false memories for events that have never taken place. Individuals are not typically aware that their memories have become contaminated and continue to report erroneous information in the mistaken belief that it is, in fact, correct. While this malleability is a natural feature of human memory, there are potential negative consequences in investigative and legal contexts, where eyewitnesses are expected to produce uncontaminated accounts about what they saw or heard. A challenge for the criminal justice system is that there are at least three categories of eyewitness statements: (1) a generally reliable account; (2) a deliberately deceptive account; or (3) a misled account containing erroneous information that has been suggested to the witness. The current chapter focuses on this third category of account, and will discuss some of the key factors affecting the reliability of eyewitness statements, including individual differences in vulnerability to suggestion. The extent to which we can distinguish between a genuine and suggested "memory" and how we can assess the likely reliability of memories is also examined. The chapter concludes with consideration of how best to minimize the negative effects of suggestibility for the criminal justice system.

That the phenomenon of suggestibility poses a threat to the work of the police and courts is in little doubt—and a number of high profile cases illustrate the impact of suggestibility within the initial investigation, or subsequently, at the trial stage. Due to the constructive nature of memory, recollections for events are easily contaminated or distorted by information encountered after the event took place (i.e., people mistakenly report information that has been suggested to them, but that they have not in reality experienced). This phenomenon—and the memorial errors that arise as a consequence—reflects suggestibility.

The murder investigation of the Swedish foreign minister, Anna Lindh, in September 2003, provides a good example of witness suggestibility impeding the immediate search for the perpetrator. Lindh was stabbed while shopping in a department store in central Stockholm. Police gathered witnesses to her murder together in a small room to prevent them leaving the scene of the crime prior to being interviewed. The witnesses admitted discussing the stabbing incident with one another while together in the room (Granhag, Ask, Rebelius, Öhma, & Mac Giolla, 2013). During these discussions, one witness mentioned to others present that the perpetrator had been wearing a camouflage-patterned military jacket. Subsequently, a number of witnesses reported this clothing description to the investigating officers. This information was then used in an immediate search for the perpetrator in the surrounding area, and also featured in the release of a national police alert. However, it later transpired that this description was incorrect, resulting in lost police time due to false investigatory leads based on incorrect information. Footage from surveillance cameras showed that the killer, Mijailo Mijailovic, was in fact wearing a grey hooded sweatshirt. Given that the witnesses were free to discuss the incident with each other at some length, it seems that co-witness influence and suggestibility was the main source of error in the immediate stages of this investigation (Granhag et al., 2013).

A second example illustrates the consequences witness suggestibility can have when contaminated evidence is presented at court. Larry Henderson was accused of a shooting in Baltimore on New Year's Day, and was later identified by a surviving witness approximately 2 weeks after the murder. Henderson was convicted for the crime. However, in a later appeal, it emerged that when showing the witness photos as part of the identification procedure, the police officers engaged in persuasive behavior (described specifically as "pressure" and "nudging") that suggested a desired response from the witness (Loftus, 2013). Furthermore, prior to the identification, the witness had consumed large amounts of wine, champagne, and crack cocaine, likely making the identification even less reliable. The appeal received national attention when the New Jersey Supreme Court ruled in 2011 that defendants who are able to show some evidence of suggestive influences on witness testimony are entitled to a court hearing in which all psychological factors bearing on that testimony are scrutinized. In such cases, if the judge still decides to admit the testimony at trial, then the jury must be provided with tailored instructions on how to consider the eyewitness evidence.[1]

The implications of the errors made by witnesses in these examples range from wasted police resources during the investigation through to a serious miscarriage of justice resulting in the mistaken conviction of an innocent person (and, concomitantly, leaving a guilty person free to commit further crimes; see www. innocenceproject.org for other examples). This latter outcome suggests that not only are witnesses whose accounts have been distorted perceived as credible by investigators, but that jurors and other legal decision makers also find their accounts compelling. Indeed, research would seem to suggest this is the case, with studies dating back almost 40 years showing that mock jurors believe witnesses who are confident, regardless of accuracy (Wells, Lindsay, & Ferguson, 1979), and recent reviews continuing to support the notion that eyewitness testimony is among the most prevalent and persuasive evidence used in the courtrooms (Howe & Knott, 2015).

ASSESSING THE CREDIBILITY AND RELIABILITY OF EYEWITNESSES

Courts have a responsibility to ensure that evidence admitted at trial is sufficiently reliable so that it may be of use to the factfinders who will draw the ultimate conclusions of guilt or innocence (Heaton-Armstrong, Shepherd, Gudjonsson, & Wolchover, 2006). In UK courts, commonly accepted tests of witness credibility and reliability include an assessment of (a) the consistency with what the witness has said on other occasions (including within the same statement); and (b) the consistency of the witness's evidence with what is agreed, or shown by other evidence, to have occurred (Bingham, 2006). As witnesses are often interviewed on more than one occasion during an investigation (Gabbert & Brown, 2015), it is relatively easy to examine the consistency of information provided across multiple interviews. In such comparisons, consistency is often interpreted as being a diagnostic cue to witness credibility. This interpretation is problematic, however, as there are different types of inconsistency, some of which simply reflect naturally occurring memory phenomena and are, as such, nondiagnostic of the reliability of the entire account (see Fisher, Brewer, & Mitchell, 2009). For example, individuals may forget information over time, or might omit information in a second interview as a result of interacting with a different interviewer or interviewing style. The reporting of new information, not reported in the first interview (i.e., reminiscent information), can be similarly innocuous. The prevalence of reminiscent details reported can be influenced by changes in retrieval cues from one interview to another, or by changes in the amount of information volunteered by witnesses based upon their perceived expectations of how much information to report (see Fisher et al., 2009; Hope, Gabbert, Fisher, & Jamieson, 2014; La Rooy, Lamb, & Pipe, 2009). On the whole, reminiscent information is reported with high levels of accuracy (Gilbert & Fisher, 2006). Another type of inconsistency is the reporting of contradictory information, where information is reported in later interviews that contradicts information reported previously (e.g., saying on one occasion that a perpetrator was clean-shaven, and on another occasion that he had a beard). At least one of the two contradictory responses must be incorrect, hence contradictory details tend to have a very low accuracy rate. In summary, rather than considering "consistency" as a single construct, investigators and triers of fact need to systematically consider the type of apparent inconsistency. Research suggests that only particular types of inconsistency are associated with an increased likelihood of memory error (e.g., contradictory details).

The second commonly accepted test of witness credibility—that a witness's evidence should be consistent with what is agreed, or shown by other evidence, to have occurred—offers some protection against accepting a witness's account in isolation. However, this test does not offer protection against falsely corroborating evidence between witnesses who have discussed their memories (see section on memory conformity later). Furthermore, it is unlikely to detect confirmation bias that may have occurred in the course of the investigation, where information is sought, or interpreted, as confirming or corroborating evidence (see Hasel & Kassin, 2009; Horry, Halford, Brewer, Milne, & Bull, 2014). Instead the seemingly corroborating evidence is simply interpreted as consistent with beliefs and, as such is not interrogated for potential bias (e.g., problems with the way the evidence was obtained; aspects that are in error or contradictory).

Inconsistency both within and between witness statements can also arise if a witness has encountered some misleading postevent information after the initial interview. As such, it is particularly important for legal decision makers to recognize the fallibility of memory, in particular, the potential for memory distortion following a suggestion (see Ridley, Gabbert, & La Rooy, 2013).

FACTORS AFFECTING THE RELIABILITY OF EYEWITNESS STATEMENTS

Exposure to Postevent Information

A sizeable literature examining the factors that affect the reliability of eyewitness statements clearly demonstrates that eyewitness recall can be influenced by "postevent information" (PEI) encountered after the original incident was encoded (see review by Frenda, Nichols, & Loftus, 2011). There are many ways in which a witness might be exposed to misleading PEI, for example, inaccurate news reports, information from co-witnesses, and suggestive or misleading questions from journalists or inexperienced investigators. Research on this "misinformation effect" has systematically demonstrated that misleading postevent suggestions, introduced after an event has been encoded, are highly likely to contaminate eyewitness memory (see Loftus, 2005). In a typical experimental misinformation paradigm, participants view a (simulated) mock-crime event, after which they are exposed to some misinformation (e.g., in the form of misleading questions or erroneous information embedded in a news report). After exposure to the misinformation, participants are tested on their memory for the witnessed event. The "misinformation effect" is the finding that, when compared with control participants who were not misinformed, participants in the misled group are likely to report the suggested information rather than the events they actually witnessed. The effect of misleading PEI is also exacerbated by a number of real world factors such as delay (witnesses are more likely to encounter misleading information the longer the delay between encoding and police interview). Furthermore, people may also be susceptible to the effects of misleading PEI following suboptimal encoding conditions such as divided attention (Lane, 2006), high stress levels (Morgan, Southwick, Steffian, Hazlett, & Loftus, 2013), and short exposure durations (Allan, Midjord, Martin, & Gabbert, 2012).

Closely related to the misinformation effect is the phenomenon of "memory conformity" (Gabbert & Hope, 2013; Gabbert, Memon, & Wright, 2003), whereby people's memories for an event become similar to each other's following a discussion. Given the importance of independent and reliable individual accounts in the investigative process and legal system, a growing body of research has investigated this form of suggestibility. The difference between the two experimental paradigms is that in memory conformity studies, the misleading PEI is usually encountered in the social context of a discussion with a co-witness. Both social and cognitive factors can play a role in susceptibility to memory conformity, meaning that exposure to misleading PEI during discussions with others results can be a particularly powerful form of suggestion (Gabbert, Memon, Allan, & Wright, 2004; Paterson & Kemp, 2006).

Understanding the potential effects of co-witness influence on the accuracy of witness accounts is important in investigative contexts. Crimes often have more than one eyewitness (Valentine, Pickering, & Darling, 2003), and surveys completed by real eyewitnesses reveal that discussion between witnesses is common. For example, Paterson and Kemp (2006) surveyed witnesses to real incidents, and found that a majority (86%) admitted to having discussed what they had seen with a co-witness who was also present. Although these witnesses may have shared the same experience, their initial perceptions, and subsequent recollections, of the event may differ for many reasons, including naturally occurring differences in attention paid to various details of the event, differences in spatial or temporal location at the scene, or perceived differences in memory ability (Gabbert, Memon, & Wright, 2006). Despite initial differences in recollections of an event, research shows that when people talk about their memories they can influence each other such that their subsequent individual memory reports become similar.

In an early study investigating memory conformity, Gabbert, Memon, and Wright (2003) showed mock-witnesses a simulated-crime event on video. Two versions of the event were prepared, each of which contained the same sequence of events but had been filmed from different angles to simulate different witness vantage points. Critically, this manipulation allowed unique features of the event to be observed by each participant. After viewing, participants were asked to recall the event either alone or in pairs. An individual recall test was then administered to examine the effects of co-witness discussion on subsequent memory reports. A significant proportion (71%) of witnesses who had discussed the event reported at least one (of two) erroneous detail acquired during the discussion with their co-witness. This finding has been replicated many times (for recent reviews see Gabbert & Hope, 2013; Gabbert & Wheeler, 2017). This memory conformity effect has been found to be larger when the co-witness is a prior acquaintance, such as a friend or partner (French, Garry, & Mori, 2008; Hope, Ost, Gabbert, Healey, & Lenton, 2008; but see also Oeberst & Seidemann, 2014).

To summarize, within both investigative and legal contexts, it is important to consider whether there has been opportunity for witnesses to encounter misleading

PEI about the target incident from a co-witness or from another source. If the target incident has been a topic of discussion or PEI has been encountered via news or social media, then the risk to the reliability of the evidence should be carefully considered. Further, seemingly consistent statements obtained from witnesses might be seized upon as valuable corroborative evidence from independent witnesses when, in fact, the evidence may instead be contaminated if the witnesses discussed their memories prior to being interviewed by the police.

Suggestions Encountered Within the Context of an Investigative Interview

Within an investigative interview, the types of questions asked, the manner in which they are asked, and the structure of the interview are all factors that impact on witness performance in terms of the amount and accuracy of information reported (Fisher, Milne, & Bull, 2011; Oxburgh, Myklebust, & Grant, 2010). The use of (mis)leading questions is particularly problematic because such questions suggest a particular answer or contain information the interviewer is seeking to have confirmed, often something that the witness has not revealed themselves. For example, the question "Was his beard black?" suggests (i) that he had a beard, and (ii) that it was black.

Witnesses of all ages can be susceptible to suggestions presented to them within the context of an investigative interview, not least because interviewees often perceive authority figures, such as an investigating officer, as more knowledgeable than themselves (Ackil & Zaragoza, 1995; Ceci & Bruck, 1993). Children are particularly vulnerable to suggestions presented by an authority figure (Lamb, La Rooy, Malloy, & Katz, 2011). The factors known to lead to children providing inaccurate reports in investigative interviews include: the use of misleading questions (Baker-Ward, Gordon, Ornstein, Larus, & Clubb, 1993; Pipe, Sutherland, Webster, Jones, & La Rooy, 2004), misleading information (Bruck, Ceci, Francoeur, & Barr, 1995), misleading props (Leichtman & Ceci, 1995), repeated questions (Krähenbühl & Blades, 2006; Poole & White, 1991, 1993;), social pressure (Melnyk & Bruck, 2004), peer pressure (Bruck, Ceci & Hembrooke, 2002; Principe & Ceci, 2002), inappropriate encouragement and praise (Bruck et al., 2002), asking about things known not to have happened (Ceci, Huffman, & Smith, & Loftus, 1994; Erdmann, Volbert, & Bohm, 2004), negative reinforcement (Powell, Jones, & Campbell, 2003), and encouraging guessing and speculation (Erdmann et al., 2004; for a review see La Rooy, Brown, & Lamb, 2013). In some of these studies, the effects of combinations of suggestive techniques were assessed; in one study, for example, as many as 73% of the children falsely agreed that fictitious events had taken place (Erdmann et al., 2004).

Prior to the early 1990s police officers typically received a very limited amount of witness interview training, and research examining the content and style of interviews identified many of the bad practices outlined previously (Fisher, Geiselman, & Raymond, 1987; George & Clifford, 1992). In response, two research-based approaches to investigative interviewing were developed: the Cognitive Interview (CI) and the National Institute of Child Health and Human Development (NICHD) Investigative Interview Protocol (see La Rooy et al., 2013). The CI technique (Fisher & Geiselman, 1992) emerged from psychological literature on the nature of episodic memory and memory retrieval processes, and incorporates the principles of social dynamics, cognition, and communication. Over the past 30 years, this technique has been fundamental in changing the manner in which witness information is elicited by police investigators. Memon et al. (2010) conducted a metaanalysis including studies published since 1999. Their analyses found that when used appropriately by skilled interviewers who fully understand and engage with the key cognitive and social principles, the CI results in a "large and significant increase in correct details" (p. 357) and reduces the use of inappropriate questioning during interviews. This metaanalysis also revealed a smaller but significant increase in the reporting of incorrect details in the CI interview. Memon, Meissner, and Fraser (2010) suggested that this increase in incorrect details may be due to variation in the version of the CI used and advocated the use of "I don't know" and "Do not guess" instructions when interviewing. Although heavily reliant on investigator resources, including time and high-quality training, the CI is effective across investigative domains (e.g., crimes, accidents, health-related experiences), interviewees (e.g., children, adults, older adults), and nationalities (e.g. U.S., U.K., Brazilian; for a review, see Fisher, 2010; see also Vrij, Hope, & Fisher, 2014).

The NICHD Protocol was developed in the mid-1990s with input from a wide range of professionals including lawyers, developmental, clinical and forensic psychologists, police officers, and social workers, and has been the focus of intensive forensic evaluation and research ever since (see Bull, 2010; Lamb, Hershkowitz, Orbach, & Esplin, 2008). It's development was prompted in part by a number of high profile child abuse cases that sparked concerns among both academics and legal professionals about the suggestive ways in which children were being interviewed. Controlled studies have repeatedly shown that the quality of interviewing reliably and dramatically improves when interviewers employ the NICHD Protocol (Lamb, Orbach, Hershkowitz, Esplin, & Horowitz, 2007). Furthermore, analysis of real child sexual abuse case data confirmed that using the NICHD protocol interview resulted in more guilty pleas and, where cases were tried, more guilty verdicts, than nonprotocol interviews (Pipe, Orbach, Lamb, & Abbott, & Stewart, 2013).

Together, these two interview techniques have significantly enhanced investigative interviewing, in part through minimizing bad practice—such as the use of suggestive techniques—by providing alternative, more effective techniques to elicit information from witnesses.

Suggestions Encountered Within the Context of a Lineup Task

Thus far, the focus in this chapter has been on the effects of suggestion on testimony based on witness recall. Another memory process is often implicated in eyewitness testimony—recognition. The positive identification of a suspect by an eyewitness can be a compelling piece of evidence for investigators and legal decision makers, including jurors. However, even inadvertently suggestive procedures can have a significant impact on recognition (and processes associated with recognition) and, hence, suspect identifications made by eyewitnesses. Research has established that recognition processes are error prone and that false identifications (and missed identifications) occur in mugshot, show-up, and lineup procedures (Gronlund & Carlson, 2013). Such mistaken identifications have been well documented in both laboratory experiments and field studies of police identification procedures (e.g., Wells, Steblay, & Dysart, 2012). Nonetheless, positive identifications made with high confidence are particularly compelling (Douglass, Neuschatz, Imprich, & Wilkinson, 2010) and, under the right conditions, mistaken identifications can also be made with high confidence. In fact, mistaken identification testimony expressed with high confidence was used to convict innocent suspects in 72% of all DNA exoneration cases (Innocence Project, 2017). Yet, laboratory research tends to suggest that there is a meaningful relationship between identification accuracy and confidence (Brewer & Wells, 2006; Sauer, Brewer, Zweck, & Weber, 2010). So how can high confidence but mistaken identifications be accounted for?

Smalarz and Wells (2015) argue that suggestive identification practices and procedures in the real world serve to falsely inflate witness confidence and in doing so undermine the reliability of identification testimony. There is a sizeable literature to support this contention. Wells and Bradfield (1998) found that witnesses who were given positive feedback (e.g., "Good, you identified the suspect") reported higher confidence and better viewing conditions than those who received no feedback (see also Douglass & Steblay, 2006). Conversely, witnesses given negative feedback were less confident and reported worse witnessing conditions. Importantly, the effects of postidentification feedback not only inflate confidence, but can also affect other potential indices of reliability (e.g., reported distance or view quality). In laboratory studies, these feedback effects have been shown to occur for both perpetrator present and perpetrator absent lineups (Bradfield, Wells, & Olson, 2002) when there are long delays between identification and feedback, and can even extend to a witness's willingness to testify (Wells & Bradfield, 1998; 1999). A recent metaanalysis (20 studies, over 7,000 witness identifications) confirmed a significant inflation of retrospective confidence following postidentification feedback (Steblay, Wells, & Douglass, 2014). Research has also identified a "distortion asymmetry" such that witnesses who make a correct identification and receive positive feedback do not display the same degree of confidence inflation as those making an incorrect identification (Smalarz & Wells, 2014). As such, mistaken witnesses are more suggestible with respect to confirmatory feedback than accurate ones (Steblay et al., 2014).

The effects of postidentification feedback are robust, far reaching, and have serious implications for the reliability of eyewitness identifications. Feedback effects also have serious implications for factfinders and jurors charged with assessing the reliability of identification evidence (Palmer, Brewer, & Weber, 2010; see also

Smalarz & Wells, 2015, for a detailed review). This challenge was starkly demonstrated by Smalarz and Wells (2015) who found that, in the absence of confirmatory feedback, evaluators were able to distinguish between accurate and mistaken witnesses at a reasonable rate, believing twice as many accurate as mistaken witnesses. However, when witnesses received confirmatory feedback, evaluators were unable to distinguish between accurate and mistaken witnesses. In short, confirmatory feedback "eliminated the evaluators' ability to discriminate between accurate and mistaken eyewitness testimony" (Smalarz & Wells, 2015, p. 122).

Beyond providing confirmatory feedback, investigators can leak information to witnesses completing identifications procedures in other ways. Ideally, lineups should take place under double-blind administration where both the witness and lineup administrator are unaware of the suspect's identity. A lineup administrator who knows which lineup member is the suspect may unintentionally transmit this knowledge to the witness (Harris & Rosenthal, 1985), increasing false identification rates if the suspect is innocent (Phillips, McAuliff, Kovera, & Cutler, 1999). Greathouse and Kovera (2009) noted that administrators displayed more biasing behaviors (such as inviting the witness to "take another look," providing overt cues as to the identity of the suspect, and exerting greater pressure on witnesses to choose) during single-blind administration procedures (i.e., when they knew the identity of the suspect) than under double-blind procedures. Research also demonstrates that witnesses may be unaware of the influence exerted by a lineup administrator (Clark, Marshall, & Rosenthal, 2009), and administrators may be unaware of the influence they are exerting (Garrioch & Brimacombe, 2001; see also Dysart, Lawson, & Rainey, 2012).

Identification decisions can also be influenced by knowledge of another witness's lineup decision, or a suggestion from a co-witness prior to viewing a lineup. Gabbert, Memon, and Wright (2007) manipulated co-witness confidence and accuracy across both target present and target absent lineups, and found that participants were more likely than controls to reject the lineup incorrectly when they were aware that the co-witness had rejected the lineup. However, participants were no more likely than controls to identify the perpetrator correctly after seeing the co-witness make an accurate identification, and the prelineup confidence expressed by the confederate did not appear to influence the witness. Zajac and Henderson (2009) examined the effect of co-witness discussion on suspect identifications from lineups, whereby half of the participants were misinformed by a confederate that the thief's accomplice had blue eyes (when in fact they were brown). Misinformed participants were significantly several times more likely than controls to describe the accomplice as having blue eyes, and twice as likely to identify someone from a culprit-absent lineup where all members had blue eyes. More recently, a study by Levett (2013) found that witnesses who simply overheard that their co-witness had chosen from the lineup were more likely to choose themselves than those who heard no information about the co-witness decision or heard the co-witness had rejected the lineup. In addition, Levett (2013) demonstrated "confidence conformity" whereby witnesses who heard co-witness decisions were also influenced by the confidence expressed by their co-witness in that decision. Thus, co-witness contamination in identification contexts can lead to a situation where legal decision makers are presented with confident, corroborating, witnesses who are actually wrong.

Finally, witnesses may bring their own biases to the identification process. For instance, witnesses often assume that the suspect apprehended by the police and presented to them in a lineup must have a high probability of being the perpetrator. Memon, Gabbert, and Hope (2004) reported that over 90% of mock witnesses expected the perpetrator to be present in a lineup. This bias is likely to be exacerbated if witnesses are presented with the task in a misleading manner (i.e., "Take a good look at the lineup and see if you can identify the offender"). Therefore, it is vital that witnesses are informed that the person they saw "may or may not be present in the lineup." Malpass and Devine (1981) demonstrated that a simple warning that the perpetrator may not be in the lineup halved the number of mistaken identifications made. These unbiased instructions may not completely attenuate the biasing effects of witnesses' expectations, but can reduce incorrect identifications from target absent lineups (see also metaanalyses by Clark, 2005; Steblay, 1997).

In sum, research amply demonstrates that eyewitness identifications are also vulnerable to suggestion and that suggestive "interventions," either by co-witnesses or investigators, not only result in mistaken identifications but can also result in falsely inflated confidence in those mistaken identifications. This section is not intended to be an exhaustive consideration of all the factors that can affect identification. Indeed, research suggests that the generation and composition of materials for identifications tasks (e.g., lineups, mugshots) can be highly suggestive (see, for example, Charman, Gregory, & Carlucci, 2009). Thus, investigators and triers of fact should be aware that witness identification decisions are also malleable and are only as reliable to the extent that the procedure used to obtain them is fair and unbiased. Indeed, in a recent field study by Wixted, Mickes, Dunn, Clark, and Wells (2016) involving actual eyewitness found that eyewitness confidence, as reported at the time of the identification decision, is a reliable indicator of accuracy for fair lineups conducted in a double-blind manner.

WHEN ARE INDIVIDUALS THE MOST VULNERABLE TO SUGGESTION?

Exposure to Postevent Information

Individuals are most susceptible to misleading PEI when they fail to notice a discrepancy between the suggested items and their original memory (see Blank 1998; Loftus, 2005; Tousignant, Hall & Loftus, 1986). Thus, people are more suggestible after a delay, when the original memory has faded (e.g., Loftus, Miller, & Burns, 1978), or when the suggested detail concerns either peripheral information (Wright & Stroud, 1998) or schema-relevant items, in comparison with low expectancy items that are more salient (Meade & Roediger, 2002; Walther, Bless, Strack, Rackstraw, Wagner, & Werth, 2002). These factors all make discrepancies particularly difficult to detect. Underwood and Pezdek (1998) showed that discrepancy detection can change over time, as memory for the PEI remains but memory for the source of the PEI is forgotten. Demonstrating this is a recent study by Horry, Colton, and Williamson (2014), who observed a large effect of retention interval on discrepancy detection and a person's ability to accurately identify the source of his or her memory. The authors therefore emphasize the importance of securing eyewitness statements as soon as possible after an event, when witnesses are best able to discriminate between information that was personally seen and information obtained from secondary sources. This recommendation is supported by earlier work showing that having a strong original memory for an event increases the likelihood that individuals notice, and reject, discrepant information (Loftus, 2005; Wright & Villalba, 2012). For example, Wright and Villalba (2012), found evidence that memory conformity is moderated by initial memory accuracy (amount correctly reported), with accurate memories being more resistant to the suggested PEI than inaccurate memories.

There are also times where individuals are suggestible because they want their report to be correct. This is particularly likely in situations where an individual doubts the accuracy of their own memory or when the information encountered from another individual convinces them that their initial judgement might be wrong (Hardin & Higgins, 1996). A memory conformity study by Allan et al. (2012) suggests that there is a strategic trade-off that balances the accuracy of our own memory with the perceived accuracy of a co-witness. This study followed on from previous work conducted by Gabbert et al. (2007) in which dyad members were led to believe that one member had viewed slides for twice the length of time of her or his partner, when in reality there was no difference in encoding duration. Despite an instruction about the importance of accuracy, participants who believed that they had seen the slides for less time than their partner were significantly more likely to conform to their partner's memory for items within the slides than those who thought they had viewed the slides for longer. Allan et al. (2012) replicated this finding using virtual confederates, as well as extending the findings to show that this effect was strongest when participants had the briefest amount of time to view a scene (30 seconds, versus 60 or 120 seconds). Thus, individuals who believed that they had an inferior memory quality to others were more likely to become influenced by, and subsequently report, items of errant PEI encountered from another person; but this reliance on others is dynamically and strategically adjusted according to knowledge of the encoding conditions of ourselves and others. Supporting this general conclusion, research has found that the overt confidence with which individuals make their assertions to each other can operate systematically as a cue that promotes conformity (Allan & Gabbert, 2008; Schneider & Watkins, 1996; Wright, Self, & Justice, 2000). Furthermore, research has found that participants are less likely to incorporate suggestions from a partner with perceived low credibility (cf. high credibility; Andrews & Rapp, 2014), or from an older adult (cf. a young adult; Davis & Meade, 2013; Thorley, 2015).

When misleading PEI is encountered, it is also common for people to make "source-monitoring" errors, whereby the PEI is remembered but the source of this information is forgotten (Johnson, Hashtroudi, & Lindsay, 1993). The source-monitoring framework (SMF; Johnson et al., 1993) describes the judgment processes that individuals employ to accurately identify the source of a memory, as well as specifying factors that are likely to promote source-monitoring errors. For example, according to the SMF, our memories contain various characteristics that provide clues to their origin. Memories from different sources tend to differ on average in the quantity and quality of the characteristics associated with them. Individuals use these differences in memory characteristics as heuristics to attribute their memories to a particular source. However, there is no single aspect of our memories that consistently specifies the true source and, as a consequence, source misattributions can occur (Johnson et al., 1993). Research on the accuracy of source monitoring has shown that source confusion errors increase when there is an overlap in the memory characteristics from two different sources (Henkel & Franklin, 1998; Markham & Hynes, 1993). This finding is particularly relevant in cases where misleading PEI is encountered during a discussion with a co-witness, as there would be a large amount of contextual overlap. For example, co-witnesses are likely to talk about what they have just seen (content overlap), they are likely to do this immediately after the crime event (temporal overlap), and it is likely that this discussion occurs at the scene, while waiting for the police to arrive, rather than at a different location (environmental overlap).

Blank's (1998) theoretical framework approaches the misinformation methodology with the premise that participants assume consistency between the event and PEI unless there is reason to doubt it. If assuming consistency, participants are unlikely to devote much attention to the source of the information at the time of the memory test. This explains why the ability to notice discrepancies is key to whether people will be misled by the suggested information or not. If the assumption of consistency is removed and individuals believe there are different versions of the facts, then increased awareness of the source, and potential accuracy of each source, become important and enter into a judgment process. Warnings can be used to reduce the misinformation effect, as they serve to remove the consistency assumption, and warn against the PEI (Blank, 1998). A recent metaanalysis of 25 postwarning studies examined whether memory could be protected against misleading PEI (Blank & Launay, 2014); warnings were found to be very effective, reducing the misinformation effect to less than half of its size on average.

Stress or Arousal and Suggestibility

A large body of literature reports that emotionally arousing events are generally remembered better than neutral events (e.g., Payne, Jackson, Ryan, Hoscheidt, Jacobs, & Nadel, 2006), with neurobiological research, in particular, suggesting that stress hormones can enhance memory performance (McGaugh, 2000; 2013; Roozendaal, 2000). However, research examining memory performance in applied contexts, including that of witnesses, both civilians and operational personnel (e.g., army, police, emergency responders), suggests the effects of stress and arousal on memory are complex. High levels of stress experienced in naturalistic settings generally impairs memory and these detrimental effects have been well-documented (e.g. Hope, Blocksidge, Gabbert, Sauer, Lewinski, Mirashi, & Atuk, 2016; Hope, Lewinski, Dixon, Blocksidge, & Gabbert, 2012; Morgan et al., 2004; 2013). In a metaanalysis, Deffenbacher, Bornstein, Penrod, and McGorty (2004) identify what they describe as a "catastrophic" decline in memory performance at higher stress levels (although see Sauerland et al., 2016). Thus, the effect of arousal on memory performance reflects an inverted U-shaped curve with memory for events best when stress levels are moderate (Morley & Farr, 2012; for a review see Finsterwald & Alberini, 2014).

Increased levels of suggestibility have been associated with stress at encoding. In a study involving over 800 soldiers taking part in survival training, Morgan et al. (2013) found that soldiers exposed to misinformation (a photo of a person who was not an interrogator) following a high-stress interrogation were 40% more likely to incorrectly identify this person as their interrogator than those who did not receive the misinformation. The soldiers' recall accounts were also vulnerable to suggestion; following exposure to misinformation, 27% soldiers mistakenly reported that their interrogator threatened them with a weapon. Similarly, in Hope et al. (2016), almost one fifth of officers in a simulated firearms scenario reported that the perpetrator pointed a weapon at them during the scenario (in fact the weapon had remained in the waistband of the perpetrator's waistband throughout the scenario). That memory for highly stressful events is suggestible is not just a feature of simulated or scenario-based training events (Morgan & Southwick, 2014). In a study of 249 soldiers who had been deployed in Afghanistan, Lommen, Engelhard, and van den Hout (2013) found that, after receiving misinformation about a fictional combat-related event, 26% of soldiers reported the misinformation several months later. Analyses suggested that lower cognitive ability and a combination of high arousal and additional stressors were associated with greater susceptibility to the misinformation effect.

Intoxication

Investigators often encounter witnesses and suspects who are under the influence of alcohol or other substances (Palmer, Flowe, Takarangi, & Humphries, 2013). The typical expectation of police and others is that the accounts provided by intoxicated witnesses are likely to be less reliable than those provided by sober individuals. Indeed, basic research on the effects of alcohol on memory tend to show memory impairment with intoxication (for a review see Mintzer, 2007). However, studies to date examining the effects of alcohol intoxication on witness memory produced somewhat inconsistent findings. Compo, Evans, Carol, Villalba, Ham, Garcia, and Rose (2012) found that intoxicated witness were no less accurate or more vulnerable to suggestion than sober witnesses in their recall of a staged event in a laboratory-based study (see also Compo, Evans, Carol, Villalba, Ham, Garcia, & Rose, 2014). However, in a field study conducted in bars, Van Oorsouw and Merckelbach (2012) noted that although the accuracy of accounts provided by intoxicated witnesses did not differ from their sober counterparts, intoxicated individuals provided significantly less information during interviews. In a subsequent field study, Van Oorsouw, Merckelbach, and Smeets (2015) found that alcohol intoxication impaired memory and increased susceptibility to suggestive questions during an immediate interview. Both effects were also present after a delay (when the participant was sober again). Of course, witnesses can be intoxicated by other means. Yuille, Tollestrup, Marxsen, Porter, and Herve's (1998) reported that witnesses who had smoked marijuana prior to witnessing an incident showed a *temporary* negative effect in terms of the amount recalled (although accuracy and recognition were not impaired).

Intoxication may also have important implications for the suggestibility of vulnerable suspects. In an analysis of suspect confessions, Sigurdsson and Gudjonsson (1994) noted high rates of drug and alcohol intoxication associated with false confessions. Extending this observation, Gudjonsson, Hannesdottir, Petursson, and Bjornsson (2002) warned that suspects who are experiencing withdrawal symptoms may be particularly vulnerable to suggestion and false confession. Thus, although some work suggests intoxicated individuals use a more conservative response bias (e.g., Mintzer, 2007), further research is needed because individuals who are intoxicated may also be at increased risk of susceptibility to suggestion.

INDIVIDUAL DIFFERENCES IN SUGGESTIBILITY

The fact that some individuals are habitually susceptible to being influenced by misinformation (Cann & Katz, 2005; Tomes & Katz, 1997) suggests there are individual differences in suggestibility. Researchers have therefore investigated whether any individual differences in personality or cognitive ability are associated with suggestibility (see Bruck & Melnyk, 2004). For example, Jaschinski and Wentura (2002) examined how working memory capacity relates to the effect of misinformation on memory. Working memory refers to a short-term memory process that is involved with online monitoring or control of information (Baddeley, 1986). It can be measured using an operation-word span test that requires not only information storage and rehearsal, but also the simultaneous processing of additional information (Conway, Kane, Bunting, Hambrick, Wilhelm, & Engle, 2005; Turner & Engle, 1989). Participants in Jaschinski and Wentura's (2002) study viewed a simulated crime event and later received misinformation about the event before being given a recall test. They found that participants with a large working memory capacity were less susceptible to the misinformation. The authors suggest that this is because people with greater memory capacity build detailed and coherent mental models of events during the encoding phase. Thus, they are able to reject misinformation because they either recognize that it contrasts with their own memory, or because their mental model that represents the event is already detailed and so additional information is ignored. More recently, Zhu, et al. (2010) and Calvillo (2014) have also found that working memory capacity is negatively associated with suggestibility and susceptibility to misinformation effects.

Age has been found to relate to suggestibility in a number of studies. In an early study, Loftus, Levidow and Duensing (1992) found in general that the oldest (over 65 years of age) and youngest (5–10 years of age) participants had the poorest memory, and were more likely to report misinformation (see also Davis & Loftus, 2005). In the older sample, this tendency is likely because older adults generally have poorer episodic memory than younger adults (Nyberg, Cabeza, & Tulving, 1996; Umanath & Marsh, 2014) and are more likely to make source monitoring errors (Mitchell, Johnson, & Mather, 2003). A recent study by Dodson, Powers, and Lytell (2015) asked younger and older adults to view a simulated robbery, then presented them with misleading information about the event before interviewing them with the CI about their memory for the robbery. Older adults were disproportionately more confident than younger adults in the accuracy of incorrect information that they reported than in the accuracy of correct information. This overconfidence occurred even in comparison with younger adults who were matched with older adults on the overall amount and accuracy of the information remembered about the robbery. In summary, there appears to be a relationship between suggestibility and cognitive/memory ability; a factor that can vary naturally between individuals (as an individual, and/or developmental, difference), as well as one that can be experimentally manipulated (based upon the amount of attention paid at encoding, the delay between encoding and retrieval, etc.). However, a recent series of studies by Otgaar, Howe, Brackmann, and Smeets (2016) shows that other factors can influence susceptibility to suggested information, and that misinformation effects in children and adults are malleable, depending on the context. As such, age is not always a reliable predictor for developmental patterns in suggestibility.

Suggestibility is also sometimes conceived of by researchers as a trait; for example, Gudjonsson's research examines the extent to which some individuals are more susceptible to "interrogative suggestibility" than others, that is, suggestibility that occurs in the presence of inappropriate questioning plus pressure, either in the form of negative feedback and/or coercive interview techniques. His findings have led to the development of the Gudjonsson Suggestibility Scales (Gudjonsson, 1983; 1984; 1997) and a model of interrogative suggestibility (Gudjonsson & Clark, 1986; Gudjonsson 2003). Gudjonsson's Suggestibility Scale enables measurement of individuals' vulnerability to suggestive influence, or to give erroneous accounts when interviewed, particularly in forensic contents. Scores on the Gudjonsson Suggestibility Scale enable comparison of an individual's suggestibility to normative groups[2] (see Gudjonsson, 2013, for a recent review). Furthermore, the scale is apparently resistant to exaggeration or feigning of interrogative suggestibility: First, it is presented in the form of a memory test (rather than a test of suggestibility); second, a study by Baxter and Bain (2002) demonstrated that even when individuals were informed that the test measures suggestibility, and were told to feign suggestibility on the test, only one of the outcome scores (the first yield score) was susceptible to faking.

When examining differences in suggestibility, an important distinction can be made between *immediate* and *delayed* suggestibility (see Eisen, Morgan,

& Mickes, 2002; Ridley et al., 2013; Schooler & Loftus, 1986). For example, between the immediate acceptance of misleading information contained in a leading question (Gudjonsson's interrogative suggestibility), and delayed suggestibility due to exposure to misleading information that is incorrectly reported in a subsequent test (Loftus's misinformation paradigm). It is likely that distinct individual differences are associated with each type of suggestibility. Eisen et al. (2002) reported that imagery ability, field dependence/locus of control, and the tendency to dissociate were related to delayed but not immediate acceptance of misleading information, whereas acquiescence, agreeableness, and intelligence were associated with immediate but not delayed suggestibility. Based on these findings, the authors concluded that immediate suggestibility is the result of social pressure, whereas delayed suggestibility is due to confusion between what was actually witnessed and what was suggested (i.e., a failure in discrepancy detection).

In sum, much research and debate has attempted to establish whether suggestibility is a trait (i.e., some people are inherently more suggestible than others), or whether suggestibility is merely the result of situational factors that can be manipulated. It seems that suggestibility is not a unified construct. Nevertheless, what both approaches have in common is the fact that they consider suggestibility from the point of view of its impact on the accuracy and reliability of memory reports (see Nash & Ost, 2017; Ridley & Gudjonsson, 2013). Being able to distinguish between a genuine memory (i.e., a reliable memory for an event that did actually occur) and a suggested "memory" (i.e., a distorted, false, or otherwise contaminated erroneous memory) would be very beneficial for both the investigative and legal process. Indeed, the search for discriminating markers between accurate (true) and inaccurate (false) memories has been the focus of researchers for some time (Bernstein & Loftus, 2009; Heaps & Nash, 2001). However, despite highlighting some differences, no consistently reliable markers have emerged.

WHAT CAN BE DONE TO MINIMIZE THE NEGATIVE EFFECTS OF SUGGESTIBILITY?

Given that a delay between witnessing an incident, and reporting memories about it, increases the opportunity that witnesses will be exposed to potentially misleading PEI, the authors propose that the first important step toward minimizing the negative effects of suggestibility is to interview witnesses as soon as possible. A good quality preliminary interview will strengthen a witness's memory, thus offering protection against exposure to misleading PEI encountered in the form of suggestive questions or from other sources such as discussions with a co-witness (Gabbert & Hope, 2013; Gabbert, Hope, Carter, Boon, & Fisher, 2015). As mentioned, this is because having a "strong" original memory for an event increases the likelihood that individuals detect, and are therefore able to reject, discrepancies between their original memories for the event and any PEI received.

Geiselman, Fisher, Cohen, Holland, and Surtes (1986) found that mock witnesses were less susceptible to the effects of misleading questions when a CI had been administered prior to the misleading questions being encountered. In contrast, a CI given after the leading and misleading questions conferred no benefits with respect to attenuating witness vulnerability to misleading questions. Similar conclusions were reached by Memon, Zaragoza, Clifford, and Kidd (2010), who gave mock witnesses a CI either prior to, or immediately after, a suggestive interview where they were encouraged to confabulate in order to provide responses to "impossible" questions. One week later, all participants returned for a final interview. It was found that participants who had been given a CI prior to (but not following) the suggestive interview reported significantly fewer forced fabrications in their final interview, leading the researchers to conclude that a CI given prior to misleading information has protective benefits. Although Memon et al. did not draw explicitly on the notion of discrepancy detection, their findings support the idea that participants are better able to be vigilant against discrepancies if their memory for a target event is strengthened (though see LaPaglia, Wilford, Rivard, Chan, & Fisher, 2014; Putnam, Sungkhassettee, & Roediger, 2016).

More recently, Gabbert, Hope, Fisher, and Jamieson (2012) investigated whether an early recall opportunity, in the form of a Self-Administered Interview (SAI©), protected against the negative consequences of exposure to misleading PEI. The SAI© is a generic reporting tool comprising several sections and drawing on a number of key memory and cognition principles to support both the quality and quantity of retrieval. These include: facilitating the witness's retrieving the encoded event from memory (e.g., by reinstating the encoding context, encouraging multiple and varied retrieval), promoting high accuracy responses (by discouraging witnesses from guessing, and not asking leading questions), and not overloading the witness's limited capacity to process information, and providing clear instructions. In initial tests of the SAI©, participants viewed a mock crime event, after which half immediately recorded their account using the SAI©. Control participants did not have an immediate recall opportunity. Following a delay, participants were presented with misinformation encountered either in a misleading news report (Study 1) or in the form of misleading cued-recall questions (Study 2). Study 1 found that completing an SAI© shortly after witnessing an event significantly increased the amount of accurate information reported in a delayed recall test, in comparison with the performance of control participants. Almost twice as many accurate details were reported after a delay by SAI© than control participants. Furthermore, SAI© participants were significantly less likely than controls to errantly report items of misleading PEI that had been encountered in the news report during the delay period. Study 2 also found that participants who had an opportunity to complete a SAI© after witnessing a mock-crime event had a better memory than control participants, and that SAI© participants were less likely to attempt to answer misleading questions by reporting confabulated responses (see also Huff, Weinsheimer, & Bodner, 2016, for similar findings).

Taken together, these studies suggest that a good quality preliminary interview can decrease the likelihood of the undesirable effects of exposure to misinformation or suggestive questions. Of course, this conclusion presupposes that police investigators are trained to a high standard to ensure professional and effective practice when eliciting evidence from witnesses.

A second important step toward minimizing the negative effects of suggestibility is to ensure that investigators and legal decision makers are aware of the ways in which a witness's memory might be the product of suggestion rather than a veridical memory. While it is difficult to know for sure if a witness's evidence is reliable, having knowledge and awareness of the individual and situational variables that can lead to increased suggestibility can help identify potential risk factors. This, in turn, can enable factfinders to evaluate the evidence being presented. For example, for some cases it might be important to assess the quality, and adherence to best practice guidelines, of interview and identification procedures. In other cases it might be important to examine potential exposure to PEI, perhaps where there has been a delay between witnessing an event and reporting evidence, or a delayed allegation case where it is sensible to examine the factors leading up to the disclosure. Overall, albeit not as easy as it seems (see Powell, 2008), the authors suggest that it is vital that police training is continually informed by the latest research in their investigative methods; that legal decision makers keep pace with relevant scientific outcomes; and that researchers work to inform, innovate, and educate in the applied context.

NOTES

1. www.judiciary.state.nj.us/criminal/ModelCrimJuryChargeCommHENDERSON REPORT.pdf
2. It should be noted that normative data are based upon populations in Great Britain and Iceland.

REFERENCES

Ackil, J. K., & Zaragoza, M. (1995). Developmental differences in eyewitness suggestibility and memory for source. *Journal of Experimental Child Psychology*, *60*, 57–83.

Allan, K., & Gabbert, F. (2008). I still think it was a banana: Memorable lies and forgettable truths. *Acta Psychologica*, *127*, 299–308.

Allan, K., Midjord, J. P., Martin D., & Gabbert, F. (2012). Memory conformity and the perceived accuracy of Self versus Other. *Memory & Cognition*, *40*, 280–286.

Andrews, J. J., & Rapp, D. N. (2014). Partner characteristics and social contagion: Does group composition matter? *Applied Cognitive Psychology*, *28*, 505–517.

Baddeley, A. (1986). *Working memory*. New York: Oxford University Press.

Baker-Ward, L., Gordon, B. N., Ornstein, P. A., Larus, D., & Clubb, P. (1993). Young children's long-term retention of a pediatric examination. *Child Development*, *56*, 1103–1119.

Baxter, J., & Bain, S. (2002). Faking interrogative suggestibility: The truth machine. *Legal and Criminological Psychology*, *7*, 219–225.

Bernstein, D. M., & Loftus, E. F. (2009). The consequences of false memories for food preferences and choices. *Perspectives on Psychological Science*, *4*, 135–139.

Bingham, T. (2006). Assessing contentious eyewitness evidence: A judicial view. In A. Heaton-Armstrong, E. Shepherd, G. Gudjonsson, & D. Wolchover (Eds.), *Witness testimony. Psychological, investigative and evidential perspectives* (pp. 327–343). Oxford: Oxford University Press.

Blank, H., & Launay, C. (2014). How to protect eyewitness memory against the misinformation effect: A meta-analysis of post-warning studies. *Journal of Applied Research in Memory and Cognition, 3,* 77–88.

Blank, H. (1998). Memory states and memory tasks: An integrative framework for eyewitness memory and suggestibility. *Memory, 6,* 481–529.

Bradfield, A. L., Wells, G. L., & Olson, E. A. (2002). The damaging effect of confirming feedback on the relation between eyewitness certainty and identification accuracy. *Journal of Applied Psychology, 87,* 112–120.

Brewer, N., & Wells, G. L. (2006). The confidence–accuracy relationship in eyewitness identification: Effects of lineup instructions, foil similarity and target-absent base rates. *Journal of Experimental Psychology: Applied, 12,* 11–30.

Bruck, M., & Melnyk, L. (2004), Individual differences in children's suggestibility: A review and synthesis. *Applied Cognitive Psychology, 18,* 947–996.

Bruck, M., Ceci, S. J., Francoeur, E., & Barr, R. J. (1995). "I hardly cried when I got my shot": Influencing children's reports about a visit to their pediatrician. *Child Development, 66,* 193–208.

Bruck, M., Ceci, S. J., & Hembrooke, H. (2002). The nature of children's true and false narratives. *Developmental Review, 22,* 520–554.

Bull, R. (2010). The investigative interviewing of children and other vulnerable witnesses: Psychological research and working/professional practice. *Legal and Criminological Psychology, 15,* 5–23.

Calvillo, D. P. (2014). Individual differences in susceptibility to misinformation effects and hindsight bias. *Journal of General Psychology, 141,* 393–407.

Cann, D. R., & Katz, A. N. (2005). Habitual acceptance of misinformation: Examination of individual differences and source attributions. *Memory and Cognition, 33,* 405–417.

Ceci, S. J., & Bruck, M. (1993). Suggestibility of the child witness: A historical review and synthesis. *Psychological Bulletin, 113,* 403–439.

Ceci, S. J., Huffman, M. L. C., Smith, E., & Loftus, E. F. (1994). Repeatedly thinking about a non-event: Source misattributions among preschoolers. *Consciousness and Cognition, 3,* 388–407.

Charman, S. D., Gregory, A. H., & Carlucci, M. (2009). Exploring the diagnostic utility of facial composites: Beliefs of guilt can bias perceived similarity between composite and suspect. *Journal Of Experimental Psychology—Applied, 15,* 76–90.

Clark, S. E. (2005). A re-examination of the effects of biased lineup instructions in eyewitness identification. *Law and Human Behaviour, 29,* 395–424.

Clark, S. E., Marshall, T. E., & Rosenthal, R. (2009). Line-up administrator influences on eyewitness identification decisions. *Journal of Experimental Psychology: Applied, 15,* 63–75.

Compo, N., Evans, J. R., Carol, R., Villalba, D., Ham, L., Garcia, T., & Rose, S. (2012). Intoxicated witnesses: Better than their reputation? *Law and Human Behavior, 36,* 77–86.

Compo, N. S., Evans, J. R., Carol, R. N., Villalba, D., Ham, L. S., Garcia, T., & Rose, S. (2012). Intoxicated eyewitnesses: Better than their reputation? *Law And Human Behavior, 36,* 77–86.

Conway, A. R. A., Kane, M. J., Bunting, M. F., Hambrick, D. Z., Wilhelm, O., & Engle, R. W. (2005). Working memory span tasks: A methodological review and user's guide. *Psychonomic Bulletin & Review, 12*, 769.

Davis, D., & Loftus, E. F. (2005). Age and functioning in the legal system: Perception memory and judgment in victims, witnesses and jurors. In I. Noy & W. Karwowski (Eds.), *Handbook of forensic human factors and ergonomics* (pp. 11-1–11-53). London: Taylor and Francis.

Davis, S. D., & Meade, M. L. (2013). Both young and older adults discount suggestions from older adults on a social memory test. *Psychonomic Bulletin & Review, 20*, 760–765.

Deffenbacher, K. A., Bornstein, B. H., Penrod, S. D., & McGorty, E. K. (2004). A meta-analytic review of the effects of high stress on eyewitness memory. *Law And Human Behavior, 28*, 687–706.

Dodson, C. S., Powers, E., & Lytell, M. (2015). Aging, confidence, and misinformation: recalling information with the cognitive interview. *Psychology and Aging, 30*, 46–61.

Douglass, A. B., & Steblay, N. (2006). Memory distortion in eyewitnesses: A meta-analysis of the post-identification feedback effect. *Applied Cognitive Psychology, 20*, 859–869.

Douglass, A. B., Neuschatz, J. S., Imrich, J., & Wilkinson, M. (2010). Does post-identification feedback affect evaluations of eyewitness testimony and identification procedures? *Law And Human Behavior, 34*, 282–294.

Dysart, J. E., Lawson, V. Z., & Rainey, A. (2012). Blind lineup administration as a prophylactic against the post-identification feedback effect. *Law and Human Behavior, 36*, 312–319.

Eisen, M. L., Morgan, D. Y., & Mickes, L. (2002). Individual differences in eyewitness memory and suggestibility: Examining relations between acquiescence, dissociation and resistance to misleading information. *Personality and Individual Differences, 33*, 553–571.

Erdmann, K., Volbert, R., & Bohm, C. (2004). Children report suggested events even when interviewed in a non-suggestive manner: What are the implications for credibility assessment? *Applied Cognitive Psychology, 18*, 589–611.

Finsterwald C., & Alberini C. M. (2014). Stress and glucocorticoid receptor-dependent mechanisms in long-term memory: From adaptive responses to psychopathologies. *Neurobiology of Learning and Memory, 112*, 17–29.

Fisher, R. P. (2010). Interviewing cooperative witnesses. *Legal and Criminological Psychology, 15*, 25–38.

Fisher, R. P., & Geiselman, R. E. (1992). *Memory-enhancing techniques for investigating interviewing: The cognitive interview.* Springfield, IL: Charles C. Thomas.

Fisher R. P., Brewer, N., Mitchell, G. (2009). The relation between consistency and accuracy of eyewitness testimony: Legal versus cognitive explanations. In: R. Bull, T. Valentine, T. Williamson. *Handbook of psychology of investigative interviewing: Current developments and future directions* (pp. 121–136). Chichester: John Wiley & Sons, Ltd.

Fisher, R. P., Geiselman, R. E., & Raymond, D. S. (1987). Critical analysis of police interviewing techniques. *Journal of Police Science & Administration, 15*, 177–185.

Fisher, R. P., Milne, R., & Bull, R. (2011). Interviewing cooperative witnesses. *Current Directions in Psychological Science, 20*, 16–19.

French, L., Garry, M., & Mori, K. (2008). You say tomato? Collaborative remembering leads to more false memories for intimate couples than for strangers. *Memory, 16,* 262–273.

Frenda, S. J., Nichols, R. M., & Loftus, E. F. (2011). Current issues and advances in misinformation research. *Current Directions In Psychological Science, 20,* 20–23.

Gabbert, F., & Brown, C. (2015). Interviewing for face identification. In T. Valentine, & J. P. Davis, (Eds.), *forensic facial identification: Theory and practice of identification from eyewitnesses, composites and CCTV* (pp. 17–41). Chichester, UK: Wiley-Blackwell.

Gabbert, F., & Hope, L. (2013). Suggestibility and memory conformity. In A. M. Ridley, F. Gabbert, & D. J. La Rooy (Eds.). *Suggestibility in legal contexts: Psychological research and forensic implications* (pp. 63–84). London: Wiley-Blackwell.

Gabbert, F., Hope, L., Carter E., Boon, R., & Fisher, R. (2015). The role of initial witness accounts within the investigative process. In G. Oxburgh, T. Myklebust, T. Grant, & R. Milne (Eds.). *Communication in investigative and legal contexts: Integrated approaches from forensic psychology, linguistics and law enforcement* (pp. 107–133). Chichester, UK: Wiley-Blackwell.

Gabbert, F., Hope, L., Fisher, R. P., & Jamieson, K. (2012). Protecting against susceptibility to misinformation with the use of a Self-Administered Interview. *Applied Cognitive Psychology, 26,* 568–575.

Gabbert, F., Memon, A., Allan, K., & Wright, D. B. (2004). Say it to my face: Examining the effects of socially encountered misinformation. *Legal & Criminological Psychology, 9,* 215–227.

Gabbert, F., Memon, A., & Wright, D. (2003). Memory conformity: Can eyewitnesses influence each other's memories for an event? *Applied Cognitive Psychology, 17,* 533–543.

Gabbert, F., Memon, A., & Wright, D. B. (2006). Memory conformity: Disentangling the steps towards influence during a discussion. *Psychonomic Bulletin & Review, 13,* 480–485.

Gabbert, F., Memon, A., & Wright, D. B. (2007). I saw it for longer than you: The relationship between perceived encoding duration and memory conformity. *Acta Psychologica, 124,* 319–331.

Gabbert, F., & Wheeler, R. (October, 2017). Memory conformity. In M. L. Meade, A. J., Barnier, P. Van Bergen, C. B. Harris, & J. Sutton (Eds.), *Collaborative remembering: How remembering with others influences memory.* Oxford: Oxford University Press.

Garrioch, L., & Brimacombe, C. A. (2001). Lineup administrators' expectations: Their impact on eyewitness confidence. *Law and Human Behavior, 25,* 299–314.

Geiselman, R. E., Fisher, R. P., Cohen, G., Holland, H., & Surtes, L. (1986). Eyewitness responses to leading and misleading questions under the cognitive interview. *Journal of Police Science and Administration, 14,* 31–39.

George, R. C., & Clifford, B. (1992). Making the most of witnesses. *Policing, 8,* 185–198.

Gilbert, J. A. E., & Fisher, R. P. (2006). The effects of varied retrieval cues on reminiscence in eyewitness memory. *Applied Cognitive Psychology, 20,* 723–739.

Granhag, P. A., Ask, K., Rebelius, A., Öhman, L., & Mac Giolla, E. (2013). 'I saw the man who killed Anna Lindh!' An archival study of witnesses' offender descriptions. *Psychology Crime and Law, 19,* 921–931.

Greathouse, S. M., & Kovera, M. B. (2009). Instruction bias and lineup presentation moderate the effects of administrator knowledge on eyewitness identification. *Law and Human Behavior, 33,* 70–82.

Gronlund, S. D., & Carlson, C. A. (2013). System-based research on eyewitness identification. In T. Perfect and D. S. Lindsay (Eds.), *Handbook of applied memory* (pp. 595–613). Thousand Oaks, CA: Sage Publishing.

Gudjonsson, G. H. (1983). Suggestibility, intelligence, memory recall and personality: An experimental study. *British Journal of Psychiatry, 142,* 35–37.

Gudjonsson, G. H. (1984). A new scale of interrogative suggestibility. *Personality and Individual Difference, 5,* 303–314.

Gudjonsson, G. H. (1997). *The Gudjonsson Suggestibility Scales manual.* Hove, UK: Psychology Press.

Gudjonsson, G. H. (2003). *The Psychology of interrogations and confessions. A handbook.* Chichester, UK: John Wiley & Sons.

Gudjonsson, G. H. (2013). Interview suggestibility: Theory, research and applications. In A. M. Ridley, F. Gabbert, & D. J. La Rooy (Eds.). *Suggestibility in legal contexts: Psychological research and forensic implications* (pp. 45–61). London: Wiley-Blackwell.

Gudjonsson, G. H., & Clark, N. K. (1986). Suggestibility in police interrogation: A social psychological model. *Social Behaviour, 1,* 83–104.

Gudjonsson, G. H., Hannesdottir, K. Petursson, H., & Bjornsson, G. (2002). The effects of alcohol withdrawal on mental state, interrogative suggestibility, and compliance: An experimental study. *Journal of Forensic Psychology, 13,* 53–67.

Hardin, C. D., & Higgins, E. T. (1996). Shared reality: How social verification makes the subjective objective. In E. T. Higgins & R. M. Sorrentino (Eds.), *Handbook of motivation and cognition: the interpersonal context* (Vol. 3, pp. 28–84). New York: Guilford Press.

Harris, M. J., & Rosenthal, R. (1985). Mediation of interpersonal expectancy effects: 31 meta-analyses. *Psychological Bulletin, 97,* 363–386.

Hasel, L. E., & Kassin, S. M. (2009). On the presumption of evidentiary independence: Can confessions corrupt eyewitness identifications? *Psychological Science, 20,* 122–126.

Heaps, C. M., & Nash, M. (2001). Comparing recollective experience in true and false autobiographical memories. *Journal of Experimental Psychology: Learning, Memory, and Cognition, 4,* 920–930.

Heaton-Armstrong, A., Shepherd, E., Gudjonsson, G., & Wolchover, D. (Eds.). (2006). *Witness testimony: Psychological, investigative and evidential perspectives.* Oxford: Oxford University Press.

Henkel, L. A., & Franklin, N. (1998). Reality monitoring of physically similar and conceptually related objects. *Memory and Cognition, 26,* 659–673.

Hope, L., Blocksidge, D., Gabbert, F., Sauer, J. D., Lewinski, W., Mirashi, A., & Atuk, E. (2016). Memory and the operational witness: Police officer recall of firearms encounters as a function of active response role. *Law and Human Behavior, 40,* 23–35.

Hope, L., Gabbert, F., Fisher, R. P., & Jamieson, K. (2014). Protecting and enhancing eyewitness memory: The Impact of an initial recall attempt on performance in an investigative interview. *Applied Cognitive Psychology, 28,* 304–313.

Hope, L., Lewinski, W., Dixon, J., Blocksidge, D., Gabbert, & F. (2012). Witnesses in action: The effect of physical exertion on recall and recognition. *Psychological Science, 23,* 386–390.

Hope, L., Ost, J., Gabbert, F., Healey, S., & Lenton, E. (2008). "With a little help from my friends . . . ": The role of co-witness relationship in susceptibility to misinformation. *Acta Psychologica, 127,* 476–484.

Horry, R., Colton, L. M., & Williamson, P. (2014). Confidence-accuracy resolution in the misinformation paradigm is influenced by the availability of source cues. *Acta Psychologica, 151,* 164–173.

Horry, R., Halford, P., Brewer, N., Milne, R., & Bull, R. (2014). Archival analyses of eye-witness identification test outcomes: What can they tell us about eyewitness memory? *Law and Human Behavior, 38,* 94–108.

Howe, M. L., & Knott, L. M. (2015). The fallibility of memory in judicial processes: Lessons from the past and their modern consequences, *Memory, 23,* 633–656.

Huff, M. J., Weinsheimer, C. C., & Bodner, G. E. (2016). Reducing the misinformation effect through initial testing: Take two tests and recall me in the morning? *Applied Cognitive Psychology, 30,* 61–69.

Innocence Project. (2017). *Eyewitness misidentification.* Retrieved from http://www.innocenceproject.org/understand/Eyewitness-Misidentification.php

Jaschinski, U., & Wentura, D. (2002). Misleading postevent information and working memory capacity: An individual differences approach to eyewitness memory. *Applied Cognitive Psychology, 16,* 223–231.

Johnson, M. K., Hashtroudi, S., & Lindsay, D. S. (1993). Source monitoring. *Psychological Bulletin, 114,* 3–28.

Krähenbühl, S., & Blades, M. (2006). The effect of question repetition within interviews on young children's eyewitness recall. *Journal of Experimental Child Psychology, 94,* 57–67.

La Rooy, D. J., Brown, D., & Lamb, M. E. (2013). Suggestibility and witness interviewing using the Cognitive Interview and NICHD Protocol. In A. M. Ridley, F. Gabbert, & D. J. La Rooy (Eds.). *Suggestibility in legal contexts: Psychological Research and forensic implications.* (pp. 197–216). London: Wiley-Blackwell.

La Rooy, D., Lamb, M. E., & Pipe, M-E. (2009). Repeated interviewing: A critical evaluation of the risks and potential benefits. In K. Kuehnle & M. Connell (Eds.) *The evaluation of child sexual abuse allegations: A comprehensive guide to assessment and testimony* (pp. 327–361). Hoboken, NJ: Wiley.

Lamb, M. E., Hershkowitz, I., Orbach, Y., & Esplin, P. W. (2008). *Tell me what happened.* Chichester, UK: Wiley.

Lamb, M. E., La Rooy, D. J., Malloy, L. C., & Katz, C. (Eds.). (2011). *Children's Testimony: A handbook of psychological research and forensic practice* (2nd ed). London: Wiley-Blackwell.

Lamb, M. E., Orbach, Y., Hershkowitz, I., Esplin, P. W., & Horowitz, D. (2007). Structured forensic interview protocols improve the quality and informativeness of investigative interviews with children: A review of research using the NICHD Investigative Interview Protocol. *Child Abuse and Neglect, 31,* 1201–1231.

Lane, S. M. (2006). Dividing attention during a witnessed event increases eyewitness suggestibility. *Applied Cognitive Psychology, 20,* 199–212.

LaPaglia, J. A., Wilford, M. M., Rivard, J., Chan, J. C. K., & Fisher, R. P. (2014). Misleading suggestions can alter later memory reports even following a cognitive interview. *Applied Cognitive Psychology, 28,* 1–9.

Leichtman, M. D., & Ceci, S. J. (1995). The effects of stereotypes and suggestions on preschoolers' reports. *Developmental Psychology, 31,* 568–578.

Levett, L. M. (2013). Co-witness information influences whether a witness is likely to choose from a lineup. *Legal and Criminological Psychology, 18*, 168–180.

Loftus, E. (2005). Planting misinformation in the human mind: A 30-year investigation of the malleability of memory. *Learning & Memory, 12*, 361–366.

Loftus, E. F. (2013). Psychological memory science and legal reforms. *Association for Psychological Science Observer, 26*, 10–11.

Loftus, E. F., Levidow, B., & Duensing, S. (1992). Who remembers best? Individual difference in memory for events that occurred in a science museum. *Applied Cognitive Psychology, 6*, 93–107.

Loftus, E. F., Miller, D. G., & Burns, H. J. (1978). Semantic integration of verbal information into a visual memory. *Journal of Experimental Psychology: Human Learning and Memory, 4*, 19–31.

Lommen, M. J. J., Engelhard, I. M., & van den Hout, M. A. (2013). Susceptibility to long-term misinformation effect outside of the laboratory. *European Journal of Psychotraumatology, 4*, 19864.

Malpass, R. S., & Devine, P. G. (1981). Eyewitness identification: Lineup instructions and the absence of the offender. *Journal of Applied Psychology, 66*, 482–489.

Markham, R., & Hynes, L. (1993). The effect of vividness of imagery on reality monitoring. *Journal of Mental Imagery, 17*, 159–170.

McGaugh, J. L. (2000). Memory—a century of consolidation. *Science, 287*, 248–251.

McGaugh, J. L. (2013). Making lasting memories: Remembering the significant. *Proceedings of the National Academy of Sciences, 110*, 10401–10407.

Meade, M. L., & Roediger, H. L., III. (2002). Explorations in the social contagion of memory. *Memory & Cognition, 30*, 995–1009.

Melnyk, L., & Bruck, M. (2004). Timing moderates the effects of repeated suggestive interviewing on children's eyewitness memory. *Applied Cognitive Psychology, 18*, 613–631.

Memon, A., Gabbert, F., & Hope, L. (2004). The aging eyewitness. In J. R. Adler (Ed.), *Forensic psychology, current concepts and debates* (pp. 96–112). Portland, OR: Willan Forensic Psychology Series.

Memon, A., Meissner, C. A., & Fraser, J. (2010). The cognitive interview: A meta-analytic analysis and study space analysis of the past 25 years. *Psychology, Public Policy & Law, 16*, 340–372.

Memon, A., Zaragoza, M., Clifford, B. R., & Kidd, L. (2010). Inoculation or antidote? The effects of cognitive interview timing on false memory for forcibly fabricated events. *Law and Human Behavior, 34*, 105–117.

Mintzer, M. Z. (2007). The acute effects of alcohol on memory: A review of laboratory studies in healthy adults. *International Journal On Disability And Human Development, 6*, 397–403.

Mitchell, K. J., Johnson, M. K., & Mather, M. (2003). Monitoring and suggestibility to misinformation: Adult age-related differences. *Applied Cognitive Psychology, 17*, 107–119.

Morgan, C. A., III, Hazlett, G. A., Doran, A., Garrett, S., Hoyt, G., Thomas, P., et al. (2004). Accuracy of eyewitness memory for persons encountered during exposure to highly intense stress. *International Journal of Law and Psychiatry, 27*, 265–279.

Morgan, C. A., III, & Southwick, S. (2014). I believe what I remember, but it may not be true. *Neurobiology of Learning and Memory, 112*, 101–103.

Morgan, C. A., III, Southwick, S., Steffian, G., Hazlett, G. A., Elizabeth F., & Loftus, E. F. (2013) Misinformation can influence memory for recently experienced, highly stressful events. *International Journal of Law and Psychiatry, 36*, 11–17.

Morley J. E., & Farr S. A. (2012). Hormesis and amyloid-beta protein: Physiology or pathology? *Journal of Alzheimer's Disease, 29*, 487–492.

Nash, R. A., & Ost, J. (Eds.) (2017). *False and distorted memories.* Abingdon, UK: Psychology Press.

Nyberg, L., Cabeza, R., & Tulving, E. (1996). PET studies of encoding and retrieval: The HERA Model. *Psychonomic Bulletin and Review, 3*, 134–147.

Oeberst, A., & Seidemann, J. (2014). Will your words become mine? Underlying processes and cowitness intimacy in the memory conformity paradigm. *Canadian Journal of Experimental Psychology, 68*, 84.

Otgaar, H., Howe, M. L., Brackmann, N., & Smeets, T. (2016). The malleability of developmental trends in neutral and negative memory illusions. *Journal of Experimental Psychology: General, 145*, 31–55.

Oxburgh, G. E., Myklebust, T., & Grant, T. (2010). The question of question types in police interviews: A review of the literature from a psychological and linguistic perspective. *The International Journal of Speech, Language, and the Law, 17*, 45–66.

Palmer, M. A., Brewer, N., & Weber, N. (2010). Postidentification feedback affects subsequent eyewitness identification performance. *Journal of Experimental Psychology: Applied, 16*, 387–398.

Palmer, F. T., Flowe, H. D., Takarangi, M. K., & Humphries, J. E. (2013). Intoxicated witnesses and suspects: An archival analysis of their involvement in criminal case processing. *Law and Human Behavior, 37*, 54–59.

Paterson, H. M., & Kemp, R. I. (2006). Co-witnesses talk: A survey of eyewitness discussion. *Psychology Crime and Law, 12*, 181–191.

Payne, J. D., Jackson, E. D., Ryan, L., Hoscheidt, S., Jacobs, W. J., & Nadel, L. (2006). The impact of stress on neutral and emotional aspects of episodic memory. *Memory, 14*, 1–16.

Phillips, M. R., McAuliff, B. D., Kovera, M. B., & Cutler, B. L. (1999). Double-blind photo-array administration as a safeguard against investigator bias. *Journal of Applied Psychology, 84*, 940–951.

Pipe, M., Orbach, Y., Lamb, M. E., Abbott, C. B., & Stewart, H. (2013). Do case outcomes change when investigative interviewing practices change? *Psychology Public Policy and Law, 19*, 179–190.

Pipe, M.-E., Sutherland, R., Webster, N., Jones, C. H., & La Rooy, D. (2004). Do early interviews affect children's long-term recall? *Applied Cognitive Psychology, 18*, 1–17.

Poole, D. A., & White, L. T. (1991). Effects of question repetition on the eyewitness testimony of children and adults. *Developmental Psychology, 27*, 975–986.

Poole, D. A., & White, L. T. (1993). Two years later: Effects of question repetition and retention interval on the eyewitness testimony of children and adults. *Developmental Psychology, 29*, 844–853.

Powell, M. B. (2008). Designing effective training programs for investigative interviews of children. *Current Issues in Criminal Justice, 20*, 189.

Powell, M. B., Jones, C. H., & Campbell, C. (2003). A comparison of preschoolers' recall of experienced versus non-experienced events across multiple interviews. *Applied Cognitive Psychology, 17*, 935–952.

Principe, G. F., & Ceci, S. J. (2002). "I saw it with my own ears": The effects of peer conversations on preschoolers reports of non-experienced events. *Journal of Experimental Child Psychology, 83*, 1–25.

Putnam, A. L., Sungkhassettee, V., & Roediger, H. L. (2016). When misinformation improves memory: The effects of recollecting change. *Psychological Science, 28*, 36–46.

Ridley, A. M., & Gudjonsson, G. H. (2013). Suggestibility and individual differences in psychosocial and memory measures. In A. M. Ridley, F. Gabbert, & D. J. La Rooy (Eds.). *Suggestibility in legal contexts: Psychological research and forensic implications* (pp. 85–106). London: Wiley-Blackwell.

Ridley, A. M., Gabbert, F., & La Rooy, D. J. (Eds.) (2013). *Suggestibility in legal contexts: Psychological research and forensic implications.* London: Wiley-Blackwell.

Roozendaal, B. (2000). Glucocorticoids and the regulation of memory consolidation. *Psychoneuroendocrinology, 25*, 213–238.

Sauer, J. D., Brewer, N., Zweck, T., & Weber, N. (2010). The effect of retention interval on the confidence-accuracy relationship for eyewitness identification. *Law and Human Behavior, 34*, 337–347.

Sauerland, M., Raymaekers, L. H. C., Otgaar, H., Memon, A., Waltjen, T. T., Nivo, M., Slegers, C. Broers, N. J., & Smeets, T. (2016). Stress, stress-induced cortisol responses, and eyewitness identification performance. *Behavioral Sciences & the Law, 34*, 580–594.

Schneider, D. M., & Watkins, M. J. (1996). Response conformity in recognition testing. *Psychonomic Bulletin and Review, 3*, 481–485.

Schooler, J. W., & Loftus, E. F. (1986). Individual differences and experimentation: Complementary approaches to interrogative suggestibility. *Social Behaviour, 1*, 105–112.

Sigurdsson, J. F., & Gudjonsson, G. H. (1994). Alcohol and drug intoxication during police interrogation and the reasons why suspects confess to the police. *Addiction, 89*, 985–997.

Smalarz, L., & Wells, G. L. (2014). Post-identification feedback to eyewitnesses impairs evaluators' abilities to discriminate between accurate and mistaken testimony. *Law and Human Behavior, 38*, 194–202.

Smalarz, L., & Wells, G. L. (2015). Contamination of eyewitness self-reports and the mistaken-identification problem. *Current Directions in Psychological Science, 24*, 120–124.

Steblay, N. (1997). Social influence in eyewitness recall: A meta-analytic review of lineup instruction effects. *Law and Human Behavior, 21*, 283–297.

Steblay, N. M., Wells, G. L., & Douglass, A. L. (2014). The eyewitness post-identification feedback effect 15 years later: Theoretical and policy implications. *Psychology, Public, Policy, and Law, 20*, 1–18.

Thorley, C. (2015). Blame conformity: Innocent bystanders can be blamed for a crime as a result of misinformation from a young, but not elderly, adult co-witness. *PLoS ONE, 10*, e0134739. doi: 10.1371/journal.pone.0134739.

Tomes, J. L., & Katz, A. N. (1997). Habitual susceptibility to misinformation and individual differences in eyewitness memory. *Applied Cognitive Psychology, 11*, 233–251.

Tousignant, J. P., Hall, D., & Loftus, E. F. (1986). Discrepancy detection and vulnerability to misleading post-event information. *Memory & Cognition, 14*, 329–338.

Turner, M. L., & Engle, R. W. (1989). Is working memory capacity task dependent? *Journal of Memory and Language, 28*, 127–154.

Umanath, S., & Marsh, E. J. (2014). Understanding how prior knowledge influences memory in older adults. *Perspectives of Psychological Science*, 9, 408–426.

Underwood, J., & Pezdek, K. (1998). Memory suggestibility as an example of the sleeper effect. *Psychonomic Bulletin & Review*, 5, 449–453.

Valentine, T., Pickering, A., & Darling, S. (2003). Characteristics of eyewitness identification that predict the outcome of real lineups. *Applied Cognitive Psychology*, 17, 969–993.

van Oorsouw, K., & Merckelbach, H. (2012). The effect of alcohol on crime-related amnesia: A field study. *Applied Cognitive Psychology*, 26, 82–90.

Van Oorsouw, K., Merckelbach, H., & Smeets, T. (2015). Alcohol intoxication impairs memory and increases suggestibility for a mock crime: A field study. *Applied Cognitive Psychology*, 29, 493–501.

Vrij, A., Hope, L., & Fisher, R. P. (2014). Eliciting reliable information in investigative interviews. *Policy Insights from Behavioral and Brain Sciences*, 1, 129–136.

Walther, E., Bless, H. Strack, F. Rackstraw, P., Wagner, D., & Werth, L. (2002). Conformity effects in memory as a function of group size, dissenters and uncertainty. *Applied Cognitive Psychology*, 16, 793–810.

Wells, G. L., & Bradfield, A. L. (1998). 'Good, you identified the suspect': Feedback to eyewitnesses distorts their reports of the witnessing experience. *Journal of Applied Psychology*, 83, 360–376.

Wells, G. L., & Bradfield, A. L. (1999). Measuring the goodness of lineups: Parameter estimation, question effects, and limits to the mock witness paradigm. *Journal of Applied Psychology*, 13, 527–539.

Wells, G. L., Lindsay, R. C. L., & Ferguson, T. J. (1979). Confidence, accuracy, and juror perceptions in eyewitness identification. *Journal of Applied Psychology*, 64, 440–448.

Wells, G. L., Steblay, N. K., & Dysart, J. E. (2012). Eyewitness identification reforms: Are suggestiveness-induced hits and guesses true hits? *Perspectives on Psychological Science*, 7, 264–271.

Wixted, J. T., Mickes, L., Dunn, J, C., Clark, S. E., & Wells, W. (2016). Estimating the reliability of eyewitness identifications from police lineups. *Proceedings of the National Academy of Sciences of the United States of America*, 113, 304–309.

Wright, D. B., Self, G., & Justice, C. (2000). Memory conformity: Exploring misinformation effects when presented by another person. *British Journal of Psychology*, 91, 189–202.

Wright, D. B., & Stroud, J. N. (1998). Memory quality and misinformation for peripheral and central objects. *Legal and Criminological Psychology*, 3, 273–286.

Wright, D. B., & Villalba, D. K. (2012). Memory conformity affects inaccurate memories more than accurate memories. *Memory*, 20, 254–265.

Yuille, J. C., Tollestrup, P., Marxsen, D., Porter, S., & Hervé, H. (1998). Some effects of marijuana on eyewitness memory. *International Journal of Law and Psychiatry*, 20, 1–23.

Zajac R., & Henderson N. (2009). Don't it make my brown eyes blue: Co-witness misinformation about a target's appearance can impair target-absent line-up performance. *Memory*, 17, 266–278.

Zhu, B., Chen, C., Loftus, E. F., Lin, C., He, Q., Chen, C., Li, H., Xue, G., Lu, Z., & Dong, Q. (2010). Individual differences in false memory from misinformation: Cognitive factors. *Memory*, 18, 43–55.

4

When Spontaneous Statements Should Not Be Trusted

False Memories in Children and Adults

HENRY OTGAAR AND MARK L. HOWE

On the evening of July 14 2016 in Nice, a crowd of people celebrating Bastille Day were taken by surprise when a cargo truck deliberately drove into the crowd on the promenade. The terrorist attack caused many casualties; 85 people died and more then 300 people were injured. During the attack many eyewitnesses, children and adults, viewed the event from a distance. Some of them were later interviewed by the media and police. A crucial issue here is when a child's statement is compared with one from an adult, whose statement should the police put more weight on?

This question is not an exceptional one. In many legal cases, this question is pivotal during the police investigation. For example, in many child sexual abuse cases, often all the police have to go on is the statement of a child (the alleged victim) against the statement of an adult (alleged perpetrator) (e.g., Brackmann, Otgaar, Sauerland, & Jelicic, 2016). When such cases are brought to court, those involved in the legal system (e.g., judges, jurors, attorneys) are faced with a difficult situation, especially when statements by children and adults conflict. For the most part, those involved in the legal system hold the default belief that children's eyewitness statement are less reliable and lower in accuracy than those of adults (Knutsson & Allwood, 2014). The "reasoning" behind this is that children's reports are more likely to be tainted by memory errors, including errors of omission and errors of commission (i.e., false memories), than those of adults' and hence, children are more likely to provide an inaccurate account of what ostensibly occurred.

This chapter demonstrates that this belief is not just naïve and potentially dangerous when it comes to judicial process, but is seriously flawed inasmuch as it fails to take into account important scientific findings from research on the development of false memories. The chapter begins by outlining the different types of false memories. Following this, it explains how eyewitness memory operates and whether eyewitnesses and victims frequently err when describing traumatic events. It then demonstrates that different types of false memories appear to have different developmental trajectories but that these developmental trajectories are sensitive to systematic variation in factors that change the underlying nature of the source of false memory, variation that is predictable based on theoretical principles. Finally, the chapter turns to the issue of when spontaneous statements by children and adults should be regarded as trustworthy and how memory experts might play a vital role in deciding this issue.

FALSE MEMORIES

False memories are not created equal, as they come in a number of different forms. They can be about persons or objects, personally relevant or unrelated details, and about the recent or distant past. However, what false memories have in common is that they refer to memories of details or events that were not experienced. Broadly speaking, false memories can be categorized as *suggestion-induced* and *spontaneous* false memories (e.g., Otgaar & Candel, 2011). The first type has received immense empirical attention and involves false memories that arise because of external suggestive pressure. The second type is increasingly receiving empirical interest and results from internal memory processes (e.g., spreading activation) that give rise to false memories without any external suggestive pressure.

There are several methods of experimentally evoking suggestion-induced false memories. One of the most popular ways is the misinformation paradigm (Loftus, 2005). This paradigm consists of three stages. In the first stage, participants are presented with stimuli such as pictures or videos (e.g., bank robbery) or are involved in an interactive event. Then, they receive misinformation concerning the event (e.g., stating that the culprit was carrying a gun while in fact he had a knife). Misinformation can be given in different ways such as a narrative or by suggestive questioning. In the final stage, participants' memory is tested. The prototypical finding is that many participants adopt the misinformation and insert it in their statements about the original event, thereby producing false memories.

There are also paradigms that have been designed to mimic more real-life forensic circumstances in which people produce false memories for *entire events*. In the false memory implantation paradigm, participants receive narratives about fictitious events (Otgaar, Scoboria, & Smeets, 2013). More specifically, unbeknownst to the participants, experimenters contact the participants' parents and ask whether their child has experienced a certain event (e.g., hot air balloon ride). If not, participants will be suggestively interviewed and told that their parents stated that they did experience this false event. Participants are asked to elaborate on this fabricated event during multiple suggestive interviews. The basic finding is that about 30% to 40% of the participants claim to remember the fictitious event and even come up with additional information (not supplied by the interviewer) about that experience (Wade et al., 2007).

There are also other procedures to foster false memories in which more subtle forms of suggestion are applied. One notable example is the memory conformity paradigm (Wright, Memon, Skagerberg, & Gabbert, 2009). In one version of this paradigm, a pair of participants look at several stimuli (e.g., pictures). The participants assume that they are looking at the same stimuli, but in fact, the participant pairs are looking at slightly different versions of the stimuli. After being presented with the stimuli, participants are asked to engage in a collaborate recall phase in which the task is to recall together what they have seen. Following this, participants are separated and are individually asked about what they can recollect about the presented stimuli. The interesting result is that during the individual recall tests, many participants report having seen details that were actually mentioned by the other participant.

Spontaneous false memories are commonly elicited by means of the Deese-Roediger-McDermott (DRM) paradigm (Deese, 1959; Roediger & McDermott, 1995). In this paradigm, a list of associatively related words (e.g., butter, baker, crust) is shown to participants. These words are all related to a nonpresented word called *the critical lure* (e.g., bread). The standard finding is that during memory tests, a significant proportion of participants falsely recall or recognize the critical lure.

As was documented, there are a variety of procedures that can be used to experimentally induce suggestion-induced or spontaneous false memories. Before explaining how children and adults react to the production of such false memories, it is important to elaborate on whether accounts of children or adults contain any false memories when no suggestive influences have been encountered. In other words, the next section discusses field studies on the reliability of accounts of eyewitnesses and victims that were given spontaneously.

FIELD STUDIES OF EYEWITNESS MEMORY

When working on criminal cases, legal professionals oftentimes want to know the accuracy of statements provided by eyewitnesses to crimes. That is, they are interested in whether the content of statements correctly reflects what truly unfolded. However, in the majority of such cases the ground truth is unknown, meaning that the accuracy of a report cannot be determined. In such cases, the consistency of statements across eyewitnesses is often relied upon to provide an index of the overall reliability of the individual statements (Brewer, Potter, Fisher, Bond, & Luszcz, 1999). However, there are a minority of cases in which objective evidence (i.e., ground truth) in the form of videos or photographs was present at the crime scene. In such unique cases, the accuracy of statements can be examined and hence, it can be determined whether eyewitness statements contain memory errors.

In one of the first field studies of this kind, Yuille and Cutshall (1986) analyzed eyewitness interviews of a shooting incident. The incident involved a thief entering a gun shop and stealing money and armoury. Outside the gun shop, the store owner and thief were in a gun fight and the store owner fatally shot the thief. Many adult witnesses were able to view the gun shooting, and 21 witnesses were interviewed by the police after the incident. Thirteen of them were later also interviewed by experimenters in the field study. The accuracy of their statements could be examined because many details were known by the police (e.g., weapons, thief's automobile). When the eyewitness statements were examined, the most striking result was the high accuracy rates, ranging from 76% (accuracy rate of person descriptions) to 89% (accuracy rate of object descriptions). Furthermore, the authors found that very few errors were produced in the eyewitness accounts.

Subsequent field research confirmed the high accuracy rates found in adult eyewitness testimony. For example, Christianson and Hubinette (1993) examined eyewitness reports from several bank robberies. The researchers contacted witnesses who had observed a bank robbery as a victim (bank teller) or a bystander (customer) and asked them to complete a questionnaire concerning their memory for the crime. When looking at the responses, they found a mean accuracy rate of 81%. Together, these results show that for adults, eyewitness statements contain a high degree of accuracy and low rates of errors.

Furthermore, Alexander and colleagues (2005) investigated the memory accuracy for adolescent and adult victims of sexual abuse 12 to 21 years after the abuse ended. Detailed information was present for these victims including details regarding the abuse (e.g., abuse duration, victim–perpetrator relationship) and information on children's legal experiences (e.g., the degree of legal involvement). The victims were interviewed and their answers were compared with the available information. Interestingly, memory accuracy was very high (i.e., proportion correct was .72), and errors of commission and omission were rather low (i.e., proportion commission was .14 and proportion omission was .14).

Such field studies have also been done with child victims of, for example, sexual abuse. In one of the first studies, Orbach and Lamb (1999) compared a 13-year-old child's statements of sexual abuse with an audio recording of the last in a series of sexually abusive incidents. The authors found that of the 189 reported details, 50.8% (n = 96) was validated by the audio recording. In this case, there was a minority of details (7% of central details) that were not corroborated by the audio recording and could be potential memory errors. In subsequent research by Bidrose and Goodman (2000), sexual abuse statements of four girls (8 to 15 years old) were compared with photographic and audiotaped records of the abuse instigated by eight adult men. Although high levels of omissions were found in the children's statements, a striking 80% of the allegations could be supported by the objective evidence.

Since these pioneering studies on child sexual abuse, follow-up field studies have found similar results. For example, Leander, Granhag, and Christianson (2005) found that children who were exposed to obscene telephone calls omitted much information in their testimony, but what they reported was highly accurate. Indeed, children oftentimes find it difficult to talk about their abusive experiences and delay disclosure of the traumatic incidents. However, what they report contains a high degree of accuracy (e.g., Leander, Christianson, & Granhag, 2007; Sjoberg & Lindblad, 2002a, 2002b). Taken together, research has consistently demonstrated that both children and adults are highly accurate when they provide an eyewitness account of highly emotional negative events (e.g., robberies, shooting incidents, sexual abuse). Based on these findings, one might argue that such memories are unlikely to be distorted and that false memories are unlikely to occur when experiencing an event. However, what follows will show the conditions under which false memories can be easily elicited for emotional events in both children and adults.

FALSE MEMORY DEVELOPMENT

A commonly held view among legal professionals and memory researchers concerning the development of false memories is that younger children are more likely to form false memories than older children and adults. Although the authors will argue that this view is overly simplistic, there is some face value to this idea. To understand why, we have to resort to the development of different types of false memories (suggestion-induced versus spontaneous). As we will see, developmental trajectories in the production of these false memories are different.

Suggestion-Induced False Memories

If we take a closer look at false memory development that is induced suggestively, then there exists an abundance of studies that show suggestion is more likely to contaminate children's memory compared with that of adults'. One of the first developmental misinformation studies was performed by Ceci, Ross, and Toglia (1987). They tested children ranging from 3 to 12 years of age (Experiment 1). Children were read a short story about a girl going to her first day at school. During the presentation, children received information that the girl had a bad stomach ache. One day later, some children were presented with misinformation suggesting that the little girl had a headache. Two days after the exposure to misinformation, all children received a recognition test. The most notable finding was that the youngest children (3- to 4-year-olds) were the most susceptible to accepting the misinformation whereas the oldest group (11- to 12-year-olds) were the least prone to misinformation acceptance.

This developmental misinformation finding has been replicated many times since this original study (e.g., Kulkofsky & Klemfuss, 2008; Roebers & Schneider, 2005; see also Loftus, 2005). In one of our studies using the misinformation paradigm, 4- to 5-year-olds and 8- to 11-year-olds were instructed to remove three pieces of clothing of a puppet (Otgaar, Candel, Smeets, & Merckelbach, 2010). Of relevance for the current discussion is that half of the children received false evidence suggesting that they took off four pieces of clothing. Then, during three follow-up interviews separated by 1-week intervals, children had to state which pieces of clothing they had removed. Younger children were more likely to falsely state that they removed four pieces of clothing than older children.

Developmental false memory studies have also been performed using the false memory implantation paradigm. We falsely suggested to 7- to 8- and 11- to

12-year-olds that they were abducted by a UFO or that they almost choked on a candy when they were 4 years old (Otgaar, Candel, Merckelbach, & Wade, 2009). We asked children what they could remember about these events during two interviews separated by a 1-week interval. We found that at the second interview, implanted false memory rates were higher in the younger than older children. The same effect was observed in another developmental false memory implantation experiment (Otgaar, Candel, Scoboria, & Merckelbach, 2010), where children (7- to 8-year-olds versus 11- to 12-year-olds) were falsely told that they received a rectal enema or that their fingers got stuck in a mousetrap during two follow-up interviews. Again, we showed that at the second interview, false events were more likely to be implanted in younger than older children's memory.

Memory conformity effects also seem to occur more often in younger children than in older children. Candel, Memon, and Al-Harazi (2007) had younger (6- to 7-year-olds) and older children (11- to 12-year-olds) view a video in dyads. The dyads believed they received the same video, whereas in fact the children were presented with two different versions. The authors demonstrated that for cued recall, memory conformity effects were stronger for younger than older children (but see also McGuire, London, & Wright, 2015 for contrasting results). Taken together, the available literature on false memories induced by suggestion shows that susceptibility to false memories decreases with age. However, the next section shows that the opposite developmental pattern occurs for spontaneous false memories.

Spontaneous False Memories

Most of the work on spontaneous false memories has been conducted using the DRM paradigm. A plethora of research has shown that when using this procedure, adults are more likely to produce false memories than children, a phenomenon also called developmental reversal (Brainerd, Reyna, & Ceci, 2008). Developmental reversals in false memories are important, as they provide a different picture concerning children's testimonial accuracy. Several false memory theories have been put forward that can accommodate this developmental pattern.

Fuzzy-trace Theory (FTT) stipulates that people store two opponent memory traces when experiencing an event (Brainerd, 2013; Brainerd et al., 2008). Gist traces capture the essential meaning or semantics of an event, whereas verbatim traces are involved in storing item-specific details of an event. For example, if a person is an eyewitness to an armed robbery, then gist traces could be involved in the storage of what happens in general during a crime (e.g., the use of a weapon such as a gun or knife), whereas verbatim traces relate to specific details that are stored of the robbery (e.g., that the weapon was a gun that was black). Verbatim traces fade faster than gist traces and hence, after some passage of time, people rely on gist traces during memory retrieval. When gist traces are extracted, people are likely to rely on the underlying meaning of an event, which can increase the retrieval of false memories (e.g., that the robber fired his weapon, which in fact did not occur). Indeed, according to FTT, false memories are the result of retrieving gist traces when verbatim traces are unavailable. Furthermore, the ability to extract gist traces improves significantly with age and hence, FTT predicts that false memories ought to increase with age across childhood.

An alternative theoretical variant to predict the development of false memories is associative-activation theory (AAT; Howe, Wimmer, Gagnon, & Plumpton, 2009; Otgaar, Howe, Brackmann, & Smeets, 2016). AAT relies on the notion of spreading activation to explain the formation of false memories. That is, when people experience an event, it will activate nodes (i.e., concepts) in a network of information in one's knowledge base (also called the mental lexicon). This spreading activation will be more efficient when relations between nodes are stronger and faster. The core theme here is that during this associative activation, nodes will be activated that are related to an event but were not actually experienced (e.g., that there was gun fire), thereby leading to false memories. AAT postulates that from childhood to adulthood, people acquire more knowledge, which can change the structure of knowledge, strengthen relations between nodes, and make associative activation more rapid. The net result is that associative activation becomes more automatic. Thus, this developmental process will enhance false memory proneness and hence, AAT predicts that adults are more likely to form false memories than children.

As has been noted, developmental DRM studies have consistently found an age-related increase in false memories. One of the more forensically relevant findings in this research line are studies showing that emotionally valenced material is more likely to give rise to false memories than neutral material. For example, Howe, Candel, Otgaar, Malone, and Wimmer (2010; also see Howe, 2007) presented children and adults with neutral and negative-emotional DRM lists and investigated false memory rates for these lists immediately and after 1 week. Interestingly, false recognition rates were significantly higher for the negative than neutral lists for both children and adults. Moreover, negative false memories increased over time, while neutral false memories remained stable after 1 week. The finding that negative false memories are more easily elicited than neutral false memories has been replicated in other studies as well (for a review, see Bookbinder & Brainerd, 2016).

Furthermore, this result has also been shown to occur in suggestion-induced false memories. For example, the authors provided 7-year-old children with false narratives suggesting that they copied off their neighbors' homework (negative false story) or that they had to move to another classroom (neutral false story) (Otgaar, Candel, & Merckelbach, 2008). The key finding was that negative false memories were more easily implanted than neutral ones. That emotion can catalyze spontaneous *and* suggestion-based false memory is of high forensic relevance because the core of many criminal investigations concerns emotionally negative events. Even more important, recent research has revealed that maltreated children are even more likely to produce negative spontaneous false memories than children without a maltreatment history (Baugerud, Howe, Magnussen, & Melinder, 2016; Goodman, Quas, & Ogle, 2010; Otgaar, Howe, & Muris, 2016). Why this is so important is that children in legal cases not only have to talk about negative events on many occasions, but many of them have faced severe trau-matic incidents (e.g., sexual abuse). Such children might even be more at risk of producing negative spontaneous false memories than children with no such adverse experiences. The story seems, however, to be different for suggestion-induced false memories. Here, research does not provide strong support that mal-treatment affects children's willingness to accept suggestive pressure (e.g., Chae, Goodman, Eisen, & Qin, 2011; Eisen, Goodman, Qin, Davis, & Crayton, 2007). Besides the effects of emotion and trauma on false memories, empirical interest has recently been increasingly concerned with whether developmental trends in false memories can be changed. The reason why this is critical is because we need to know whether false memory development is fixed or whether it can be altered in predictable ways, given theories about memory and its development during childhood.

Changing False Memory Development

A core element of AAT is the use of theme nodes when experiencing an event. That is, a theme node captures the essence of an experienced event. The key point is that children do not have as many theme nodes as adults because they lack the specific knowledge about a diversity of situations. Based on this theoretical tenet, AAT predicts that when stimuli are presented where the theme of the event is eas-ily identified, children will be equally susceptible to false memories, or perhaps even more susceptible than adults, who already possess such theme nodes in their knowledge base. If so, then such stimuli might lead to changes in developmental trends in false memories (Howe et al., 2009).

To examine this possibility, instead of presenting DRM lists, an alterna-tive procedure was used to foster spontaneous false memories (Otgaar, Howe, Peters, Smeets, & Moritz, 2014). More specifically, we gave children (7- to 8- and 11- to 12-year-olds) pictures containing different themes (e.g., beach, classroom). The pictures consisted of associatively related details (e.g., sand castle in the beach scene) that were related to critical nonpresented items (e.g., beach ball). After the presentation of these pictures, children and adults received a recognition task containing presented items and critical nonpre-sented items. The most interesting finding was that children's spontaneous false memory rates were higher than that of adults'. So, although one might expect that when associatively related stimuli are presented to children and adults, that the typical "DRM-like" developmental reversal should be obtained, it waas found that such reversals can even be "reversed" when stimuli used contain easily identifiable ("child-friendly") themes.

This finding was replicated by using another type of stimuli with obvious themes (Otgaar, Howe, Peters, Sauerland, & Raymaekers, 2013). More precisely, 6- to 8-year-olds, 10- to 12-year-olds, and adults were presented with a video false memory paradigm in which several events were shown (e.g., video of a street fight). Here, too, the videos contained several associatively related details that were linked to critical nonpresented items (e.g., police riding in a car). After this, participants received a recognition task composed of presented and critical non-presented items. The standard DRM paradigm was also included in this experiment. Here again, the experiment demonstrated that when associatively related stimuli were used containing obvious themes, children were most susceptible to the formation of spontaneous false memories and, as such, a reversal of the developmental reversal was observed. Equally important, when looking at the production of DRM false memories, the standard developmental reversal effect was found.

So, the crucial message here is that when associatively related material is presented to children and adults in which the theme is obvious, then age-related changes in false memories occur. Indeed, this dovetails nicely with research showing that when DRM lists are embedded in stories, developmental reversal effects are reversed as well (Dewhurst, Pursglove, & Lewis, 2007; Howe & Wilkinson, 2011). What these results tell us is that for spontaneous false memories, developmental trends can change in predicable ways and that such trends are not fixed. That is, in such circumstances, children are more susceptible than adults to false memories when the theme or meaning of the event is something they understand (i.e., part of their knowledge base).

So, if developmental trends in *spontaneous* false memories are malleable, so too should be developmental trends in *suggestion-induced* false memories. However, the finding that susceptibility to suggestive pressure decreases with age has been accepted as established science (Brainerd, 2013). Importantly, the authors have performed several experiments showing that this is not established at all. Based on theories such as FTT and AAT, the recipe for changing developmental trends in suggestion-induced false memories is the following: (1) Present younger, older children, and adults with stimuli containing associatively-related details; (2) provide suggestive pressure in which the associative structure is preserved; and (3) test children's and adults' memory for presented and nonpresented details. The logical prediction would be that adults and older children would be more likely to link the suggestion with their knowledge base than younger children and hence, be most susceptible to making incorrect associations and thus, creating false memories.

This prediction was tested in a series of four misinformation experiments (Otgaar, Howe, Brackmann, & Smeets, 2016). Neutral (postwomen bringing mail) and emotionally-negative (robbery) videos were presented to participants from different age groups. Based on pilot work, the authors made sure that the videos contained associatively related details. For example, in the negative video, the culprit wore black clothes and stole money. After the presentation of the videos, participants received misinformation in which related, but not presented details were presented during the video (e.g., that the culprit had a pistol, while in fact he did not have a weapon). Then, participants underwent a recognition task. The key result was that when this adapted misinformation procedure was used, older children and adults were more likely to succumb to suggestive pressure and produce false memories than younger children. So, a developmental reversal effect was found for suggestion-induced false memories.

The story so far is that the development of false memories—spontaneous or suggestion-induced—is not a given fact and that age is probably not the best predictor for false memory formation. Other factors such as changes in one's knowledge base might be better suited to make predictions concerning the development of false memories. The previously-stated findings are of particular relevance for memory experts in court whose task is to judge the reliability of children's and adults' testimony. How memory experts should do this task and what happens when expert witnesses are not memory experts in court are discussed next.

MEMORY EXPERTS AND FALSE MEMORIES

As has been shown, the development of false memories can vary in predictable ways and both spontaneous and suggestion-induced false memories can increase and decrease with age. Such specific knowledge is important for memory researchers working as expert witnesses in court. Expert witnesses who have to provide an index of the reliability of statements are faced with a daunting exercise. To begin with, expert witnesses have a slightly different role depending upon in which country they need to testify and which criminal legal system is used in that country. In general, there are two main criminal law systems active across the world: Inquisitorial and adversarial (De Ruiter & Kaser-Boyd, 2015). The inquisitorial approach is used in the strictest sense in the Netherlands, whereas the adversarial system is active in countries such as England, Canada, and the United States. In the adversarial system, legal cases can be seen as contests between two equivalent parties: the defense and prosecution (Van Koppen, 2007). These parties provide their arguments in a rather similar role in front of the judge and sometimes also a jury. Furthermore, in this system, a judge needs to have a neutral role during the case and only mediates in case of conflicts.

In the inquisitorial approach, parties are not equal and a jury is also absent. In this system, the main purpose is to find the truth (Van Koppen & Penrod, 2003). Compared with the adversarial system, in the inquisitorial method, the judge acts professionally based on special training that he/she has received. Such training involves courses on judicial training, but also on psychology and law (Van Koppen, 2007). Also in this legal system, the judge has an active role and leads the investigation. This means it is not the prosecution and defense asking the majority of questions in the courtroom, but the judge.

Expert witnesses play an important role in each of these systems. In both systems, experts can be asked to write a report on the reliability of statements and can be asked to appear in court. Also, in both legal systems, both the prosecution and defense can ask for expert witness assistance. However, one fundamental difference between the two systems is that in the adversarial legal system, the chance that expert witnesses are biased toward the side that hired them is higher than in the inquisitorial method. Such allegiance biases can lead to expert witnesses "battling" about their reports in the courtroom in front of the judge and jury (Murrie, Boccaccini, Guarnera, & Rufino, 2013). In the inquisitorial legal system, expert witnesses are assumed to be completely independent (Saks, 2003) and do not have to appear frequently in the courtroom to explain their report. Nonetheless, in the inquisitorial system, experts do often end up battling against each other in the legal arena.

Part of the reason for this boils down to which type of expert witnesses are admitted in court. For example, in the United States, only expert witnesses are allowed who meet certain criteria (i.e., Frye or Daubert criteria: e.g., known error rate, subjected to peer review; Saks & Faigman, 2005). Such criteria are generally lacking in, for example, the Netherlands, yet scientific databases do exist containing expertise of various disciplines (e.g., forensic psychology, DNA-analysists). Such databases are generally embraced by the scientific community and should guard against biased expert witnesses appearing in court making flawed judgments regarding a certain case. Of course, such a barrier is not error proof and occasionally, flawed expert testimony does enter the courtroom.

To illustrate such a case, the first author (HO) was recently asked to provide an expert opinion concerning statements made by a 6-year-old girl (Brackmann, Otgaar, Sauerland, & Jelicic, 2016). The girl claimed to have seen her mother being murdered by her father. The core conclusion of the expert report was that there were no strong reasons to question the statements of the young girl. The defense, however, asked another expert, a clinical psychologist, who reached a different conclusion. The clinical psychologist postulated that the girl had a spontaneous false memory of the event and that hence, there were severe reasons to discount her statements. However, during the trial, HO argued that spontaneous false memories are not necessarily elicited with ease in young children, something that the clinical psychologist was unaware of. Such disagreements lead to the question of how expert witnesses dealing with memory questions should handle such cases and write objective reports.

This question is not a new one and has been raised by other memory scholars as well (e.g., Zajac, Garry, Goodyear-Smith, & Hayne, 2013). In the authors' opinion, to be considered as a memory expert, the following issues are relevant. First, memory experts should be part of the scientific community on memory research. They should, for example, attend conferences on memory, publish on memory research, and review papers related to memory. Second, their sole practice is the science of memory, and not clinical practice. Although this is by no means an exhaustive list, such requirements make sure that experts are up to date concerning the latest findings in their field. This is especially relevant for the current discussion on spontaneous and suggestion-induced false memories. That is, knowledge about the particularities by which spontaneous and suggestion-induced false memories develop across age protects us from making the false assumption that children are necessarily inferior eyewitnesses. As shown in the current chapter, even young children can provide extremely accurate statements of highly arousing and negative events such as sexual abuse (e.g., Orbach & Lamb, 1999). Furthermore, our synopsis of the literature has demonstrated that children, under very specific circumstance, can be the least susceptible to making spontaneous false memories (e.g., Otgaar & Candel, 2011; Otgaar et al., 2013, 2016). Taken together, such findings can be of special relevance for memory experts, as these findings show that when there are indications in a legal case that children spontaneously disclosed a certain incident, then this can be a strong sign that the disclosure refers to a truly experienced event. Of course, our discussion also shows that in certain situations, spontaneous statements made by adults might be contaminated by errors. Such a situation could occur when adults experience events that are all closely related to each other. Sexual abuse might be seen as such an event. During sexual abuse, a perpetrator might touch the victim on several places and when questioned about it, the victim might misremember being touched somewhere that they were not touched as well (see also Holliday, Reyna, & Brainerd, 2008).

Besides being up to date with the recent literature on memory, the authors' opinion is also that certain safeguards should be taken into account when writing expert witness reports. One recommendation is that expert witness should construct at least two scenarios when looking at the reliability of statements (Otgaar, De Ruiter, Howe, Hoetmer, & Van Reekum, in press). Specifically, they should look for evidence in the case files for the guilty scenario (i.e., statements are accurate) and the innocent scenario (i.e., statements are fabricated). Doing such scenario building might protect the expert witness from confirmation bias (Kassin, Dror, & Kukucka, 2013). Second, expert witnesses should always look for the first disclosure and investigate under which circumstances this was made. As has been mentioned, suggestion can taint disclosures, but spontaneous disclosures, especially in children, can be highly accurate. Finally, to make sure expert witnesses have not fallen prey to confirmation biases and flawed reasoning, another expert who has not seen the case files should carefully look at the report and comment critically on it.

CONCLUSION

This chapter outlined recent evidence showing that developmental trends in false memories are not fixed and can be radically altered based on clear theoretical principles. Specifically, it has shown that, depending on certain theoretical conditions, children and adults can be both the least and most prone to false memory illusions. Such results are highly relevant because in many child sexual abuse cases, oftentimes the sole evidence is the testimony of a child against the testimony of an adult. The take-home message here is that age should not be used to make judgments about the reliability of one's statements. Instead, the authors' argue that memory experts should search for elements (e.g., suggestive pressure, spontaneous disclosure) in the case file of which the science of memory has shown might be beneficial or perilous for statements. Only by doing such a task can memory experts give a balanced and objective report about whether spontaneous or suggestion-induced false memories have been present in a case.

REFERENCES

Baugerud, G. A., Howe, M.L., Magnussen, S., & Melinder, A. (2016). Maltreated and non-maltreated children's true and false memories of neutral and emotional word lists in the Deese/Roediger-McDermott task. *Journal of Experimental Child Psychology, 143*, 102–110.

Bookbinder, S. H., & Brainerd, C. J. (2016). Emotion and false memory: The context-content paradox. *Psychological Bulletin*, *142*, 1315–1351.

Brackmann, N., Otgaar, H., Sauerland, M., & Jelicic, M. (2016). When children are the least vulnerable to false memories: A true report or a case of autosuggestion? *Journal of Forensic Sciences*, *61*, S271–S275.

Brainerd, C. J. (2013). Developmental reversals in false memory: A new look at the reliability of children's evidence. *Current Directions in Psychological Science*, *22*, 335–341. doi: 10.1177/0963721413484468

Brainerd, C. J., Reyna, V. F., & Ceci, S. J. (2008). Developmental reversals in false memory: A review of data and theory. *Psychological Bulletin*, *134*, 343–382. doi: 10.1037/0033-2909.134.3.343

Brewer, N., Potter, R., Fisher, R. P., Bond, N., & Luszcz, M. A. (1999). Beliefs and data on the relationship between consistency and accuracy of eyewitness testimony. *Applied Cognitive Psychology*, *13*, 297–231.

Ceci, S. J., Ross, D. F., & Toglia, M. P. (1987). Suggestibility of children's memory: Psycholegal implications. *Journal of Experimental Psychology: General*, *116*, 38–49.

Chae, Y., Goodman, G. S., Eisen, M. L., & Qin, J. (2011). Event memory and suggestibility in abused and neglected children: Trauma-related psychopathology and cognitive functioning. *Journal of Experimental Child Psychology*, *110*, 520–538.

Deese, J. (1959). On the prediction of occurrence of particular verbal intrusions in immediate recall. *Journal of Experimental Psychology*, *58*, 17–22.

De Ruiter, C., & Kaser-Boyd, N. (2015). *Forensic psychological assessment in practice: Case studies*. New York and London: Routledge.

Dewhurst, S. A., Pursglove, R. C., & Lewis, C. (2007). Story contexts increase susceptibility to the DRM illusion in 5-year-olds. *Developmental Science*, *10*, 374–378.

Eisen, M. L., Goodman, G. S., Qin. J., Davis, S., & Crayton, J. (2007). Maltreated children's memory: Accuracy, suggestibility, and psychopathology. *Developmental Psychology*, *43*, 1275–1294.

Goodman, G. S., Quas, J. A., & Ogle, C. M. (2010). Child maltreatment and memory. *Annual Review of Psychology*, *61*, 325–351.

Holliday, R. E., Reyna, V. F., & Brainerd, C. J. (2008). Recall of details never experienced: Effects of age, repetition, and semantic cues. *Cognitive Development*, *23*, 67–78.

Howe, M. L. (2007). Children's emotional false memories. *Psychological Science*, *18*, 856–860.

Howe, M. L., & Wilkinson, S. (2011). Using story contexts to bias children's true and false memories. *Journal of Experimental Child Psychology*, *108*, 77–95.

Howe, M. L., Candel, I., Otgaar, H., Malone, C., & Wimmer, M. C. (2010). Valence and the development of immediate and long term false memory illusions. *Memory*, *18*, 58–75.

Howe, M. L., Wimmer, M. C., Gagnon, N., & Plumpton, S. (2009). An associative-activation theory of children's and adults' memory illusions. *Journal of Memory and Language*, *60*, 229–251.

Kassin, S. M., Dror, I. E., & Kukucka, J. (2013). The forensic confirmation bias: Problems, perspectives, and proposed solutions. *Journal of Applied Research in Memory and Cognition*, *2*, 42–52.

Knutsson, J., & Allwood, C. M. (2014). Opinions of legal professionals: Comparing child and adult witnesses' memory report capabilities. *The European Journal of Psychology Applied to Legal Context*, *6*, 79–89. doi: 10.1016/j.ejpal.2014.06.001

Kulkofsky, S., & Klemfuss, J. Z. (2008). What the stories children tell can tell about their memory: Narrative skill and young children's suggestibility. *Developmenal Psychology*, *44*, 1442–1456.

Leander, L., Christianson, S. A., & Granhag, P. A. (2007). A sexual abuse case study: Children's memories and reports. Psychiatry. *Psychology and Law*, *14*, 12–129.

Loftus, E.F. (2005). Planting misinformation in the human mind: A 30-year investigation of the malleability of memory. *Learning & Memory*, *12*, 361–366.

Murrie, D. C., Boccaccini, M. T., Guarnera, L. A., & Rufino, K. A. (2013). Are forensic experts biased by the side that retained them? *Psychological Science*, *24*, 1889–1897.

Orbach, Y., & Lamb, M. E. (1999). Assessing the accuracy of a child's account of sexual abuse: A case study. *Child Abuse & Neglect*, *23*, 91–98.

Otgaar, H., & Candel, I. (2011). Children's false memories: Different false memory paradigms reveal different results. *Psychology, Crime & Law*, *17*, 513–528. doi: 10.1080/10683160903373392

Otgaar, H., Candel, I., & Merckelbach, H. (2008). Children's false memories: Easier to elicit for a negative than for a neutral event. *Acta Psychologica*, *128*, 350–354. doi: 10.1016/j.actpsy.2008.03.009

Otgaar, H., Candel, I., Merckelbach, H., & Wade, K. A. (2009). Abducted by a UFO: Prevalence information affects young children's false memories for an implausible event. *Applied Cognitive Psychology*, *23*, 115–125. doi: 10.1002/acp.1445

Otgaar, H., Candel, I., Scoboria, A., & Merckelbach, H. (2010). Script knowledge enhances the development of children's false memories. *Acta Psychologica*, *133*, 57–63. doi: 10.1016/j.actpsy.2009.09.002

Otgaar, H., Candel, I., Smeets, T., & Merckelbach, H. (2010). "You didn't take Lucy's skirt off": The effect of misleading information on omissions and commissions in children's memory reports. *Legal and Criminological Psychology*, *15*, 229–241. doi: 10.1348/135532509X471951

Otgaar, H., de Ruiter, C., Howe, M. L., Hoetmer, L., & van Reekum, P. (2017). A case concerning children's false memories of abuse: Recommendations regarding expert witness work. *Psychiatry, Psychology and Law*.

Otgaar, H., Howe, M.L., Peters, M., Sauerland, M., & Raymaekers, L. (2013). Developmental trends in different types of spontaneous false memories: Implications for the legal field. *Behavioral Sciences & the Law*, *31*, 666–682.

Otgaar, H., Howe, M.L., Peters, M., Smeets, T., & Moritz, S. (2014). The production of spontaneous false memories across childhood. *Journal of Experimental Child Psychology*, *121*, 28–41.

Otgaar, H., Scoboria, A., & Smeets, T. (2013). Experimentally evoking nonbelieved memories for childhood events. *Journal of Experimental Psychology: Learning, Memory, and Cognition*, *39*, 717–730.

Roebers, C. M., & Schneider, W. (2005). The strategic regulation of children's memory and suggestibility. *Journal of Experimental Child Psychology*, *91*, 24–44.

Roediger, H. L., & McDermott, K. B. (1995). Creating false memories: Remembering words not presented in lists. *Journal of experimental psychology: Learning, Memory, and Cognition*, *21*, 803.

Saks, M. J. (2003). Expert witnesses in Europe and the United States. In P. J. Van Koppen & S. D. Penrod (Eds.), *Adversarial versus inquisitorial justice: Psychological perspectives on criminal justice systems*. New York.

Saks, M. J., & Faigman, D. L. (2005). Expert evidence after Daubert. *Annual Review of Law and Social Science, 1*, 105–130.

Sjoberg, R. L., & Lindblad, F. (2002a). Limited disclosure of sexual abuse whose experiences were documented by videotape. *The American Journal of Psychiatry, 159*, 312–314.

Sjoberg, R. L., & Lindblad, F. (2002b). Delayed disclosure and disrupted communication during forensic investigation of child sexual abuse: A study of 47 corroborated cases. *Acta Paediatrica, 91*, 1391–1396.

Van Koppen, P. J. (2007). Miscarriages of justice in inquisitorial and accusatorial legal systems. *The Journal of the Institute of Justice & International Studies, 7*, 50–58.

Van Koppen, P. J., & Penrod, S. D. (2003). Adversarial or inquisitorial: Comparing systems. In P. J. Van Koppen & S. D. Penrod (Eds.), *Adversarial versus inquisitorial justice: Psychological perspectives on criminal justice systems*. New York: Springer Science & Business Media.

Wade, K. A., Sharman, S. J., Garry, M., Memon, A., Mazzoni, G., Merckelbach, H., & Loftus, E. F. (2007). False claims about false memory research. *Consciousness and Cognition, 16*, 18–28.

Wright, D. B., Memon, A., Skagerberg, E. M., & Gabbert, F. (2009). When eyewitnesses talk. *Current Directions in Psychological Science, 18*, 174–178. doi:10.1111/j.1467-8721.2009.01631.x

Yuille, J. C., & Cutshall, J. L. (1986). A case study of eyewitness memory of a crime. *Journal of Applied Psychology, 71*, 291–301.

Zajac, R., Garry, M., London, K., Goodyear-Smith, F., & Hayne, H. (2013). Misconceptions about childhood sexual abuse and child witnesses: Implications for psychological experts in the courtroom. *Memory, 21*, 1–9.

5

A Neurobiological Account of False Memories

VINCENT VAN DE VEN, HENRY OTGAAR, AND MARK L. HOWE

Memory is a reconstructive, rather than a reproductive, system (Loftus, 1991; Nader, Schafe, & Ledoux, 2000; Roediger & McDermott, 1995; Schacter & Loftus, 2013; Schacter, Norman, & Koutstaal, 1998). As a result, we can experience considerable difficulty when trying to distinguish between true and false memories. More specifically, as memories can contain fragments of what was originally experienced, along with (schema-driven) elements that were not experienced but are meaningfully associated with those fragments, it is difficult to decide which parts of our recollections are true and which parts are false. This aspect of memory can lead to harmless or amusing results in discussing anecdotal recollections with friends and family. However, in judicial situations such as in court it can have dire consequences such as false allegations (Loftus, 1993; Roediger & McDermott, 2000), especially when memory serves as (the only) evidence (Howe, 2013; Schacter & Loftus, 2013).

Over the last few decades, human functional neuroimaging studies have increasingly contributed to the understanding of the brain's mechanisms underlying false memories (Mitchell & Johnson, 2009; Schacter & Slotnick, 2004). A neuroscientific description of the brain's memory mechanisms is important to obtain a complete understanding about how human memory works and how memory illusions can arise. Neuroimaging research of false memories addresses the question as to whether brain activity of a true memory can be distinguished from that of a false memory. This chapter reviews developments and advances in this field of research, and discusses possibilities and pitfalls in translating neuroscientific findings to the courtroom.

Neuroimaging methods, and particularly functional magnetic resonance imaging (fMRI) and electro-/magnetoencephalography, have been used to map memory-related processes on localized brain areas and structures. A plethora of neuroimaging studies have revealed that memory formation and retrieval activate a distributed brain-wide network of cortical areas and subcortical structures that support associative processes (medial temporal lobe, including hippocampus [Paller & Wagner, 2002; Squire, 1992]), auditory (e.g., Rauschecker &

Scott, 2009) and visual perception (Tootell, Hadjikhani, Mendola, Marrett, & Dale, 1998), attentional selection and enhancement of processing (e.g., frontal and parietal areas [Corbetta & Shulman, 2002; Hopfinger, Buonocore, & Mangun, 2000]), cognitive control and executive functions (frontal areas [Van Veen & Carter, 2002; Weissman, Roberts, Visscher, & Woldorff, 2006]), and social and emotional information processing (amygdala [(Phelps & LeDoux, 2005] and medial ventromedial frontal cortex [Schilbach, Eickhoff, Rotarska-Jagiela, Fink, & Vogeley, 2008]). Figure 5.1 provides an overview of the anatomical locations of many of these brain areas. Many studies have shown that the brain areas that are associated with false memories, for a large part, overlap with those of accurate memory judgments (Buckner & Wheeler, 2001; Schacter & Slotnick, 2004), in line with the notion that true and false memories rely on shared memory mechanisms. However, there are some indications that brain activity for false memories can be distinguished from true memories under certain experimental conditions.

Many excellent reviews about the cognitive neuroscience of false memories have already been published (Buckner & Wheeler, 2001; M. K. Johnson, Raye, Mitchell, & Ankudowich, 2012; Mitchell & Johnson, 2009; Schacter & Slotnick, 2004). This chapter reviews previous findings, but also extends previously published reviews to include more recent developments in cognitive neuroscience, as well as a few examples from molecular neuroscience. First, it discusses relevant findings from human brain imaging research that show the involvement of various cortical areas and brain structures in true and false memories. Second, it

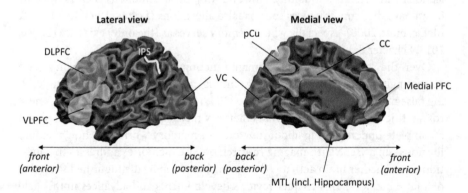

Figure 5.1 Anatomical locations of brain areas and structures related to true and false memories. Shown is a computer-generated representation of the left hemisphere from a lateral (seen outside looking inward) and medial view (seen from in-between the hemispheres outward). The "hills and valleys" (i.e., gyri and sulci) of the cortical curvature are slightly exaggerated. Dark gray areas are valleys (sulci) and lighter gray areas are hills (gyri). Drawn on top of the curvature are representations of the various brain areas and structures. Abbreviations: DLPFC, dorsolateral prefrontal cortex; VLPFC, ventrolateral prefrontal cortex; VC, visual cortex; pCu, precuneus; CC, cingulate cortex; MTL, medial temporal lobe. (See Color Plate.)

discusses what neuroscience studies can and cannot tell us about false memories in laboratory settings and in real life. Third, it briefly describes efforts in fundamental and molecular neuroscience that demonstrate how principles of synaptic connectivity may be associated with the generation of false memories. The chapter concludes with a few critical considerations about the possible role of neuroimaging in the courtroom.

A NEUROBIOLOGICAL ACCOUNT OF FALSE MEMORIES

False memories are recollections of events that did not happen, or that did not happen in the remembered context (Roediger & McDermott, 1995, 2000). The term *false memory* does not refer to a theoretical framework or model about memory, but rather to the phenomenon of reporting events from memory for which there is no evidence of an external correlate. There is strong consensus that the mechanisms of false memories are largely similar to those of accurate memory formation and retrieval (Mitchell & Johnson, 2000; Roediger & McDermott, 1995; Schacter & Slotnick, 2004). Rather than a separate class of memories, false memories reflect the erroneous decision that a mental experience derives from a recollection of a previously experienced event.

Understanding False Memories as Misassociations

A key notion in understanding memory, both true and false, is that it is associative in nature (Howe, Wimmer, Gagnon, & Plumpton, 2009; Tulving & Craik, 2000). Typically, false memories pertain to episodic or autobiographical memories, which are recollections of perceptual or emotional events that are embedded within a spatial, temporal, or cognitive context in which the events occurred. Furthermore, recollection from episodic or autobiographical memory is considered to be cue dependent, that is, current mental experiences can lead to recollections of previous mental experiences from memory. Cues can be explicit items or impressions (such as the face of a friend recalls fun times) or implicit contextual information (such as doing a memory test in the same room that you studied for the test facilitates your performance). A prominent cognitive framework about the contextual nature of memory is the Source Monitoring Framework (SMF) (M. K. Johnson, Hashtroudi, & Lindsay, 1993; Mitchell & Johnson, 2000). The SMF states that the recollection of an event is an attribution about a current mental experience, which is based on the association between (previous) mental experiences of an event that have been bound together (paraphrased from p. 20 in M. K. Johnson et al., 2012). These mental experiences can include sensory/perceptual experiences, semantic information, contextual information, emotions, and information about cognitive operations, as well as physiological states, which influence the judgment about the source of a current mental experience, as "different sources differ on these dimensions" (M. K. Johnson et al., 2012, p. 20). The notion of *source* can refer to the spatiotemporal origin of an event (the time or place in which something occurred), the acting agent from which the event occurred (events that you caused yourself or by someone else) or some other context that is relevant to the event (e.g., a semantic "source"). This framework predicts that false memories result from misattributing or erroneously associating a mental experience to an unrelated context. The SMF has a strong theoretical basis because it provides testable predictions about how episodic memories are formed and how this could lead to false memories (M. K. Johnson et al., 2012; Mitchell & Johnson, 2009). In what follows, the text will refer back to the SMF when interpreting the presented fMRI studies.

Mapping the Neural Correlates of Memory

The workings and applications of fMRI are well explained to the nonexpert reader in a number of excellent publications (Amaro & Barker, 2006; Huettel, Song, & McCarthy, 2004; Logothetis, 2008; Poldrack et al., 2008). This chapter skips methodological details and considers only the key conceptual components. The common approach to investigating the neural correlates of true and false memory is to interpret changes in amount of brain activity (or fMRI *signal amplitude*) in relation to some memory function or judgment. Brain areas that show increased activity during moments of recollection compared with moments of rest (in which there is no memory recollection) are interpreted as being associated with memory recollection. At the same time, brain areas that show increased activity during recollection *and* during another mental act could indicate that the respective brain area supports a function that is shared between mental processes. For example, increased activity during recollection in brain areas that are associated with visual perception could indicate perception-related processes during memory recollection, such as the imagining of visual details of the remembered event. Figure 5.2 provides a schematic overview of this approach. Crucial to this approach is the ability with which the investigator can identify the process of interest (e.g., whether a participant is recalling a mental event from memory), but also the ability to identify some control process in which the process of interest is missing (e.g., doing a mathematical assignment). The difference in amount of brain activity as a function of the difference between the targeted and control process can then serve as evidence to whether the brain area is associated with the process of interest. Clearly, choices that affect how the targeted and control processes are manifested will strongly influence the outcome and interpretability of the findings.

In false memory research, investigators are arguably interested in two brain activity scenarios. In the first scenario, the premise is that false memories are not the same as true memories, and the aim is to find brain areas that are more activated during the encoding or retrieval of true memories than for false memories. Identification of such brain areas could elucidate how false memories can be distinguished from true memories on a cognitive or neural level. Importantly, such a true/false memory distinction at the level of brain activity does not mean that the participant is conscious of, or somehow has unconscious access to, this distinction.

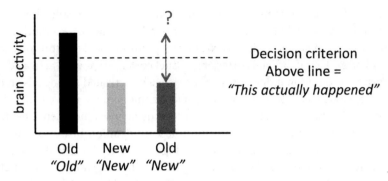

Figure 5.2 Schematic representation of the differential amplitude approach in mapping memory functions on brain areas. The premise is that memory-related areas show increased activity for true memory formation and/or retrieval (Old items that the participant judges as "old," black bar), in comparison with seeing items that were not memorized from a previous experience (New items that the participant judges as "new," gray bar). These brain areas can respond to false memories (New items judged as "old," red bar) in various ways (indicated by red question mark). Brain areas that process true memories different from false memories show less activity for false memories than for true memories. Brain areas that do not dissociate between true and false memories show activity similar to that of true memories. A false recollection can be judged as a true memory if brain activity surpasses a certain threshold (dashed horizontal line) and becomes similar to that of true memories.

In the second scenario, the premise is that false memories are misinterpreted as being true memories because of some shared property between the two memory types. Here, the aim is to find brain areas in which activity for false memories matches the activity for true memories. Thus, if brain activity of a mental event becomes more similar to the pattern of activity that is associated with a true memory, then that mental event is more likely to be interpreted as a true memory.

Neural Correlates of False Recollections

In cognitive psychological research, the Deese-Roediger-McDermott (DRM) paradigm has often been used to elicit false memories in healthy participants (Deese, 1959; Roediger & McDermott, 1995). In the DRM task, participants are presented with lists of words that are related to an unpresented concept (e.g., candy, chocolate, icing, sugar, nice, sour, and cake are related to the unpresented item SWEET). During subsequent recall or recognition testing, participants often report the unpresented item, also termed *the critical lure*, along with items from the previously presented lists.

In a number of early neuroimaging studies, brain activity was measured while participants completed a recognition test of previously learned auditorily presented items from several associatively-related DRM word lists (Schacter et al., 1996; Schacter, Buckner, Koutstaal, Dale, & Rosen, 1997). Participants made *old–new judgments* on items presented during the test phase. Results showed that many brain areas, including the medial temporal lobe (MTL)—comprising the hippocampus and neighboring cortex, anterior prefrontal and orbitofrontal areas, insular cortex, lateral parietal cortex, and visual cortex—that were activated during correct recognition judgments ("hits") were also activated during false recognition ("false alarms"). This indicated that false memory judgments relied, in large part, on similar brain mechanisms as those for true memory judgments. Evidence for differential brain activity for true and false recognition in DRM items was inconclusive, with some studies reporting higher activity for hits than for false alarms (Kim & Cabeza, 2007), but other studies showing no differential effect (Cabeza, Rao, Wagner, Mayer, & Schacter, 2001; Paz-Alonso, Ghetti, Donohue, Goodman, & Bunge, 2008; Schacter et al., 1997). Thus, the neural mechanisms underlying false recollections largely overlap with those of true recollections.

In these studies, false memories were inferred from the old–new judgments that participants made. Such judgments provide little information about the subjective mental experience during recollections. To ascertain whether false memory judgments are based on memory processes rather than response bias, participants can be asked about the quality of their recollective experience. People tend to discriminate true from false memories by judging the amount of perceptual or contextual detail or "evidence" that is associated with recollections (M. K. Johnson et al., 1993; Roediger & McDermott, 2000). True recollections tend to have more recollective detail than false recollections. To obtain information about recollective detail, participants must provide a memory judgment based on perceptual or contextual detail in addition to old-true judgments (Tulving, 1985). The *Remember/Know paradigm* (R/K) has been used to address this issue (Rajaram, 1993; Roediger & McDermott, 1995; Tulving, 1985). In this paradigm, participants make Remember/Know judgments for those items they report to have recognized from a previously studied list (i.e., old/new judgment), which provide information about whether participants have explicit knowledge of item features or contextual details ("recollection") or have a more implicit sense of the experience in memory ("familiarity").

Generally, participants report less phenomenological detail with falsely recognized items compared with accurately recognized items. That is, false memory judgments are associated with more Know than Remember responses, which indicates that false memories possess less perceptual detail or associative context (Rajaram, 1993; Tulving, 1985). However, participants are more likely to make Remember endorsements with false memories if their recollections come to mind more easily or are made more distinctive from other memories (Roediger & McDermott, 1995). One way that this effect is achieved could be through increased sensory or mnemonic processing prior to recognition testing.

Functional neuroimaging studies that used the R/K paradigm have shown greater MTL activity during memory retrieval for Remember judgments compared with Know judgments (Eldridge, Knowlton, Furmanski, Bookheimer, & Engel, 2000; Wheeler & Buckner, 2004). This finding fits well with the long recognized role of the MTL in episodic memory formation (Milner, Squire, & Kandel,

1998; Scoville & Milner, 1957; Squire, 1992). Several decades of clinical research has shown dense anterograde and retrograde amnesia for episodic events in patients with bilateral hippocampal lesions (Milner et al., 1998; Scoville & Milner, 1957). At the same time, research in rodents has shown that hippocampal neural cells also encode for contextual features in perception and memory, such as space (Burgess, Maguire, & O'Keefe, 2002) and time (Eichenbaum, 2014), which indicates that the MTL is particularly associated with encoding associative information. The MTL's place within the brain's anatomical architecture further supports the associative processing role of the MTL: It is strongly interconnected with many cortical and subcortical structures (Burgess et al., 2002; Squire, 1992), which suggests that it may be well suited to bind inputs from various neural sources that represent different mental experiences. This description of the MTL as an associative module fits well with the notion that episodic memories are inherently associative, that is, episodic memories are context-dependent mental experiences (Moscovitch et al., 2005). Indeed, several fMRI studies showed greater MTL activity when participants correctly recalled items in context, such as the source of an item or the spatial or temporal configuration of a set of items, compared with recalling or recognizing single items (Cansino, Maquet, Dolan, & Rugg, 2002; Weis et al., 2004). The MTL may thus contribute to the activation of contextual associations that underlie Remember endorsements of true recollections.

In addition, Remember responses for correctly recognized items are also related to increased activity in the sensory perception cortex in comparison with Know responses for such items (Wheeler & Buckner, 2004). This suggests that the act of remembering recruits perceptual content stored in memory, with the degree of sensory cortical activity during memory retrieval possibly indicating the perceptual vividness of the recollection. More generally, this finding points to the suggestion that memory for perceptual details is stored in those brain areas that encode perceptual information (Buckner & Wheeler, 2001). Indeed, human neuroimaging studies have shown that recalling visual objects from memory activates early and higher order visual cortex, including object-related brain areas (Slotnick & Schacter, 2006; Wheeler, Petersen, & Buckner, 2000), whereas recalling sounds or tunes activates content-related auditory cortex (Halpern & Zatorre, 1999; Linden et al., 2011). These findings appear in line with a series of case reports (Penfield & Perot, 1963) in which patients who were to undergo brain surgery to treat intractable epilepsy received intracortical brain stimulation to sensory cortical sites while they were awake and conscious. Local stimulation of the visual cortex resulted in several patients reporting seeing faces or scenes from previous experiences, comparable to a hallucinatory-like experience. Likewise, stimulation of the auditory cortex resulted in some patients reporting hearing voices, sounds, or music from previous experiences. In recent years, noninvasive brain stimulation techniques, such as transcranial magnetic stimulation, have been applied to visual cortical sites in healthy participants while they performed a memory task (Silvanto, Muggleton, & Walsh, 2008; van de Ven & Sack, 2013). When administered over the occipital cortex during moments of short-term memory retention, participants showed impaired subsequent recognition performance, indicating that brain stimulation interfered with memory representations in visual cortex (Cattaneo, Vecchi, Pascual-Leone, & Silvanto, 2009; van de Ven, Jacobs, & Sack, 2012).

These latter findings are controversial because they contrast the more traditional, modular view of brain processing in which sensory brain areas are passive encoders of incoming sensory information and memories are stored in MTL and higher order processing areas. Instead, there is strong evidence that the neural representation of memory is distributed across the entire brain, with functionally specialized brain areas supporting encoding as well as storage of respective content or cognitive information. Activation of parts of the distributed neural traces could spread to other parts of the memory representation, that is, reactivate the neural network that represents the memory of the experience (Kandel, Dudai, & Mayford, 2014). These findings provide further support for postulations about how memories are formed that were made more than a century ago (James, 1890).

However, other studies have shown that the link between sensory cortical activity and memory retrieval may not be straightforward. In one study (Slotnick & Schacter, 2004), participants learned a list of visual abstract items, which activated the early visual cortex. During the testing phase, visual cortical activity for correctly recognized items was not different than for missed items. Another study used a method to analyze distributed patterns of activity (for more information on this method, see later) that were measured when participants provided R/K-like judgments (J. D. Johnson, McDuff, Rugg, & Norman, 2009). Results showed that the pattern of brain activity during retrieval was similar to that of encoding for both types of judgment, indicating that reactivation occurred irrespective of participants' memory decisions. These findings suggest that putative memory traces in the sensory cortex may not always be used in—or be accessible for—memory judgments.

Neural Correlates of False Memory Creation: A Role for Encoding

Many of the aforementioned studies focused on false memory retrieval. In fact, false memory judgments may also stem from processing mechanisms prior to retrieval, that is, during the encoding and storage of perceptual experiences in memory. As already stated by William James, the functional role of encoding is to facilitate the "liability to recall" (James, 1890). In other words, encoding mechanisms can facilitate the endurance of a memory. Importantly, the memory encoding mechanisms are constructive in nature and thus play an active role in how information is processed. Manipulation of encoding processes can thus alter the fate of memories. Faulty encoding of current mental experiences and their associations could result in memories that are unrelated to the initial experience. Indeed, there are ample examples of behavioral studies that demonstrated an increased likelihood for false memory judgments under certain encoding conditions (Gallo & Roediger, 2002; Howe et al., 2009; Roediger & McDermott, 2000).

It is well known that the hippocampus and other MTL structures are important for memory encoding. Hippocampal damage can lead to complete loss of the ability to form new memories (Milner et al., 1998). Further, functional imaging studies in healthy participants have shown that MTL activity increases under contextual encoding conditions. For example, tasks that require participants to pair or bind items together during encoding activate the hippocampus more strongly compared with when participants encode individual items (Davachi & Wagner, 2002; Giovanello, Schnyer, & Verfaellie, 2004). The MTL has also been shown to process temporal contexts, such as temporal proximity or temporal regularity between visual items, during encoding (Ezzyat & Davachi, 2014; Staresina & Davachi, 2009; Tubridy & Davachi, 2011). Furthermore, the strength of MTL activity during encoding predicts subsequent retrieval success (Davachi & Wagner, 2002; Kim & Cabeza, 2007), which indicates that the associative role of the MTL is important in facilitating the endurance of memories. Further, it is well known that attention facilitates encoding of sensory events (Desimone & Duncan, 1995; Kastner & Ungerleider, 2000; Treisman & Gelade, 1980). FMRI studies have shown increased sensory cortical activity when selectively attending visual or auditory objects, resulting in more information processing to optimize task performance and decision making (see Kastner & Ungerleider, 2000).

Not all items presented during encoding will be processed in the same way. Changes in mental or neurophysiological states at different moments in time will alter how individual items are processed. To better understand the brain processes that underlie the subsequent fate of memories, investigators have used trial sorting approaches to group encoding trials according to retrieval success. In this approach, which has also been termed the *subsequent memory paradigm* (Paller & Wagner, 2002), encoding trials are sorted posthoc according to participants' subsequent retrieval success, thereby contrasting brain activity of encoding trials that resulted in successful retrieval to those encoding trials that resulted in failed retrieval (see Figure 5.3 for a schematic overview). Brain areas that show differential encoding activity for items that are later successfully retrieved could then be important in facilitating memory processes. Furthermore, the approach allows investigation of how moment-to-moment variations in mental or physiological conditions during encoding increase the endurance of memories within participants, such as changing levels of attention, working memory performance, or behavioral goals (for a review, see Paller & Wagner, 2002).

The relevance of subsequent memory sorting of encoding trials has been used in a number of fMRI studies that used a *reality monitoring paradigm*, in which during the encoding phase, participants either saw pictures of objects or had to mentally imagine the object that was cued only by name. Encoding was implicit, that is, participants made semantic decisions about the seen or imagined object without instructions to remember the object. In a subsequent recognition test, participants had to make an old/new judgment and judge the source of the item, that is, if they had seen it ("external source") or had imagined it ("internal source"). Correct source judgments constituted an external source judgment for items they had previously seen. A false memory constituted an external source judgment for items they had actually previously imagined. FMRI studies that used this paradigm showed stronger activity in sensory areas for items that were seen during

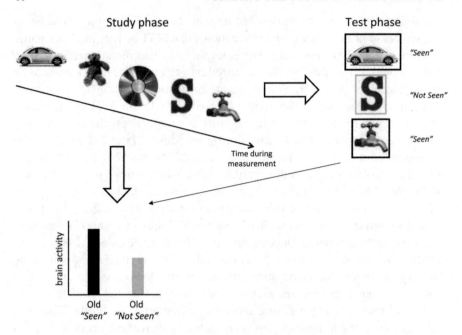

Figure 5.3 Trial sorting approach to analyze how encoding-related activity predicts subsequent successful memory retrieval. See main text for more details.

the encoding phase compared with imagined items (Kensinger & Schacter, 2005), a finding that is in line with other studies on mental imagery of visual objects (Goebel, Khorram-Sefat, Muckli, Hacker, & Singer, 1998; Kosslyn, Thompson, Kim, & Alpert, 1995; O'Craven & Kanwisher, 1999). However, imagined items that subsequently led to a false memory judgment showed more activity in perceptual processing areas during encoding than imagined items that did not lead to false memories (Gonsalves & Paller, 2000; Gonsalves et al., 2004; Kensinger & Schacter, 2005). A comparable finding was also reported for an auditory-based reality monitoring task, in which increased left inferior frontal cortex activity during auditory imagery of words was associated with subsequent judgments that these words were acoustically presented to participants during encoding (Sugimori, Mitchell, Raye, Greene, & Johnson, 2014). These findings suggest that increased sensory cortical activity during mental imagery of objects during encoding could increase the likelihood of subsequent source misattributions. Possibly, increased sensory cortex during encoding could indicate enhanced processing of perceptual features, which are subsequently encoded into memory. In other words, the subjective vividness in a recollected experience may contribute to the decision about whether that recollection is predicated on a sensory-based experience. There is some empirical support for this postulation, with one fMRI study showing increased sensory cortical activity for recollections that were erroneously judged to be based on sensory experiences when they were in fact mentally

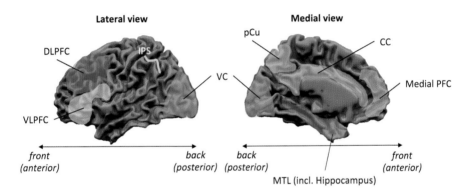

Figure 5.1 Anatomical locations of brain areas and structures related to true and false memories. Shown is a computer-generated representation of the left hemisphere from a lateral (seen outside looking inward) and medial view (seen from in-between the hemispheres outward). The "hills and valleys" (i.e., gyri and sulci) of the cortical curvature are slightly exaggerated. Dark gray areas are valleys (sulci) and lighter gray areas are hills (gyri). Drawn on top of the curvature are representations of the various brain areas and structures. Abbreviations: DLPFC, dorsolateral prefrontal cortex; VLPFC, ventrolateral prefrontal cortex; VC, visual cortex; pCu, precuneus; CC, cingulate cortex; MTL, medial temporal lobe.

imagined during encoding (Kensinger & Schacter, 2006). Thus, it is possible that a false memory constitutes too rich or vivid a recollection of perceptual features.

In sum, fMRI studies of false memories have shown a substantial overlap between the neural networks that support true and false memories. This is in accordance with the notion that true and false memories arise from the same cognitive operations. Further, fMRI studies of memory encoding showed that overly increased activity in brain areas associated with perception and higher cognitive functions increase the likelihood of subsequent false memory judgments. Thus, false memories could arise when the encoding of the respective mental events incidentally becomes more similar to that of encoding of true memories, which suggests that memory encoding processes—including sensory perception, attention, associative encoding, and other cognitive functions—may play a crucial role in false memory generation.

Attentional Selection and Control of Memory Formation and Retrieval

In addition to the MTL and sensory cortical areas, activity in higher-order cortical areas in the frontal and parietal lobes has also been associated with true and false memories. Studies in patients have shown that damage to the prefrontal cortex (PFC) may lead to various memory problems, including deficits in working memory (Owen, Downes, Sahakian, Polkey, & Robbins, 1990; Ranganath & Knight, 2002), memory recall (Gershberg & Shimamura, 1995; Shimamura, Janowsky, & Squire, 1990), and source misattributions or confusions—arguably types of false memory (Janowsky, Shimamura, & Squire, 1989; Moscovitch & Melo, 1997). FMRI of healthy participants has shown increased PFC activity during retention of items in working memory (Courtney, Ungerleider, Keil, & Haxby, 1997; Jiang, Haxby, Martin, Ungerleider, & Parasuraman, 2000; Linden et al., 2003; Todd & Marois, 2004), as well as directing attention to mental representations in short- and long-term memory (Blumenfeld & Ranganath, 2007; Ranganath, Johnson, & D'Esposito, 2003). Generally, the PFC has been associated with many higher order cognitive functions, including executive control (Courtney et al., 1997; Munk et al., 2002), error monitoring (Van Veen & Carter, 2002), and planning and attentional selection (Nelissen, Stokes, Nobre, & Rushworth, 2013; Zanto & Gazzaley, 2009; Zanto, Rubens, Thangavel, & Gazzaley, 2011), which indicates that the PFC exerts cognitive control over memory functions. Further, PFC areas are anatomically and functionally interconnected to hippocampal structures, thereby exerting control over the associative process of items in memory.

The PFC has a heterogenous organization that includes several functional and anatomical subdivisions, many of which remain to be conclusively mapped to cognitive functions. There is some evidence that different PFC areas contribute differentially to memory of item or source information. The dorsolateral PFC (DLPFC) shows greater activity for encoding the relational features between items than for encoding item identity (Blumenfeld, Parks, Yonelinas, & Ranganath, 2011; Munk et al., 2002; Murray & Ranganath, 2007). This could be related to the putative functional role of the DLPFC in the executive functions of working memory, particularly the manipulation and prioritization of information in memory. The ventrolateral PFC (VLPFC) has been found to be related to the selection of goal-relevant information or the inhibition of goal-irrelevant information (Blumenfeld & Ranganath, 2007). Further, VLPFC activity during encoding may predict subsequent memory recognition for items that were bound during encoding (Staresina & Davachi, 2006; Staresina, Gray, & Davachi, 2009; Sugimori et al., 2014). During memory testing, there is greater activity in both the DLPFC and VLPFC for contextually processed items than for item identity, but the contributions to memory retrieval may be different. There is some evidence for a hemispheric lateralization to contextual memory processing in the PFC, with the left PFC related to retrieval of contextual (source) memory and the right PFC related to retrieval of item memory (Ranganath, Johnson, & D'Esposito, 2000; Rugg, Fletcher, Chua, & Dolan, 1999; Slotnick, Moo, Segal, & Hart, 2003). An fMRI study using the DRM paradigm found increased activity of the left VLPFC in both true and false recognition (Paz-Alonso et al., 2008), which fits with the suggestion that the left PFC supports contextual memory processing. However, it is also possible that lateralized differentiation of the PFC may be associated with how information is monitored in memory, with the left PFC being associated with strategic monitoring of specific information and the right PFC being associated with more heuristic memory judgments (Blumenfeld & Ranganath, 2007). This differentiation has some overlap with the recollection versus familiarity ratings in R/K paradigms, for which there is also some evidence for a respective left versus right PFC differentiation (Ranganath et al., 2000).

Parietal areas have been associated with a variety of perceptual and higher order cognitive functions, including top-down attentional control (Hopfinger et al., 2000), mapping salience of perceptual items (Gottlieb, Kusunoki, & Goldberg, 1998), comparison of an internal template with perceptual evidence (Ploran et al., 2007), and decision making (Platt & Glimcher, 1999). Many of these functions also interplay with memory functions (Ranganath & Rainer, 2003; Wagner, Shannon, Kahn, & Buckner, 2005), although the exact mechanism of interaction remains unclear.

Several studies showed increased activity in lateral parietal areas, particularly at and around the intraparietal sulcus (IPS) during memory processes, including number of items retained in (short-term) memory (Todd & Marois, 2004), successful encoding of stimulus features into memory (Uncapher & Wagner, 2009), and retrieval of episodic events from memory (Buckner & Wheeler, 2001). However, contrary to sensory cortical areas, the parietal cortex does not seem to be specifically involved in memory for sources or other contexts per se. Rather, the IPS may serve attentional allocation functions that prioritize internal representations or perceptual features for further processing (Cabeza, Ciaramelli, Olson, & Moscovitch, 2008), much like attentional enhancement of incoming sensory stimuli from an external source. This internal attentional role of the parietal cortex could also be associated with the integration of perceptual and contextual information in order to guide decision-making (Platt & Glimcher, 1999; Ploran et al., 2007). Neuropsychological studies in patients with parietal lobe damage provide support for this account, where these patients show no impairment in source memory judgments, but do show lower confidence in their judgments (Simons, Peers, Mazuz, Berryhill, & Olson, 2010).

At the same time, medial parietal areas, including posterior cingulate cortex and the precuneus, have been associated with processing of information relevant to the "self" (Cavanna & Trimble, 2006; Rameson, Satpute, & Lieberman, 2010; Spreng, Mar, & Kim, 2009). Medial parietal areas are activated during encoding and retrieval of autobiographical information (Buckner & Wheeler, 2001; Spreng et al., 2009). The integrative account of lateral parietal cortex could be extended to include the integration of perceptual information from the external world with self-referential information in order to optimize decision making in favor of one's own goals and beliefs. Finally, the parietal cortex is strongly interconnected with MTL structures, including the hippocampus (Sestieri, Corbetta, Romani, & Shulman, 2011; Vincent et al., 2006), which further supports the integrative account of the parietal cortex in memory formation and retrieval.

In summary, lateral and medial frontal and parietal areas underlie cognitive control and attentional selection that support memory formation and retrieval. In this manner, these areas control and guide content-related and associative processing in perceptual and MTL areas, respectively. Attentional processes prioritize target and contextual information during an experience, related to information from the external world as well as self-referential, which are then bound in memory through activity in the hippocampus and perceptual content areas. However, these processes would not act differently for true and false memories, thereby making it difficult for fMRI to detect false memory-related activity in these areas.

Recent Advances: Mapping Distributed Memory Representations

The studies described have examined how strength or amplitude of brain activity differs for various memory encoding and retrieval conditions. Recently, computational methods for fMRI analysis have been developed that go beyond the mapping of amplitudes and analyze how distributed patterns of brain activity are associated with classes of mental states (Norman, Polyn, Detre, & Haxby, 2006). With this approach, a computer algorithm first learns how best to classify two or more brain states according to the patterns of activity that are associated with these states. Then, the classification information is used to predict the classification of the same brain states with new data. The approach has been referred to by various names, such as multivoxel pattern analysis (MVPA) or, more colloquially, "brain reading," as the method has been able to differentiate brain activity between perceptual or mental conditions that are otherwise not detectable with standard methods (Haxby, Connolly, & Guntupalli, 2014). For example, several research groups were able to dissociate brain activity in the sensory cortex between different subliminal perceptions, which could not be performed with standard approaches (Haynes & Rees, 2005; Kamitani & Tong, 2005). More sensational demonstrations of this method have been the classification of brain activity patterns of particular sensory content in dream states (Horikawa, Tamaki, Miyawaki, & Kamitani, 2013) and optimizing how a participant learns a visual skill without actually seeing the stimuli that must be learned (Shibata, Watanabe, Sasaki, & Kawato, 2011). An in-depth treatment of this application is beyond the scope of this chapter, and the reader is referred to several excellent reviews on the topic (Haxby et al., 2014; Norman et al., 2006; Rissman & Wagner, 2012).

MVPA's sensitivity to distributed patterns of activity makes it very interesting for use in classifying brain states related to memory functions or phenomenal content (Rissman & Wagner, 2012). For example, MVPA has been used to reveal the contents of short-term memory in visual cortex when participants retained previously seen visual information in mind (Harrison & Tong, 2009; Serences, Ester, Vogel, & Awh, 2009). Moreover, MVPA of brain activity during short-term memory retention shows that parietal cortex does not represent perceptual contents, but rather represents information that is relevant for stimulus matching and decision making (Christophel, Hebart, & Haynes, 2012).

In recent years, Wagner and colleagues used MVPA to address the issue of whether false memories can be reliably detected in the absence of participant reports about their memories (Rissman & Wagner, 2012). In one study (Kuhl, Rissman, Chun, & Wagner, 2011), the authors investigated brain activity when two memories competed for retrieval. Participants first learned paired associations between words and pictures of either faces or scenes. Symbolically, learning followed *AB* pairing, comprising memory cues *A* and paired associates *B*. During the experiment, however, the association was altered, such that participants learned to associate the same words with new pictures (*C*), following an *AC* pairing. Specifically, if in the *AB* pairing the associate was a face, then in the *AC* pairing the associate was a scene. Thus, during the experiment the same cue became associated with two different associates in memory. This led to competition of retrieval between the associates when the cue was presented. In addition, participants learned noncompeting cue–associate pairings (*DE* pairings). During test phases, participants were shown the cue and had to indicate if they had specific (that is, similar to an R/K Remember response) or general knowledge (similar to a Know response) about the associate or if they did not know about the associate.

The choice for faces or scenes as associates was crucial, as it utilized the common finding that anatomically different brain areas process faces (Kanwisher, McDermott, & Chun, 1997) and visual scenes (Epstein, Harris, Stanley, & Kanwisher, 1999). Thus, whether during testing a cue elicits recall of a face or a scene can be inferred from the peak activity in either the brain areas that processes faces or that processes scenes. Further, the authors reasoned that confusion in recalling the associate could result in activity in both face and scene processing areas.

MVPA was used to classify activity for the retrieval of faces or scenes in the MTL and higher order visual processing areas. Results showed MVPA could classify faces versus scenes more accurately for *AB* and *DE* cues during retrieval than for the *AC* cues. The authors interpreted this finding as indicating that recall after *AC* pairing suffered from competition from the previously learned *AB* pairings.

Furthermore, classification accuracy was higher for trials in which participants reported having specific knowledge about the associate (similar to Remember), compared with reports of having general information (similar to Know), which fits with differential brain activity for recollection versus familiarity ratings. Thus, these findings show how patterns of brain activity change as a function of competition between items in memory. Further, they suggest that it could be possible to map false memories—as misassociations between different mental events—by the distributed pattern of activity, given that one knows the original source material on which memories were based.

However, it was subsequently shown that using MVPA to predict memory-related brain states may be limited to particular situations. In another study (Rissman, Greely, & Wagner, 2010), the authors used MVPA to classify previously seen from novel faces during an *explicit* recognition task, in which participants gave an old/new judgment to each presented face. Classification accuracy was above 80% for hits versus correct rejections, indicating good separability of whether participants recognized a face. Interestingly, MVPA classification seemed to rely mostly on frontal and parietal areas, with comparatively little contribution from MTL regions. More importantly, the authors conducted a second experiment in which participants *incidentally* encoded faces and then completed an implicit recognition task. This scenario is of particular interest, as it mimics real-life cases in which participants are not aware that their memory will be tested in the future. In this second experiment, MVPA classification dropped to chance performance, indicating that there was no reliable separation between patterns of brain activity for previously seen versus novel faces in implicit memory scenarios. Thus, although it is possible to harvest more information from the brain when participants make explicit memory judgments, fMRI is insensitive to whether a mental experience is implicitly associated with a perceptual memory.

Recent Advances: Manipulating Memories

Ultimately, the brain mechanisms for true and false memories are arguably best described at the level of neural interactions. Although recent developments in fMRI technology have made it possible to measure brain activity at very high spatial and temporal resolution, the inherent workings of fMRI preclude direct measurement of neural activity. For this endeavor, neurophysiological and molecular animal research currently remains the only option.

Recent advances in animal molecular neuroscience studies have provided an innovative insight into the creation of false memories. More specifically, using the methodology of optogenetics (Fenno, Yizhar, & Deisseroth, 2011), researchers obtain experimental control over the activity of *mnemonically specific* neural populations in the hippocampus and create a false memory of fear in living and freely exploring mice. In optogenetics, researchers shine light through an implanted fiber optic cable on neurons that have been genetically manipulated to express light-sensitive receptors on their membranes. The genetic manipulation is required because neurons are not inherently programmed to express light-sensitive receptors (the manipulation is done in vivo and without otherwise altering neural functioning). Activation of the light-sensitive receptors by turning on the light source causes neurons to increase or decrease their activity, according to experimental parameters such as the type of receptors and frequency of the light.

Pioneering optogenetics work in mice showed that it is possible to activate hippocampal neurons that had become part of a fear memory. In this work, mice were allowed to explore two environments, where in one of the environments the animal received a shock that caused a fear response and activated hippocampal cells, resulting in the formation of a fear memory (Liu et al., 2012). Hippocampal cells were genetically prepared to express light-sensitive receptors when they showed increased activity. As a result of these manipulations, hippocampal cells that were activated during fear learning expressed light-sensitive receptors. In other words, these hippocampal cells became tagged as a result of memory formation. The animal was then returned to the neutral environment, in which it never received a shock. In this neutral environment, turning on the light source resulted in increased activity of the receptor-expressing hippocampal cells, which resulted in fear responses in the mouse. The animal thus behaved as if it responded to being in the fearful environment. Thus, by controlling the activity of the neural ensemble that supported a fear memory, the mouse could be made to retrieve the fearful memory under experimental control.

This approach was also used to create a false memory in mice (Ramirez et al., 2013). Here, hippocampal cells were functionally tagged for optogenetic manipulation using a neutral environment. Subsequently, the mice were put in a new, fearful environment. Crucially, during fear learning, the previously tagged hippocampal cells that coded for the neutral environment were optogenetically activated, which resulted in activation of the memory of the neutral environment concomitant to experiencing the fearful environment. The coactivation of the two environments resulted in them being associated in memory. When put back in the neutral environment, mice that had undergone the optogenetic treatment showed more fear responses than mice that went through fear conditioning without concomittant optogenetic manipulation. This finding demonstrated that false memories can result from associations between cues of different mental experiences. In other words, these findings provide evidence at the level of neural interactions in support of an associative account of false memory creation (Mitchell & Johnson, 2000; Roediger & McDermott, 2000). How to translate this paradigm to human research is an immediate challenge for future studies.

Neuroscience in the Courtroom

This chapter started by asking whether neuroscience could help those in the judiciary (police, prosectors, jurors, and judges) to distinguish between true and false memories. Although the research we have reviewed has considerable promise, there are a number of limitations to the use of neuroscience in the courtroom at this juncture. It is important to stress that fMRI images have played a role in

some cases regarding the reliability of statements. Specifically, legal professionals have become interested in whether fMRI might be useful in the detection of
deception;[1] something which is related to true and false memories. Although we
will not elaborate on such cases, we do want to make the point that several words
of caution are warranted when neuroscience is used to differentiate between true
and false memories.

To begin, an often overlooked fact, by scientists and laypeople alike, is that
fMRI results represent the output of carefully designed and controlled experiments in combination with a series of decisions about data acquisition, prepro-
cessing, and analysis (Amaro & Barker, 2006; Logothetis, 2008). As previously
described, typical fMRI studies of true and false memories require participants
to attend to carefully selected stimulus materials under controlled contextual and
environmental parameters. Brain activity is then analyzed as a function of the
experimental parameters. In other words, experimenters know, or at least have a
fairly good sense, about what the participant saw and what he or she ideally did
with the information mentally. Typically, in a courtroom one does not have this
level of control or knowledge about what the eyewitness experienced.

A further complication is that in many (but not all) fMRI studies, the presented
results are statistical summaries of population effects; that is, they rely on the distribution of brain responses from the sampled participants. This approach gives a
description about the general pattern of brain activity but does not (necessarily)
provide a description of brain activity in a single participant. Recent methodological advances indicate that it is possible, under certain circumstances, to obtain
impressions from fMRI images that indicate what a single participant experienced
while the experimenter is blind to the content of the experience. However, while
intriguing and scientifically innovative, these findings require participant cooperation and carefully controlled experimental conditions. Furthermore, even under
these controlled circumstances, the results are not reliable enough to be held as
judicial evidence in court.

Finally, fMRI is inherently correlational, which means that it provides no basis
for a broadly causal interpretation of the findings (Logothetis, 2008; Poldrack,
2008). An often made error is to infer a brain or mental state from observing
a change in brain activity: *Because there is activity in the hippocampus, I know
that the participant is now remembering what previously happened.* This inferential
problem has been termed the reverse inference problem, because it reverses the
chain of events in the experimental design (Poldrack, 2008). Brain activity in a
particular area can show a change in level of activity when a participant reports
recognizing a stimulus from a previously shown list of items: *On average there is
activity in the hippocampus when I ask the participant to now try and remember
what previously happened.* This does not mean that seeing the same change of
brain activity in the same brain area at a different moment in time means that the
participant is now recalling the same stimulus from memory.

Thus, while fMRI research can provide important insights into how cognitive functions are generally mapped onto the brain, the method is not suitable to
provide case-specific judgments about whether a person provides a true or false

memory statement at high accuracy (Schacter & Loftus, 2013). As with many other previously proposed techniques, fMRI does not provide an unbiased and objective window into the mental landscape of an individual person in order to unveil private or subjective mental states.

CONCLUSION

In sum, this chapter has described relevant human neuroimaging research that has provided insights into how false memories arise in the brain. The neural and cognitive mechanisms of false memories are largely the same as those for true memory formation and retrieval. The brain forms memories of perceptual or emotional events through the interaction of widely-distributed networks of functionally specialized brain areas. Sensory processing areas encode and store perceptual content of experiences. Frontal and parietal areas control and monitor stimulus processes by implementing goal-directed selection and processing strategies, and prioritize processing of items and relational features for encoding into as well as retrieval from memory. Medial parietal areas and MTL structures encode the relational features of stimuli or mental experiences into memory. Memory retrieval relies for a large part on reactivation of the encoding pathways, under prefrontal executive control. The hippocampus and other MTL areas can erroneously create associations between unrelated items and contexts during encoding as well as during retrieval. Further, overactivity in the sensory cortex during encoding mentally imagined visual objects can lead to subsequent false memory judgments that these objects were actually seen. It remains to be investigated when and how sensory overactivity comes about during mental imagery, and how it affects relational memory processing (e.g., in the hippocampus) and memory decision making (e.g., in parietal cortex).

NOTE

1. See for example http://www.wired.com/2009/03/noliemri/ or http://www.wired.com/2010/05/fMRI-in-court-update/

REFERENCES

Amaro, E., & Barker, G. J. (2006). Study design in fMRI: Basic principles. *Brain and Cognition*, 60(3), 220–232.

Blumenfeld, R. S., Parks, C. M., Yonelinas, A. P., & Ranganath, C. (2011). Putting the pieces together: The role of dorsolateral prefrontal cortex in relational memory encoding. *Journal of Cognitive Neuroscience*, 23(1), 257–265.

Blumenfeld, R. S., & Ranganath, C. (2007). Prefrontal cortex and long-term memory encoding: An integrative review of findings from neuropsychology and neuroimaging. *The Neuroscientist*, 13(3), 280–291.

Buckner, R. L., & Wheeler, M. E. (2001). The cognitive neuroscience of remembering. *Nature Reviews Neuroscience*, 2(9), 624–634.

Burgess, N., Maguire, E. A., & O'Keefe, J. (2002). The human hippocampus and spatial and episodic memory. *Neuron, 35*(4), 625–641.

Cabeza, R., Ciaramelli, E., Olson, I. R., & Moscovitch, M. (2008). The parietal cortex and episodic memory: An attentional account. *Nature Reviews Neuroscience, 9*(8), 613–625.

Cabeza, R., Rao, S. M., Wagner, A. D., Mayer, A. R., & Schacter, D. L. (2001). Can medial temporal lobe regions distinguish true from false? An event-related functional MRI study of veridical and illusory recognition memory. *Proceedings of the National Academy of Sciences of the United States of America, 98*(8), 4805–4810.

Cansino, S., Maquet, P., Dolan, R. J., & Rugg, M. D. (2002). Brain activity underlying encoding and retrieval of source memory. *Cerebral Cortex, 12*, 1048–1056.

Cattaneo, Z., Vecchi, T., Pascual-Leone, A., & Silvanto, J. (2009). Contrasting early visual cortical activation states causally involved in visual imagery and short-term memory. *European Journal of Neuroscience, 30*(7), 1393–1400.

Cavanna, A. E., & Trimble, M. R. (2006). The precuneus: A review of its functional anatomy and behavioural correlates. *Brain, 129*(3), 564–583.

Christophel, T. B., Hebart, M. N., & Haynes, J.-D. (2012). Decoding the contents of visual short-term memory from human visual and parietal cortex. *Journal of Neuroscience, 32*(38), 12983–12989.

Corbetta, M., & Shulman, G. L. (2002). Control of goal-directed and stimulus-driven attention in the brain. *Nature Reviews Neuroscience, 3*(3), 201–215.

Courtney, S. M., Ungerleider, L. G., Keil, K., & Haxby, J. V. (1997). Transient and sustained activity in a distributed neural system for human working memory. *Nature, 386*, 608–611.

Davachi, L., & Wagner, A. D. (2002). Hippocampal contributions to episodic encoding: insights from relational and item-based learning. *Journal of Neurophysiology, 88*(2), 982–990.

Deese, J. (1959). On the prediction of occurence of particular verbal intrusions in immediate recall. *Journal of Experimental Psychology, 58*, 17–22.

Desimone, R., & Duncan, J. (1995). Neural mechanisms of selective visual attention. *Annual Review of Neuroscience, 18*(1), 193–222.

Eichenbaum, H. (2014). Time cells in the hippocampus: A new dimension for mapping memories. *Nature Reviews Neuroscience, 15*(October), 732–744.

Eldridge, L. L., Knowlton, B. J., Furmanski, C. S., Bookheimer, S. Y., & Engel, S. A. (2000). Remembering episodes: A selective role for the hippocampus during retrieval. *Nature Neuroscience, 3*(11), 1149–1152.

Epstein, R., Harris, A., Stanley, D., & Kanwisher, N. (1999). The parahippocampal place area: Recognition, navigation, or encoding? *Neuron, 23*(1), 115–125.

Ezzyat, Y., & Davachi, L. (2014). Similarity breeds proximity: pattern similarity within and across contexts is related to later mnemonic judgments of temporal proximity. *Neuron, 81*(5), 1179–1189.

Fenno, L. E., Yizhar, O., & Deisseroth, K. (2011). The development and applications of optogenetics. *Annual Review of Neuroscience, 34*, 389–412.

Gallo, D. A., & Roediger, H. L. (2002). Variability among word lists in eliciting memory illusions: Evidence for associative activation and monitoring. *Journal of Memory and Language, 47*(3), 469–497.

Gershberg, F. B., & Shimamura, A. P. (1995). Impaired use of organizational strategies in free recall following frontal lobe damage. *Neuropsychologia, 13*(10), 1305–1333.

Giovanello, K. S., Schnyer, D. M., & Verfaellie, M. (2004). A critical role of the anterior hippocampus in relational memory: Evidence from an fMRI study comparing associative and item recognition. *Hippocampus, 14*(1), 5–8.

Goebel, R., Khorram-Sefat, D., Muckli, L., Hacker, H., & Singer, W. (1998). The constructive nature of vision: Direct evidence from functional magnetic resonance imaging studies of apparent motion and motion imagery. *European Journal of Neuroscience, 10*(5), 1563–1573.

Gonsalves, B., & Paller, K. A. (2000). Neural events that underlie remembering something that never happened. *Nature Neuroscience, 3*(12), 1316–1321.

Gonsalves, B., Reber, P. J., Gitelman, D. R., Parrish, T. B., Mesulam, M.-M., & Paller, K. A. (2004). Neural evidence that vivid imagining can lead to false remembering. *Psychological Science, 15*(10), 655–660.

Gottlieb, J. P., Kusunoki, M., & Goldberg, M. E. (1998). The representation of visual salience in monkey parietal cortex. *Nature, 391*(6666), 481–484.

Halpern, A. R., & Zatorre, R. J. (1999). When that tune runs through your head: A PET investigation of auditory imagery for familiar melodies. *Cerebral Cortex, 9,* 697–704.

Harrison, S. A., & Tong, F. (2009). Decoding reveals the contents of visual working memory in early visual areas. *Nature, 458*(7238), 632–635.

Haxby, J. V, Connolly, A. C., & Guntupalli, J. S. (2014). Decoding neural representational spaces using multivariate pattern analysis. *Annual Review of Neuroscience, 37,* 435–456.

Haynes, J.-D., & Rees, G. (2005). Predicting the orientation of invisible stimuli from activity in human primary visual cortex. *Nature Neuroscience, 8*(5), 686–691.

Hopfinger, J. B., Buonocore, M. H., & Mangun, G. R. (2000). The neural mechanisms of top-down attentional control. *Nature Neuroscience, 3*(3), 284–291.

Horikawa, T., Tamaki, M., Miyawaki, Y., & Kamitani, Y. (2013). Neural decoding of visual imagery during sleep. *Science, 340*(6132), 639–642.

Howe, M. L. (2013). Memory development: Implications for adults recalling childhood experiences in the courtroom. *Nature Reviews Neuroscience, 14*(12), 869–876.

Howe, M. L., Wimmer, M. C., Gagnon, N., & Plumpton, S. (2009). An associative-activation theory of children's and adults' memory illusions. *Journal of Memory and Language, 60*(2), 229–251.

Huettel, S. A., Song, A. W., & McCarthy, G. (2004). *Functional magnetic resonance imaging. Book* (Vol. 23).

James, W. (1890/1950). *The principles of psychology* (Vol. 1). New York: Dover Publishers, Inc.

Janowsky, J. S., Shimamura, A. P., & Squire, L. R. (1989). Source memory impairment in patients with frontal lobe lesions. *Neuropsychologia, 27*(8), 1043–1056.

Jiang, Y., Haxby, J. V, Martin, A., Ungerleider, L. G., & Parasuraman, R. (2000). Complementary neural mechanisms for tracking items in human working memory. *Science, 287*(5453), 643–646.

Johnson, J. D., McDuff, S. G. R., Rugg, M. D., & Norman, K. A. (2009). Recollection, familiarity, and cortical reinstatement: A multivoxel pattern analysis. *Neuron, 63*(5), 697–708.

Johnson, M. K., Hashtroudi, S., & Lindsay, D. S. (1993). Source monitoring. *Psychological Bulletin, 114*(1), 3–28.

Johnson, M. K., Raye, C. L., Mitchell, K. J., & Ankudowich, E. (2012). The cognitive neuroscience of true and false memories. In R. F. Belli (Ed.), *True and false recovered memories: Toward a reconciliation of the debate* (Vol. 58, pp. 15–52). : Springer.

Kamitani, Y., & Tong, F. (2005). Decoding the visual and subjective contents of the human brain. *Nature Neuroscience, 8*(5), 679–685.

Kandel, E. R., Dudai, Y., & Mayford, M. R. (2014). The molecular and systems biology of memory. *Cell, 157*(1), 163–186.

Kanwisher, N., McDermott, J., & Chun, M. M. (1997). The fusiform face area: A module in human extrastriate cortex specialized for face perception. *Journal of Neuroscience, 17*(11), 4302–4311.

Kastner, S., & Ungerleider, L. G. (2000). Mechanisms of visual attention in the human cortex. *Annual Review of Neuroscience, 23*, 315–341.

Kensinger, E. A., & Schacter, D. L. (2005). Emotional content and reality-monitoring ability: fMRI evidence for the influences of encoding processes. *Neuropsychologia, 43*(10), 1429–1443.

Kensinger, E. A., & Schacter, D. L. (2006). Neural processes underlying memory attribution on a reality-monitoring task. *Cerebral Cortex, 16*(8), 1126–1133.

Kim, H., & Cabeza, R. (2007). Differential contributions of prefrontal, medial temporal, and sensory-perceptual regions to true and false memory formation. *Cerebral Cortex, 17*(9), 2143–2150.

Kosslyn, S. M., Thompson, W. L., Kim, I. J., & Alpert, N. M. (1995). Topographical representations of mental images in primary visual cortex. *Nature, 378*, 496–498.

Kuhl, B. A., Rissman, J., Chun, M. M., & Wagner, A. D. (2011). Fidelity of neural reactivation reveals competition between memories. *Proceedings of the National Academy of Sciences of the United States of America, 108*(14), 5903–5908.

Linden, D. E. J., Bittner, R. A., Muckli, L., Waltz, J., Kriegeskorte, N., Goebel, R., ... Munk, M. H. J. (2003). Cortical capacity constraints for visual working memory: Dissociation of fMRI load effects in a fronto-parietal network. *NeuroImage, 20*(3), 1518–1530.

Linden, D. E. J., Thornton, K., Kuswanto, C. N., Johnston, S. J., van de Ven, V., & Jackson, M. C. (2011). The brain's voices: Comparing nonclinical auditory hallucinations and imagery. *Cerebral Cortex, 21*(2), 330–337.

Liu, X., Ramirez, S., Pang, P. T., Puryear, C. B., Govindarajan, A., Deisseroth, K., & Tonegawa, S. (2012). Optogenetic stimulation of a hippocampal engram activates fear memory recall. *Nature, 484*(7394), 381–385.

Loftus, E. F. (1991). Made in memory: Distortions in recollection after misleading information. *Psychology of Learning and Motivation, 27*(C), 187–215.

Loftus, E. F. (1993). The reality of repressed memories. *American Psychologist, 48*(5), 518–537.

Logothetis, N. K. (2008). What we can do and what we cannot do with fMRI. *Nature, 453*(7197), 869–878.

Milner, B., Squire, L. R., & Kandel, E. R. (1998). Cognitive neuroscience and the study of memory. *Neuron, 20*, 445–468.

Mitchell, K. J., & Johnson, M. K. (2000). Source monitoring: Attributing mental experiences. In E. Tulving & F. Craik (Eds.), *The Oxford handbook of memory* (pp. 179–195). New York: Oxford University Press.

Mitchell, K. J., & Johnson, M. K. (2009). Source monitoring 15 years later: What have we learned from fMRI about the neural mechanisms of source memory? *Psychological Bulletin, 135*(4), 638–677.

Moscovitch, M., & Melo, B. (1997). Strategic retrieval and the frontal lobe: Evidence from confabulation and amnesia. *Neuropsychologia, 35*(7), 1017–1034.

Moscovitch, M., Rosenbaum, R. S., Gilboa, A., Addis, D. R., Westmacott, R., Grady, C., ... Nadel, L. (2005). Functional neuroanatomy of remote episodic, semantic and spatial memory: A unified account based on multiple trace theory. *Journal of Anatomy, 207*(1), 35–66.

Munk, M. H. J., Linden, D. E. J., Muckli, L., Lanfermann, H., Zanella, F. E., Singer, W., & Goebel, R. (2002). Distributed cortical systems in visual short-term memory revealed by event-related functional magnetic resonance imaging. *Cerebral Cortex, 12*(8), 866–876.

Murray, L. J., & Ranganath, C. (2007). The dorsolateral prefrontal cortex contributes to successful relational memory encoding. *Journal of Neuroscience, 27*(20), 5515–5522.

Nader, K., Schafe, G. E., & Ledoux, J. E. (2000). The labile nature of consolidation theory. *Nature Reviews Neuroscience, 1*(3), 216–219.

Nelissen, N., Stokes, M. G., Nobre, A. C., & Rushworth, M. F. S. (2013). Frontal and parietal cortical interactions with distributed visual representations during selective attention and action selection. *Journal of Neuroscience, 33*(42), 16443–16458.

Norman, K. A., Polyn, S. M., Detre, G. J., & Haxby, J. V. (2006). Beyond mind-reading: multi-voxel pattern analysis of fMRI data. *Trends in Cognitive Sciences, 10*(9), 424–430.

O'Craven, K. M., & Kanwisher, N. (1999). Mental imagery of faces and places activates corresponding stimulus-specific brain regions. *Journal of Cognitive Neuroscience, 12*(6), 1013–1023.

Owen, A. M., Downes, J. J., Sahakian, B. J., Polkey, C. E., & Robbins, T. W. (1990). Planning and spatial working memory following frontal lobe lesions in man. *Neuropsychologia, 28*(10), 1021–1034.

Paller, K. A., & Wagner, A. D. (2002). Observing the transformatioin of experience into memory. *Trends in Cognitive Sciences, 6*(2), 93–102.

Paz-Alonso, P. M., Ghetti, S., Donohue, S. E., Goodman, G. S., & Bunge, S. A. (2008). Neurodevelopmental correlates of true and false recognition. *Cerebral Cortex, 18*(September), 2208–2216.

Penfield, W., & Perot, P. (1963). The brain's record of auditory and visual experience. *Brain, 86*(4), 595–696.

Phelps, E. A., & LeDoux, J. E. (2005). Contributions of the amygdala to emotion processing: From animal models to human behavior. *Neuron, 48*(2), 175–187.

Platt, M. L., & Glimcher, P. W. (1999). Neural correlates of decision variables in parietal cortex. *Nature, 400*(6741), 233–238.

Ploran, E. J., Nelson, S. M., Velanova, K., Donaldson, D. I., Petersen, S. E., & Wheeler, M. E. (2007). Evidence accumulation and the moment of recognition: Dissociating perceptual recognition processes using fMRI. *Journal of Neuroscience, 27*(44), 11912–11924.

Poldrack, R. A. (2008). The role of fMRI in Cognitive Neuroscience: Where do we stand? *Current Opinion in Neurobiology, 18*(2), 223–227.

Poldrack, R. A., Fletcher, P. C., Henson, R. N. A., Worsley, K. J., Brett, M., & Nichols, T. E. (2008). Guidelines for reporting an fMRI study. *NeuroImage, 40*(2), 409–414.

Rajaram, S. (1993). Remembering and knowing: Two means of access to the personal past. *Memory & Cognition, 21*(1), 89–102.

Rameson, L. T., Satpute, A. B., & Lieberman, M. D. (2010). The neural correlates of implicit and explicit self-relevant processing. *NeuroImage, 50*(2), 701–708.

Ramirez, S., Liu, X., Lin, P.-A., Suh, J., Pignatelli, M., Redondo, R. L., . . . Tonegawa, S. (2013). Creating a false memory in the hippocampus. *Science, 341*(6144), 387–391.

Ranganath, C., Johnson, M. K., & D'Esposito, M. (2000). Left anterior prefrontal activation increases with demands to recall specific perceptual information. *Journal of Neuroscience, 20 (22)*(108), 1–5.

Ranganath, C., Johnson, M. K., & D'Esposito, M. (2003). Prefrontal activity associated with working memory and episodic long-term memory. *Neuropsychologia, 41*, 378–389.

Ranganath, C., & Knight, R. T. (2002). Prefrontal cortex and episodic memory: Integrating findings from neuropsychology and functional brain imaging. In A. Parker, T. J. Bussey, & E. L. Wilding (Eds.), *The cognitive neuroscience of memory: Encoding and retrieval* (Vol. 1, pp. 83–99). Hove, UK: Psychology Press.

Ranganath, C., & Rainer, G. (2003). Neural mechanisms for detecting and remembering novel events. *Nature Reviews Neuroscience, 4*(3), 193–202.

Rauschecker, J. P., & Scott, S. K. (2009). Maps and streams in the auditory cortex: Nonhuman primates illuminate human speech processing. *Nature Neuroscience, 12*(6), 718–724.

Rissman, J., Greely, H. T., & Wagner, A. D. (2010). Detecting individual memories through the neural decoding of memory states and past experience. *Proceedings of the National Academy of Sciences of the United States of America, 107*(21), 9849–9854.

Rissman, J., & Wagner, A. D. (2012). Distributed representations in memory: Insights from functional brain imaging. *Annual Review of Psychology, 63*, 101–128.

Roediger, H. L., & McDermott, K. B. (1995). Creating false memories: Remembering words not presented in lists. *Journal of Experimental Psychology: Learning, Memory, and Cognition, 21*(4), 803–814.

Roediger, H. L., & McDermott, K. B. (2000). Distortions of memory. In E. Tulving & F. I. Craik (Eds.), *Oxford handbook of memory* (pp. 149–162). Oxford: Oxford University Press.

Rugg, M. D., Fletcher, P. C., Chua, P. M., & Dolan, R. J. (1999). The role of the prefrontal cortex in recognition memory and memory for source: An fMRI study. *NeuroImage, 10*(5), 520–529.

Schacter, D. L., Buckner, R. L., Koutstaal, W., Dale, A. M., & Rosen, B. R. (1997). Late onset of anterior prefrontal activity during true and false recognition: An event-related fMRI study. *NeuroImage, 6*(4), 259–269.

Schacter, D. L., & Loftus, E. F. (2013). Memory and law: What can cognitive neuroscience contribute? *Nature Neuroscience, 16*(2), 119–123.

Schacter, D. L., Norman, K. A., & Koutstaal, W. (1998). The cognitive neuroscience of constructive memory. *Annual Review of Psychology, 49*, 289–318.

Schacter, D. L., Reiman, E., Curran, T., Yun, L. S., Bandy, D., Mcdermott, K. B., & Roediger III, H. L. (1996). Neuroanatomical correlates of veridical and illusory recognition memory: Evidence from positron emission tomography. *Neuron, 17*, 267–274.

Schacter, D. L., & Slotnick, S. D. (2004). The cognitive neuroscience of memory distortion. *Neuron, 44*, 149–160.

Schilbach, L., Eickhoff, S. B., Rotarska-Jagiela, A., Fink, G. R., & Vogeley, K. (2008). Minds at rest? Social cognition as the default mode of cognizing and its putative relationship to the "default system" of the brain. *Consciousness and Cognition, 17*(2), 457–67.

Scoville, W. B., & Milner, B. (1957). Loss of recent memory after bilateral hippocampal lesions. *The Journal of Neurology, Neurosurgery & Psychiatry, 20*(11), 11–21.

Serences, J. T., Ester, E. F., Vogel, E. K., & Awh, E. (2009). Stimulus-specific delay activity in human primary visual cortex. *Psychological Science, 20*(2), 207–214.

Sestieri, C., Corbetta, M., Romani, G. L., & Shulman, G. L. (2011). Episodic memory retrieval, parietal cortex, and the default mode network: Functional and topographic analyses. *Journal of Neuroscience, 31*(12), 4407–4420.

Shibata, K., Watanabe, T., Sasaki, Y., & Kawato, M. (2011). Perceptual learning incepted by decoded fMRI neurofeedback without stimulus presentation. *Science, 334*(6061), 1413–1415.

Shimamura, A. P., Janowsky, J. S., & Squire, L. R. (1990). Memory for the temporal order of events in patients with frontal lobe lesions and amnesic patients. *Neuropsychologia, 28*(8), 803–813.

Silvanto, J., Muggleton, N. G., & Walsh, V. (2008). State-dependency in brain stimulation studies of perception and cognition. *Trends in Cognitive Sciences, 12*(12), 447–454.

Simons, J. S., Peers, P. V, Mazuz, Y. S., Berryhill, M. E., & Olson, I. R. (2010). Dissociation between memory accuracy and memory confidence following bilateral parietal lesions. *Cerebral Cortex, 20*(2), 479–485.

Slotnick, S. D., Moo, L. R., Segal, J. B., & Hart, J. (2003). Distinct prefrontal cortex activity associated with item memory and source memory for visual shapes. *Cognitive Brain Research, 17*, 75–82.

Slotnick, S. D., & Schacter, D. L. (2004). A sensory signature that distinguishes true from false memories. *Nature Neuroscience, 7*(6), 664–672.

Slotnick, S. D., & Schacter, D. L. (2006). The nature of memory related activity in early visual areas. *Neuropsychologia, 44*(14), 2874–2886.

Spreng, R. N., Mar, R. A., & Kim, A. S. N. (2009). The common neural basis of autobiographical memory, prospection, navigation, theory of mind, and the default mode: A quantitative meta-analysis. *Journal of Cognitive Neuroscience, 21*(3), 489–510.

Squire, L. R. (1992). Memory and the hippocampus : A synthesis from findings with rats, monkeys, and humans. *Psychological Review, 99*(2), 195–231.

Staresina, B. P., & Davachi, L. (2006). Differential encoding mechanisms for subsequent associative recognition and free recall. *Journal of Neuroscience, 26*(36), 9162–9172.

Staresina, B. P., & Davachi, L. (2009). Mind the gap: Binding experiences across space and time in the human hippocampus. *Neuron, 63*, 267–276.

Staresina, B. P., Gray, J. C., & Davachi, L. (2009). Event congruency enhances episodic memory encoding through semantic elaboration and relational binding. *Cerebral Cortex, 19*(May), 1198–1207.

Sugimori, E., Mitchell, K. J., Raye, C. L., Greene, E. J., & Johnson, M. K. (2014). Brain mechanisms underlying reality monitoring for heard and imagined words. *Psychological Science, 25*(2), 403–413.

Todd, J. J., & Marois, R. (2004). Capacity limit of visual short-term memory in human posterior parietal cortex. *Nature, 428*(6984), 751–754.

Tootell, R. B. H., Hadjikhani, N. K., Mendola, J. D., Marrett, S., & Dale, A. M. (1998). From retinotopy to recognition. *Trends in Cognitive Sciences, 2*(5), 174–183.

Treisman, A. M., & Gelade, G. (1980). A feature-integration theory of attention. *Cognitive Psychology, 12*(1), 97–136.

Tubridy, S., & Davachi, L. (2011). Medial temporal lobe contributions to episodic sequence encoding. *Cerebral Cortex, 21*(2), 272–280.

Tulving, E. (1985). Memory and consciousness. *Canadian Psychologist, 26*, 1–12.

Tulving, E., & Craik, F. I. (Eds.). (2000). *The Oxford handbook of memory*. Oxford: Oxford University Press.

Uncapher, M. R., & Wagner, A. D. (2009). Posterior parietal cortex and episodic encoding: Insights from fMRI subsequent memory effects and dual-attention theory. *Neurobiology of Learning and Memory, 91*(2), 139–154.

van de Ven, V., Jacobs, C., & Sack, A. T. (2012). Topographic contribution of early visual cortex to short-term memory consolidation: A transcranial magnetic stimulation study. *Journal of Neuroscience, 32*(1), 4–11.

van de Ven, V., & Sack, A. T. (2013). Transcranial magnetic stimulation of visual cortex in memory: Cortical state, interference and reactivation of visual content in memory. *Behavioural Brain Research, 236*, 67–77.

Van Veen, V., & Carter, C. S. (2002). The anterior cingulate as a conflict monitor: fMRI and ERP studies. *Physiology and Behavior, 77*(4-5), 477–482.

Vincent, J. L., Snyder, A. Z., Fox, M. D., Shannon, B. J., Andrews, J. R., Raichle, M. E., & Buckner, R. L. (2006). Coherent spontaneous activity identifies a hippocampal-parietal memory network. *Journal of Neurophysiology, 96*(6), 3517–3531.

Wagner, A. D., Shannon, B. J., Kahn, I., & Buckner, R. L. (2005). Parietal lobe contributions to episodic memory retrieval. *Trends in Cognitive Sciences, 9*(9), 445–453.

Weis, S., Specht, K., Klaver, P., Tendolkar, I., Willmes, K., Ruhlmann, J., . . . Fernández, G. (2004). Process dissociation between contextual retrieval and item recognition. *Neuroreport, 15*(18), 2729–2733.

Weissman, D. H., Roberts, K. C., Visscher, K. M., & Woldorff, M. G. (2006). The neural bases of momentary lapses in attention. *Nature Neuroscience, 9*(7), 971–978.

Wheeler, M. E., & Buckner, R. L. (2004). Functional-anatomic correlates of remembering and knowing. *NeuroImage, 21*(4), 1337–1349.

Wheeler, M. E., Petersen, S. E., & Buckner, R. L. (2000). Memory's echo: Vivid remembering reactivates sensory-specific cortex. *Proceedings of the National Academy of Sciences of the United States of America, 97*(20), 11125–11129.

Zanto, T. P., & Gazzaley, A. (2009). Neural suppression of irrelevant information underlies optimal working memory performance. *Journal of Neuroscience, 29*(10), 3059–3066.

Zanto, T. P., Rubens, M. T., Thangavel, A., & Gazzaley, A. (2011). Causal role of the prefrontal cortex in top-down modulation of visual processing and working memory. *Nature Neuroscience, 14*(5), 656–661.

PART II

Children in the Courtroom

6

Assessing the Veracity of Children's Forensic Interviews

Implications for the Courtroom

HAYDEN M. HENDERSON AND SAMANTHA J. ANDREWS

The numbers of children (that is, individuals under the age of 18 years) experiencing contact with legal systems around the world as victims and witnesses of maltreatment represent "a large and growing legal constituency" (Bruck, Ceci, & Principe, 2006, p. 777; see Lamb, Malloy, Hershkowitz, & La Rooy, 2015). For example, in the United States, around 3 million investigations of suspected child maltreatment are carried out annually (Gelles & Brigham, 2011), with nearly 800,000 children classified as victims of maltreatment in 2007 (U.S. Department of Health and Human Services, Administration on Children, Youth, and Families, 2009). This alarming situation is shared internationally. In 2013–2014, over 650,000 children in England were referred to local authority children's social care services by individuals who had concerns about their welfare (HM Government, March 2015). In 2012, across the United Kingdom, more than 66,000 children were the subjects of child protection plans, and thus considered to be at risk for physical, emotional, or sexual abuse and neglect (NSPCC, May 25, 2013). Furthermore, in Australia, between 2001–2002 and 2005–2006, the number of child protection notifications almost doubled from 138,000 to 267,000 (Australian Institute of Health and Welfare, 2007), while in Canada, approximately 236,000 child maltreatment investigations were conducted in 2008, 36% of which were substantiated by child protection workers (Trocmé et al., 2010).

Most children who are suspected victims or witnesses of maltreatment are forensically interviewed. Forensic interviewing is one of the first steps in most child protection investigations, with the child being questioned by a neutral professional. In addition to yielding the information needed to make a determination about whether maltreatment has occurred, forensic interviews may produce evidence that will stand up in court if the investigation leads to criminal prosecution (see Child Advocacy Centre, 2016). Forensic interviews play a particularly important role in child maltreatment investigations because children are often the only witnesses of the alleged events and medical evidence is often lacking (e.g., in the case of fondling) (World Health Organization, 2006). If children are called to court to testify, the contents of their prerecorded forensic interviews can be played to the court in some jurisdictions (e.g., New Zealand, England, and Wales) and referred to throughout direct examination (or evidence-in-chief) by the prosecution, as well as challenged during cross-examination by the defense.

Given the number of children involved in the legal system, and the importance of forensic interviews in the investigative process, much experimental and applied research since the early 1980s has focused on investigating the diverse developmental factors—cognitive, emotional, and social—and interviewing practices that can enhance or seriously compromise children's effective participation during interviews (see Lamb et al., 2015, for reviews). Such collaborative research focus has resulted in the development of evidence-based best practice guidelines for conducting forensic interviews, such as the National Institute of Child Health and Human Development (NICHD) Investigative Interview Protocol (see Lamb, Hershkowitz, Orbach, & Esplin, 2008). Such guidelines minimize the risk of eliciting erroneous information from children and increase their response productivity by encouraging interviewers to maximally rely on free-recall open-ended prompts (e.g., "Tell me what happened"), advising against the use of closed-ended "yes/no" questions (e.g., "Did it happen once?"), and strongly discouraging suggestive utterances and techniques that imply the expected response (e.g., "He hit you, didn't he?") (see also, APSAC, 2012; Home Office, 2011, section 3.44).

However, given the nature and complexities of such cases, even when questioned using best-practice techniques to ensure that interview quality is high, the veracity of children's accounts cannot be completely assured. Children may be reluctant to disclose abuse or certain aspects of it for a variety of reasons (see Pipe, Lamb, Orbach, & Cederborg, 2007). For example, children may be fearful to disclose the perpetrators' abusive behavior for fear of repercussions, they may be motivated to protect or cover for family members, or they may find sexual matters difficult and embarrassing to talk about. As well as false omissions, children may erroneously recollect information or knowingly report information that is not true. Some children may fabricate or exaggerate the entirety or parts of their evidence, may be coached by an outside influence (e.g., family member) into falsely disclosing abuse, or may have the motivation to exacerbate the accused's sentence. For various reasons, therefore, experts are sometimes asked to assess the credibility of the allegations made by children in forensic interviews, and triers of fact, such as judges and juries in common law courts, must make such determinations.

This chapter begins with a brief review of developmental trajectories in the principal domains of development known or likely to affect the assessments of children's credibility in forensic interviews. It then reviews the effectiveness of, and problems associated with, various methodological approaches attempting to assess veracity, including Reality Monitoring (RM) and Criteria-Based Content Analysis (CBCA). This discussion of methodology ends by considering how measures of forensic interview quality must be considered when attempting to assess children's credibility. The subsequent section reviews the interplay, usefulness, and potential of considering both forensic interview quality and the veracity of children's accounts when assessing credibility. The chapter then turns to the implications this relationship has for children in court. It first considers the importance of reliable forensic interviews in the legal context. It then discusses how accurate credibility assessments, by triers of fact, of children's testimony given both during direct- and cross-examinations may be much more difficult to establish than in forensic interviews because lawyers use techniques and practices that violate best-practice principles for eliciting truthful testimony. The chapter ends with an examination of the key questions to which researchers should turn their attention in order to better understand how to assess the truthfulness of children's accounts, both in forensic interviews and in court, so that justice can be effectively achieved.

WHAT CAPABILITIES AND VULNERABILITIES DO CHILDREN BRING TO FORENSIC SETTINGS?

In order to effectively assess testimonial credibility, it is critical that triers of fact consider the vulnerabilities and capabilities that children present in the legal system. Before considering the various methods that have been used to assess veracity, the chapter briefly reviews the principal domains of development known or likely to affect credibility assessments, including, but not limited to, memory development, language and communication, suggestibility, and deception.

Memory Development

The process of memory is not fully understood, but researchers agree that memory is a complex and reconstructive process of encoding, storage, and retrieval (Erdelyi, 1996; Howe, 2011; Lamb et al., 2015; Melton, 1963). Thus, when evidence provided from memory is introduced in legal proceedings, critical limitations must be considered. For example, what is encoded and later retrieved from memory can be affected (or contaminated) by a multitude of factors. Such factors include, but are not limited to, the extent to which witnesses attended to particular stimuli/events, what information is already stored in memory, witnesses' expectations of stimuli/events and retrieval, and witness emotional states (see Howe & Knott, 2015). Therefore, because memories are often fragmentary and piecemeal, rather than complete and coherent, the reliability and completeness of evidence provided from memory should be questioned (Howe, 2013).

Although memories are fallible for children, adolescents, and adults, age is the largest determinant of the quantity and quality of details encoded and stored in memory (Flin, Boon, Knox, & Bull, 1992; Lamb, Hershkowitz, Orbach, & Esplin, 2011). Young children only remember a fraction of their experiences but, with age, experiences are remembered for longer; thus older children have better recall than younger children (Howe, 2011; Ornstein,

Gordon, & Larus, 1992). Throughout childhood, children develop episodic (the who, what, where, when, why, and how of events) and semantic (factual information independent of events) memory encoding, storage, and retrieval strategies in parallel; thus younger children typically encode fewer episodic and semantic details than older children and adults (Brainerd & Reyna, 2005; Howe, 2011, 2013). Additionally, experiences are more likely to be encoded and stored when they make sense (e.g., Lamb et al., 2015; Tulving, 1974). Thus, young children may remember less information, particularly in forensic contexts, because the events under examination may not make sense to them (e.g., sexual abuse) (see La Rooy, Malloy, & Lamb, 2011). Last, information is more likely to be encoded and stored when associations exist between other past experiences (Walsh & Ungson, 1991), and, again, younger children are disadvantaged relative to older children and adults because they have had fewer past experiences (see Lamb et al., 2015; La Rooy et al., 2011).

In particular, children are vulnerable to a problem known as *source monitoring*, in which memories from different sources (e.g., a thought vs. a speech act) are confused when the sources are similar to one another (e.g., identifying what speaker [left/right] played the words spoken by a woman; Lindsay, Johnson, & Kwon, 1991). Source monitoring ability improves with age (Foley, Johnson, & Raye, 1983; McIntyre & Craik, 1987), although researchers have found that children can perform as well as adults when the sources are relatively discriminable (Foley, Durso, Wilder, & Friedman, 1991; Foley & Johnson, 1985; Foley, Santini, & Sopasakis, 1989; Foley et al., 1983; Lindsay et al., 1991). When interviewed, young children's contradictory or nonsensical responses might thus be a result of source monitoring errors, rather than deliberate deceit.

Despite these limitations, children can provide coherent accounts and be effective witnesses in the legal system when questioned using strategies that do not exceed or exploit children's developing memory abilities (Lamb, Orbach, Hershkowitz, Horowitz, & Abbott, 2007b; Lamb et al., 2011, 2015). Indeed, fieldwork has found that, although children under 5 years old do not provide as many informative details in response to free-recall episodic memory questions (e.g., "Tell me what happened") as do older children, even very young children (3-year-olds) are able to recall important information about events in response to questions that provide slightly more structure, in that they tap cued-recall episodic memory (e.g., "What did he do?") and their responses are no less accurate than those of older children (Hershkowitz, Lamb, Orbach, Katz, & Horowitz, 2012; for reviews, see Lamb et al., 2011, 2015). In sum, children's memories can be accurate and reliable when procedures are adapted to their capabilities (Lamb et al., 2011, 2015).

Language and Communication

A second domain likely to affect credibility assessments is the development of language and communication. Although young children may know as many as 6,000 to 8,000 words, their vocabulary is still much more idiosyncratic and less descriptive than that of adults (Dale, 1976; de Villiers & de Villiers, 1979). In addition, interviewers may misinterpret children's statements because young children do not always articulate individual sounds appropriately (Reich, 1986). Furthermore, children, and even adolescents, struggle with both conventional adult vocabulary (Saywitz, 2002) and the legal language ("legalese") that may be used during forensic questioning (Hanna, Davies, Henderson, Crothers, & Rotherham, 2010). Even simple concepts like "always," "some," "yesterday," "before," or "touch" may be misused or misunderstood (Saywitz, 2002).

Moreover, adults typically overestimate children's comprehension of grammatically and linguistically complex sentences (Hanna et al., 2010). This is particularly troublesome because researchers have found that the accuracy of children's accounts is affected by question complexity (Carter, Bottoms, & Levine, 1996; Imhoff & Baker-Ward, 1999; Perry et al., 1995; Zajac, Gross, & Hayne, 2003). As children grow older, their comprehension increases, as does the length, informativeness, and complexity of their responses (Fivush, 1997; Saywitz & Camparo, 1998; Schneider & Pressley, 1997). Thus, misunderstandings may frequently occur for both children and interviewers, which is an issue that is considerably worsened by children's propensity not to seek clarification (Zajac et al., 2003). Children's deficient understanding of their role as informants (Lamb & Sim, 2013; Lamb, Orbach, Warren, Esplin, & Hershkowitz, 2007) and their reticence toward unfamiliar adult interviewers (Carter et al., 1996), coupled with limited vocabulary to describe experiences, may increase the likelihood that the veracity of children's statements will be misinterpreted.

Suggestibility

The veracity of children's statements may be further affected by their suggestibility, that is, the degree to which encoding, storage, retrieval, and reporting of events can be influenced by a range of social and psychological factors (Ceci & Bruck, 1993). There are developmental differences in susceptibility to suggestion; however, they are not yet clearly understood. Researchers often find that younger children are more susceptible to suggestion than older children (Eisen, Goodman, Qin, Davis, & Crayton, 2007). However, recent research has also shown that in certain occasions, younger children can be less susceptible to suggestion than older children and adults, a phenomenon dubbed *developmental reversal* (Otgaar, Howe, Brackman, & Smeets, 2016). Because false memories may be rooted in connections to previous events, studies have found that age increases reports of false memories, and sometimes decreases the net accuracy of memories (Brainerd, Reyna, & Ceci, 2008). Regardless of age, it seems that suggestibility is a threat to accurate veracity assessments, particularly due to the suggestive questioning styles often used in forensic settings (Lamb et al., 2011; Spencer & Lamb, 2012).

Interviewers are often suggestive: introducing new details, implying expected responses, and posing the same questions repeatedly (see Lamb, La Rooy, Malloy, & Katz, 2011). Strategies such as referring to the interviewer's high status (e.g., police officer), peer pressure, promises of threats or rewards, requests that children pretend or imagine, and the use of anatomical dolls also influence children's testimony suggestively (Pipe, Lamb, Orbach, & Esplin, 2004).

Strategies employed by lawyers while questioning children in court are particularly suggestive and contaminating. In cross-examination, researchers have found that the use of complex and leading questions, credibility challenges, and expressions of disbelief result in the majority of children changing at least one answer provided in direct-examination (e.g., Szojka, Andrews, Lamb, Stolzenberg, & Lyon, 2017; Zajac & Hayne, 2003). Option posing (e.g., yes/no) and suggestive questions are strongly discouraged and are even more contaminating when they are repeated. One study showed that 17% of prosecutor utterances and 33% of defense attorney utterances were repeated and were significantly more likely to be option posing or suggestive (Andrews, Lamb, & Lyon, 2015). When interviewers encourage children to answer truthfully; admit that they "don't know" when appropriate; employ open-ended questions; and avoid misleading, suggestive, and repetitive questions, children provide more meaningful and accurate responses (Pipe et al., 2004).

Deception

The last major issue to discuss when considering the capabilities and vulnerabilities children bring to forensic settings is deception. Researchers and legal practitioners are often concerned that children may lie about alleged events. However, lie-telling abilities develop alongside other cognitive and social abilities, and children below the age of 7 do not possess the appropriate skills to be effective liars (Polak & Harris, 1999; Talwar, Gordon, & Lee, 2007; Talwar & Lee, 2002). Children acquire the ability to make false statements around the age of 3.5 (Ahern, Lyon, & Quas, 2011) and they progressively learn to control nonverbal behavior, conceal their knowledge or feign ignorance, and maintain consistency in their lies (Polak & Harris, 1999; Talwar & Crossman, 2012; Talwar et al., 2007). These key developmental changes appear to begin around the age of 7 (Talwar & Crossman, 2011).

Lie detection in children is equally difficult for laypersons and trained professionals. Studies have shown that both groups only detect lies told by children accurately around 50% of the time (Vrij, 2008, p. 157, see Table 6.2; Vrij, 2008, p. 167, see Table 6.4). This may be because children make shorter responses, thus giving fewer verbal cues. In addition, younger children may experience less negative emotion when lying (e.g., fear of being caught, guilt) and thus may not show as many nonverbal cues of deceit (Vrij, 2008). Because it is difficult to detect deception in children, researchers have studied the efficacy of children's oaths in promoting honesty in the legal system. Researchers have found that, when children promise to tell the truth, they provide more honest answers (e.g., Lyon, 1999).

Taken together, research has shown that children, on average, bring more vulnerabilities to forensic settings—in relation to memory, language and communication, suggestibility, and deception—than adults do. However, research has also shown that when questioned appropriately and in accordance with best-practice guidelines, even very young children can nevertheless provide reliable and productive responses. By adjusting questioning practices to accommodate children's capabilities, interviewers can facilitate better communication, and thus obtain better evidence to help secure just verdicts.

METHODOLOGY: ASSESSING VERACITY

In the criminal justice system, eyewitness testimony has been described as the single most effective predictor of case outcomes (Colwell, Hiscock, & Memon, 2002). Regardless of accuracy, jurors are overwhelmingly convinced by eyewitness testimony; of concern, they are particularly influenced by eyewitness confidence rather than case facts, cross-examination, or judicial instructions (Penrod & Cutler, 1995). Thus, researchers have spent decades developing several nonverbal and verbal ways of assessing the veracity of statements made by witnesses. Because the only evidence available is typically the child's statement, it is critical that veracity can be assessed reliably so that justice can be served (Lamb, Sternberg, Orbach, Hershkowitz, & Esplin, 1999). The field has worked extensively to develop measures that assess veracity using both verbal and nonverbal cues. However, as both laboratory and field studies often have limitations (e.g., ecological validity, and lack of control, respectively) that affect the generalizability of their findings, the field still lacks a fully accurate and objective measure that can be applied in the criminal justice system (Lamb et al, 1997; Vrij, 2005).

Nonverbal Cues to Deception

Lies can be detected by focusing on both nonverbal and verbal cues. With regard to nonverbal cues, some researchers hypothesize that the emotions often associated with lying (e.g., guilt, fear of being caught, physiological arousal) can "leak" through and affect the liar's behavior (DePaulo et al., 2003; Ekman & Friesen, 1969). Researchers have thus measured physical responses such as eye contact and shifts, body movement, and facial expressions for cues of deception. A metaanalysis by DePaulo et al. (2003) identified visual and verbal cues that were significantly correlated with veracity (e.g., liars are more likely to speak in a high pitch; truth tellers are more likely to move fingers, hands, and arms to modify and/or supplement what is being said) (see DePaulo et al., 2003; see also Vrij, 2008).

However, nonverbal cues are only probabilistically correlated with veracity and cannot differentiate on an individual basis whether a particular statement was true or false. Thus, due to this degree of uncertainty and unreliability, further evidence is needed to definitively determine an account's veracity (DePaulo et al., 2003). It is important to note that only 2 of the 11 studies included in the metaanalysis employed the high-stake emotion eliciting paradigm (i.e., lies of consequence more similar to real world scenarios, often accompanied by strong emotions) Therefore, the metaanalysis may underrepresent the value of emotional cues that signal lying. More serious lies may stir up greater emotion, thus interfering with cognitive processes and leaking more emotional cues (DePaulo et al.,

2003). Unfortunately, research on emotional cues has not adequately assessed high stakes lying, so further research is needed.

Other researchers using "lower-stake" paradigms have found that "no single cue to deception, such as Pinocchio's growing nose, exists" (Vrij & Mann, 2005, p. 64) and that people hold incorrect views about the way liars behave (Vrij & Mann, 2005). Studies have shown that accuracy rates for detecting deceit via nonverbal cues range between 45% and 60%, close to chance (Raskin, Honts, & Kircher, 2013; Vrij, Edwards, Roberts, & Bull, 2000). For these reasons, veracity assessments may be more reliable when attempting to detect deception using verbal cues.

Verbal Cues to Deception

Several methods to measure the verbal cues used in deception currently exist, in particular RM and CBCA. Only a handful of studies have compared the discriminant validity of CBCA and RM using the same material (Sporer, 1997; Vrij, Akehurst, Soukara, & Bull, 2004a; Vrij et al., 2000). Proponents of the RM approach argue that it is based on substantive empirical research and that it involves fewer criteria than the CBCA technique (Strömwall, Bengtsson, Leander, & Granhag, 2004) but the paucity of research precludes determination of either approach as "better" than the other. In addition, as explained in the following, both have serious weaknesses that need to be addressed before either could be employed in forensic contexts.

Reality Monitoring

The RM approach, developed by Johnson and Raye (1981), attempts to assess veracity based on verbal differences between truthful and deceptive statements (Alonso-Quecuty, 1992; Sporer, 1997). RM theory proposes that truthful memories contain more perceptual information (sounds, smells, sights, physical sensations), contextual information (details about where and when the event took place), and affective information (details about how something felt). By contrast, RM theory posits that imagined or fantasized events are derived only from internal sources, and that deceptive verbal statements thus make more references to cognitive operations like thoughts and reasoning (Strömwall et al., 2004). Sporer (1997) later extended this theory and developed eight criteria reflecting veracity: (1) clarity, (2) sensory information, (3) spatial information, (4) temporal information, (5) emotions and feelings, (6) reconstructability of the story, (7) realism, and (8) cognitive operations.

Originally, Johnson and colleagues (1988) developed the Memory Characteristics Questionnaire (MCQ), a self-report questionnaire that participants could use to rate the quality of past memories. As predicted by RM theory, memories of experienced events rated using the MCQ contained more contextual, perceptual, and affective information than memories of imagined events (Johnson, Foley, Suengas, & Raye, 1988). However, because the MCQ was a self-report measure, a modified version was still needed so that forensic interviewers and other third-party observers could use RM to discriminate between children's reports of experiences. Thus, the MCQ was adapted into the RCQ (the Report Characteristics Questionnaire), which has two parts: general characteristics (e.g., complexity, clarity) and specific characteristics (e.g., perceptual and contextual information) (Roberts & Lamb, 2010' Roberts, Lamb, & Randall, 1997).

The RCQ has only been tested infrequently, and these studies have found conflicting results. For example, contrary to predictions, researchers have found that children's truthful accounts may actually provide less visual information (Strömwall & Granhag, 2005), fewer contextual and semantic details (Alonso-Quecuty, 1995), and less affective information (Santtila, Roppola, & Niemi, 1999) than their imagined counterparts. In contrast, when Otgaar and colleagues (2010) examined the RM criterion separately, they found that children provided more visual information in true accounts than in false accounts, but similarly found that the RM theory failed to distinguish between true and false accounts (Otgaar, Candel, Memon, & Almerigogna, 2010). In addition, when children have been coached, they may provide more spatial details than children who actually experienced the event (Joffe, 1994; see Roberts & Lamb, 2010). As a result, the RM approach, and the RCQ, in particular, require further research before it can be considered sufficiently valid and reliable to be used in legal contexts.

Criteria-Based Content Analysis

The second technique, CBCA, is currently the most popular method for assessing the veracity of children's statements in legal settings (Vrij, 2005). It was developed specifically to evaluate statements made by children in sexual abuse investigations (Honts, 1994), and consists of three parts: the semi-structured interview, CBCA, and a contextual evaluation called the Statement Validity Assessment (SVA). In the semi-structured interview, children provide their accounts of the allegation(s) (Raskin & Esplin, 1991b). It is critical that these details are obtained without any influence from the interviewer (Raskin & Esplin, 1991b), because research shows that children are highly susceptible to interviewer suggestion (Ceci & Bruck, 1993). In addition, appropriate prompts such as open-ended, free-recall questions should be employed, and risky closed-ended and suggestive prompts strongly discouraged (Lamb, Sternberg, & Esplin, 1994; Vrij, 2005). Afterwards, the transcripts of the interviews are coded for the 19 CBCA criteria developed from the "Undeutsch Hypothesis" (1967) by Raskin and Esplin (1991a) (Figure 6.1). The *Undeutsch hypothesis* posits that statements derived from the memories of actual experiences will differ in content and quality from accounts of events that were not directly experienced (see Undeutsch, 1989 for a brief history) (Steller & Köhnken, 1989), and the criteria on the CBCA checklist refer to those elements likely to be more characteristic of the former.

Proponents of CBCA assume that the elements referenced in criteria 1 to 13 are too difficult to fabricate, and thus that their presence indicates truthfulness. Then, criteria 14 to 18 refer to differing motivations for telling the truth or lying

(Köhnken 1996, 1999, 2004). For example, truth tellers will be more likely to spon-taneously correct or add to their statement because actual experiences are seldom recalled in a strict, chronological sequence. On the other hand, liars typically cre-ate and adhere to relatively simple scripts, thus avoiding errors of omission or commission that they believe may detract from their credibility. Therefore, when corrections and additions are spontaneously offered, these indicate truthfulness (Raskin & Esplin, 1991b). The last criterion concerns whether the descriptions of the event(s) are typical and/or expected for victims of that specific crime (e.g., a child describes feelings that professionals know are typical for victims of parental sexual abuse) (Raskin & Esplin, 1991a, 1991b; Vrij, 2005).

The third and final stage is the SVA determination, involving an evaluation of the CBCA score in the context of other information about the alleged event. For example, CBCA scores may be affected by factors other than truthfulness (e.g., age, cognitive abilities, and quality of the interview) (Köhnken 2004; Raskin & Esplin, 1991b; Vrij, 2005). As noted by Raskin and Esplin (1991b), the purpose of the SVA is not to assess the credibility of the witness, but to assess the valid-ity of the statement. Thus, the validity checklist refers to factors that may affect the CBCA score and should thus be noted in the evaluation. Several versions exist, and these lists refer to issues such as: (a) mental capability (particularly of a child); (b) the interviewee's susceptibility to suggestion; (c) evidence of sugges-tive, leading, or coercive questioning; (d) overall adequacy of the interview; and (e) pressures to report falsely (e.g., suggestion, coaching, or pressure by some-one) (Köhnken, 2004; Steller, 1989; Steller & Boychuk, 1992). In the final stage of the SVA evaluation, an evaluator considers these external factors and their

General Characteristics
1. Logical structure
2. Unstructured production
3. Quantity of details
Specific Contents
4. Contextual embedding
5. Descriptions of interactions
6. Reproduction of conversation
7. Unexpected complications during the incident
8. Unusual details
9. Superfluous details
10. Accurately reported details misunderstood
11. Related external associations
12. Accounts of subjective mental state
13. Attribution of perpetrator's mental state
Motivation-Related Contents
14. Spontaneous corrections
15. Admitting lack of memory
16. Raising doubts about one's own testimony
17. Self-deprecation
18. Pardoning the perpetrator
Offense-Specific Elements
19. Details characteristic of the offense

Figure 6.1 Content criterion.

implications for interpretation of the CBCA score (Köhnken, 2004; Raskin & Esplin, 1991b; Vrij, 2005).

A field study by Esplin, Boychuk, & Raskin (1988) grouped child statements as "confirmed cases" and "doubtful cases" and found significantly different scores with no overlap in CBCA scores between the two groups. However, despite these overwhelmingly promising results, the study was heavily criticized by Wells and Loftus (1991), who pointed out three critical problems: (1) only one evaluator scored the transcripts, (2) the results could have simply reflected the ages of the children, and (3) the determination of whether the statement was "confirmed" or "doubtful" was not independent of the statement itself. Esplin et al. (1988) used case facts such as "judicial dismissal," "no prosecution," or "persistent denial by accused" to determine "ground truth." This means that the same factors (e.g., a poor statement) could have explained both the poor CBCA scores and a decision not to prosecute, regardless of whether or not the incident had taken place (Wells & Loftus, 1991). In response, Raskin and Esplin (1991c) reclassified "doubtful cases" as those in which at least two of the following criteria were met: (1) lack of medical evidence; (2) recantation, (3) "truthful" polygraph by the accused. Reanalysis of their findings still yielded significant differences between the "confirmed" and "doubtful" groups (Raskin & Esplin, 1991c).

Subsequent studies addressing the criticisms of Esplin et al.'s study, also found differences in the expected direction (Boychuk, 1991; Craig, Scheibe, Raskin, Kircher, & Dodd, 1999; Lamb et al., 1997; Parker & Brown, 2000). For example, Lamb et al. (1997) used a very thorough and explicit coding scheme (e.g., medical and other physical evidence, corroborative statements by the suspect or other witnesses) to group the cases along a continuum from "Very Unlikely" to "Very Likely" to incidents that had happened on the basis of information entirely independent of the children's statements. Although there were significantly more CBCA criteria present in statements provided by children whose allegations were deemed "Likely" or "Very Likely" to have happened, the differences were much smaller than in Esplin et al.'s study. In addition, many of the "implausible" statements contained many CBCA criteria, and the distributions were overlapping, leading the researchers to caution against applying CBCA in forensic settings (Lamb et al., 1997).

Craig et al. (1999) found that their confirmed cases included only slightly more criteria than the doubtful cases but the study used recantations and confessions to establish case veracity. Boychuck (1991) used three masked raters and included a third group, "likely abused," to address some of the criticisms of Esplin et al.'s (1988) study. She found significant differences between the "confirmed" and "likely abused" groups, on the one hand, and "doubtful" cases on the other. Parker and Brown (2000) found significant group differences when CBCA was applied to adult rape allegations. However, only one rater was used, and the criteria for establishing veracity of statements was either too vague or not independent of case facts (e.g., "convincing evidence of rape") (for reviews, see Parker & Brown, 2000; Vrij, 2005) making the findings equivocal.

Compared with the field studies mentioned, laboratory studies control for truth and lie-telling, and thus have undeniable knowledge of veracity. An additional benefit of laboratory studies is the ability to determine whether CBCA can distinguish between truth-telling children and coached children, as children are often asked to lie in laboratory studies. A metaanalysis on laboratory studies found fewer significant differences between liars and truth tellers; however, the differences were still in the expected direction consistent with the *Undeutsch hypothesis* (Vrij, 2005). Looking empirically at each of the 19 criteria, Vrij found that quantity of details (Criterion 3) appeared most often in truthful accounts, followed by unstructured production (Criterion 2), contextual embedding (Criterion 4), and reproduction of conversation (Criterion 6). However, the motivational criteria received little support, especially self-deprecation (17), which has received no empirical support to date (Vrij, 2005). Despite these findings by Vrij, a recent metaanalysis by Oberlader et al. (2016) found that CBCA could distinguish between truthful and false accounts significantly better when all 19 criteria were used. This derives from classical test theory, which states that test validity increases when measuring a higher number of converging yet conceptually distinct facets. Laboratory studies may not be able to measure all 19 criteria because some criteria may be difficult to implement (e.g., pardoning the perpetrator), potentially affecting score validity. However, there is still a known error rate of 30% in laboratory studies, and an indeterminable error rate in field studies (Vrij, 2005). Thus, until the error rate can be reduced, CBCA is clearly too imprecise to be useful in forensic contexts.

Further Weaknesses of Existing Verbal Veracity Assessment Tools

In order for MCQ and CBCA scores to be useful, evaluators need to have access to statements that comprise, in the main, narrative accounts provided by the children, but all of the field studies described earlier acknowledged that they had to work with many poor interviews, the quality of which undermined the informativeness of any assessments. Not surprisingly, researchers have found that open-ended questions yield more CBCA criteria than more direct questions (Craig et al., 1999; Hershkowitz, Lamb, Sternberg, & Esplin, 1997). Facilitators (i.e., non-suggestive words of encouragement) (Hershkowitz et al., 1997), verbal affirmations ("Yes," "I see"), and confirming comments are also positively correlated with higher CBCA scores (Davies, Westcott, & Horan, 2000). To date, no researchers have used CBCA or RCQ to distinguish between true and false accounts elicited in high-quality interviews of the type described in the next section.

Further, the RM approach has two additional weaknesses that ultimately restrict its applicability in the legal system. Firstly, RM scores are positively correlated with word count, meaning the greater the number of words, the higher the RM score (Elntib, Wagstaff, & Wheatcroft, 2015). Sporer (2004) has suggested that standardizing the RM score will improve veracity determination and eliminate inaccurate assessments by controlling for the number of words when scoring. However, this is problematic in light of the prediction by RM theory that truthful accounts will contain "more perceptual, spatial, temporal, semantic, and affective information," and thus will be richer in detail and word count (Johnson, Hashtroudi, & Lindsay, 1993, p. 4). So, by standardizing the word count, researchers would be altering one of the predicted qualities of lies, namely, that they contain less information (Colwell et al., 2002; Memon, Fraser, Coldwell, Odinot, & Mastroberardino, 2010; Vrij, Akehurst, Soukara, & Bull, 2004b).

Second, RCQ scale scores are significantly affected by developmental differences. When word count is standardized, truthful reports given by older children contain a higher number of the criteria than truthful reports given by younger children, suggesting that children's abilities to answer significantly affect RCQ scores. Furthermore, truthful and doubtful accounts given by older children were indistinguishable using the RCQ (Roberts & Lamb, 2010). The same problem bedevils use of the CBCA approach, with statements provided by older children getting higher scores than those provided by younger children in both field and laboratory analogue contexts (Anson, Golding, & Gully, 1993; Boychuk, 1991; Craig et al., 1999; Esplin et al., 1988; Horowitz et al., 1997; Lamb et al., 1997; Santtila, Roppola, Runtti, & Niemi, 2000; Strange & Hayne, 2013; Vrij, Akehurst, Soukara, & Bull, 2002).

Coaching may also affect the scores assigned to children's statements. Vrij et al. (2002) found that, when told how to tell a convincing story, children (both 10–11 and 14–15-year-olds) obtained higher CBCA scores than untrained children. Coached liars of all ages never scored significantly lower than coached or uncoached truth tellers on the CBCA (Vrij et al., 2002). In a similar study by Blandon-Gitlin and colleagues (2005), children (ages 9 to 12 years) who were familiarized, or "coached," about an account received significantly higher CBCA scores regardless of veracity; meanwhile, account veracity was not significantly correlated with CBCA score. Therefore, for multiple reasons, we must conclude that neither of the standardized methods for assessing children's truthfulness are sufficiently reliable to be used in forensic contexts.

Can Best-Practice Interviewing Elicit More Accurate Verbal Cues to Deception?

Earhart, La Rooy, and Lamb (2016) have argued, as the authors have, that traditional psychometric tools such as the CBCA and the RM approach cannot be used to determine whether a child has been abused or is telling the truth. However, there is some evidence that veracity can be assessed more accurately when children provide narrative accounts in the course of interviews adhering to the best-practice guidelines. Reliance on open-ended questions (in accordance with best-practice guidelines) elicits free recall responses from children that are more elaborate and richer in detail. When presented with interviews of that sort, raters were better able to identify plausible and implausible accounts than when presented with poorly conducted interviews (Hershkowitz, Fisher, Lamb, & Horowitz, 2007).

As noted by Earhart et al. (2016), "the only way to assess interviews is to focus not on whether the children are telling the truth, but on what the interviewers have done during the interview, and whether the conditions are right for obtaining accurate statements." Thus, focusing on the extent to which interviewers encourage children to provide narrative accounts, and minimize possible sources of contamination, would likely provide richer, more complete statements for which triers of fact could more accurately assess children's credibility.

LESSONS LEARNED FROM FORENSIC INTERVIEWING

Structured investigative interviewing protocols have been developed to encourage witnesses to provide complete and accurate accounts of the alleged event(s). Particularly in cases of alleged abuse, children's testimony is likely to be critical (Brown, Lamb, Pipe, & Orbach, 2008). Researchers have identified several factors that can enhance or hinder the capabilities of children to provide accurate testimony, and have considered these factors when designing structured investigative interviewing protocols, particularly the NICHD Protocol (Lamb, Orbach, Hershkowitz, Esplin, & Horowitz, 2007a).

Best-Practice Guidelines—the NICHD Investigative Interview Protocol

The creation of the NICHD Protocol was informed by abundant research conducted in the wake of day care abuse scandals in the 1980s and 1990s (Lamb et al., 2007a). For example, in one of the most infamous cases, the McMartin Preschool Case, seven teachers were accused of sexually abusing several children in the preschool. After one of the longest and most expensive criminal trials in the history of California, all charges were ultimately dropped due to heavy criticism of the videotaped forensic interviews played at trial. Specifically, interviewers behaved so suggestively (e.g., introducing new information, giving praise or criticism, including information from other witnesses, and inviting speculation) that jurors deemed the allegations unreliable. Jurors, the media, and academic experts publicly criticized the leading nature of the forensic interviews (Schreiber et al., 2006).

Research conducted after the McMartin trial and other highly publicized cases found that, like adults, children can provide informative and complete accounts of events they have experienced. One of the most important factors, however, concerns the interviewer's capabilities to appropriately elicit information from the child and the child's willingness and ability to cooperate, rather than the child's memory (or lack thereof) of the event (Lamb et al., 2007a). Thus, the NICHD Protocol was developed to translate research findings (Ceci & Bruck, 1993, 1995; Lamb et al., 2008; Poole & Lamb, 1998) into a standardized but flexible set of guidelines that could be followed by forensic interviewers when questioning children (Lamb et al., 2007a). Laboratory research on best-practice questioning styles has consistently found that responses to open-ended questions are more accurate (Dale, Loftus, & Rathbun, 1978; Ceci & Bruck, 1993). Although accuracy is more difficult to determine in field studies, it is inferred based on other case facts such as corroborating statements from the suspect

(Lamb et al., 2007b), physical evidence (i.e., audio recording) (Orbach & Lamb, 1999), or internal inconsistencies in the form of self-contradictions (e.g., Lamb & Fauchier, 2001; Orbach & Lamb, 2001). Research from field studies has also consistently confirmed that open-ended questions are more likely to elicit accurate responses, while closed-ended questions are more likely to elicit erroneous responses or self-contradictions (Lamb & Fauchier, 2001; Lamb et al., 2007b; Sternberg, Lamb, Orbach, Esplin, & Mitchell, 2001). Suggestive techniques such as the use of closed-ended questions that introduce information not previously disclosed, leading questions that communicate the expected responses, repeated questions, coaching, and the use of props can detrimentally contaminate child responses (Andrews & Lamb, 2014; Ceci & Bruck, 1995; Lamb et al., 2007al., 2007b; Poole, Bruck, & Pipe, 2011; Vrij et al., 2002). On the other hand, nonsuggestive techniques such as the use of open-ended questions, rapport-building, and interviewer supportiveness can encourage not only more complete recall, but also more accurate recall (Ceci & Bruck, 1995; Lamb et al., 2007a; Brown et al., 2008; Cyr & Lamb, 2009; Lamb et al., 2009).

Question Types

The first issue to be addressed concerns the questioning styles used in forensic interviews. The NICHD Protocol encourages the use of open-ended questions whenever possible (e.g., "Tell me what happened"). However, if the interviewee fails to report crucial details in response to exhaustive free-recall questions, directives and option-posing questions may be employed. Directive questions are narrow questions referring to information previously mentioned by the child as a cue (e.g., "What color was the shirt?" [when the child had previously mentioned a shirt]). Option-posing questions, prompting recognition memory, may be asked sparingly if crucial details are still missing after multiple open-ended prompts. Option-posing questions are typically formed as yes/no prompts (e.g., "Was your mum in the car?") or forced choice prompts (e.g., "Did he touch you over or under your clothes?" [when the child had previously mentioned being touched]) (Lamb et al., 2007a). Such closed-ended questions are potentially problematic because children may simply agree or disagree with the line of questioning regardless of whether or not they actually remember (Ahern et al., 2011). Interviewers are universally advised not to ask suggestive questions, which communicate to the child an expected response (e.g., "It hurt, didn't it?" [when the child had not previously mentioned feeling pain]) or introduce details not yet mentioned by the child (e.g., "Did he take his trousers down?" [when the child had not previously mentioned that he was wearing trousers]) (Lamb et al., 2007a).

By encouraging the use of open-ended questions and avoiding close-ended and suggestive prompts, researchers elicit more productive responses and higher quality (e.g., less contaminated) accounts of the alleged abuse, which can assist interviewers in making more reliable veracity assessments (Hershkowitz et al., 2007). By contrast, interviews largely composed of close-ended questions yield less information and information of poorer quality (Hershkowitz et al., 2007). For example, one study found that no self-contradictions were elicited by open invitations, while 86% of the self-contradictions were elicited using option posing and suggestive questions (Lamb & Fauchier, 2001).

Independent field studies in four different counties (i.e., the United States, Israel, Canada, and the United Kingdom) have shown that use of the NICHD Protocol significantly improves the quality of information obtained in interviews with alleged victims (Cyr & Lamb, 2009; Lamb et al., 2009; Orbach et al., 2000; Sternberg et al., 2001). Interviewers trained to use the NICHD Protocol offered three times as many open-ended prompts and half as many option-posing and suggestive prompts as they did when not using the Protocol. In addition, 80% of the initial disclosures and half of the forensically relevant details were provided in response to free-recall prompts, even by children as young as preschool age (Lamb et al., 2007a). NICHD Protocol interviewers also offered more free-recall cued prompts before asking any more focused questions (Lamb et al., 2007a). These findings are important because, not only were young children able to provide forensically relevant information, but the information was more likely to be accurate because it was elicited using open-ended prompts. Thus, it is critical for forensic interviewers to use option-posing questions sparingly and to avoid suggestive questions entirely so that the evidence elicited is likely to be as accurate as possible.

Repeated Questions

The veracity of children's statements can also be negatively affected by repeated questions. Poole and White (1991) speculated that children may interpret repeated questions as indications that their initial answers were incorrect, and thus change their responses to accommodate interviewers. There is ample evidence that repeating questions decreases response accuracy and elicits self-contradictions (Gelman, Meek, & Merkin, 1986; Moston, 1987). Similarly, Poole and White (1991) found that, although repeated open-ended questions had little to no effect on accuracy and consistency, repeated closed-ended (e.g., option-posing) questions were significantly more likely to elicit self-contradictions. Another study by Andrews and Lamb (2014) found that option-posing questions elicited 64% of the self-contradictions ($n = 36$) in interviews, while suggestive questions elicited 19% of the self-contradictions. Although question repetition does not always elicit inaccurate information, repetition is particularly problematic in some circumstances (e.g., suggestive interviews, younger age, longer delay, social pressure), and the inaccurate information they elicit can further contaminate children's later reports (Goodman & Quas, 2008). Thus, repeated questions, particularly repeated close-ended utterances, negatively affect children's perceived credibility because they elicit self-contradictions. In addition, because individuals, including interviewers and jurors, place strong emphasis on response consistency when assessing veracity, it is best that repeated questions be used sparingly (Semmler & Brewer, 2002).

Use of Props

The use of props in forensic interviews can also be highly suggestive and thus likely to diminish children's veracity. The use of props, such as anatomically correct dolls and body maps, is controversial, and thus discouraged in many guidelines, although proponents believe that props may assist children struggling to disclose—due to motivational factors (e.g., embarrassment), linguistic issues (e.g., restricted understanding of the word "touch" and a limited vocabulary for describing abuse), and/or memory problems (e.g., failure to remember target memories without cues)—allowing them to provide information they cannot verbalize (Russell, 2008). In fact, interviews conducted using props do not yield more information and the information they do yield can be hard to evaluate (Brown et al., 2008; Bruck, Kelley, & Poole, 2016; Poole & Bruck, 2012; Poole et al., 2011). The effective use of props requires highly complex cognitive abilities that young children may not have developed, thus limiting their suitability for younger children (see Deloache, 2000; Poole et al., 2011). For example, DeLoache and Marzolf (1995) found that the majority of 2.5 year olds failed to replicate sticker placement on a doll when the sticker was still present on themselves, suggesting this was a much more complex task for younger children than originally believed (only 5 of the 41 children accurately placed 3 of the 4 stickers on the doll). In addition, children often rejected the doll as a representation of themselves, were distracted by the doll, or did not know how to use it, thus providing less responsive accounts than children who gave direct reports alone. In addition, a field study found that when questioned with dolls, younger children were more likely to provide inconsistent and inaccurate responses, and older children did not provide additional details, but merely repeated details already disclosed earlier in the interview (Thierry, Lamb, Orbach, & Pipe, 2005).

The use of body diagrams in forensic interviews may be associated with increases in the number of details reported by children (Aldridge et al., 2004) but there is also an increased risk of false reports by young children (Bruck et al., 2016). In addition, it is not clear whether the use of body diagrams, the retrieval cues, or the more specific questions accounts for increases in the numbers of details (Poole et al., 2011). To address problems of generalization due to the innocuous touches typically employed in laboratory studies, a recent study by Bruck et al. (2016) asked children ages 3 to 8 about "sexual" touches that occurred during a medical examination. The touches were not actually "sexual," but the children did experience anal and or/genital touches during medical examinations (i.e., sexual abuse clinics, gastrointestinal appointments). Researchers found a concerning high number of falsely reported sexual touches during interviews conducted using body diagrams; 50% of the three-year-olds ($n = 50$) and 33% of the 4–year-olds ($n = 57$) incorrectly reported genital touching. Thus, there is no compelling evidence that the use of props, such as dolls and body maps, facilitates higher quality or more detailed reports (Poole et al., 2011). In addition, their use significantly increases the chances that children will falsely report touches (Bruck et al., 2016; Pipe &

Salmon, 2009; Poole et al., 2011; Willcock, Morgan, & Hayne, 2006). Thus, the use of props may result in less reliable accounts, adversely affecting the ability of interviewers and triers of fact to determine what if anything happened to the child in question.

Unlike dolls and body maps, the use of drawing in forensic interviews may increase the amount of details provided for a variety of reasons (e.g., interviews that include a drawing element are typically longer; see Macleod, Gross, & Hayne, 2013). Researchers are currently exploring the implications that drawing may have in forensic interviews, as well as procedures for eliciting both episodic detail and evaluative information (Butler, Gross, & Hayne, 1995; Gross & Hayne, 1999; Macleod et al., 2013; Otgaar, Ansem, Pauw, & Horselenberg, 2016). For example, in one study, children who drew during a forensic interview were more accurate and provided more details than children who did not draw, particularly in response to direct questions (Butler et al., 1995). This effect was seen in 5- to 6-year-old children even after a 1-month delay (Butler et al., 1995). Similarly, in another study, children who drew in an interview reported twice as many details compared with those children who were asked to tell only (Gross & Hayne, 1999). However, a third study found that children who drew during interviews provided more complete accounts, but the completeness was associated with increased commission errors and decreased accuracy (Otgaar et al., 2016). Furthermore, as with other props, factors such as age and interviewer prompts may affect the efficacy of drawing. More specifically, drawing has been shown to not aid children under the age of 4 years old in providing additional details (Butler, et al., 1995). In addition, there are conflicting results regarding the most appropriate questioning styles to use with drawing, but it is typically found to be most productive when combined with relatively specific but nonleading prompts (Butler, et al., 1995; Gross & Hayne, 1999; Salmon, 2001). Last, the generalizability of drawing to forensic contexts is still limited, as the majority of studies have been conducted in laboratory settings. Thus, the use of drawings to facilitate productive interviews seems promising; however, more research in the field is necessary.

Rapport Building and Supportiveness

Although some "rapport-building" practices can be suggestive, researchers have also identified some strategies that facilitate productive and reliable disclosures by child witnesses. The NICHD Protocol encourages interviewers to build rapport before the substantive questioning begins, to create a relaxed and supportive environment. By asking children open-ended questions about neutral topics, children can become accustomed to the types of open-ended questions used in the substantive phases as well as the richness of specific details interviewers would welcome (Lamb et al., 2007; Sternberg et al., 1997). There is evidence that rapport building can increase the accuracy and amount of details disclosed during the substantive phase, especially if the interviewer employs open-ended questions (Roberts, Lamb, & Sternberg, 2004; Sternberg et al., 1997) or if the child is initially reluctant to disclose (Hershkowitz, Lamb, & Katz, 2014; Wood, McClure,

& Birch, 1996). Thus, when interviewers engage in rapport building, they may increase the amount of details the child provides that, in turn, contribute to veracity assessment.

Interviewer supportiveness during the substantive phase of questioning can also be helpful. Although support must be provided nonsuggestively (e.g., Carter et al., 1996; Davis & Bottoms, 2002; Goodman, Bottoms, Schwartz-Kenney, & Rudy, 1991), investigators can show support neutrally by commenting on the effort the child is making (e.g., "I can tell this is hard for you") or by showing the child small acts of kindness (e.g., offering a glass of water or a tissue) (Earhart et al., 2016). Supportiveness increases response accuracy and resistance to misleading questions (Carter et al., 1996; Goodman et al., 1991). Ultimately, the improvement in interview quality resulting from interview supportiveness may also contribute to more accurate veracity assessments.

Informed by the results of research conducted during the last three decades, improvements have been made in the ways that children are questioned in forensic interviews (see Cyr & Lamb, 2009; Lamb et al., 1996, 2007, 2009; Orbach et al., 2000; Sternberg et al., 2001). However, the forensic interview is seldom the final stage in the criminal prosecution of child sexual abuse cases. Spencer and Lamb (2012) explain that the questioning styles encouraged by the NICHD Protocol should be encouraged—if not required—by lawyers in the trial setting as well. If the case is considered prosecutable, children must be deemed credible by both interviewers in the forensic interview as well as judges and jurors in their courtroom testimony. This underlines the need, not only for high-quality forensic interviews, but also for fair and effective examination at trial. If defense lawyers conducting cross-examinations undermine the credibility of child witnesses using the same leading, suggestive, and repetitive questioning styles discouraged in forensic interviews, jurors may doubt the veracity of the testimony (Semmler & Brewer, 2002; Spencer & Lamb, 2012). Ultimately, children must be deemed truthful in first, the forensic interview, and later, in court, for justice to be achieved.

IMPLICATIONS FOR THE DIRECT- AND CROSS-EXAMINATION OF CHILDREN IN COURT

Because courtroom testimony poses significant challenges for vulnerable witnesses, many legal systems are now implementing special measures to accommodate young witnesses in the courtroom (e.g., live links, intermediaries, etc.). However, the process is often still traumatizing and stressful for children (Plotnikoff & Woolfson, 2009). Many countries, like the United Kingdom and New Zealand, permit video-recorded forensic interviews to replace the children's evidence-in-chief (Spencer & Lamb, 2012). Thus, children are spared from having to fully recount potentially traumatic and embarrassing experience(s), once again, in court (Plotnikoff & Woolfson, 2009). However, the use of the forensic interview in the courtroom emphasizes the crucial importance of high-quality interviews so that triers of fact can effectively assess the testimony.

Although children may be spared from giving their evidence-in-chief, they typically must still be cross-examined in court. Courtroom questioning, and in particular the cross-examination, differs drastically from forensic interviewing and can present significant difficulties for child witnesses. Because the court setting is inherently "adversarial" and there are fewer restrictions on the use of certain types of questions, risky questions that exploit children's developmental limitations (e.g. suggestive questions, repeated questions) are employed frequently (Andrews & Lamb, 2016; Andrews et al., 2015). This leads to increases in the numbers of inaccurate responses (e.g., self-contradictions, contamination through leading questions). Thus, the current procedure for cross-examination may not be "the greatest legal engine ever invented for the discovery of truth" (Wigmore, 1974, p. 32), but may actually limit our system's ability to achieve justice. Instead, the most efficient means "for the discovery of truth" may involve simply employing developmentally appropriate questioning strategies in both the forensic interview and direct- and cross-examination.

To facilitate reliable decision making, both the forensic interviewers and courtroom examiners should elicit as many uncontaminated details as possible. Question types discouraged by the NICHD Protocol (e.g., closed-ended, repeated, and suggestive), which diminish response accuracy and productivity, unfortunately still predominate in many forensic interviews (Lamb et al., 2007). A recent study using an English sample found that 50% of forensic interviewer utterances were either suggestive questions, forced choice questions, compound questions, or statements (Phillips, Oxburgh, Gavin, & Myklebust, 2012), underlining the need to improve practice.

The problem is more severe when examining the questioning strategies employed by attorneys in court, where leading, suggestive, and repeated questions are frequently used in child direct- and cross-examinations. For example, one study found that of the questions asked by prosecutors ($n = 26,548$), 68% were option posing or suggestive, and only 3% were invitations (Andrews, Lamb, & Lyon, 2015). Of the questions asked by defense attorneys ($n = 22,168$), 46% percent were option posing and 42% were suggestive; there were no invitations at all (Andrews et al., 2015). Despite the number of risky questions asked, interventions by attorneys, judges, or intermediaries are infrequent (Andrews et al., 2015; Plotnikoff & Woolfson, 2009).

As previously mentioned, it is difficult for experts and laypersons alike to assess veracity (Vrij, 2008). This problem is confounded when both forensic interviewers and courtroom examiners do not use the types of questions likely to elicit accurate information. Because triers of fact must determine guilt or innocence based on the evidence presented, it behooves us to provide them with the most reliable evidence possible.

First, forensic interviewing procedures must be improved. As Earhart and colleagues (2016) concluded, and as is recommended by the NICHD Protocol, the best way to elicit accurate information involves open-ended, non-suggestive questioning strategies. "High quality interviewing is not an art form; it is a science . . ." and "if children are interviewed under ideal conditions, we can have reasonable faith in what they have said" (Earhart et al., 2016, p. 330). If procedures are improved (for example, training in the use of the NICHD Protocol), children's responses are more likely to be both detailed and reliable. Pipe, Orbach, Lamb, Abbott, and Stewart (2013) determined that, when forensic interviewers employed the NICHD Protocol, charges were more likely to be filed and convictions were more likely to be obtained than when other interview methods were employed.

Second, the questioning procedures employed in court should be better regulated, particularly during the cross-examination of vulnerable witnesses. Researchers have begun to question whether cross-examination is less a "forensic tool for exposing a dishonest witness" and more "a procedure to manufacture false evidence" (Cossins, 2012, p. 102). Studies have shown that children often misunderstand leading and closed questions asked by defense attorneys, and as a result are highly compliant in their responses (Zajac et al., 2003). In one study, over three quarters of the children changed their testimony as a result of cross-examination (Zajac et al., 2003). In a follow-up study, the researchers found that children were just as likely to change initially correct answers during cross examination as they were to change initially incorrect answers, showing that cross-examination did not expose dishonest child witnesses effectively (Zajac & Hayne, 2003). By asking misleading questions and inducing self-contradictions, attorneys are hindering jurors' and judges' abilities to reliably assess child witnesses' credibility. Thus, "the question is whether it is in the public interest for jurors to make decisions based on what amounts to manufactured inaccuracies [i.e., cross-examination]," because "if a fair trial necessarily involves preventing the contamination of a child's evidence then there is a need to consider the ways in which the cross-examination process can be reformed" (Cossins, 2012, p. 105). Such reforms have been implemented gradually in many court systems worldwide, particularly in Australia, New Zealand, and the United Kingdom (e.g., restricting the defendant from personally cross-examining a victim of sexual assault/abuse, allowing testimony to be provided by live-link or from behind a screen, using the forensic interview as evidence-in-chief, removing wigs and robes) (Cossins, 2012; Spencer & Lamb, 2012).

A recently implemented special measure in the United Kingdom, known as Section 28 of the Youth Justice and Criminal Evidence Act (1999), permits the prerecording of the cross-examination for vulnerable witnesses (similar policies have also been employed in Australia; Home Office, 1989). The special measure allows the child's participation in the legal system to end months earlier, and ensures that the questions can be more thoroughly scrutinized and preapproved before the proceeding. A week prior to the cross-examination, a Ground Rules Hearing takes place. In this hearing, prosecuting and defense attorneys meet with the judge and intermediary (if one has been appointed) to set rules for questioning that will ensure fair and effective communication. Critical issues such as the duration, manner, content, and style of questioning are addressed (Rafferty, 2016). Thus, the Section 28 procedures aim to improve courtroom questioning not only by creating a more efficient and less prolonged experience for witnesses, but also by improving the quality of evidence obtained.

Section 28 has only recently been implemented, but preliminary analyses have shown that Section 28 cross-examinations were significantly briefer and that the delays between the forensic interviews and the conclusion of the children's participation were significantly shorter than in cases conducted without benefit of the new procedures (Henderson & Lamb, 2017). It remains to be seen whether similar benefits will be obtained when a larger number of judges and courts are involved. Improvement is dependent on the nature of the "rules" established in the Ground Rules Hearings, as well as on the extent to which the judges demand adherence.

Intermediaries can also serve as third-party participants whose role is to ensure coherent and accurate communication among the children, attorneys, and triers of fact; however, their level of involvement varies greatly across countries (Henderson, 2012). Proponents of the intermediary system believe that their involvement offers a range of benefits, including facilitating communication, helping witnesses cope with the stress of court, assisting in bringing offenders to justice, and identifying prosecutable cases (thus saving court time and money). By ensuring effective communication with vulnerable witnesses, the most reliable evidence possible should be presented to triers of fact. However, as the role is still relatively new, there remains considerable variability in the levels of expertise and the actual behavior of intermediaries, and training is variable (Plotnikoff & Woolfson, 2007). More fundamentally, in a conventional cross-examination, it is difficult and slightly unrealistic to expect intermediaries to intervene when every risky question is asked. However, in many parts of the United Kingdom, Ground Rules Hearings are now required in all cases involving serious sexual allegations, so the work of intermediaries in child sexual abuse cases will be facilitated (Rafferty, 2016).

Special measures such as these are designed to encourage fair, reliable, and coherent communication among participants in legal settings, with the ultimate aim of achieving justice. Whether designed to ease the witness's anxiety and fear (e.g., screens, live-link), ensure developmentally appropriate communication (e.g., training of forensic interviewers, employing intermediaries), and/or restrict the use of risky question types (e.g., Ground Rules Hearings), significant steps have been made to elicit more reliable testimony. However, the success of many of these special measures still depends entirely on legal practitioners recognizing and employing appropriate utterances (e.g., forensic interviews as Evidence-in-Chief, intermediaries, Ground Rules Hearings, Section 28).

CONCLUSION

Millions of children are abused worldwide each year. Even very young children have the capacity to provide the evidence necessary to prosecute these cases. However, instead, of fostering effective communication, children's vulnerabilities are often exploited in a criminal justice system that has only recently begun to make accommodations for young victims. In the last few decades, researchers have determined that the strategies commonly used in forensic interviews and courtroom examinations, particularly risky questioning styles, have been contaminating testimony rather than encouraging accurate, complete, and coherent accounts. These questioning strategies not only produce less reliable evidence, but also, hinder accurate assessments of veracity.

Progress has been made in improving the quality of questioning used in both forensic interviews as well as in courtrooms. However, the system is still far from ideal, and considerable improvement remains necessary, whether in forensic interview practices or in developmentally appropriate cross-examination strategies. Additional special measures need to be identified and implemented so the evidence can remain uncontaminated and more reliable (e.g., intermediaries, Ground Rules Hearings). In addition, education and training for all parties involved in the criminal justice system should be encouraged. Contamination of testimony can begin as early as the initial police reports, and every individual who interacts with the child has the potential to foster or diminish accuracy. Many of the special measures rely on an improvement in questioning procedures so as to reap their full benefit. However, forensic interviewers, judges, advocates, and intermediaries all must have reasonable knowledge and comprehension of appropriate and risky practices. We have come a long way in the treatment of child witnesses, but we still have far to go if we wish to provide justice for both defendants and victims alike.

REFERENCES

Ahern, E. C., Lyon, T. D., & Quas, J. A. (2011). Young children's emerging ability to make false statements. *Developmental Psychology, 47*, 61–66.

Aldridge, J., Lamb, E., Sternberg, K. J., Orbach, Y., Esplin, P. W., & Bowler, L. (2004). Using human figure drawings to elicit information from alleged victims of child sexual abuse. *Journal of Consulting and Clinical Psychology, 72*, 304–316.

Alonso-Quecuty, M. L. (1992). Deception detection and reality monitoring: A new answer to an old question? In F. Lösel, D. Bender, & T. Bliesener (Eds.), *Psychology and law: International perspectives* (pp. 328–332). Berlin: Walter de Gruyter:.

Alonso-Quecuty, M. L. (1995). Detecting fact from fallacy in child and adult witness accounts. In G. Davies, S. Lloyd-Bostock, M. McMurran, & C. Wilson (Eds.), *Psychology, law, and criminal justice: International developments in research and practice* (pp. 74–80). Berlin: Walter de Gruyter.

American Professional Society on the Abuse of Children, APSAC. (2012). *Practice guidelines: Investigative interviewing in cases of alleged child abuse.* Retrieved from: http://www.apsac.org/

Andrews, S. J., & Lamb, M. E. (2014). The effects of age and delay on responses to repeated questions in forensic interviews with children alleging sexual abuse. *Law and human behavior, 38*, 171–180.

Andrews, S. J., & Lamb, M. E. (2016). How do lawyers examine and cross-examine children in Scotland? *Applied Cognitive Psychology, 30*, 953–971.

Andrews, S. J., Lamb, M. E., & Lyon, T. D. (2015). Question types, responsiveness and self- contradictions when prosecutors and defense attorneys question alleged victims of child sexual abuse. *Applied Cognitive Psychology, 29*, 253–261.

Anson, D. A., Golding, S. L., & Gully, K. J. (1993). Child sexual abuse allegations: Reliability of criteria-based content analysis. *Law and Human Behavior, 17,* 331–341.

Australian Institute of Health and Welfare. (2007). *Child protection Australia 2005-2006* (Cat no. CWS 28, Child welfare series no. 40). Canberra, Australia: Author.

Blandon-Gitlin, I., Pezdek, K., Rogers, M., & Brodie, L. (2005). Detecting deception in children: An experimental study of the effect of event familiarity on CBCA ratings. *Law and Human Behavior, 29,* 187–197.

Brainerd, C. J., & Reyna, V. F. (2005). *The science of false memory.* New York: Oxford University Press.

Brainerd, C. J., Reyna, V. F., & Ceci, S. J. (2008). Developmental reversals in false memory: A review of data and theory. *Psychological bulletin, 134,* 343–382.

Brown, D., Lamb, M. E., Pipe, M. E., & Orbach, Y. (2008). Pursuing 'the truth, the whole truth, and nothing but the truth': Forensic interviews with child victims or witnesses of abuse. In M. Howe, G. S. Goodman, & D. Cicchetti, (Eds.), *Stress, trauma, and children's memory development: Neurobiological, cognitive, clinical, and legal perspectives* (pp. 267–301). Oxford: Oxford University Press.

Boychuk, T. D. (1991). Criteria-based content analysis of children's statements about sexual abuse: A field-based validation study. Unpublished doctoral dissertation. Arizona State University, Tempe, AZ.

Bruck, M., & Ceci, S. J., Principe, G. (2006). The child and the law. In K. A. Renninger & I. E. Sigel (Vol. Eds.), *Child psychology in practice* (Vol. 5). In W. Damon & R. Lerner (Gen. Eds.), *Handbook of child psychology* (6th ed.). Hoboken, NJ: Wiley.

Bruck, M., Kelley, K., & Poole, D. A. (2016). Children's reports of body touching in medical examinations: The benefits and risks of using body diagrams. *Psychology, Public Policy, and Law, 22,* 1–11.

Butler, S., Gross, J., & Hayne, H. (1995). The effect of drawing on memory performance in young children. *Developmental Psychology, 31,* 597–608.

Carter, C. A., Bottoms, B. L., & Levine, M. (1996). Linguistic and socioemotional influences on the accuracy of children's reports. *Law and Human Behavior, 20,* 335–356.

Ceci, S. J., & Bruck, M. (1993). Suggestibility of the child witness: A historical review and synthesis. *Psychological bulletin, 113,* 403–439.

Ceci, S. J., & Bruck, M. (1995). *Jeopardy in the courtroom: A scientific analysis of children's testimony.* Washington, DC: American Psychological Association.

Child Advocacy Centre. (2016). Retrieved from: http://www.nationalcac.org

Craig, R. A., Scheibe, R., Raskin, D. C., Kircher, J. C., & Dodd, D. H. (1999). Interviewer questions and content analysis of children's statements of sexual abuse. *Applied Developmental Science, 3,* 77–85.

Colwell, K., Hiscock, C. K., & Memon, A. (2002). Interviewing techniques and the assessment of statement credibility. *Applied Cognitive Psychology, 16,* 287–300.

Cossins, A. (2012). Cross examining the child complainant in Australia. In J. R. Spencer & M. E. Lamb (Eds.), *Children and cross-examination: Time to change the rules?* Oxford; Hart Publishing.

Cyr, M., & Lamb, M. E. (2009). Assessing the effectiveness of the NICHD investigative interview protocol when interviewing French-speaking alleged victims of child sexual abuse in Quebec. *Child Abuse & Neglect, 33,* 257–268.

Dale, P. (1976). *Language development: Structure and function* (2nd ed.). New York: Holt, Rinehart and Winston.

Dale, P. S., Loftus, E. F., & Rathbun, L. (1978). The influence of the form of the question on the eyewitness testimony of preschool children. *Journal of Psycholinguistic Research, 7*, 269–277.

Davis, S., & Bottoms, B. (2002). Effects of social support on children's eyewitness reports: A test of the underlying mechanism. *Law and Human Behavior, 26*, 185–214.

Davies, G. M., Westcott, H. L., & Horan, N. (2000). The impact of questioning style on the content of investigative interviews with suspected child sexual abuse victims. *Psychology, Crime, and Law, 6*, 81–97.

DeLoache, J. S. (2000). Dual representation and young children's use of scale models. *Child Development, 71*, 329–338.

DeLoache, J. S., & Marzolf, D. P. (1995). The use of dolls to interview young children: Issues of symbolic representation. *Journal of Experimental Child Psychology, 60*, 155–173.

DePaulo, B. M., Lindsay, J. J., Malone, B. E., Muhlenbruck, L., Charlton, K., & Cooper, H. (2003). Cues to deception. *Psychological bulletin, 129*, 74–118.

de Villiers, P. A., & de Villiers, J. G. (1979). *Early language. The developing child series*. Cambridge, MA: Harvard University Press.

Earhart, B., La Rooy, D., & Lamb, M. E. (2016). Assessing the quality of forensic interviews with child witnesses. In W. T. O'Donohue & M. Fanetti (Eds.), *Forensic interviews regarding child sexual abuse* (pp. 317–335). Cham, Switzerland: Springer International Publishing.

Eisen, M. L., Goodman, G. S., Qin, J., Davis, S., & Crayton, J. (2007). Maltreated children's memory: Accuracy, suggestibility, and psychopathology. *Developmental Psychology, 43*, 1275–1294.

Ekman, P., & Friesen, W. V. (1969). Nonverbal leakage and clues to deception. *Psychiatry, 32*, 88–106.

Elntib, S., Wagstaff, G. F., & Wheatcroft, J. M. (2015). The role of account length in detecting deception in written and orally produced autobiographical accounts using reality monitoring. *Journal of Investigative Psychology and Offender Profiling, 12*, 185–198.

Erdelyi, M. H. (1996). *The recovery of unconscious memories: Hypermnesia and reminiscence*. Chicago: University of Chicago Press.

Esplin, P. W., Boychuk, T., & Raskin, D. C. (1988, June). *A field validity study of Criteria-Based Content Analysis of children's statements in sexual abuse cases*. Paper presented at the NATO Advanced Study Institute on Credibility Assessment, Maratea, Italy.

Fivush, R. (1997). Event memory in early childhood. In N. Cowan (Ed.), *The development of memory in children*. Hove, UK: Psychology Press.

Flin, R., Boon, J., Knox, A., & Bull, R. (1992). The effect of a five-month delay on children's and adults' eyewitness memory. *British Journal of Psychology 83*, 323–336.

Foley, M. A., Durso, F. T., Wilder, A., & Friedman, R. (1991). Developmental comparisons of explicit versus implicit imagery and reality monitoring. *Journal of Experimental Child Psychology, 51*, 1–13.

Foley, M. A., & Johnson, M. K. (1985). Confusions between memories for performed and imagined actions: A developmental comparison. *Child development, 56*, 1145–1155.

Foley, M. A., Johnson, M. K., & Raye, C. L. (1983). Age-related changes in confusion between memories for thoughts and memories for speech. *Child development, 54*, 51–60.

Foley, M. A., Santini, C., & Sopasakis, M. (1989). Discriminating between memories: Evidence for children's spontaneous elaborations. *Journal of Experimental Child Psychology, 48*, 146–169.

Gelman, R., Meek, E., & Merkin, S. (1986). Young children's numerical competence. *Cognitive Development, 1*, 1–29.

Gelles, R., & Brigham, R. (2011). Child protection considerations in the United States. In M. E. Lamb, D. J. La Rooy, L. C. Malloy, & C. Katz (Eds.), *Children's testimony: A handbook of psychological research and forensic practice* (pp. 15–48). Oxford: Wiley- Blackwell.

Goodman, G. S., Bottoms, B. L., Schwartz-Kenney, B. M., & Rudy, L. (1991). Children`s testimony about a stressful event: improving children's reports. *Journal of Narrative and Life History, 1*, 69–99.

Goodman, G. S. & Quas, J. A. (2008). Repeated interviews and children's memory it's more than just how many. *Current Directions in Psychological Science, 17*, 386–390.

Gross, J. & Hayne, H. (1999). Drawing facilitates children's verbal reports after long delays. *Journal of Experimental Psychology: Applied, 5*, 265–283.

Hanna, K. M., Davies, E., Henderson, E., Crothers, C., & Rotherham, C. (2010). *Child witnesses in the New Zealand criminal courts: A review of practice and implications for policy*. Wellington, New Zealand: New Zealand Law Foundation.

Henderson, E. (2012). Alternative routes: Other accusatorial jurisdictions on the slow road to best evidence. In J. R. Spencer & M. E. Lamb (Eds.), *Children and cross-examination: Time to change the rules?* Oxford: Hart Publishing.

Henderson, H. M., & Lamb, M. E. (2017). Pre-Recording Children's Testimony: Effects on Case Progression. *Criminal Law Review, 5*, 345.

Hershkowitz, I., Fisher, S., Lamb, M. E., & Horowitz, D. (2007). Improving credibility assessment in child sexual abuse allegations: The role of the NICHD investigative interview protocol. *Child Abuse & Neglect, 31*, 99–110.

Hershkowitz, I., Lamb, M. E., & Katz, C. (2014). Allegation rates in forensic child abuse investigations: Comparing the revised and standard NICHD Protocols. *Psychology, Public Policy, and Law, 20*, 336–344.

Hershkowitz, I., Lamb, M. E., Orbach, Y., Katz, C., & Horowitz, D. (2012). The development of communicative and narrative skills among preschoolers: Lessons from forensic interviews about child abuse. *Child Development, 83*, 611–622.

Hershkowitz, I., Lamb, M. E., Sternberg, K. J., & Esplin, P. W. (1997). The relationships among interviewer utterance type, CBCA scores and the richness of children's responses. *Legal and Criminological Psychology, 2*, 169–176.

HM Government (2015, March). *Working together to safeguard children: A guide to inter- agency working to safeguard and promote the welfare of children*. Retrieved from: https://www.gov.uk/government/uploads/system/uploads/attachment_data/file/419595/Working_Together_to_Safeguard_Children.pdf

Home Office (1989). *Report of the advisory group on video evidence*. London: Chairman His Honour Judge Thomas Pigot, QC.

Home Office. (2011). *Achieving the best evidence in criminal proceedings: Guidance on interviewing victims and witnesses, and guidance on using special measures*. Retrieved from: http://www.cps.gov.uk/publications/docs/best_evidence_in_criminal_proceedings.pdf

Honts, C. R. (1994). Assessing children's credibility: Scientific and legal issues in 1994. *North Dakota Law Review, 70*, 879–903.

Horowitz, S. W., Lamb, M. E., Esplin, P. W., Boychuk, T. D., Krispin, O., & Reiter- Lavery, L. (1997). Reliability of Criteria-Based Content Analysis of child witness statements. *Legal and Criminological Psychology, 2*, 11–21.

Howe, M. L. (2011). *The nature of early memory: An adaptive theory of the genesis and development of memory.* New York, New York: Oxford University Press.

Howe, M. L. (2013). Memory development: implications for adults recalling childhood experiences in the courtroom. *Nature Reviews Neuroscience, 14,* 869–876.

Howe, M. L., & Knott, L. M. (2015). The fallibility of memory in judicial processes: Lessons from the past and their modern consequences. *Memory, 23,* 633–656.

Imhoff, M. C., & Baker-Ward, L. (1999). Preschoolers' suggestibility: Effects of developmentally appropriate language and interviewer supportiveness. *Journal of Applied Developmental Psychology, 20,* 407–429.

Joffe, R. D. (1994). *Content-Based Criteria Analysis: An experimental investigation with children.* Unpublished doctoral dissertation, Department of Psychology. University of British Columbia, British Columbia, Canada.

Johnson, M. K., Foley, M. A., Suengas, A. G., & Raye, C. L. (1988). Phenomenal characteristics of memories for perceived and imagined autobiographical events. *Journal of Experimental Psychology: General, 117,* 371–376.

Johnson, M. K., Hashtroudi, S., & Lindsay, D. S. (1993). Source monitoring. *Psychological Bulletin, 114,* 3–29.

Johnson, M. K., & Raye, C. L. (1981). Reality monitoring. *Psychological Review, 88,* 67–85.

Köhnken, G. (1996). Social psychology and the law. In G. R. Semin & K. Fiedler (Eds.)., *Applied social psychology* (pp. 257–281). Thousand Oaks, CA: SAGE.

Köhnken, G. (1999). *Statement validity assessment.* Paper presented at the preconference programme of applied courses "Assessing credibility" organised by the European Association of Psychology and Law, Dublin, Ireland.

Köhnken, G. (2004). Statement validity analysis and the detection of the truth. In P. A. Granhag & L. A. Strömwall (Eds.), *The detection of deception in forensic contexts* (pp. 41–63). Cambridge: Cambridge University Press.

Lamb, M. E., & Fauchier, A. (2001). The effects of question type on self-contradictions by children in the course of forensic interviews. *Applied Cognitive Psychology, 15,* 483–491.

Lamb, M. E., Hershkowitz, I., Orbach, Y., & Esplin, P. W. (2008). *Tell me what happened: Structured investigative interviews of child victims and witnesses* (1st edition). Chichester, UK: Wiley.

Lamb, M. E., Hershkowitz, I., Orbach, Y., & Esplin, P. W. (2011). *Tell me what happened: Structured investigative interviews of child victims and witnesses* (2nd edition). Hoboken, NJ: John Wiley & Sons.

Lamb, M. E., Hershkowitz, I., Sternberg, K. J., Esplin, P. W., Hovav, M., Manor, T., Yudilevitch. L. (1996). Effects of investigative utterance types on Israeli children's responses. *International Journal of Behavioral Development, 19,* 627–637.

Lamb, M. E., La Rooy, D. J., Malloy, L. C., & Katz, C. (Eds.). (2011). *Children's testimony: A handbook of psychological research and forensic practice* (Vol. 53). Hoboken, NJ: John Wiley & Sons.

Lamb, M. E., Malloy, L. C., Hershkowitz, I., & La Rooy, D. (2015). Children and the law. In R. M. Lerner & M. E. Lamb (Eds.), *Handbook of child psychology and developmental science* (7th ed.). Volume 3, Social, emotional and personality development. Hoboken, NJ: Wiley:.

Lamb, M. E., Orbach, Y., Hershkowitz, I., Esplin, P. W., & Horowitz, D. (2007a). A structured forensic interview protocol improves the quality and informativeness of investigative interviews with children: A review of research using the NICHD Investigative Interview Protocol. *Child Abuse & Neglect, 31,* 1201–1231.

Lamb, M. E., Orbach, Y., Hershkowitz, I., Horowitz, D., & Abbott, C. B. (2007b). Does the type of prompt affect the accuracy of information provided by alleged victims of abuse in forensic interviews? *Applied Cognitive Psychology, 21,* 1117–1130.

Lamb, M. E., Orbach, Y., Sternberg, K. J., Aldridge, J., Pearson, S., Stewart, H. L., . . . & Bowler, L. (2009). Use of a structured investigative protocol enhances the quality of investigative interviews with alleged victims of child sexual abuse in Britain. *Applied Cognitive Psychology, 23,* 449–467.

Lamb, M. E., Orbach, Y., Warren, A. R., Esplin, P. W., & Hershkowitz, I. (2007). Enhancing performance: Factors affecting the informativeness of young witnesses. In M. P., Toglia, J. D. Read, D. F. Ross, & R. C. L. Lindsay (Eds.), *Handbook of eyewitness psychology: Memory for events* (Vol. 1, pp. 429–451). Mahwah, NJ: Erlbaum.

Lamb, M. E., & Sim, M. P. (2013). Developmental factors affecting children in legal contexts. *Youth justice, 13,* 131–144.

Lamb, M. E., Sternberg, K. J., & Esplin, P. W. (1994). Factors influencing the reliability and validity of statements made by young victims of sexual maltreatment. *Journal of Applied Developmental Psychology, 15,* 255–280.

Lamb, M. E., Sternberg, K. J., Esplin, P. W., Hershkowitz, I., Orbach, Y., & Hovav, M. (1997). Criterion-based content analysis: A field validation study. *Child Abuse & Neglect, 21,* 255–264.

Lamb, M. E., Sternberg, K. J., Orbach, Y., Hershkowitz, I., & Esplin, P. W. (1999). Forensic interviews of children. In A. Memon & R. Bull (Eds.), *Handbook of the psychology of interviewing* (pp. 253–277). Chichester, UK: John Wiley.

La Rooy, D. J. Malloy, L. C., & Lamb, M. E. (2011). The development of memory in childhood. In M. E. Lamb, D. J. La Rooy, L. C. Malloy, & C. Katz (Eds.), *Children's testimony: A handbook of psychological research and forensic practice* (pp. 49–68). Chichester, UK: Wiley-Blackwell:.

Lindsay, D. S., Johnson, M. K., & Kwon, P. (1991). Developmental changes in memory source monitoring. *Journal of Experimental Child Psychology, 52,* 297–318.

Lyon, T. D. (1999). Child witnesses and the oath: Empirical evidence. *Southern California Law Review, 73,* 1017–1074.

Macleod, E., Gross, J., & Hayne, H. (2013). The clinical and forensic value of information that children report while drawing. *Applied Cognitive Psychology, 27,* 564–573.

McIntyre, J. S., & Craik, F. I. (1987). Age differences in memory for item and source information. *Canadian Journal of Psychology/Revue Canadienne de Psychologie, 41,* 175–192.

Melton, A. W. (1963). Implications of short-term memory for a general theory of memory. *Journal of Memory and Language, 2,* 1–45.

Memon, A., Fraser, J., Colwell, K., Odinot, G., & Mastroberardino, S. (2010), Distinguishing truthful from invented accounts using reality monitoring criteria. *Legal and Criminological Psychology, 15,* 177–194.

Moston, S. (1987). The suggestibility of children in interview studies. *First Language, 7,* 67–67.

National Society for Prevention of Cruelty to Children. (2013, May 25). Statistics. Retrieved from: http://www.nspcc.org.uk/Inform/research/statistics/statistics_wda48748.html

Oberlader, V. A., Naefgen, C., Koppehele-Goseel, J., Quinten, L., Banse, R., & Schmidt, A. F. (2016). Validity of content-based techniques to distinguish true and fabricated statements: A meta-analysis. *Law and Human Behavior, 40*, 440–457.

Orbach, Y., Hershkowitz, I., Lamb, M. E., Sternberg, K.J., Esplin, P. W., & Horowitz, D. (2000). Assessing the value of structured protocols for forensic interviews of alleged abuse victims. *Child Abuse & Neglect, 24*, 733–752.

Orbach, Y., & Lamb, M. E. (1999). Assessing the accuracy of a child's account of sexual abuse: A case study. *Child Abuse & Neglect, 23*, 91–98.

Orbach, Y., & Lamb, M. E. (2001). The relationship between within-interview contradictions and eliciting interviewer utterances. *Child Abuse & Neglect, 25*, 323–333.

Ornstein, P. A., Gordon, B. N., & Larus, D. M. (1992). Children's memory for a personally experienced event: Implications for testimony. *Applied Cognitive Psychology, 6*, 49–60.

Otgaar, H., Ansem, R., Pauw, C., & Horselenberg, R. (2016). Improving children's interviewing methods? The effects of drawing and practice on children's memories for an event. *Journal of Police and Criminal Psychology, 31*, 1–9.

Otgaar, H., Candel, I., Memon, A., & Almerigogna, J. (2010). Differentiating between children's true and false memories using reality monitoring criteria. *Psychology, Crime & Law, 16*, 555–566.

Otgaar, H., Howe, M. L., Brackmann, N., & Smeets, T. (2016). The malleability of developmental trends in neutral and negative memory illusions. *Journal of Experimental Psychology: General, 145*, 31–55.

Parker, A. D., & Brown, J. (2000). Detection of deception: Statement Validity Analysis as a means of determining truthfulness or falsity of rape allegations. *Legal and Criminological Psychology, 5*, 237–259.

Penrod, S., & Cutler, B. (1995). Witness confidence and witness accuracy: Assessing their forensic relation. *Psychology, Public Policy, And Law, 1*, 817–845.

Perry, N. W., McAuliff, B. D., Tam, P., Claycomb, L., Dostal, C., & Flanagan, C. (1995). When lawyers question children: Is justice served?. *Law and Human Behavior, 19*, 609–629.

Phillips, E., Oxburgh, G., Gavin, A., & Myklebust, T. (2012). Investigative interviews with victims of child sexual abuse: The relationship between question type and investigation relevant information. *Journal of Police and Criminal Psychology, 27*, 45–54.

Pipe. M. E., Lamb, M. E., Orbach, Y., Cederborg, A-C. (2007). *Child sexual abuse: Disclosure, delay and denial.* Mahwah, NJ: Lawrence Erlbaum Associates.

Pipe, M. E., Lamb, M. E., Orbach, Y., Esplin, P. W. (2004). Recent research on children's testimony about experienced and witnessed events. *Developmental Review, 24*, 440–468.

Pipe, M. E., Orbach, Y., Lamb, M. E., Abbott, C. B., & Stewart, H. (2013). Do case outcomes change when investigative interviewing practices change? *Psychology, Public Policy, and Law, 19*, 179–190.

Pipe, M. E., & Salmon, K. (2009). Dolls, drawings, body diagrams, and other props: Role of props in investigative interviews. In K. Kuehnle, & M. Connell, (Eds.), *The evaluation of child sexual abuse allegations: A comprehensive guide to assessment and testimony* (pp. 365–395). Hoboken, NJ: Wiley.

Plotnikoff, J., & Woolfson, R. (2007). *The "go-between": Evaluation of intermediary pathfinder projects.* Hitchin: Lexicon Limited, UK.

Plotnikoff, J., & Woolfson, R. (2009). *Measuring up? Evaluating implementation of government commitments to young witnesses in criminal proceedings.* www.nspcc.org.uk/inform

Polak, A., & Harris, P. L. (1999). Deception by young children following noncompliance. *Developmental Psychology, 35,* 561–568.

Poole, D. A., & Bruck, M. (2012). Divining testimony? The impact of interviewing props on children's reports of touching. *Developmental Review, 32,* 165–180.

Poole, D. A., Bruck, M., & Pipe, M. E. (2011). Forensic interviewing aids: Do props help children answer questions about touching? *Current Directions in Psychological Science, 20,* 11–15.

Poole, D. A., & Lamb, M. E. (1998). *Investigative interviews of children: A guide for helping professionals.* Washington, DC: American Psychological Association:.

Poole, D. A., & White, L.T. (1991). Effects of question repetition on the eyewitness testimony of children and adults. *Developmental Psychology, 27,* 975–986.

Rafferty, A., QC. (2016, April). Ground rules hearings and section 28 pre-recorded cross-examination. CBA Handout.

Raskin, D. C., & Esplin, P. W. (1991a). Assessment of children's statements of sexual abuse. In J. Doris (Ed.), *The suggestibility of children's recollections* (pp. 153–164). Washington, DC: American Psychological Association.

Raskin, D. C., & Esplin, P. W. (1991b). Statement validity assessments: Interview procedures and content analyses of children's statements of sexual abuse. *Behavioral Assessment, 13,* 265–291.

Raskin, D. C., & Esplin, P. W. (1991c). Commentary: Response to Wells, Loftus, and McGough. In J. Doris (Ed.), *The suggestibility of children's recollections* (pp. 172–176). Washington, DC: American Psychological Association.

Raskin, D. C., Honts, C. R., & Kircher, J. C. (Eds.). (2013). *Credibility assessment: Scientific research and applications.* Oxford: Academic Press.

Reich, P. A. (1986). *Language development.* Englewood Cliffs, NJ: Prentice-Hall.

Roberts, K. P., & Lamb, M. E. (2010), Reality-monitoring characteristics in confirmed and doubtful allegations of child sexual abuse. *Applied Cognitive Psychology, 24,* 1049–1079.

Roberts, K. P., Lamb, M. E., & Randall, D. W. (1997). *Assessing the Plausibility of Allegations of Sexual Abuse from Children's Accounts.* Presented at the biennial meeting of the Society for Applied Research in Memory and Cognition, Toronto, Canada.

Roberts, K. P., Lamb, M. E., & Sternberg, K. J. (2004). The effects of rapport building style on children's reports of a staged event. *Applied Cognitive Psychology, 18,* 189–202.

Russell, A. (2008). Out of the woods: A case for using anatomical diagrams in forensic interviews. *National Children's Advocacy Centre Update. 21,* 2–6.

Salmon, K. (2001). Remembering and reporting by children: The influence of cues and props. *Clinical Psychology Review, 21,* 267–300.

Santtila, P., Roppola, H., & Niemi, P. (1999). Assessing the truthfulness of witness statements made by children (aged 7–8, 10–11, and 13–14) employing scales derived from Johnson and Raye's model of reality monitoring. *Expert Evidence, 6,* 273–289.

Santtila, P., Roppola, H., Runtti, M., & Niemi, P. (2000). Assessment of child witness statements using Criteria-Based Content Analysis (CBCA): The effects of age, verbal ability, and interviewer's emotional style. *Psychology, Crime, and Law, 6,* 159–179.

Saywitz, K. J. (2002). Developmental underpinnings of children's testimony. In H. L. Westcott, G. M. Davies, & R. H. C. Bull (Eds.), *Children's testimony: A handbook of psychological research and forensic practice* (pp. 3–20). Chichester, UK: John Wiley & Sons Ltd.

Saywitz, K., & Camparo, L. (1998). Interviewing child witnesses: A developmental perspective. *Child Abuse and Neglect, 22,* 825–843.

Schreiber, N., Bellah, L. D., Martinez, Y., McLaurin, K. A., Strok, R., Garven, S., & Wood, J. M. (2006). Suggestive interviewing in the McMartin Preschool and Kelly Michaels daycare abuse cases: A case study. *Social Influence, 1,* 16–47.

Schneider, W., & Pressley, M. (1997). *Memory development between two and twenty.* Mahwah, NJ: Lawrence Erlbaum Associates.

Semmler, C., & Brewer, N. (2002). Effects of mood and emotion on juror processing and judgments. *Behavioral Sciences & the Law, 20,* 423–436.

Spencer, J. R., & Lamb, M. E. (2012) (Eds.). *Children and cross-examination: Time to change the rules?*:Oxford: Hart Publishing.

Sporer, S. L. (1997). The less travelled road to truth: Verbal cues in deception detection in accounts of fabricated and self-experienced events. *Applied Cognitive Psychology, 11,* 373–397.

Sporer, S. L. (2004). Reality monitoring and detection of deception. In P. A. Granhag & L. A. Strömwall (Eds.), *Deception detection in forensic contexts* (pp. 64–102). Cambridge: Cambridge University Press:.

Steller, M. (1989). Recent developments in statement analysis. In J. C. Yuille (Ed.), *Credibility assessment* (pp. 135–154). Deventer, the Netherlands: Kluwer.

Steller, M., & Boychuk, T. (1992). Children as witnesses in sexual abuse cases: Investigative interview and assessment techniques. In H. Dent & R. Flin (Eds.), *Children as witnesses* (pp. 47–73). Hoboken, NJ: John Wiley & Sons.

Steller, M., & Köhnken, G. (1989). *Criteria-based content analysis. Psychological methods in criminal investigation and evidence.* New York: Springer-Verlag.

Sternberg, K. J., Lamb, M. E., Hershkowitz, I., Yudilevitch, L., Orbach, Y., Esplin, P. W., & Hovav, M. (1997). Effects of introductory style on children's abilities to describe experiences of sexual abuse. *Child Abuse and Neglect, 21,* 1133–1146.

Sternberg, K. J., Lamb, M. E., Orbach, Y., Esplin, P. W., & Mitchell, S. (2001). Use of a structured investigative protocol enhances young children's responses to free-recall prompts in the course of forensic interviews. *Journal of Applied Psychology, 86,* 997–1005.

Strange, D., & Hayne, H. (2013). The devil is in the detail: Children's recollection of details about their prior experiences. *Memory, 21,* 431–443.

Strömwall, L. A., Bengtsson, L., Leander, L., & Granhag, P. A. (2004). Assessing children's statements: The impact of a repeated experience on CBCA and RM ratings. *Applied Cognitive Psychology, 18,* 653–668.

Strömwall, L. A., & Granhag, P.-A. (2005). Children's repeated lies and truths: Effects on adults' judgments and reality monitoring scores. *Psychiatry, Psychology, and the Law, 12,* 345–356.

Szojka, Z. A., Andrews, S. J., Lamb, M. E., Stolzenberg, S. N., & Lyon, T. D. (2017). Challenging the credibility of alleged victims of child sexual abuse in Scottish courts. *Psychology, Public Policy, and Law, 22,* 200–210.

Talwar, V., & Crossman, A. (2011). From little white lies to filthy liars: The evolution of honesty and deception in young children. *Advances in Child Development and Behaviour, 40,* 139–179.

Talwar, V., & Crossman, A. M. (2012). Children's lies and their detection: Implications for child witness testimony. *Developmental Review, 32,* 337–359.

Talwar, V., Gordon, H. M., & Lee, K. (2007). Lying in the elementary school years: verbal deception and its relation to second-order belief understanding. *Developmental Psychology, 43*, 804–810.

Talwar, V., & Lee, K. (2002). Emergence of white-lie telling in children between 3 and 7 years of age. *Merrill-Palmer Quarterly, 48*, 160–181.

Thierry, K. L., Lamb, M. E., Orbach, Y., & Pipe, M. E. (2005). Developmental differences in the function and use of anatomical dolls during interviews with alleged sexual abuse victims. *Journal of Consulting and Clinical Psychology, 73*, 1125–1134.

Trocmé, N., Fallon, B., MacLaurin, B., Sinha, V., Black, T., Fast, E., . . . & Holroyd, J. (2010). Characteristics of children and families. In Public Health Agency of Canada (Eds.), *Canadian incidence study of reported child abuse and neglect 2008: Major findings*. Ottawa, ON, Canada: Public Health Agency of Canada.

Tulving, E. (1974). Cue-dependent forgetting: When we forget something we once knew, it does not necessarily mean that the memory trace has been lost; it may only be inaccessible. *American Scientist, 62*, 74–82.

Undeutsch, U. (1967). Beurteilung der Glaubhaftigkeit von Aussagen [Veracity assessment of statements]. In U. Undeutsch (Ed.), *Handbuch der psychologie: Vol. 11. Forensische psychologie* (pp. 26–181). Gottingen, Germany: Hogrefe.

Undeutsch, U. (1989). The development of statement reality analysis. In J. C. Yuille (Ed.), *Credibility assessment* (pp. 101–119). Springer: Netherlands.

U. S. Department of Health and Human Services, Administration on Children, Youth and Families (2009). *Child maltreatment 2007*. Washington, DC: U. S. Government Printing Office.

Vrij, A. (2005). Criteria-based content analysis: A qualitative review of the first 37 studies. *Psychology, Public Policy, and Law, 11*, 3–41.

Vrij, A. (2008). *Detecting lies and deceit: Pitfalls and opportunities*. Hoboken, NJ: John Wiley & Sons.

Vrij, A., Akehurst, L., Soukara, S., & Bull, R. (2004a). Detecting deceit via analyses of verbal and nonverbal behavior in children and adults. *Human Communication Research, 30*, 8–41.

Vrij, A., Akehurst, L., Soukara, S., & Bull, R. (2004b). Let me inform you how to tell a convincing story: CBCA and reality monitoring scores as a function of age, coaching, and deception. *Canadian Journal of Behavioural Science, 36*, 113–126.

Vrij, A., Edwards, K., Roberts, K. P., & Bull, R. (2000). Detecting deceit via analysis of verbal and nonverbal behavior. *Journal of Nonverbal Behavior, 24*, 239–263.

Vrij, A., Akehurst, L., Soukara, S., & Bull, R. (2002). Will the truth come out? The effect of deception, age, status, coaching, and social skills on CBCA scores. *Law and human behavior, 26*, 261–283.

Vrij, A., & Mann, S. (2005). Police use of nonverbal behavior as indicators of deception. In R. E. Riggio & R. S. Feldman (Eds.), *Applications of nonverbal communication* (pp. 63–94). Mahwah, NJ: Lawrence Erlbaum Associates.

Walsh, J. P., & Ungson, G. R. (1991). Organizational memory. *Academy of management review, 16*, 57–91.

Wells, G. L., & Loftus, E. F. (1991). Commentary: Is this child fabricating? Reactions to a new assessment technique. In J. Doris (Ed.), *The suggestibility of children's recollections* (pp. 168–171). Washington, DC: American Psychological Association.

Wigmore, J. H. (1974). *Evidence in trials at common law* (Vol 5). Boston: Little, Brown, and Company.

Willcock, E., Morgan, K., & Hayne, H. (2006). Body maps do not facilitate children's reports of touch. *Applied Cognitive Psychology, 20,* 607–615.

Wood, J. M., McClure, K. A., & Birch, R. A. (1996). Suggestions for improving interviews in child protection agencies. *Child Maltreatment, 1,* 223–230.

World Health Organization (2006). *Preventing child maltreatment: A guide to taking action and generating evidence.* Geneva: Author.

Youth Justice and Criminal Evidence [UK] Act 1999. Retrieved from: http://www.legislation.gov.uk/ukpga/1999/23

Zajac, R., Gross, J., & Hayne, H. (2003). Asked and answered: Questioning children in the courtroom. *Psychiatry, Psychology, and Law, 10,* 199–209.

Zajac, R., & Hayne, H. (2003). I don't think that's what really happened: The effect of cross- examination on the accuracy of children's reports. *Journal of Experimental Psychology: Applied, 9,* 187–195.

7

Putting Children's Memory and Suggestibility in their Place

An Analysis Considering Person, Topic, and Context

DEBORAH GOLDFARB, GAIL S. GOODMAN, RAKEL P. LARSON, ALEJANDRA GONZALEZ, AND MITCHELL L. EISEN

Children have the capacity to be both accurate and suggestible while responding to forensic interviews or testifying in court. As such, any discussion of children's memory and suggestibility in legal settings requires a nuanced approach to potential factors influencing children's eyewitness reports. In earlier work, we have argued that discussions of memory accuracy and inaccuracy in forensic contexts must consider not only age but also person-specific individual differences (e.g., the individual's maltreatment history or psychopathology; Goodman, Goldfarb, Chong, & Goodman-Shaver, 2014; Goodman et al., 2016; Goodman, Quas, & Ogle, 2010), the topic or nature of the event (e.g., memory for a traumatic vs. neutral event; Goodman et al., 2016; Goodman et al., 2010; McWilliams, Narr, Goodman, Mendoza, & Ruiz, 2013), and the context in which the memory is elicited (e.g., forensic interview vs. courtroom; Goldfarb, Goodman, & Lawler, 2015; Goodman et al., 2014). In this chapter, we apply our proposed framework to a discussion of children's memory and suggestibility (Figure 7.1). We first describe two cases (one real and one an amalgamation) that raise issues explored in this chapter.

Case 1: A 7-year-old girl was interviewed at a forensic center because her older sister, 12-years-old, was pregnant as a result of repeated rape by their father. (Parenthood was confirmed by genetic testing.) The father had also been violent with all the children and their mother. Despite leading questions, use of anatomical dolls, and repeated interviewing (often considered suggestive techniques), the 7-year-old denied everything—witnessing domestic violence, being beaten, and sexual abuse of the sister. It was uncovered later that the 7-year-old had been told by a grandparent not to tell anything to the authorities.

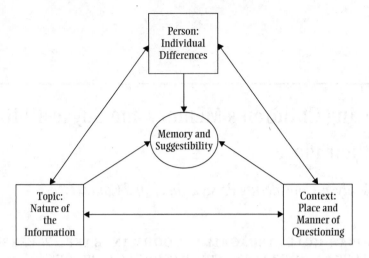

Figure 7.1 Proposed model for considering child witness memory and suggestibility within legal settings.

Case 2: A 6-year-old girl disclosed sexual abuse by her mother's live-in boy-friend. The 6-year-old told her best friend about the abuse after the girls heard a "good touches/bad touches" talk at school. Despite the 6-year-old's request that her friend keep the abuse a secret, the friend told her (own) mother, who called school officials who, in turn, notified legal authorities. The 6-year-old victim's mother was dismayed at the disclosure and was struggling to support her daughter in the criminal matter, particularly after the mother's boyfriend, the family's sole bread winner, was ordered out of the house as part of a dependency proceeding, and the mother had experienced a negative interaction with child protective services when she was previously investigated for neglect. On cross-examination during the criminal trial, the 6-year-old recanted her story and said that she had just made it all up. The fact finders were left wondering whether the recantation was correct or an omission error (i.e., inaccurately stating that something that actually did occur had not happened).

Memory and suggestibility are potentially influenced by a multitude of factors, including narrative quality (Kulkofsky & Klemfuss, 2008), source monitoring abilities (Bright-Paul & Jarrold, 2012), theory of mind (Welch-Ross, 1999), and overall level of cognitive functioning (Eisen, Goodman, Qin, Davis, & Crayton, 2007). Thus, a thorough discussion of *all* of the factors that relate to whether, on average, a child would be more or less accurate or suggestible is outside of the confines of this chapter. As such, we review here relevant literature on three particular factors that are all relevant to the cases discussed above. Specifically, consistent with Figure 7.1, we consider maltreatment history in relation to age and trauma-related psychopathology symptoms as potential *individual difference factors* (i.e., individual influences that might affect level of memory error and sug-gestibility), we consider memory for child sexual abuse allegations as the *topic* being recounted, and we consider criminal investigative settings (e.g., forensic interviews, cross-examination in court) as the *context* of the statements. Although it is not always possible to fully disentangle these three factors within the current scientific research base, we hope the distinctions still provide a useful organizational framework. Gaps in the literature and areas for future research are also mentioned.

PERSON FACTORS: INDIVIDUAL DIFFERENCES

Relations Among Child Maltreatment, Individual Differences, and Memory/Suggestibility

In our case examples, the children are alleged to have experienced abuse or neglect and also alleged to have endured or witnessed sexual abuse. A trauma history may have a facilitative or deleterious effect (or both) on memory accuracy and resistance to suggestion (Goodman et al., 2010). A small, but burgeoning body of evidence has examined actual victims' memory accuracy and suggestibility for emotional, stressful, or traumatic events (Goodman et al., 2010).

Before such research is reviewed, however, it is important to consider that, overall, children and adults who have experienced maltreatment can accurately retain and retrieve neutral or trauma-related memories; maltreatment history per se does not necessarily lead to increased accuracy, error, or susceptibility to suggestion (Chae, Goodman, Eisen, & Qin, 2011; Howe, Cicchetti, Toth, & Cerrito, 2004; Valentino, Cicchetti, Rogosch, & Toth, 2008). For instance, studies find no statistically significant differences in basic memory processes (e.g., associative recognition memory) between maltreated and nonmaltreated individuals (Howe et al., 2004; Howe, Toth, & Cicchetti, 2011; but see Otgaar, Howe, & Muris, 2017).

Although maltreatment alone may or may not explain differences seen in memory performance, there are individual difference factors, often related to child maltreatment, that play important roles in influencing memory accuracy and suggestibility (Goodman et al., 2014). These factors may operate in largely similar ways for both individuals with and without trauma histories, although some of them (e.g., psychopathology symptoms) may be more operative in one group over the other. In the following text, we review the roles of age and trauma-related psychopathology symptoms as specific individual difference factors that may affect children's memory accuracy and suggestibility, with a focus on individuals who have experienced maltreatment.

Age Differences

Age is one of the most robust individual difference predictors of children's memory accuracy and suggestibility in both maltreated and nonmaltreated samples. Although children as young as 2 years of age can provide accurate reports of emotionally arousing and personally salient events (albeit brief and fragmented; Fivush, 2002; Peterson, 2011), older children tend to provide more detailed, complete, coherent, and correct responses compared with younger children in response to free recall, specific, and misleading questions (e.g., Goodman, Bottoms, Rudy, Davis, & Schwartz-Kenney, 2001). Memory for central compared with peripheral event-related details also improves with age (Eisen et al., 2007). Developmental changes in prefrontal and hippocampal functioning, language and narrative ability, knowledge base, memory strategies, source monitoring, and metacognition likely contribute to such age differences in memory performance, including suggestibility (Ghetti & Alexander, 2004; Goodman, Ogle, McWilliams, Narr, & Paz-Alonso, 2014; Howe, 2011; Paz-Alonso, Ghetti, Donohue, Goodman, & Bunge, 2008). That said, age differences in suggestibility can be altered: For example, in some circumstances, older children and adults are more suggestible than younger children (Brainerd, Renya, & Ceci, 2008; Otgaar, Howe, Brackmann, & Sweets, 2016; Otgaar, Howe, Brackmann, & van Helvoort, 2017).

Maltreated children evince the same basic age effects in memory and suggestibility as nonmaltreated children. For example, like other children, young maltreated preschoolers (e.g., 3-year-olds) make more commission errors in answering specific and misleading questions (i.e., inaccurately stating that something occurred when it did not actually happen) than maltreated children who are older. This age trend was evident in Eisen and colleagues' (2002) research, in which 3- to 17-year-old children's memories were examined for an anogenital examination that occurred a few days prior as part of a 5-day inpatient forensic evaluation. The study included children with both substantiated cases of maltreatment as well as those without any known maltreatment history, the latter of which served as a nonabused comparison group. The questioning of the children in this study had a particularly high degree of ecological validity, as it was conducted in the context of ongoing forensic investigations, mixed in with actual forensic interviews related to allegations of abuse. These investigators examined children's performance on questions that would typically be asked during forensic interviews, which they characterized as either high inappropriate (for a doctor) abuse-related questions (e.g., "Did the doctor or nurse hit you?," when in fact neither the doctor nor nurse had done so) or low inappropriate (for a doctor) abuse-related questions. (e.g., "Did the doctor take your clothes off?" or "Did the doctor take a picture of you?"). Age-related trends emerged, such that 3- to 5-year-olds were less accurate than their older counterparts in their memory of the examination. Specific to suggestibility, older age was also associated with more resistance to false suggestion and fewer commission errors to direct questions (see also McWilliams, Harris, & Goodman, 2014). The error rate among the 3- to 5-year-olds on the low inappropriate abuse-related questions was relatively high (e.g., 55% error rate), largely because the questions were "schema consistent" with a medical examination and referred to individuals whose identities were likely confused by young children (e.g., "Did the doctor take off your clothes?" when in fact, it was a nurse who helped the children undress; young children often confuse nurses and doctors).

Central to the sort of questions children might be asked in criminal investigative settings, children were generally resistant to misleading questions that suggested highly inappropriate abuse-related behaviors on the part of the doctor or nurse (e.g., that the doctor had hit or kissed the children during the medical examination, when in fact the doctor had not). A few children in the youngest age group accounted for a large percentage of the errors. Specifically, 40% of the errors to these highly inappropriate forensically relevant questions were attributable to a small subset (3 out of 26) of the 3- to 5-year olds, suggesting that widespread susceptibility to these suggestions (even amongst this sample of maltreated children) was infrequent. Eisen et al. (2007) conducted a second, larger scale study of children being evaluated for allegations of abuse, analyzing maltreated and non-maltreated children's memory for a forensic anogenital examination and venipuncture. Although the overall commission error rate to misleading questions for preschoolers was 18%, only 4% of 3- to 16-year-old children made commission errors on abuse-related questions. Again, a subset of the youngest children largely accounted for the errors.

Trauma-Related Psychopathology Symptoms

As previously mentioned, it often may not be maltreatment itself that affects memory and suggestibility in children who have experienced trauma. Indeed, it is clear that not all children or adults respond in the same way to similar highly stressful and/or traumatic events (e.g., Berntsen et al., 2012). Instead, other factors, such as trauma-related psychopathology, may mediate relations between maltreatment, on the one hand, and memory and suggestibility, on the other hand.

In the aftermath of childhood trauma, individuals are at risk of developing heightened dissociative tendencies (American Psychiatric Association, 2013). A well-known measure of dissociation, the Dissociative Experience Scale (Bernstein & Putnam, 1986), provides insight into how psychologists think about dissociative symptoms. Of particular interest, among other items, the Dissociative Experience Scale includes questions that tap attention and memory (e.g., "Some people find that sometimes they are listening to someone talk and they suddenly realize that they did not hear part or all of what was just said," "Some people find they have no memory for some important events in their lives," "Some people have the experience of sometimes remembering a past event so vividly that they feel as if they were reliving the event"). Although nonpathological dissociative experiences are quite common, individuals with (compared to without) childhood maltreatment histories are at greater risk of developing more profound and often pathological dissociative symptoms, which may, at least in part, reflect preoccupation with traumatic memories (e.g., reliving the event). This interpretation fits with Eisen et al.'s (2002) findings that dissociation positively correlated with clinicians' ratings of the amount of information children provided in their abuse disclosures and with Sayfan, Mitchell, Goodman, Eisen, and Qin's (2008) findings that more dissociative children evinced greater distress when disclosing abuse experiences.

This preoccupation with trauma memories may make dissociative individuals more inaccurate at times about other events in their lives, including events that may raise attempts to activate defensive processes (e.g., motivated attentional avoidance, denial, memory suppression) or that motivate compliance with suggestions. Although Eisen et al. (2007) found that dissociative tendencies alone did not predict memory error in maltreated children, children who evinced high dissociative tendencies made more errors about the medical examination if the children also reported greater trauma symptoms and higher cortisol response to the stressful examination. These effects were similar for both stressful (e.g., an anogential exam and venipuncture; Eisen et al., 2007) and nonstressful life events (e.g., neutral play event in a forensic context; Chae et al., 2011). For example, Chae et al. (2011) examined a subset of children in Eisen et al.'s (2007) study who had engaged in a fun bean bag game with a research assistant also as part of their stay at the hospital unit. When interviewed about the bean bag game, among the highly dissociative children, those with greater self-reported trauma symptoms evinced more commission errors (Chae et al., 2011: Note that cortisol was not measured and thus not directly at issue in relation to the neutral event).

These data raise the possibility that dissociative tendencies disrupt memory processes when children are experiencing elevated levels of stress. However, errors on misleading questions are not always driven by memory deficits. Dissociative children experiencing elevated stress could also be more vulnerable to influence from nonmemorial factors introduced during forensic investigations, such as situational demands and pressures that can affect children's performance in these interviews. Rather than reflecting memory distortion, these errors may reflect a response bias to agree with the interviewer. A response bias also helps explain the correlation between heightened dissociation and false memory effects reported by Hyman and Billings (1998; see also Giesbrecht, Lynn, Lilienfeld, & Merkelbach, 2008). That said, the significant relation between dissociative tendencies and false memory becomes nonsignificant when parental factors are considered (Qin, Ogle, & Goodman, 2008), perhaps indicating that youth who are highly dissociative and susceptible to false memory effects have learned to agree with others in authority roles regardless of accuracy, at least in some situations.

Victims of childhood abuse may also develop symptoms associated with post-traumatic stress disorder (PTSD), which is characterized by the following symptomology: reexperiencing the trauma through distressing recollections of the event, avoidance of reminders of the trauma, and increased arousal, such as difficulty sleeping and concentrating (American Psychiatric Association, 2013). In a study of PTSD, when adults' memories of their alleged child sexual abuse were examined 12 to 21 years after maltreatment ended, participants with more rather than less PTSD symptoms had greater memory accuracy regarding their maltreatment (Alexander et al., 2005; see also Ghetti et al., 2006). This result suggests that trauma victims who experience PTSD symptomology, an individual difference factor, may accurately report the details of their maltreatment experiences.

There are, however, times when psychopathology in maltreated and nonmaltreated children is associated with greater memory error (McWilliams et al., 2014). As is seen later in this chapter, the relation between psychopathology and commission errors in memory may be most evident for certain types of information (the topic or nature of information at issue).

Summary and Future Research

Taken together, studies show that maltreatment alone does not necessarily inflate memory inaccuracy or suggestibility (Goodman et al., 2010). In fact, as seen next, for forensically relevant information regarding traumatic experiences relevant to the self, maltreatment may have quite the opposite effect. Moreover, trauma-related sequelae that manifest as a consequence of maltreatment may influence memory reports (McWilliams et al., 2014), as trauma-related psychopathology can affect response biases (Eisen et al., 2007). However, findings on dissociation and PTSD suggest that trauma-related psychopathology can also lead to heightened attention to and better memory for trauma-related information. Future studies should include and evaluate if and how trauma-related psychopathology may mediate relations between maltreatment history and memory/suggestibility in child victims.

TOPIC: THE NATURE OF THE MEMORY

Trauma-Related Memory

We have argued that the nature of the information to be remembered affects the resulting memory. The topic of child sexual abuse has been of special concern to child witness memory researchers because in child sexual abuse cases, much rests on the eyewitness reports of the children and much attention has focused on how children are interviewed. But sexual abuse is, by its nature, an emotional topic for children to discuss; we next turn to memory and suggestibility for such emotional, negative events in maltreated children.

It is widely recognized that emotional, distressing, distinctive, survival significant, consequential, and traumatic events are typically retained in memory with a special robustness compared with memory for more mundane experiences (Brown & Kulik, 1977; Christianson, 1992; Nairne & Pandeirada, 2010; Sharot, Martorella, Delgado, & Phelps, 2007). Although such memories may not be perfect, they can be enduring (Hirst & Phelps, 2016), often because personal survival relevance heightens memory (e.g., Cunningham, Brady-von den Bos, Gill, & Turk, 2013). This may include greater attention to central, survival-relevant information and decreased attention to peripheral details (Christianson, 1992), leading to better memory accuracy and resistance to suggestion for central information (Eisen et al., 2007; Paz-Alonso & Goodman, 2016).

Behind these effects is the memory-bolstering influence of self-relevance. When information activates self-referencing, rich representations result in adults and children (Klein & Kihlstrom, 1986; Rudy & Goodman, 1991; Symons & Johnson, 1997). Automatic processes, including increased attention, contribute to elaborative encoding that characterizes the richness of self-referential memories (Turk, Cunningham, & Macrae, 2008; Turk, Van Bussel, Waiter, & Macrae, 2011). In fact, the initial organization of the self in early childhood is said to initiate autobiographical memory itself (Howe & Courage, 1997). There are few, if any, more self-relevant events than those that involve personal safety.

Nevertheless, despite self-relevance, distress may interfere with encoding, retention, and/or retrieval (Edelstein et al., 2005; Quas et al., 1999). When defensive processes (e.g., motivated attempts to avoid information) arise, cognitive resources that may otherwise be used for attending to and remembering an event may be reallocated to emotion-regulating processes, including diversion of attention, suppression of thinking about or talking about the event, and avoidance of the memory, thereby reducing accurate memory performance later (Edelstein et al., 2005). For children, when their parents evince avoidance or a combination of anxiety and avoidance, memory can suffer and memory errors can emerge (e.g., Goodman, Quas, Batterman-Faunce, Ridddlesberger, & Kuhn, 1994; Qin et al., 2008).

Although such differences in processing of negative information and trauma exist, overall, maltreatment victims attend more quickly to negative and trauma-related information (e.g., Masten et al., 2008; Pollak & Tolley-Schell, 2003; Shackman, Shackman, & Pollak, 2007). Individuals with histories of childhood maltreatment may evince hyperarousal symptoms and increased attention to trauma-related details as a preparatory response for detecting potentially dangerous cues in the environment (Carlson, Furby, Armstrong, & Shales, 1997; Shackman et al., 2007). Enhanced attention to trauma-related cues should in turn have a beneficial effect on memory, particularly for emotionally arousing or stressful events, potentially bolstering resistance to false suggestion.

With increased exposure to trauma, individuals with maltreatment histories may also have a stronger knowledge base to draw upon when encoding and retrieving information about negative, emotional, or stressful events. This stronger knowledge base may lead to better memory and greater resistance to false suggestion about trauma-related information. Specifically, trauma victims may be particularly accurate and resistant to suggestion when answering interview questions about abuse-related details. Consistent with this idea, Eisen et al. (2007) found that children with sexual abuse histories were more accurate on questions about an anogenital examination compared to children without substantiated maltreatment or those who had experienced other forms of maltreatment (see also Katz, Schonfeld, Carter, Leventhal, & Cicchetti, 1995). These data indicate that children who have verifiable experiences of sexual abuse in their recent past are far less likely to accept suggestions that the doctor or nurse engaged them in some type of sexually inappropriate manner. It is possible that the children who had previous sexual contact with adults were more vigilant and attentive to potential threats during the exam, resulting in better memory for the event and more resistance to suggestions of actions that were clearly inconsistent with their well-remembered experience. These results support the idea that individuals with a prior maltreatment history may particularly attend to, process, and accurately remember trauma-related details, perhaps also in part due to a more detailed knowledge base.

This greater attention to and processing of negative information may help guard against memory error. In a recent study, Otgaar, Howe, and Muris (2017) tested memory in 4- to 12-year-olds with suspected histories of child sexual abuse and nonmaltreated comparison children, using a misinformation paradigm, in which memory for a negative videotape (i.e., a bank robbery) was examined after children were exposed to misinformation. The maltreated children were *more* accurate than the nonmaltreated children regarding the negative videotape. That is, despite misinformation, the children with histories of maltreatment evinced lower levels of suggestion-induced memory errors about the bank robbery. This finding is of particular interest for the legal system given that children typically testify about negative events. It is likely that some children who have endured highly stressful and often traumatic experiences of abuse are more attentive and otherwise especially vigilant when faced with threat-related situations. This increased vigilance may even make some children more accurate when recounting the details of threat-related actions. To the extent that this finding generalizes to Case 1 described earlier, the 7-year-old girl who had suffered physical abuse might have quite accurate memory for what she witnessed about the family violence and her older sister's rapes (even though the 7-year-old was not willing to tell authorities about it).

Although a stronger knowledge base and previous experiences of abuse can contribute in some cases to more accurate memory and greater resistance to false suggestion, in other instances they can contribute to memory distortion. It has been proposed, for example, that trauma victims may have greater difficulty than nontrauma victims in monitoring their true and false memories and in response bias effects especially for negative information (Windmann & Kruger, 1998). Otgaar, Howe, and Muris (2017) recent findings may exemplify this theoretical possibility in a study employing the Deese-Roediger-McDermott (DRM) false memory paradigm involving negative and neutral word lists. The DRM paradigm arguably taps the ability to extract meaning from basic associative memory (e.g., the semantic relations among words) as well as memory monitoring processes (e.g., distinguishing thoughts from experience during memory retrieval). In comparing DRM performance in maltreated and nonmaltreated children, although semantic processing and basic associative structure was evident for both groups, the maltreated children had higher rates of DRM-induced false memories (recognition memory for "related words") for the negative lists, likely reflecting greater semantic processing of negative information, perhaps due to a more robust knowledge base for and/or greater sensitivity to the meaning of words with negative valence. As Otgaar et al. suggest, maltreated compared with nonmaltreated children appeared to be more likely to automatically activate related but nonpresented negative information in memory. In addition, the children with maltreatment histories may have had greater difficulty with memory monitoring between true and false information during retrieval of negative words on the DRM task (see also Baugerud, Howe, Magnussen, & Melinder, 2016). A similar finding has been reported for adults with PTSD subsequent to child sexual abuse (Bremner, Shobe, & Kihlstrom, 2000). Thus, in the Otgaar et al. study, although basic associative memory was comparable regardless of maltreatment status, the content of the information mattered in terms of memory performance: The children with maltreatment histories seemed to have more difficulty monitoring their automatically activated negative semantic networks. Although the DRM task ostensibly lacks ecological validity in relation to eyewitness memory, there is a risk that lax memory monitoring may generalize to some eyewitness memory tasks (Qin et al., 2008).

Under certain conditions, children with maltreatment histories make commission errors in their memory reports not just of word lists but also of experienced or witnessed events, although not necessarily any more than do nonmaltreated children. In fact, when they do show increased errors in memory for more realistic information, it is often for positive information rather than for negative information. In an early study, Goodman et al. (2001) compared the memory reports of child maltreatment (mainly child sexual abuse) victims with that of age-matched nonmaltreated children about a babysitting event. There were no significant differences in suggestibility rates, but there were hints that the maltreated children may have been more uncomfortable interacting with the babysitter and being interviewed (e.g., they recalled less and recognized the babysitter's picture less well than did the nonmaltreated children). In addition, in the Eisen et al. (2007) and Chae et al. (2011) studies of maltreated children who experienced medical examinations (negative events) and a play event (an arguably positive event), overall, children's suggestibility was primarily predicted by age rather than abuse status, with younger children making significantly more commission errors regardless of the type of event (the two types were not directly compared statistically). Moreover, all the events took place in the traumatic context of removal from home and a forensic investigation. In a study in which memory for negative information was tested, Greenhoot, McCloskey, and Gilsky (2005) detected that children who had suffered physical abuse and witnessed domestic violence were especially accurate in remembering the abuse incidents if they had more negative attitudes toward the abuser. McWilliams et al. (2014) found that maltreated children made more commission errors about a movie showing a positive interaction, but not one in which a negative family interaction was depicted, although psychopathology likely mediated the effect. Young and Widom (2014) also reported that maltreatment was associated with less accurate memory for positive than for negative photographic images, although the children's intelligence levels also affected this relation. Overall, it is possible that maltreated children, or at least a subset thereof, are more prone to error about positive than negative stimuli.

That said, young children with trauma histories who are interviewed in a misleading manner may have the knowledge to err in ways that nonmaltreated children lack. There are hints in the literature that if young maltreated or traumatized children also have immature executive function, source monitoring difficulties, social anxiety, or psychopathology symptoms, they may at times make worrisome commission errors that are grounded in knowledge base. For example, Chae et al. (2014) reported that one 4-year-old boy in a study of memory for inoculations made false reports of child sexual abuse regarding the nurse. The boy had a traumatic background (e.g., his father was in jail) and had been inappropriately exposed to adult sexuality, providing him with sexual knowledge ordinarily beyond his years.

Another possible source of memory error for maltreated children derives from the fact that, unfortunately, maltreatment is not a singular incident for many children, and repeated and routinized experiences may lead children to form "scripts" (i.e., sets of organized expectations about routines), including scripts about a prototypical traumatic experience (Farrar & Goodman, 1992). Victims of childhood sexual abuse may well remember specific occurrences when a perpetrator performed an especially traumatic or distinctive action, particularly if the action was unique to a repeated abusive routine (Goodman et al., 2014); however, the children may conflate some crime-related details, such as temporal information (Wandrey, Lyon, Quas, & Friedman, 2012). Monitoring of one's own memories relevant to repeated maltreatment experiences may therefore be important for avoiding such errors.

Although suggestibility is of considerable concern when obtaining memory reports from maltreated and nonmaltreated children, and thus misleading questions are typically to be avoided, recent research on commission errors reveals that there are times when suggestions actually lead children and adults to be more resistant to false memories and suggestion, and that the effect of false suggestions may relate to both the memorability of the suggested detail and time delay to the interview (Putnam, Sungkhasettee, & Roediger, 2016; Quas et al., 2007). When children's memory is strong for the type of information at issue and they detect that the interviewer is suggesting false information, even young children's accuracy increases and suggestibility decreases (Goodman, Bottoms, Schwartz-Kenney, & Rudy, 1991). At older ages, the rejection of false information about memorable (e.g., negative, embarrassing, distinctive) events is bolstered by metacognitive heuristics, such as "If that happened, I would remember it" (Ghetti & Alexander, 2004). Scoboria et al. (2012) explain that suggested events that are judged to be implausible, are often evaluated and dismissed quite rapidly, and as a result are less likely to lead to memory change. Children and adults may be less trusting of interviewers who they detect making implausible suggestions, and are thus subsequently more vigilant to subsequent erroneous suggestions. Future research should investigate such processes in maltreated children (but see Otgaar, Candel, Merckelbach, & Wade, 2009; Strange, Sutherland, & Garry, 2006).

So far, this discussion has focused primarily on maltreatment in relation to memory error and suggestibility in the form of commission errors. However, another facet of suggestibility should also be considered: specifically, stating or agreeing that something did not happen when it actually did occur, that is, on suggestibility as omission errors.

Omission Errors and Suggestibility

We have argued that the nature of the information to be recounted can significantly affect children's memory and suggestibility. When the information to be recounted is child sexual abuse, the topic is not only negative and emotional, but also may be shrouded in secrecy. Children learn early that both experiencing and talking openly about sexual acts is taboo. As discussed in the following, there are numerous reasons for child victims to omit or deny that such events were experienced. Moreover, adults assume that, if children deny that an event happened, then the event likely was not experienced, even when it actually had transpired (Block et al., 2012). When children falsely deny, it is typically difficult to differentiate omission errors due to suggestibility from reticence or intentional deception on the children's part. This mix of issues is addressed next, especially in relation to concerns about child sexual abuse.

Although research on omission errors is less plentiful than that on correct responses and commission errors, recent work enhances our understanding of children's omission errors. Research has largely considered two potential types of omissions. The first type is when children are told that the event never occurred, sometimes accompanied by misleading explanations or inaccurate physical evidence. These studies are comparable to, but in effect the inverse of, ones on children's commission errors. An example legal situation would be, if in Case 2 described earlier, the mother convinced her 6-year-old daughter that she just made up and imagined (or dreamt) the entire thing. One goal of the relevant research is to determine if children's memory traces have been altered by the false suggestion. The second type involves a suggestion to children that they recant a prior disclosure (rather than suggestions that the event never occurred). An example from real cases is when children perceive or receive perpetrator or familial pressure, either by way of suggestion or demands, to recant that the events were experienced, as might also have been the situation in Case 2. Especially in intrafamilial sexual abuse cases, children's disclosures of criminal or abusive acts can cause the children substantial anxiety and guilt or be accompanied by considerable pressure by family members, such as when the children might be removed from home or punished for telling (e.g., Tashjian, Goldfarb, Goodman, Quas, & Edelstein, 2016). In such cases, children may lie to protect themselves or loved ones, and say the event never occurred, as in Case 1 in the introduction to this chapter involving the grandparent who silenced the 7-year-old grandchild. Research addressing these two types of omission errors is discussed next.

SUGGESTIONS THE EVENT NEVER OCCURRED

Early work into children's omission errors revealed that children were generally resistant to suggestions that an event did not occur. In a study by Pezdek and Roe (1997), 4- and 10-year-olds were touched by an experimenter on the hand or shoulder. The children later were read a narrative by the same experimenter that indicated the children had not been touched. When an experimenter tested the children's memory, there was no significant detrimental effect on memory of the false suggestion. However, in this study, children were simply told that the experimenter had not touched them. No false physical evidence (nor pressure or threat, as might occur in real cases) was presented.

Later work, however, demonstrated situations in which children were susceptible to omission errors due to false suggestion. Silence about an event is one such suggestion. Children (5- to 6-years of age) in Williams, Wright, and Freeman's (2002) study were susceptible to omission errors about details of an event they had experienced (making cakes with Mrs. Flour) when they then saw a videotape of the event that omitted (was "silent about") the details at issue. In Otgaar, Candel, Smeets, and Merckelbach's (2010) research, 45% of the children ($n = 27$) omitted information after being presented with false physical evidence that an action had not occurred. There, children removed certain items of clothing from a doll. After an experimenter incorrectly told the children that they had not removed a particular item and, as proof, presented the doll wearing the item (which had been surreptitiously replaced after the fact by a researcher), children adopted the suggestion that the removal of the clothing did not occur. Thus, children are responsive to omission suggestions that an event did not occur, particularly when they observe physical evidence supporting the omission, even if it likely contradicts their memory trace.

Children's omission errors, however, are not necessarily stable. Omission errors decrease over time and, at least in one study, at a faster rate than commission errors (Otgaar et al., 2010). Indeed, in that study, when children were questioned by a parent more than a week after the event occurred, on average, 4- to 5-year-old and 8- to 11-year-old participants' rates of omission were around 13% ($n = 6$). Errors rates for the children in a commission condition, however, remained at around 42% ($n = 14$). Surprisingly, there were no age-related differences for the rate of omission errors, but younger children made more commission errors than older children at all interviews.

Omission errors' lack of stability may support the proposition that these errors are not memory based (Otgaar et al., 2010); omission errors may instead be due to social pressure by the interviewer, which dissipates after the interview has concluded. In a follow-up to the Otgaar et al. (2010) doll study discussed above, the same children saw a number of images of clothing items and were asked to state whether they previously removed the items from the doll (Otgaar, Meijer, et al., 2010). The children's responses indicated that their memory was still intact. Similar findings occurred in Candel, Hayne, Strange, and Prevoo's (2009) study, where children were more likely to endorse omission errors during a suggestive interview but less likely to incorrectly report on a later recognition test. These findings support the argument that omission errors in prior memory interviews are not reflective of and do not generally alter the original correct memory. Rather, the children seem to be succumbing to the social pressure and false information provided. (Of course, the same can be said about commission errors at times.)

SUGGESTIONS THAT A CHILD RECANT
Another type of omission error is when children recant, even though the crime or abuse did occur, in response to the suggestion that the children should withdraw their prior disclosures. In child sexual abuse cases, there are myriad reasons why adults would make such a suggestion (familial economic pressures, cultural shame, etc.). These suggestions may spark or exacerbate children's fears, for example, that disclosure will bring shame to a family, cause additional abuse to occur, or bring to light abuse that other victims wish to stay hidden. Children are susceptible to these pressures and often delay disclosure in unsupportive situations (Hershkowitz

et al., 2007) or abusive environments (Tashjian et al., 2016). It is largely unknown how such omissions affect memory in adulthood.

Although rates of recantation in actual child sexual abuse cases are debated, some case file review studies find as many as 23.1% of children recant these allegations (Malloy, Lyon, & Quas, 2007). Children are more likely to recant (or omit the alleged abuse) in subsequent interviews where there are external pressures encouraging such actions, including a lack of caregiver supportiveness (Malloy, Mugno, Rivard, Lyon, & Quas, 2016). Experimental research has confirmed these case file findings, showing that 23.3% of children recant prior disclosures and, when a mother is unsupportive of a disclosure, the rates shoot up as high as 46% (Malloy & Mugno, 2016).

Given the highly sensitive nature of the topics children are asked to describe in forensic interviews and in court (e.g., sexual abuse, parental domestic violence), societal or cultural attitudes may be enough, without any explicit statement requesting that the children omit information, to discourage disclosure. This reluctance may be further compounded by unspoken pressures, including discouraging discussion of private family matters or feeling shame toward prior sexual acts. In studies where children's sexual abuse was documented, children have been found to omit a number of sexual or sensitive details of the abuse (indeed sometimes all such details) and instead default toward more neutral information (Leander, 2010; Leander, Granhag, & Christianson, 2005). Some children, especially older ones, when asked about a prior genital examination similarly failed to disclose the sensitive touch, despite documented evidence that it had occurred (Saywitz, Goodman, Nicholas, & Moan, 1991). Even when children retain a memory trace of the event at issue, they may be reluctant to disclose initially but may do so over time (e.g., the second or third interview) or not at all (Goodman et al., 2003; Hershkowitz, Horowitz, & Lamb, 2007).

Summary and Future Research

Research supports the view that the nature of the information to be remembered affects children's eyewitness memory performance, including suggestibility. Memory is typically heightened for negative life incidents, especially when they relate to the self and activate personal survival concerns. That said, commission errors can occur in both maltreated and nonmaltreated children. Commission errors may result from memory monitoring deficits and response biases. However, it is likely that many children, maltreated or not, are explicitly told or are old enough to understand that, in forensic interviews and courtroom testimony, accuracy and strict memory monitoring are required ("Don't guess," "Do you promise to tell the truth?").

Moreover, children can and do omit information when adults or others suggest that the event did not occur or that they should not report. When the omission is suggested to a child and supported by physical evidence, it is possible that the child's memory for the event will become distorted, at least over time. Although experimental studies are understandably confined by ethical considerations, in real sexual abuse cases, children may have emotional forces, such as feelings of embarrassment, complicity, or guilt that might undermine otherwise robust memory and lead to stable omission errors, eventually affecting the memory trace. Further research on omission errors in children, particularly errors that are salient to or due in part to experiences related to the forensic context, is still an area ripe for future study.

Additional developmental research should similarly consider whether children are particularly likely to omit certain types of memories (including manipulating both the centrality and the sensitivity of the memory) under certain conditions. Further, the authors are not aware of any study thus far that has empirically combined both a suggestion that an event never occurred with a suggestion that children should not disclose (e.g., "That didn't happen did it? If you said it did, your uncle would get in a lot of trouble.") to determine if such statements affect the rates of disclosure. Studies have also not considered the import of the role of the individual who suggests that an event did not occur. When parents suggest that an event did not occur and also should not be disclosed, or that the children should just forget about it, the parents are in a trustworthy position of authority, which may make the suggestion particularly strong. Future work should consider the intersection of these variables and how they affect children's choice to disclose and the children's later memory.

In this chapter, we contend that the topic of the information to be remembered and recounted can have a profound effect on the accuracy and suggestibility of children's reports. Using child sexual abuse as an example, sexual acts are likely quite memorable and yet uncomfortable for children to discuss. The topic to be recounted, along with associated pressures on children, can promote commission errors, but at other times, they can promote omission errors instead. The pressures are particularly high when children testify in court.

CONTEXT: FORENSIC INTERVIEWS AND COURTROOM CROSS-EXAMINATION

The third part of our conceptualization concerns the context in which children are questioned (see Figure 7.1). This context can affect a child's memory report and suggestibility. As proof, Saywitz and Nathanson (1993) tested 8- to 10-year-old children's memory in a courtroom or in a school environment. As they note:

> Children questioned at court showed impaired memory performance when compared with agemates questioned at school. They also rated certain court-related experiences as more stressful than peers interviewed at school. Furthermore, children's perceptions of courtroom stress were negatively correlated with completeness of accurate free recall, suggesting a relation between court-related stress and eyewitness memory (p. 613).

Child Advocacy Centers, where many children are interviewed for forensic purposes, are specifically designed to be child friendly in hopes that the context will support children's comfort and ease of talking fully and truthfully about their experiences (Goldfarb et al., 2015). In contrast, children's accuracy is decreased and their suggestibility increased when they are interviewed in an intimidating context (e.g., Carter, Bottoms, & Levine, 1996; Goodman et al., 1998; Goodman et al., 1991). The criminal court is a particularly intimidating context.

In the United States criminal courtroom, testifying child victims face the daunting task of recounting what happened to them, no matter how embarrassing or upsetting, while seeing the defendant (Goodman et al., 1992; Hobbs et al., 2014). These children must also withstand cross-examination by the defendant's attorney. Early in this chapter, we described in Case 2, the possibility that, during cross examination, children may withdraw prior allegations regarding sexual abuse. Cross-examination (via the Sixth Amendment right to confrontation in the United States) is thought to bring about more truthful and accurate testimony, and thus decrease the likelihood that an innocent person goes to jail. Research on cross-examination, however, suggests that cross-examination sometimes has the opposite effect on children's testimony.

Child witnesses in a laboratory setting often change their testimony when subjected to cross-examination, even when initially they are correctly testifying about an event that occurred (Zajac & Hayne, 2003, 2006). Although cross-examination can help increase more accurate accounts where children have been directed to lie about an event occurring (either commission or omission errors) (Fogliati & Bussey, 2015; Zajac, Irvine, Ingram, & Jack, 2016), cross-examination is harmful for children whose original (direct examination) testimony was accurate. These children often incorrectly change their answers when pressured by questioning.

These changes in testimony, however, are not necessarily diagnostic of the truthfulness of the original statements. Zajac and colleagues (2016) found that a change in testimony is not indicative of the veracity of the prior statements. Further, even when children have been prepared for cross-examination (which has shown promise in helping children resist incorrectly changing their responses; Righarts, O'Neill, & Zajac, 2013), this line of questioning still decreases children's accuracy. At the end of the day, all we know from cross-examination resulting in a change of testimony is that children may have been encouraged to reveal a more truthful account or, conversely, felt bullied or pressed to lie. Thus, the context in which children are questioned can be crucial for the accuracy of their statements.

Summary and Future Research

Research has shown that children's memory and suggestibility are affected by the interviewing context. Children's reluctance to answer questions, their inconsistency, and their suggestibility increase, on average, when they face intimidating questioning in the adversarial context of criminal court trials (e.g., Goodman et al., 1992; Goodman et al., 1998; Zajac et al., 2016). It is not surprising then that children may change their testimony under the pressures of cross-examination and that adults likely cannot deduce the truthfulness of the original statement from such a change, especially if it leads to a false denial (Block et al., 2012).

Instead, one can simply know that the children have retracted a prior allegation. What we do not know from previous experimental research is whether cross-examination is particularly deleterious when children face low levels of support (and potentially even encouragement not to disclose) at home or elsewhere (e.g., Goodman et al., 1992). Future work should consider the context of the questioning of the children and how the presence of overlapping pressures increases the likelihood of adopting false suggestions that an event did or did not occur.

CONCLUSION

Children who enter forensic settings to testify come with their own unique backgrounds and circumstances that may influence the likelihood that they will be accurate and adopt or resist suggestions. Rather than blanket statements about children's memory and suggestibility, here we build on important recent research revealing that whether children are accurate or not is influenced by a number factors. We thus put forth a model that allows one to place children's memory and suggestibility within individuals' unique circumstances. Specifically, we propose that when discussing memory and suggestibility that one consider at least three important factors: the person, the topic to be discussed, and the context in which the memory is recounted. Each one of these factors plays an important role in any statement regarding the potential for memory error and suggestibility in a particular situation.

We do not mean to imply that the current state of the research permits experts or others to testify with any guarantee about the suggestibility of the individual child at question. Indeed, here we purposefully chose to critically analyze a few key individual and contextual factors in depth, but a number of other variables are likely to influence a child's eyewitness memory performance, and currently there is a lack sufficient research that considers the many overlaps between them. Without such research, we simply lack a model predictive or sensitive to an individual child and can only speak in broad generalizations. Such testimony, although at times permitted under the rules of evidence, should thus come with appropriate caveats (Faigman, Monahan, & Slobogin, 2014).

Finally, here we also considered susceptibility to suggestion such as in the form of pressure-induced omission errors. Children's commission errors are highly disconcerting for the legal system, as they may lead to the incarceration of innocent individuals. Others have noted, however, that we should also be vigilant to the harm incurred by children's omission errors (Otgaar et al., 2010). When relatives or legal authorities falsely suggest to child victims that criminal or abusive acts were not witnessed or experienced, or pressure the children into believing or simply stating a criminal act did not occur when it did, children are not given an adequate opportunity to have a voice and participate in the legal system. This may lead to children feeling that the system is illegitimate and not worthy of trust and utilization (Fagan & Tyler, 2005). Just as a system cannot stand when the innocent are jailed, justice also cannot function when victims feel that they cannot come forward. A rich understanding of children's commission and omission errors, including for children who suffered maltreatment and who will be required to face the often daunting prospect of testifying, thus helps us better serve child victims specifically, and the legal system and society more generally.

AUTHORS' NOTE

This manuscript is based in part on work supported by the National Science Foundation (1424420) and the National Institute of Justice (2013-IJ-CX-0104). Any opinions, findings, conclusions, or recommendations expressed in this article are those of the authors and do not necessarily reflect the views of the National Science Foundation or the National Institute of Justice. Direct correspondence to: Dr. Gail S. Goodman, Department of Psychology, University of California, One Shields Avenue, Davis, CA 95616; E-mail: ggoodman@ ucdavis.edu

REFERENCES

Alexander, K., Quas, J., Goodman, G. S., Ghetti, S., Edelstein, R., Redlich, A., Cordon, I., & Jones, D. P. H. (2005). Traumatic impact predicts long-term memory of documented child sexual abuse. *Psychological Science, 16*, 33–40.

American Psychiatric Association. (2013). *Diagnostic and statistical manual of mental disorders* (5th ed.). Arlington, VA: American Psychiatric Publishing.

Baugerud, G. A., Howe, M. L., Magnussen, S., & Melinder, A. M. D. (2016). Maltreated and non-maltreated children's true and false memories of neutral and emotional word lists in the DRM task. *Journal of Experimental Child Psychology, 143*, 102–110.

Bernstein, E. M., & Putnam, F. W. (1986). Development, reliability and validity of a dissociation scale. *Journal of Nervous & Mental Diseases, 174*, 727–735.

Berntsen, D., Johannessen, K. B., Thomsen, Y. D., Bertelsen, M., Hoyle, R. H., & Rubin, D. (2012). Peace and war: Trajectories of posttraumatic stress disorder symptoms before, during, and after military deployment in Afghanistan. *Psychological Science, 23*, 1557–1565.

Block, S. D., Shestowsky, D., Segovia, D. A., Goodman, G. S., Schaaf, J. M., & Alexander, K. W. (2012). "That never happened": Adults' discernment of children's true and false memory reports. *Law and Human Behavior, 36*, 365–374.

Brainerd, C. J., Reyna, V. F., & Ceci, S. J. (2008). Developmental reversals in false memory: A review of data and theory. *Psychological Bulletin, 134*, 343–382.

Bremner, J. D., Shobe, K. K., & Kihlstrom, J. F. (2000). False memories in women with self-reported childhood sexual abuse: An empirical study. *Psychological Science, 11*, 333–337.

Bright-Paul, A., & Jarrold, C. (2012). Children's eyewitness memory: Repeating postevent misinformation reduces the distinctiveness of a witnessed event. *Memory, 20*, 818–835.

Brown, R., & Kulik, J. (1977). Flashbulb memories. *Cognition, 5*, 73–99.

Candel, I., Hayne, H., Strange, D., & Prevoo, E. (2009). The effect of suggestion on children's recognition memory for seen and unseen details. *Psychology, Crime & Law, 15*, 29–39.

Carlson, E. B., Furby, L., Armstrong, J., & Shales, J. (1997). A conceptual framework for the long-term psychological effects of traumatic child abuse. *Child Maltreatment, 2,* 272–295.

Carter, C. A., Bottoms, B. L., & Levine, M. (1996). Linguistic and socioemotional influences on the accuracy of children's reports. *Law and Human Behavior, 20,* 335–358.

Chae, Y., Goodman, G. S., Eisen, M. L., & Qin, J. (2011). Event memory and suggestibility in abused and neglected children: Trauma-related psychopathology and cognitive functioning. *Journal of Experimental Child Psychology, 110,* 520–538.

Chae, Y., Goodman, G. S., Larson, R. P., Augusti, E. M., Alley, D., VanMeenen, K. M., . . . Coulter, K. P. (2014). Children's memory and suggestibility about a distressing event: The role of children's and parents' attachment. *Journal of Experimental Child Psychology, 123,* 90–111.

Christianson, S. Å. (1992). Emotional stress and eyewitness memory: A critical review. *Psychological Bulletin, 112,* 284–309.

Cunningham, S., Brady-Van den Bos, M., Gill, L., & Turk, D. J. (2013). Survival of the selfish: Contrasting self-referential and survival based encoding. *Consciousness and Cognition, 22,* 237–244.

Edelstein, R., Ghetti, S., Quas, J. A., Goodman, G. S., Alexander, K., Redlich, A., & Cordon, I. (2005). Avoidant attachment and memory for child sexual abuse. *Personality and Social Psychology Bulletin, 31,* 1549–1560.

Eisen, M. L., Goodman, G. S., Qin, J., Davis, S., & Crayton, J. (2007). Maltreated children's memory: Accuracy, suggestibility, and psychopathology. *Developmental Psychology, 43,* 1275–1294.

Eisen, M. L., Qin, J., Goodman, G. S., & Davis, S. L. (2002). Memory and suggestibility in maltreated children: Age, stress arousal, dissociation, and psychopathology. *Journal of Experimental Child Psychology, 83,* 167–212.

Fagan, J., & Tyler, T. R. (2005). Legal socialization of children and adolescents. *Social Justice Research, 18,* 217–241.

Faigman, D. L., Monahan, J., & Slobogin, C. (2014). Group to individual (G2i) inference in scientific expert testimony. *University of Chicago Law Review, 81,* 417–480.

Farrar, M. J., & Goodman, G. S. (1992). Developmental changes in event memory. *Child Development, 63,* 173–187.

Fivush, R. (2002). The development of autobiographical memory. In H. L. Westcott, G. M. Davies, & R. H. C. Bull (Eds.), *Children's testimony: A handbook of psychological research and forensic practice* (pp. 3–19). Chichester, UK: Wiley.

Fogliati, R., & Bussey, K. (2015). The effects of cross-examination on children's coached reports. *Psychology, Public Policy, and Law, 21,* 10–23.

Giesbrecht, T., Lynn, S. J., Lilienfeld, S. O., & Merckelbach, H. (2008). Cognitive processes in dissociation: An analysis of core theoretical assumptions. *Psychological Bulletin, 134,* 617–647.

Ghetti, S., & Alexander, K. W. (2004). "If it happened, I would remember it": Strategic use of event memorability in the rejection of false autobiographical events. *Child Development, 75,* 542–561.

Ghetti, S., Edelstein, R. S., Goodman, G. S., Cordon, I. M., Quas, J. A., Alexander, K.W., Jones, D. P. H. (2006). What can subjective forgetting tell us about memory for childhood trauma? *Memory & Cognition, 34,* 1011–1025.

Goldfarb, D. A., Goodman, G. S., & Lawler, M. (2015). Children's evidence and the Convention on the Rights of the Child: Improving the legal system for children. In S. Mahmoudi, A. Leviner, A. Kaldal, & K. Lainpelto (Eds.), *Child-friendly justice: A quarter of a century of the UN Convention on the Rights of the Child* (pp. 85–109). Leiden, The Netherlands: Koninklijke Brill NV.

Goodman, G. S., Bottoms, B. L., Schwartz-Kenney, B. M., & Rudy, L. (1991). Children's testimony about a stressful event: Improving children's reports. *Journal of Narrative & Life History, 1,* 69–99.

Goodman, G. S., Bottoms, B. L., Rudy, L., Davis, S. L., & Schwartz-Kenney, B. (2001). Effects of past abuse experiences on children's eyewitness memory. *Law and Human Behavior, 25,* 269–298.

Goodman, G. S., Ghetti, S., Quas, J. A., Edelstein, R. S., Alexander, K. W., Redlich, A. D., ... Jones, D. P. H. (2003). A prospective study of memory for child sexual abuse: New findings to the repressed-memory controversy. *Psychological Science, 14,* 113–118.

Goodman, G. S., Goldfarb, D. A., Chong, J., & Goodman-Shaver, L. (2014). Children's eyewitness memory: The influence of cognitive and socio-emotional factors. *Roger Williams University Law Review, 19,* 476–512.

Goodman, G. S., Goldfarb, D., Quas, J. A., Narr, R. K., Milojevich, H., & Cordon, I. M. (2016). Memory development, emotion regulation, and trauma-related psychopathology. In D. Cicchetti (Ed.), *Developmental psychopathology* (3rd ed., pp. 555–890). Hoboken, NJ: Wiley & Sons.

Goodman, G. S., Ogle, C. M., McWilliams, K., & Narr, R. K., & Paz-Alonso, P. (2014). Memory development in the forensic context. In P. J. Bauer, & R. Fivush (Eds.), *The Wiley handbook on the development of children's memory* (pp. 920–941). Chichester, UK: John Wiley & Sons.

Goodman, G. S., Quas, J. A., Batterman-Faunce, J. M., Riddlesberger, M. M., & Kuhn, J. (1994). Predictors of accurate and inaccurate memories of traumatic events experienced in childhood. *Consciousness and Cognition, 3,* 269–294.

Goodman, G. S., Quas, J. A., & Ogle, C. M. (2010). Child maltreatment and memory. *Annual Review of Psychology, 61,* 325–351.

Goodman, G. S., Taub, E. P., Jones, D. P., England, P., Port, L. K., Rudy, L., ... Prado, L. (1992). Testifying in criminal court: Emotional effects on child sexual assault victims. *Monographs of the Society for Research in Child Development, 57,* 1–159.

Goodman, G. S., Tobey, A. E., Batterman-Faunce, J. M., Orcutt, H., Thomas, S., Shaprio, C., & Sachsenmaier, T. (1998). Face-to-face confrontation: Effects of closed-circuit technology on children's eyewitness testimony and jurors' decisions. *Law and Human Behavior, 22,* 165–203.

Greenhoot, A. F., McCloskey, L., & Gilsky, E. (2005). A longitudinal study of adolescents' recollections of family violence. *Applied Cognitive Psychology, 19,* 719–743.

Hershkowitz, I., Horowitz, D., & Lamb, M. E. (2007). Individual and family variables associated with disclosure and nondisclosure of child abuse in Israel. In M.-E. Pipe, M. E. Lamb, Y. Orbach, & A.-C. Cederborg (Eds.), *Child sexual abuse: Disclosure, delay and denial* (pp. 63–76). New York: Taylor & Francis.

Hirst, W., & Phelps, E. A. (2016). Flashbulb memories. *Current Directions in Psychological Science, 25,* 36–41.

Hobbs, S. D., Goodman, G. S., Block, S. D., Oran, D., Quas, J. A., Park, A., Widaman, K., & Baumrind, N. L. (2014). Child abuse victims' responses to appearing in dependency and criminal courts. *Children & Youth Services Review, 44,* 407–416.

Howe, M. L. (2011). *The nature of early memory: An adaptive theory of the genesis and development of memory.* New York: Oxford University Press.

Howe, M. L., Cicchetti, D., Toth, S. L., & Cerrito, B. M. (2004). True and false memories in maltreated children. *Child Development, 75,* 1402–1417.

Howe, M. L., & Courage, M. L. (1997). The emergence and early development of autobiographical memory. *Psychological Review, 104,* 499–523.

Howe, M. L., Toth, S. L., & Cicchetti, D. (2011). Can maltreated children inhibit true and false memories for emotional information? *Child Development, 82,* 967–981.

Hyman, I. E., & Billings, F. J. (1998). Individual differences and the creation of false childhood memories. *Memory, 6,* 1–20.

Katz, S. M., Schonfeld, D. J., Carter, A. S., Leventhal, J. M., & Cicchetti, D. V. (1995). The accuracy of children's reports with anatomically correct dolls. *Journal of Developmental & Behavioral Pediatrics, 16,* 71–76.

Klein, S. B., & Kihlstrom, J. F. (1986). Elaboration, organization, and the self-reference effect in memory. *Journal of Experimental Psychology: General, 115,* 26–38.

Kulkofsky, S., & Klemfuss, J. Z. (2008). What the stories children tell can tell about their memory: Narrative skill and young children's suggestibility. *Developmental Psychology, 44,* 1442–1456.

Leander, L. (2010). Police interviews with child sexual abuse victims: Patterns of reporting, avoidance and denial. *Child Abuse & Neglect, 34,* 192–205.

Leander, L., Granhag, P. A., & Christianson, S. Å. (2005). Children exposed to obscene phone calls: What they remember and tell. *Child Abuse & Neglect, 29,* 871–888.

Malloy, L. C., Lyon, T. D., & Quas, J. A. (2007). Filial dependency and recantation of child sexual abuse allegations. *Journal of the American Academy of Child & Adolescent Psychiatry, 46,* 162–170.

Malloy, L. C., & Mugno, A. P. (2016). Children's recantation of adult wrongdoing: An experimental investigation. *Journal of Experimental Child Psychology, 145,* 11–21.

Malloy, L. C., Mugno, A. P., Rivard, J. R., Lyon, T. D., & Quas, J. A. (2016). Familial influences on recantation in substantiated child sexual abuse cases. *Child Maltreatment, 21,* 256–261.

Masten, C. L., Guyer, A. E., Hodgdon, H. B., McClure, E. B., Charney, D.S., Ernst, M., . . . Monk, C. S. (2008). Recognition of facial emotions among maltreated children with high rates of post-traumatic stress disorder. *Child Abuse & Neglect, 32,* 139–153.

McWilliams, K., Harris, L. S., & Goodman, G. S. (2014). Child maltreatment, trauma-related psychopathology, and eyewitness memory in children and adolescents. *Behavioral Sciences & the Law, 32,* 702–717.

McWilliams, K., Narr, R., Goodman, G. S., Mendoza, M., & Ruiz, S. (2013). Children's memory for their mother's murder: Accuracy, suggestibility, and resistance to suggestion. *Memory, 21,* 591–598.

Nairne, J. S., & Pandeirada, J. N. S. (2010). Adaptive memory: Ancestral priorities and the mnemonic value of survival processing. *Cognitive Psychology, 61,* 1–22.

Otgaar, H., Candel, I., Merckelbach, H., & Wade, K. (2009): Abducted by a UFO: Prevalence information affects young children's false memories for an implausible event *Applied Cognitive Psychology, 23,* 115–125.

Otgaar, H., Candel, I., Smeets, T., & Merckelbach, H. (2010). 'You didn't take Lucy's skirt off': The effect of misleading information on omissions and commissions in children's memory reports. *Legal and Criminological Psychology, 15,* 229–241.

Otgaar, H., Howe, M. L., Brackmann, N., & Sweets, T. (2016). The malleability of developmental trends in neutral and negative memory illusions. *Journal of Experimental Psychology: General, 145*, 31–55.

Otgaar, H., Howe, M. L., Brackmann, N., & van Helvoort, D. H. J. (2017). Eliminating age differences in children's and adults' suggestibility and memory conformity effects. *Developmental Psychology, 53*, 962–970.

Otgaar, H., Howe, M. L., & Muris, P. (2017). Maltreatment increases spontaneous false memories but decreases suggestion-induced false memories in children. *British Journal of Developmental Psychology*, Jan 17, doi: 10.1111/bjdp.12177. [Epub ahead of print].

Otgaar, H., Meijer, E. H., Giesbrecht, T., Smeets, T., Candel, I., & Merckelbach, H. (2010). Children's suggestion-induced omission errors are not caused by memory erasure. *Consciousness and Cognition, 19*, 265–269.

Paz-Alonso, P., Ghetti, S., Donohue, S., Goodman, G. S., & Bunge, S. (2008). Neurodevelopmental correlates of true and false recognition. *Cerebral Cortex, 18*, 2208–2216.

Paz-Alonso, P., & Goodman, G. S. (2016). Developmental differences across middle childhood in memory and suggestibility for negative and positive events. *Behavioral Sciences & the Law, 34*, 30–54.

Peterson, C. (2011). Children's memory reports over time: Getting both better and worse. *Journal of Experimental Child Psychology, 109*, 275–293.

Pezdek, K., & Roe, C. (1997). The suggestibility of children's memory for being touched: Planting, erasing, and changing memories. *Law and Human Behavior, 21*, 95–106.

Pollak, S. D., & Tolley-Schell, S. A. (2003). Selective attention to facial emotional in physically abused children. *Journal of Abnormal Psychology, 112*, 323–338.

Putnam, A. L., Sungkhasettee, V. W., & Roediger, H. L. (2016). When misinformation improves memory: The effects of recollecting change. *Psychological Science, 6*, 253–271.

Qin, J., Ogle, C. M., & Goodman, G. S. (2008). Adults' memories of childhood: True and false memory reports. *Journal of Experimental Psychology: Applied, 14*, 373–391.

Quas, J. A., Goodman, G. S., Bidrose, S., Pipe, M. E., Craw, S., & Ablin, D. S. (1999). Emotion and memory: Children's long-term remembering, forgetting, and suggestibility. *Journal of Experimental Child Psychology, 72*, 235–270.

Quas, J. A., Malloy, L. C., Melinder, A. M. D., Goodman, G. S., D'Mello, M., & Schaaf, J. (2007). Developmental differences in the effects of repeated interviews and interviewer bias on young children's event memory and false reports. *Developmental Psychology, 43*, 823–837.

Righarts, S., O'Neill, S., & Zajac, R. (2013). Addressing the negative effect of cross-examination questioning on children's accuracy: Can we intervene? *Law and Human Behavior, 37*, 354–365.

Rudy, L., & Goodman, G. S. (1991). Effects of participation on children's reports: Implications for children's testimony. *Developmental Psychology, 27*, 1–26.

Sayfan, L., Mitchell, E., Goodman, G. S., Eisen, M. L., & Qin, J. (2008). Predictors of expressed emotion during disclosure of child maltreatment. *Child Abuse & Neglect, 32*, 1026–1036.

Saywitz, K. J., Goodman, G. S., Nicholas, E., & Moan, S. F. (1991). Children's memories of a physical examination involving genital touch: Implications for reports of child sexual abuse. *Journal of Consulting and Clinical Psychology, 59*, 682–691.

Saywitz, K. J., & Nathanson, R. (1993). Children's testimony and their perceptions of stress in and out of the courtroom. *Child Abuse & Neglect, 17*, 613–22.

Scoboria, A., Mazzoni, G., Jarry, J., & Shapero, D. (2012). Implausibility inhibits but does not eliminate false autobiographical beliefs. *Canadian Journal of Experimental Psychology, 66*, 259–267.

Shackman, J. E., Shackman, A. J., & Pollak, S. D. (2007). Physical abuse amplifies attention to threat and increases anxiety in children. *Emotion, 7*, 838–852.

Sharot, T., Martorella, E. A., Delgado, M. R., & Phelps, E. A. (2007). How personal experience modulates the neural circuitry of memories of September 11. *Proceedings of the National Academy of Sciences, 104*, 389–394.

Strange, D., Sutherland, R., & Garry, M. (2006). Event plausibility does not determine children's false memories. *Memory, 14*, 937–951.

Symons, C. S., & Johnson, B. T. (1997). The self-reference effect in memory: A meta-analysis. *Psychological Bulletin, 121*, 371–394.

Tashjian, S. M., Goldfarb, D., Goodman, G. S., Quas, J. A., & Edelstein, R. (2016). Delay in disclosure of non-parental child sexual abuse in the context of emotional and physical maltreatment: A pilot study. *Child Abuse & Neglect, 58*, 149–159.

Turk, D. J., Cunningham, S. J., & Macrae, C. N. (2008). Self-memory biases in explicit and incidental encoding of trait adjectives. *Consciousness and Cognition, 17*, 1040–1045.

Turk, D. J., van Bussel, K., Waiter, D. D., & Macrae, C. N. (2011). Mine and me: Exploring the neural basis of object ownership. *Journal of Cognitive Neuroscience, 23*, 3657–3668.

Valentino, K., Cicchetti, D., Rogosch, F. A., & Toth, S. L. (2008). True and false recall and dissociation among maltreated children: The role of self-schema. *Development and Psychopathology, 20*, 213–232.

Wandrey, L., Lyon, T. D., Quas, J. A., & Friedman, W. J. (2012). Maltreated children's ability to estimate temporal location and numerosity of placement changes and court visits. *Psychology, Public Policy, and Law, 18*, 79–104.

Welch-Ross, M. K. (1999). Interviewer knowledge and preschoolers' reasoning about knowledge states moderate suggestibility. *Cognitive Development, 14*, 423–442.

Williams, S.-J., Wright, D. B., & Freeman, N. H. (2002). Inhibiting children's memory of an interactive effect: The effectiveness of a cover-up. *Applied Cognitive Psychology, 16*, 651–664.

Windmann, S., & Krüger, T. (1998). Subconscious detection of threat as reflected by an enhanced response bias. *Consciousness and Cognition, 7*, 603–633.

Young, J. C., & Widom, C. S. (2014). Long-term effects of child abuse and neglect on emotion processing in adulthood. *Child Abuse & Neglect, 38*, 1369–1381.

Zajac, R., & Hayne, H. (2003). I don't think that's what really happened: The effect of cross-examination on the accuracy of children's reports. *Journal of Experimental Psychology: Applied, 9*, 187–195.

Zajac, R., & Hayne, H. (2006). The negative effect of cross-examination style questioning on children's accuracy: Older children are not immune. *Applied Cognitive Psychology, 20*, 3–16.

Zajac, R., Irvine, B., Ingram, J. M., & Jack, F. (2016). The diagnostic value of children's responses to cross-examination questioning. *Behavioral Sciences & the Law, 34*, 160–177.

PART III

Deception in the Courtroom

8

Nonverbal Detection of Deception

ALDERT VRIJ

Throughout history it has been assumed that lying is accompanied by specific nonverbal behaviors; various sources still claim that nonverbal behavior is very revealing about deception. Systematic research, however, examining nonverbal cues to deceit has shown that nonverbal cues to deceit are faint and unreliable. This chapter starts with discussing under which circumstances people pay attention to nonverbal behavior and provides reasons why they do so. This is followed by a theoretical background of nonverbal cues to deception and discussions of the (weak) empirical evidence about (1) the relationship between nonverbal cues and deception, including the empirical evidence regarding the Behavior Analysis Interview (BAI) and Ekman's approach of observing facial expressions; and (2) people's (poor) ability to detect deceit when paying attention to nonverbal behavior. Despite the popularity of observing nonverbal behavior to detect deception, analyzing speech content provides more accurate results, particularly when specific interview protocols are used. Prime examples are the Strategic Use of Evidence (discussed elsewhere in this book) and the Verifiability Approach and cognitive lie detection, which are briefly outlined in the final part of this chapter.

NONVERBAL DETECTION OF DECEPTION

Throughout history, it has long been assumed that lying is accompanied by specific nonverbal behaviors. The underlying assumption was that the fear of being detected was an essential element of deception (Trovillo, 1939a). A Hindu writing from 900 BC mentioned that liars rub the great toe along the ground and shiver, and that they rub the roots of their hair with their fingers (Trovillo, 1939a); and Münsterberg (1908) described the utility of observing posture, eye movements, and knee jerks for lie detection purposes (Trovillo, 1939b). Freud, although not a deception researcher, also expressed his view about the topic *"He who has eyes to see and ears to hear may convince himself that no mortal can keep a secret. If his lips are silent, he chatters with his finger-tips; betrayal oozes out of him at every pore"* (Freud, 1959, p. 94).

Various sources claim that nonverbal behavior is very revealing about deception. There are numerous articles in popular magazines expressing this idea, as does the popular TV series "Lie to Me." Many books are conveying this idea, including *Lie spotting* (Meyer, 2010) and *Spy the lie* (Houston, Floyd, & Carnicero, 2012). (American) police manuals typically pay considerably more attention to nonverbal cues than to verbal cues to deceit (Vrij & Granhag, 2007), and nonverbal lie detection tools such as the BAI (Horvath, Blair, & Buckley, 2008; Horvath, Jayne, & Buckley, 1994) and Ekman's (1985) approach of observing facial expressions and involuntary body language are frequently taught to practitioners, including police and intelligence personnel.

Systematic research examining nonverbal cues to deceit emerged in the second half of the 20th century with Reid and Arther's (1953) analysis of the behavior of more than 800 suspects. This research, although pioneering, was problematic because the ground truth was unknown, that is, it could not be established who of those 800 suspects were actually truth tellers and who were liars. Research after Reid and Arther (1953), overwhelmingly experimental laboratory research in which the ground truth was known, showed that nonverbal cues to deceit are faint and unreliable (DePaulo & Morris, 2004; DePaulo et al., 2003).

This chapter starts with discussing under which circumstances people pay attention to nonverbal behavior and provides reasons why they do so. This is followed by a theoretical background of nonverbal cues to deception and the empirical evidence about (1) the relationship between nonverbal cues and deception, including the empirical evidence regarding the BAI and Ekman's approach of observing facial expressions; and (2) people's ability to detect deceit when paying attention to nonverbal behavior.

Despite the popularity of observing nonverbal behavior to detect deception, analyzing speech content provides more accurate results, particularly when specific interview protocols are used (Vrij & Granhag, 2012). A prime example is the Strategic Use of Evidence (Granhag & Hartwig, 2008, 2015; Hartwig, Granhag, & Luke, 2014), which is discussed in detail elsewhere in this book (chapter 9). Other examples are the Verifiability Approach and cognitive lie detection, which is briefly outlined in the final part of this chapter.

THE RELATIVE IMPORTANCE OF SPEECH CONTENT AND NONVERBAL BEHAVIOR WHEN ATTEMPTING TO DETECT DECEIT

There are specific circumstances in which observers merely rely on speech content when they attempt to detect deceit. First, when they know the facts that are discussed by the target person. In such cases the observer typically compares what s/he knows with what the target person says. Police detectives could easily establish that a suspect, later convicted for murder, was lying about his whereabouts on a particular day when he said that he went to a market. Unknown to the suspect, but known to the detectives, the market was cancelled on that particular day (Vrij & Mann, 2001). To examine what cues people use to detect lies in daily life, college students were asked to recall an instance in their life in which they had detected that another person had lied to them and how they had discovered the lie (Park, Levine, McCornack, Morrison, & Ferrara, 2002). The main method of detecting lies was by comparing someone's speech content with other sources of information (third parties and physical evidence).

Second, observers are also typically inclined to pay attention to speech content when they have access to more than one statement. They may have obtained statements about an event from different people or more than one statement from the same person. In such cases, observers check for consistency between the different statements (Strömwall, Granhag, & Jonsson, 2003; Vredeveldt, van Koppen, & Granhag, 2014). Third, observers rely on verbal cues when these cues are distinctive. For example, people rely on speech when they find a story implausible (this is seen as suspicious, Kraut, 1978), or when a statement appears to be against the self-interest of the storyteller (this is seen as honest; Noller, 1985).

When observers are unaware of factual information, have no statements to compare, and when the speech content is not distinctive, they are inclined to pay more attention to behavior than to speech content. For example, in a lie detection experiment, 99 British police officers saw 54 videotaped fragments of police interviews with suspects who were suspected of rape, arson, or murder. They told in each fragment a verified truth or lie (Mann, Vrij, & Bull, 2004). The police officers made veracity judgements after each fragment and reported the cues on which they based their decisions. The vast majority of the cues the police officers reported (78%) were nonverbal, with "gaze aversion" being the most frequently mentioned cue (73% of the officers reported this cue). Some real-life observations further demonstrate the importance of behavior in judging whether someone is lying. In Florida, Tom Sawyer, accused of sexual assault and murder, was interrogated for 16 hours. The detectives issued threats and extracted a, probably false, confession. Sawyer became a prime suspect because he appeared embarrassed and his face was flushed during an initial interview in which he denied involvement in the crime (Meissner & Kassin, 2002). In another American case, 14-year-old Michael Crowe was submitted to lengthy interrogations and confessed to having stabbed his sister to death. He became a prime suspect because the detectives believed that he did not appear upset in reaction to his sister's death. The charge against the boy was later dropped (Kassin, 2005).

There are several reasons why observers pay so much attention to nonverbal behavior (Vrij, 2008b). First, people are used to making inferences from nonverbal behavior. By observing behavior alone, people can determine with reasonable accuracy someone's personality trait (e.g., extraversion and sociability), masculinity, femininity, or sexual orientation. From behavior, it is also possible to discern information about status, dominance, and romantic involvement (Ambady, Bernieri, & Richeson, 2000; DePaulo, 1992). Having good experience with such judgements, people may think that deception can also be detected by observing someone's behavior. That has proved to be very difficult, as will be discussed.

Second, expectancies about the truthfulness of a person may influence what people pay attention to. Police officers readily assume that a suspect is guilty

(Kassin, 2005; Moston, Stephenson, & Williamson, 1992). Analyses of police interviews in England showed that in 73% of cases the police interviewers were "certain" of the suspect's guilt before interviewing them (Moston et al., 1992). Saul Kassin (2005, p. 216), who over the years has asked many American police officers whether they are concerned that their persuasive interrogation methods may make innocent people confess, reported that the most common reply he received is: "No, because I do not interrogate innocent people." When lying is expected, police officers may have little interest in listening to a suspect's flat denials and prefer to look at bodily signs to detect deceit (Millar & Millar, 1995).

Third, conducting interviews in criminal investigations is a mentally taxing task, as the investigator has to simultaneously listen to the suspect's story and think of the next question to ask. When a task is difficult, people tend to rely on behavior because it is more suited than speech content for the use of simple, mentally less taxing judgemental rules, such as "liars are often nervous" (Reinhard & Sporer, 2008).

Fourth, the preference of examining nonverbal behaviors may be the result of the dominance in writing about nonverbal cues to deception. American police manuals pay more attention to nonverbal cues than to speech content—and to visual nonverbal cues in particular—when discussing cues to deceit (Vrij & Granhag, 2007; Vrij, Granhag, & Porter, 2010). This is justified with quotes such as "according to various social studies as much as 70% of a message communicated between persons occurs at a nonverbal level" (Inbau, Reid, Buckley, & Jayne, 2013, p. 122). This claim is taken out of context and, as such, misleading. It is largely based on Mehrabian's (1971) work on the communication of single spoken words (such as the expression of emotions through single words like "dear" or "terrible"). Obviously, if someone says little, verbal behavior cannot have much influence on the impression information. This does not mean that Mehrabian's findings can be applied to police interviews or any other interview setting, where interviewees say considerably more than a single word. Mehrabian has personally addressed the incorrect citation of his work. In an email on October 31, 2002 to the author Dr. Max Atkinson (2005, pp. 343–345), known from his commentaries on public communications, he wrote: "I am obviously uncomfortable about misquotes of my work. From the very beginning I have tried to give people the correct limitations of my findings. Unfortunately the field of self-styled 'corporate image consultants' or 'leadership consultants' has numerous practitioners with very little psychological expertise."

Last, perhaps observers pay so much attention to nonverbal behavior because they assume that people are less aware of their behavior than their speech and therefore will leak the information they are trying to hide through nonverbal channels (Vrij, 2008b, 2014b). Four factors contribute to this idea (DePaulo & Kirkendol, 1989; Vrij, 2008b, 2014b). First, there are certain automatic links between strongly felt emotions and behavior. For example, the moment people become afraid, their bodies jerk backwards; and anger results in narrowing of the lips (Ekman, 1985). Similarly, tone of voice is difficult for senders to control (Ekman, 1981), because the autonomic nervous system controls the relevant features of the voice in moments of high stress (Hocking & Leathers, 1980). In contrast, automatic links between emotions and speech content do not exist.

Second, people are less practiced in using behavior than in using words because people exchange information predominantly via words. When asked to report their activities of a particular day, people mostly choose to use words to describe what they have done. People therefore concentrate more on their speech and tend to neglect their behavior somewhat.

Third, people are less aware of how they are behaving than what they are saying. Unless they look in the mirror or watch a videotape of themselves, they do not actually see themselves. And since the exchange of information predominantly happens via words, they are not aware of their behavior most of the time. Lack of insight into nonverbal behavior may make people sometimes unaware of subtle changes that take place in it.

Fourth, verbally, people can pause and think what to say, whereas nonverbally people cannot be silent. Suppose a guilty suspect realizes during a police interview that the police know more than he thought about his involvement in the crime. This may throw the suspect off guard and he may need time to recompose himself, which may affect the suspect's behavior.

Two comments are relevant here. First, these reasons may suggest that there are large and easy identifiable differences in nonverbal behavior between truth tellers and liars. This is not the case, as will be outlined later. Second, these reasons seem to underestimate the difficulty of telling a convincing and plausible lie and ignore that investigators can make lying verbally difficult by using the appropriate interview techniques, as is discussed in the last section of this chapter.

THEORIES ABOUT THE RELATIONSHIP BETWEEN NONVERBAL BEHAVIOR AND DECEPTION

Zuckerman, DePaulo, and Rosenthal's Multifactor Model

All three deception theories discussed in this section have one important feature in common: The mere fact that people lie will not necessarily affect their nonverbal behavior. Sometimes, however, liars may show different behaviors than do truth tellers. According to Zuckerman, DePaulo, and Rosenthal (1981), three factors could influence cues to deception: (1) emotional reactions, (2) content complexity, and (3) attempted behavioral control. Each of these factors may influence a liar's nonverbal behavior and emphasize a different aspect of deception.

EMOTIONAL REACTIONS

Telling a lie is associated most commonly with three different emotions: guilt, fear, or delight (Ekman, 1985). Liars might feel guilty because they are lying, might be afraid of getting caught, or might be excited about having the opportunity to fool someone. The strength of these emotions depends on the personality of the liar and on the circumstances under which the lie takes place (Ekman, 1985; Vrij, 2008a). Guilt might result in gaze aversion if the liar does not dare to look the target straight in the eye while telling a lie. Fear and excitement might result in signs of stress, such as an increase in movements, an increase in speech hesitations (mm's and errrr's) and speech errors (stutters, repetition of words, omission of words), or a higher pitched voice.

CONTENT COMPLEXITY

Lying in interview settings can be more cognitively demanding than truth telling (Vrij, 2014a, 2015; Vrij et al., 2008). Liars needs to invent a story and must monitor their fabrication so that it is plausible and adheres to everything the observer(s) know or might find out. Moreover, liars must remember what they have said to whom in order to maintain consistency. Liars should also refrain from providing new leads (Vrij, 2008a). Second, liars are typically less likely than truth tellers to take their credibility for granted (Kassin, Appleby, & Torkildson-Perillo, 2010). As such, liars will be more inclined than truth tellers to monitor and control their demeanour in order to appear honest to the investigator (as emphasized in the attempted control process later). Third, because liars do not take credibility for granted, they may monitor the *investigator's* reactions carefully in order to assess whether they appear to be getting away with their lie (Buller & Burgoon, 1996). Fourth, liars may be preoccupied with the task of reminding themselves to role-play (DePaulo et al., 2003). Fifth, deception requires a justification, whereas truth telling does not (Levine, Kim, & Hamel, 2010). People often lie because they are too embarrassed to tell the truth (psychological reasons) or they lie to make money or to avoid punishment (material reason) (DePaulo, Kashy, Kirkendol, Wyer, & Epstein, 1996). Sixth, liars also have to suppress the truth while they are fabricating and this is cognitively demanding (Spence et al., 2001). Finally, whereas activation of the truth often happens automatically, activation of the lie is more intentional and deliberate (Walczyk, Roper, Seemann, & Humphrey, 2003).

The extent to which lying is demanding often depends on the type of lie (Sporer & Schwandt, 2006). Telling an outright lie might be more cognitively challenging than concealing information, and telling an elaborate lie might well be more demanding than providing short yes or no answers. Lying may also be more demanding when the lie is not well prepared or rehearsed. Walczyk, Igou, Dixon, and Tcholakian (2013) list several factors that add cognitive load to truth telling, including when memories have not been accessed for a long time, or when a truthful response requires elaboration or qualification, or the generation of a novel opinion.

Several nonverbal behaviors are related to cognitive load. People engaged in cognitively complex tasks make more speech hesitations (e.g., stutters) and speech errors, speak slower, pause more, and wait longer before giving an answer (Goldman-Eisler, 1968). Cognitive complexity also leads to fewer hand and arm movements because energy is spent on the brain (Ekman & Friesen, 1972), and to more gaze aversion because looking the conversation partner in the eye can be distracting (Doherty-Sneddon, Bruce, Bonner, Longbotham, & Doyle, 2002).

ATTEMPTED BEHAVIORAL CONTROL

Liars may realize that observers pay attention to their behavioral reactions to judge whether they are lying and may, therefore, attempt to control their behavior to appear credible. To be successful, typically, liars must suppress their nervousness, masking evidence of having to think hard, and should also avoid displaying "dishonest-looking" behaviors and replace them with "honest-looking" behaviors (Hocking & Leathers, 1980). This means that liars may need to act, but they must also avoid behavior appearing planned, rehearsed, and lacking in spontaneity. According to this theoretical perspective, liars' motivation and efforts to control their behavior will increase when the stakes (negative consequences of getting caught or positive consequences of succeeding) increase (Ekman, 1985).

DePaulo's Self-Presentational Perspective

Zuckerman et al.'s (1981) perspective predicts that the more liars experience one or more of the three factors (emotion, content complexity, behavioral control), the more likely it is that cues to deception will occur. These factors are present only to a limited extent in the majority of lies that people tell (DePaulo, Kashy, Kirkendol, Wyer, & Epstein, 1996). In her self-presentational perspective, DePaulo (1992; DePaulo, et al., 2003) argues that emotions, content complexity, and behavioral control might also influence *truth tellers'* behavior. Thus, liars may be afraid of not being believed in high-stakes situations, but so will truth tellers, because they too could face negative consequences if they fail to convince others. Given the similarities between liars and truth tellers, this perspective thus predicts that clear, diagnostic nonverbal cues to deception are unlikely to exist.

According to DePaulo et al. (2003), liars and truth tellers will only succeed in their social interaction goals if they appear sincere. The difference between lying and truth telling is that the liar's claim to honesty is illegitimate, and this lack of legitimacy has two implications. First, deceptive self-presentations might be less embraced as truthful self-presentations (e.g., because liars have moral scruples, lack emotional investment in their false claims, or lack the knowledge and experience to back up their deceptive statements convincingly). Second, liars typically experience a greater sense of awareness and deliberateness in their performances than truth tellers, because they may take their credibility less for granted than truth tellers. Trying to appear convincing deliberately might be counterproductive.

Buller and Burgoon's Interpersonal Deception Theory

A third perspective on deception, Buller and Burgoon's (1996) interpersonal deception theory (IDT), postulates that during face-to-face encounters, liars must accomplish numerous communication tasks simultaneously. They must produce a credible verbal message while projecting credible nonverbal behavior simultaneously. They must also manage their emotions, attend to their conversation partner while keeping the dialogue running smoothly, send desired relational messages to their conversation partner and respond appropriately to what they say, and be discreet about any intentions to deceive their partner.

IDT embraces Zuckerman et al.'s (1981) factors (emotion, content complexity, and attempted behavior control) as underlying reasons for cues to deceit (Burgoon, Buller, White, Afifi, & Buslig, 1999). In addition, it emphasizes that when deception occurs in interactive contexts, both liar and receiver mutually influence each other (Burgoon, Buller, Floyd, & Grandpre, 1996). According to IDT, target persons' behavior may influence senders' behavioral displays both directly, via synchrony, and indirectly, because it may trigger behavioral adjustments (Burgoon et al., 1999). Regarding the direct effects, when people communicate with each other, matching and synchrony may take place. People may mirror each other's posture, or they may converge in how quickly and how loudly they speak. They may also reciprocate each other's gazing, nodding, accents, and smiling behavior (DePaulo & Friedman, 1998). Furthermore, the indirect effects are related to feedback from the target person: When liars are exposed to negative feedback from the target person, expressed through either verbal comments or through nonverbal behavior, liars might realize that their performance is lacking credulity. Consequently, liars might respond by making behavioral adjustments to diminish suspicions (Burgoon et al., 1999).

Summary

The three perspectives discussed here make clear that the relationship between lying and deceptive behavior is complex. Zuckerman et al.'s (1981) assumptions that liars might show signs of emotions and cognitive load seem straightforward, yet liars often do not experience emotions and high cognitive load (DePaulo et al., 1996) and DePaulo et al.'s (2003) self-presentation perspective stresses that such experiences are not the exclusive domain of liars. Truth tellers may experience them as well, and, as a result, may also display nonverbal cues associated with emotion or cognitive load. The attempted behavioral control prediction is not straightforward given that the behaviors shown by deceptive senders, as a result of this deliberate control, will depend on both their perceptions of what constitutes a credible nonverbal display and their acting skills in performing this display. Finally, IDT's interactive approach implies that deceptive behavior might be influenced directly by the behavior of the target person, as a result of the nonconscious mimicry of the postures, mannerisms, facial expressions, and other behaviors of one's interaction partners (the so-called "chameleon effect)", or indirectly influenced by the suspicions raised by the target person (Burgoon et al., 1999). This complex relationship between nonverbal communication and deception makes it unlikely that clear, diagnostic, nonverbal cues to deception exist. Deception research, summarized in the next section, has supported this view.

NONVERBAL CUES TO DECEIT: THE EMPIRICAL EVIDENCE

DePaulo et al.'s Meta-analysis

DePaulo et al.'s (2003) meta-analysis of cues to deception is the most compre-hensive review of nonverbal cues to deception to date. It included 116 studies, although not all of them focused on nonverbal cues to deception, and involved 102 different nonverbal cues. Most of the studies were experimental studies where university students lied or told the truth for the sake of the experiment. Sometimes efforts were made to motivate the participants, for example, by promising them a financial reward if they were convincing.

Significant findings emerged for 23 of the 102 nonverbal cues, and these are listed in Table 8.1. Nine of those cues, listed in the bottom half of Table 8.1, were investigated in only a few studies and will not be discussed further. The cues are ranked in terms of their effect sizes. Cohen (1977) suggested that effect sizes of .20, .50, and .80 should be interpreted as small, medium, and large effects, respec-tively. The highest effect sizes were found in the cues that were not often investi-gated (bottom half of Table 8.1), but focusing on the cues that were investigated more often it can be concluded that the effects are small. The largest effect size was found for verbal and vocal immediacy, $d = .55$ and the lowest for facial pleasant-ness, $d = .12$. The average effect size for these 13 significant cues combined was .27, which represents a small effect size, the equivalent of the difference in height between a 15- and 16-year-old girl. Given this, combined with the finding that the majority of cues (79 of the 102 investigated cues) did not show any relationship with deception at all, we can conclude that the relationship between nonverbal cues and deception is faint and unreliable.

Three observations merit attention. First, the most diagnostic cue, verbal and vocal immediacy, is not just a nonverbal cue but a combination of verbal and non-verbal cues. In fact, only 3 of the 13 cues refer to actual nonverbal behaviors (pupil dilation, pitch of voice, and illustrators [movements tied to speech directly and serving to illustrate what is being said verbally; Ekman & Friesen, 1972]), whereas the other 10 cues involve a cluster of nonverbal cues or a mixture of nonverbal and verbal cues. Second, most cues in Table 8.1 consist of a cluster of cues rather than a single cue, which means that deception can be more easily detected from multiple cues than from single cues, see also Hartwig and Bond (2014). Third, the cues people typically associate with deception (gaze aversion, increase of move-ments, inconsistency) (the Global Deception Team, 2006; Strömwall, Granhag, & Hartwig, 2004) are, in fact, not actually related to deception. See DePaulo et al., 2003 for all effect sizes, information about the individual studies, definitions of the nonverbal cues, and the impact of several moderating factors on these cues.

SUPPORT FOR THE THEORETICAL PERSPECTIVES

Although the differences between truth tellers and liars are typically very small, they occur in alignment with the theoretical perspectives discussed previously. Several cues (pupil dilation, nervousness, vocal tension, and pitch) indicate

Table 8.1. Nonverbal Cues to Deception

	d (Effect Size)
verbal and vocal immediacy	−.55
pupil dilation	.39
talking time	−.35
discrepant/ambivalent	.34
verbal and vocal uncertainty	.30
nervous, tense	.27
vocal tension	.26
chin raise	.25
words and phrase repetitions	−.21
pitch, frequency	.21
lip pressing	.16
illustrators	−.14
facial pleasantness	−.12
Cues based on a small number of studies	
changes in foot movements	1.05
pupillary changes	.90
genuine smile	−.70
indifferent, unconcerned	.59
interrupted words and repeated words	.38
specific hand and arm movements	−.36
seems planned, not spontaneous	.35
intensity of facial expression	−.32
direct orientation	−.20

Derived from DePaulo et al. (2003).

NOTE: Positive *d*-scores mean that the cue occurs more when lying than truth telling, whereas negative *d*-scores mean the cue occurs more when truth telling than lying.

that liars may be a little bit tenser than are truth tellers. The findings that liars talk less, make more word and phrase repetitions, and make fewer illustrators suggest that lying is somewhat more cognitively demanding than truth telling. The remaining cues reveal that liars appear somewhat less spontaneous, more ambivalent, less involved, and more uncertain. This fits well with the predictions that liars endorse their statements less convincingly than do truth tellers (DePaulo et al., 2003) and that liars often fail to control their behavior in a convincing manner (DePaulo et al., 2003; Zuckerman et al., 1981).

Since in the overwhelming majority of deception studies no interaction took place between sender and receiver, Buller and Burgoon's (1996) IDT could not be tested. Studies in which an interactional interview style has been employed have provided mixed results regarding whether liars avoid displaying suspicious behaviors (Levine & McCornack, 1996). It might be that liars aim to suppress all behaviors that they believe are suspicious, but they often do not succeed (Buller, Stiff, & Burgoon, 1996; Vrij, 2008a).

REASONS WHY NONVERBAL CUES TO DECEIT ARE FAINT AND UNRELIABLE

The complex relationship between nonverbal behavior and deception, outlined previously, already predicted that research would reveal only a few, and usually weak, relationships between nonverbal cues and deception. There are more explanations for why the relationship between nonverbal behavior and deception appears to be weak, and three of them are discussed in this section.

Individual Differences

Perhaps nonverbal cues to deceit occur on an individual level, that is, different individuals may give their lies away in different ways (DePaulo et al., 2003). Empirical studies present results at a group level rather than at an individual level and therefore such studies, as well as a meta-analysis based on such studies, cannot capture signs of deceit at an individual level and idiosyncratic cues do not become apparent. It is debatable whether this is a serious limitation, as it is unknown how useful idiosyncratic cues are for practitioners who try to detect deceit. Idiosyncratic cues imply that each individual displays an almost unique set of cues to deceit, without a practitioner knowing which cues these actually are for each individual they assess.

Situational Differences

It has been argued that cues to deceit are more likely to occur when the stakes are high rather than low (Ekman, 1985; Frank & Svetieva, 2012; O'Sullivan, Frank, Hurley, & Tiwana, 2009). In high-stakes situations, when the consequences of being caught out are serious, liars may feel stronger emotions, may experience more cognitive demand, and may be more motivated to manage their behavior to appear credible. In their meta-analysis, Hartwig and Bond (2014) examined the detectability of lies based on nonverbal cues and compared settings that elicit strong emotions with settings of a more trivial nature. No difference was found in the detectability of lies between these two settings. The same meta-analysis did not find an effect for motivation either: Lies were equally detectable when the senders were unmotivated as when they were highly motivated. The reason for these null effects is that emotion and motivation will also affect truth tellers. For example, liars may be more likely to display nervous behaviors when the stakes are high, but so are truth tellers (Bond & Fahey, 1987; Ofshe & Leo, 1997), which means that the difference between them will not change.

Same Experiences and Same Strategies

Perhaps differences in nonverbal behavior between truth tellers and liars are weak because of the similarities between them. This refers to both their experiences and their strategies to appear convincing. As DePaulo's self-presentational perspective emphasized, emotions, content complexity, and behavioral control are not the sole domain of liars, they may also influence truth tellers and their behavior. Apart for having similar experiences, truth tellers and liars also appear to have the same nonverbal strategy when they try to come across as being honest. That is, both truth tellers and liars will attempt to avoid displaying nervous nonverbal behaviors and will try to replace this by nonverbal behaviors that appear more sincere (e.g., look someone into the eye, try to sit still) (Hartwig, Granhag, Strömwall, & Doering, 2010; Vrij, Mann, Leal, & Granhag, 2010).

The Behavior Analysis Interview and Observing Facial Expressions of Emotions

The BAI is a set of 15 predetermined standardized questions designed to elicit differential responses from innocent and guilty suspects at the outset of an investigative interview (Inbau et al., 2013). It is believed to be one of the two most commonly taught questioning methods in the United States (Colwell, Miller, Lyons, & Miller, 2006). BAI forms an important first step in police interviewing. Police investigators who are reasonably certain of a suspect's guilt may submit the suspect to persuasive interrogation techniques meant to break down the suspect's resistance. Since such interrogation techniques may lead to false confessions, it is important not to submit innocent suspects to these techniques. The BAI is meant to inform investigators about the innocence or guilt of suspects.

The BAI interview includes questions such as: "Did you commit the crime?," and "And what do you think should happen to the person who committed the crime?"

Despite its name, *behavior* analysis interview, the BAI predicts that guilty and innocent suspects will differ in their nonverbal behavior and also in their verbal responses, but in this chapter the focus is on the nonverbal responses. It is assumed that liars feel more uncomfortable than truth tellers in police interviews. Guilty suspects should therefore display more nervous behaviors such as crossing their legs, shifting about in their chairs, performing grooming behaviors, or looking away from the investigator. However, none of these nonverbal cues emerged as a diagnostic cue to deceit in DePaulo's et al.'s meta-analysis, whiuch means that the BAI lacks empirical support.

Supporters of the BAI refer to a single study, a field study by Horvath, Jayne and Buckley (1994). In that study, 60 suspects were interviewed by four BAI-trained detectives via the BAI protocol, and these detectives made veracity judgements after completing each interview. High-accuracy scores emerged, but the ground truth (which suspects were actually lying and which ones were actually telling the truth) was lacking. In fact, ground truth was established in only two out of 60 cases. This is a serious limitation of this study, also acknowledged by the authors themselves: They concluded that "If it were possible to develop ground truth criteria in a large number of cases such as occurred in these two instances, the interpretation of findings would be less problematic" (p. 805). If we disregard this study, no empirical support for the BAI protocol exists.

Over the years Paul Ekman has argued that facial expressions of emotion betray liars (Ekman, 1985/2001). According to Ekman, aspects of facial communication are beyond control and can betray a deceiver's true emotion via microexpressions (lasting 1/25 to 1/5 of a second) of that emotion. The method became known to the public through the fictional character Dr. Cal Lightman, who successfully uses this method to catch liars in the American crime drama TV series *Lie to Me*. Ekman has claimed that his system of lie detection can be taught to anyone, with an accuracy of more than 95% (*New York Times Magazine*, February 5, 2006; see also *Washington Post*, October 29, 2006 for a similar statement). However, Ekman has never published empirical data to back up this claim. That is, he has not published data showing that observers achieve this accuracy; neither has he published data showing that facial expressions of emotions are a diagnostic indicator of deceit. Regarding the latter, Porter and ten Brinke (2008) found that microexpressions only occurred in 14 out of the 697 analyzed expressions, and that 6 of those 14 expressions were displayed by truth tellers. Perhaps we should read Ekman's 95% claim differently. Perhaps it does not suggest that someone who is taught the method can classify correctly 95% of truth tellers and liars. Perhaps it merely suggests that people who are taught the method can spot microexpressions with 95% accuracy, which is an entirely different claim. In any case, there is no empirical support for Ekman's lie detection method, and we should consider *Lie to Me* and Dr. Cal Lightman's achievements in the drama series as fiction.

PEOPLE'S LIE-DETECTING SKILLS WHEN OBSERVING NONVERBAL BEHAVIOR

Laypersons' Lie Detection in Strangers

In a typical lie detection study, observers (normally undergraduate students) are shown video clips of strangers who are either lying or telling the truth. They are asked to indicate after each clip whether the person was lying or telling the truth. The observers have received no training in lie detection and there is no opportunity for them to check the veracity of the statement via physical evidence, third parties, and so on. The only source of information is the verbal and nonverbal behavior displayed in the videos. In such a study, simply guessing whether the person lied or spoke the truth would result in an accuracy rate (percentage of correct classifications) of 50%.

Bond and DePaulo (2006) carried out a meta-analysis regarding people's ability to detect truth and lies. This meta-analysis included 206 samples with almost 25,000 observers and revealed an average accuracy rate of 54% in correctly classifying truth tellers and liars. Deception can be judged via visual cues (video), auditory cues (audio), or via a combination of visual and auditory cues (audiovisual), and Bond and DePaulo (2006) examined the ability to detect truths and deceit through these different mediums separately. The results revealed that the lowest accuracy rates were obtained through the video channel (52% accuracy) followed by the audiovisual channel (56%) and audio channel (63%). The video channel revealed significantly lower results than the audio and audiovisual channels, whereas the latter two did not differ from each other. These findings demonstrate that switching off the sound makes lie detection worse.

Professionals' Lie Detection in Strangers

Vrij (2008a) reviewed 28 studies in which the observers in the lie detection studies were professionals (e.g., police officers, law enforcement, parole officers) rather than laypersons. The same paradigm was used as with laypersons: The professionals were shown video clips of strangers who were either lying or telling the truth and were asked to indicate after each clip whether the person was lying or telling the truth. The accuracy rate of these professionals was 56%, similar to the 54% that was obtained with laypersons. The main difference that emerged between professionals and laypersons was in confidence: Professionals were more confident in their decision making than students.

Why Are People Poor Lie Detectors When Observing Nonverbal Behavior

There are two compelling reasons as to why observers perform poorly in lie detection tests. The first reason is that the task is difficult because, as outlined previously, differences between the truth tellers and liars are typically very small. The second reason is that observers look for the wrong cues and fail to spot differences that actually exist. For example, observers frequently report that they based their decision on whether or not the person they observed showed gaze aversion (Mann, Vrij, & Bull, 2004), but gaze aversion is not actually related to deception. In their meta-analysis, Hartwig and Bond (2011) examined these two possibilities and concluded that people perform poorly because the differences between truth tellers and liars are too small to make the task achievable (the first explanation). This also explains why training people to detect lies, by informing them about "diagnostic nonverbal cues to deceit," has hardly any effect (Frank & Feeley, 2003; Hauch, Sporer, Michael, & Meissner, 2014; Vrij, 2008a).

VERBAL LIE DETECTION

Verbal lie detection has more potential than nonverbal lie detection. First, the DePaulo et al. (2003) meta-analysis showed that verbal cues are more diagnostic cues to deceit than nonverbal cues. In that meta-analysis, 38 verbal cues ands 49 nonverbal cues were included in the main analyses (Tables 3 to 7). The average effect size (d) for the verbal cues ($M = .20$, $SD = .15$, 95% CI [.16,.24]) was significantly larger than the average effect size for the nonverbal cues ($M = .11$, $SD = .11$, 95% CI [.07,.14]), $F(1, 85) = 10.39$, $p = .002$, $eta^2 = .11$, and this difference in effect sizes was substantial ($d = .69$). Second, a meta-analysis about the effect of training in "cues to deceit" on trainees' ability to detect truths and lies revealed that training in verbal cues yielded better results than training in nonverbal cues (Hauch, Sporer, Michael, & Meissner, 2014). Third, although nonverbal strategies to make an honest impression do not differ from each other, verbal strategies between truth tellers and liars do differ. Truth tellers are inclined to "tell it all," whereas liars are inclined to stay vague and keep it simple (Hartwig, Granhag, & Strömwall, 2007; Hartwig, Granhag, Strömwall, & Doering, 2010; Strömwall, Hartwig, & Granhag, 2006; Vrij, Mann, Leal, & Granhag, 2010). This difference in strategy explains why liars are often less detailed than truth tellers (DePaulo et al., 2003; Vrij, 2008a). Liars are less detailed because they lack the imagination to fabricate the same amount of detail that truth tellers actually experienced and reported, or are reluctant to provide detail because they are afraid that these details may give leads to investigators to detect their lies (Nahari, Vrij, & Fisher, 2014a, b; Vrij, 2008a).

The final reason why verbal lie detection has more potential than nonverbal lie detection is because, as research has shown, specific interview protocols can be employed that enhance the differences in verbal cues between truth tellers and liars. No research is published in which specific interview protocols enhanced the differences between truth tellers and liars in nonverbal cues. One of such interview protocols that enhance the verbal differences between truth tellers and liars is the Verifiability Approach, which is based on two assumptions. First, liars prefer to provide many details because they are aware that accounts rich in detail are more likely to be believed (Bell & Loftus, 1989). Second, liars also prefer to avoid mentioning too many details out of fear that investigators will check such details (Nahari, Vrij, & Fisher, 2012). A strategy that compromises both motivations is to provide details that cannot be verified. This was indeed found in all six Verifiability Approach studies published to date (Harvey, Vrij, Nahari, & Ludwig, 2017; Nahari & Vrij, 2014; Nahari, Vrij, & Fisher, 2014a, b; Nahari, Leal, Vrij, Warmelink, & Vernham, 2014; Vrij, Nahari, Isitt, & Leal, 2016). Liars choose to provide details that are difficult to verify (e.g., "Several people walked by when I sat there") and avoid providing details that are easy to verify (e.g., "I phoned my friend Zvi at 10.30 this morning"). The accuracy rates in these studies ranged from 61% to 88%. Intriguingly, research has shown that the verifiability effect became stronger when interviewees were informed about the lie detection method, that is, when they were informed that the investigator would read their statement carefully and would check whether or not the details they provided could be verified (Harvey et al., 2017, Nahari et al., 2014b). Truth tellers who received this instruction included more verifiable details into their account than truth tellers who did not receive this instruction, whereas this instruction had no or a lesser effect on liars. See Vrij and Nahari (2016) for an overview of the Verifiability Approach.

A second approach that enhances verbal differences between truth tellers and liars is the cognitive lie detection approach, which consists of three parts: Imposing cognitive load, encouraging interviewees to say more, and asking unexpected questions (Vrij, 2014, 2015; Vrij, Fisher, & Blank, 2017; Vrij, Leal, Mann, Vernham, & Brankaert, 2015). Imposing cognitive load is based on the well-established empirical finding that in interview settings lying is typically more mentally taxing than truth telling (see for example fMRI research, Christ et al., 2009; Vrij & Ganis, 2014). Imposing cognitive load refers to investigators' interventions aimed at making the interview setting mentally even more difficult. Liars, who require more cognitive resources than truth tellers, will have fewer cognitive resources left over. If cognitive demand is further raised, which could be achieved by making additional requests, such as asking interviewees to recall their stories in reverse order or engaging interviewees in a second unrelated task (e.g., driving a car) while conducting the interview, liars are less able than truth tellers to cope with these additional requests.

Regarding encouraging interviewees to provide more information, it will help truth tellers if they provide much information, because the richer an account is perceived to be in detail, the more likely it is to be believed. Moreover, the additional information truth tellers provide could give leads to investigators to check. As explained earlier, liars may lack the imagination to fabricate the same amount of detail that truth tellers actually experienced and reported or may be reluctant to do so out of fear that this gives leads to investigators to detect their lies. Therefore, techniques to encourage interviewees to say more, which include letting them listen to an example of a detailed statement at the beginning of the interview, using a supportive interviewer, and mimicking the posture of the interviewee, lead to truth tellers adding more (plausible) detail than liars.

A consistent finding in the deception literature is that liars prepare themselves for anticipated interviews by preparing possible answers to questions they expect to be asked (e.g., Hartwig, Granhag, & Strömwall, 2007). Preparing for answers has a limitation, as it will be fruitful only if liars correctly anticipate which questions will be asked. Investigators can exploit this limitation by asking questions that liars do not anticipate. Though liars can refuse to answer unexpected questions by saying "I don't know" or "I can't remember," such responses will create suspicion if they are about central aspects of the target event. A liar, therefore, has little option other than to fabricate a plausible answer on the spot, which is cognitively demanding. For liars, expected questions should be easier to answer than unexpected questions, because liars can give their planned and rehearsed answers to the expected questions but they need to fabricate answers to the unexpected questions. The difference liars experience in cognitive load while answering these two sets of questions should become evident in their verbal responses. In contrast, truth tellers experience similar levels of cognitive load while answering expected and unexpected questions, and they should produce more comparable answers to the expected and unexpected questions than liars. Research supports the unexpected questions approach, and examples of unexpected questions include spatial questions, questions about processes (e.g., planning of a trip) rather than outcomes (e.g., purpose of a trip), and asking the same question twice in different formats.

A meta-analysis of cognitive lie detection showed support for the approach. The ability to distinguish between truth tellers and liars (results of human judges and objective criteria assessments combined) was significantly higher in interviews where cognitive lie detection techniques were utilized (71%) than in the standard control conditions (56%) (Vrij, Fisher, & Blank, 2017). In addition, in a training study UK police detectives received 1 day training in cognitive lie detection, after which they were asked to use these techniques in an interview with a mock suspect (either a truth teller or liar). In the control condition, UK police detectives who did not receive this training interviewed a mock suspect in the way they would normally do (Vrij, Leal, Mann, Vernham, & Brankaert, 2015). The accuracy rates of correctly classifying truth tellers and liars was significantly higher among the trained detectives (74%) than the untrained detectives (59%).

One final point about verbal lie detection merits attention. Verbal lie detection is strongly linked with the core aspect of investigative interviewing: to gather information from an interviewee (Bull, 2010; Fisher, 2010: Vrij, Hope, & Fisher, 2014). This becomes perhaps most evident in the encouraging interviewees to say more approach (which prompts truth tellers to provide more information) and the verifiability approach (which prompts truth tellers to provide more checkable information). Therefore, verbal lie detection simultaneously fulfills two aims of an interview: to gather information and to detect deceit. In contrast, nonverbal lie detection focuses on detecting deceit only. In addition, since it is cognitively difficult to focus on someone's behavior and speech at the same time (Vrij, 2008a), it could be that investigators who examine nonverbal cues do not listen carefully to what the interviewee says, resulting in missing vital information and/or not being able to ask adequate follow-up questions. This would mean that the quality of an interview is better if investigators are engaged in verbal lie detection compared with nonverbal lie detection. This hypothesis merits attention from deception researchers.

CONCLUSION

People pay considerable attention to nonverbal behavior when attempting to detect deceit, in part because they believe that nonverbal behavior is more difficult to control than speech content. Research has shown that nonverbal cues to deceit are faint and unreliable, and there is no evidence that popular nonverbal lie detection tools such as the BAI or observing facial expressions of emotions actually work. The reasons why nonverbal behaviors are faint are that (1) the underlying mechanisms for nonverbal cues to deceit (emotions, content complexity, attempted behavioral control) also influence truth tellers, and (2) when truth tellers and liars attempt to appear convincing they use the same nonverbal strategies. Verbal cues to deceit have more potential because (1) truth tellers and liars pursue different verbal strategies and (2) interview protocols can be employed that enhance the verbal differences between truth tellers and liars.

REFERENCES

Ambady, N., Bernieri, F. J., & Richeson, J. A. (2000). Toward a histology of social behaviour: Judgmental accuracy from thin slices of the behavioural stream. *Advances in Experimental Social Pxychology, 32,* 201–271.

Atkinson, M. (2005). *Lend me your ears.* New York: Oxford University Press.

Bell, B. E., & Loftus, E. F. (1989). Trivial persuasion in the courtroom: The power of (a few) minor details. *Journal of Personality and Social Psychology, 56,* 669–679. doi: 10.1037//0022-3514.56.5.669

Bond, C. F., & DePaulo, B. M. (2006). Accuracy of deception judgements. *Personality and Social Psychology Review, 10,* 214–234. doi: 10.1207/s15327957pspr1003_2

Bond, C. F., & Fahey, W. E. (1987). False suspicion and the misperception of deceit. *British Journal of Social Psychology, 26,* 41–46. doi: 10.1111/j.2044-8309.1987.tb00759.x

Bull, R. (2010). The investigative interviewing of children and other vulnerable witnesses: Psychological research and working/professional practice. *Legal and Criminological Psychology, 15,* 5–24. doi: 10.1348/014466509X440160

Buller, D. B., & Burgoon, J. K. (1996). Interpersonal deception theory. *Communication Theory, 6,* 203–242. doi: 10.1111/j.14682885.1996.tb00127.x

Buller, D. B., Stiff, J. B., & Burgoon, J. K. (1996). Behavioral adaptation in deceptive transactions. Fact or fiction: A reply to Levine and McCornack. *Human Communication Research, 22,* 589–603.

Burgoon, J. K., Buller, D. B., Floyd, K., & Grandpre, J. (1996). Deceptive realities: Sender, receiver, and observer perspectives in deceptive conversations. *Communication Research, 23,* 724–748.

Burgoon, J. K., Buller, D. B., White, C. H., Afifi, W., & Buslig, A. L. S. (1999). The role of conversation involvement in deceptive interpersonal interactions. *Personality and Social Psychology Bulletin, 25,* 669–685.

Christ, S., E., Van Essen, D. C. Watson, J. M., Brubaker, L. E., & McDermott, K. B. (2009). The Contributions of Prefrontal Cortex and Executive Control to Deception: Evidence from Activation Likelihood Estimate Meta-analyses. *Cerebral Cortex, 19,* 1557–1566. doi:10.1093/cercor/bhn189.

Cohen, J. (1977). *Statistical power analysis for the behavioral sciences.* New York: Academic Press.

Colwell, L. H., Miller, H. A., Lyons, P. M., & Miller, R. S. (2006). The training of law enforcement officers in detecting deception: A survey of current practices and suggestions for improving accuracy. *Police Quarterly, 9,* 275–290.

DePaulo, B. M. (1992). Nonverbal behavior and self-presentation. *Psychological Bulletin, 111,* 203–243.

DePaulo, B. M., & Friedman, H. S. (1998). Nonverbal communication. In D. T. Gilbert, S. T. Fiske, & G. Lindzey (Eds.), *The handbook of social psychology* (pp. 3–40). Boston: McGraw-Hill.

DePaulo, B. M., Kashy, D. A., Kirkendol, S. E., Wyer, M. M., & Epstein, J. A. (1996). Lying in everyday life. *Journal of Personality and Social Psychology, 70,* 979–995. doi: 10.1037/0022-3514.70.5.979

DePaulo, B. M., & Kirkendol, S. E. (1989). The motivational impairment effect in the communication of deception. In J. C. Yuille (Ed.), *Credibility assessment* (pp. 51–70). Dordrecht, the Netherlands: Kluwer.

DePaulo, B. M., Lindsay, J. L., Malone, B. E., Muhlenbruck, L., Charlton, K., & Cooper, H. (2003). Cues to deception. *Psychological Bulletin, 129*, 74–118. doi: 10.1037/0033-2909.129.1.74

DePaulo, B. M., & Morris, W. L. (2004). Discerning lies from truths: Behavioural cues to deception and the indirect pathway of intuition. In P. A. Granhag & L. A. Strömwall (Eds.), *Deception detection in forensic contexts* (pp. 15–40). Cambridge: Cambridge University Press.

Doherty-Sneddon, G., Bruce, V., Bonner, L., Longbotham, S., & Doyle, C. (2002). Development of gaze aversion as disengagement of visual information. *Developmental Psychology, 38*, 438–445.

Ekman, P. (1981). Mistakes when deceiving. *Annals of the New York Academy of Sciences, 364*, 269–278.

Ekman, P. (1985). *Telling lies: Clues to deceit in the marketplace, politics and marriage.* New York: W. W. Norton. (Reprinted with some additional new chapters in 1992, 2001, and 2009.)

Ekman, P., & Friesen, W. V. (1972). Hand movements. *Journal of Communication, 22*, 353–374.

Fisher, R. P. (2010). Interviewing cooperative witnesses. *Legal and Criminological Psychology, 15*, 25–38. doi: 10.1348/135532509X441891

Frank, M. G., & Feeley, T. H. (2003). To catch a liar: Challenges for research in lie detection training. *Journal of Applied Communication Research, 31*, 58–75. doi: 10.1080/00909880305377

Frank, M. G., & Svetieva, E. (2012). Lies worth catching involve both emotion and cognition: Commentary of Vrij and Granhag (2012). *Journal of Applied Research in Memory and Cognition, 1*, 131–133.

Freud, S. (1959). *Collected papers.* New York: Basic Books.

The Global Deception Team (2006). A world of lies. *Journal of Cross-Cultural Psychology, 37*, 60–74. doi: 10.1177/0022022105282295

Goldman-Eisler, F. (1968). *Psycholinguistics: Experiments in spontaneous speech.* New York: Doubleday.

Granhag, P.A., & Hartwig, M. (2008). A new theoretical perspective on deception detection: On the psychology of instrumental mind-reading. *Psychology, Crime & Law, 14*, 189–200. Doi: 10.1080/10683160701645181

Granhag, P. A., & Hartwig, M. (2015). The Strategic Use of Evidence (SUE) technique: A conceptual overview. In P. A. Granhag, A. Vrij, & B. Verschuere (Eds.), *Deception detection: Current challenges and new approaches* (pp. 231–251). Chichester, UK: Wiley.

Hartwig, M., & Bond, C. F. (2011). Why do lie-catchers fail? A lens model meta-analysis of human lie judgments. *Psychological Bulletin, 137*, 643–659. doi: 10.1037/a0023589

Hartwig, M., & Bond, C. F. (2014). Lie detection from multiple cues: A meta-analysis. *Applied Cognitive Psychology, 28*, 661–667. doi: 10.1002/acp.3052

Hartwig, M., Granhag, P. A., & Luke, T. (2014). Strategic use of evidence during investigative interviews: The state of the science. In: Raskin, D. C., Honts, C. R., Kircher, J. C. (Eds.), *Credibility assessment: Scientific research and applications* (pp. 1–36). San Diego, CA: Academic Press.

Hartwig, M., Granhag, P. A., & Strömwall, L. (2007). Guilty and innocent suspects' strategies during police interrogations. *Psychology, Crime, & Law, 13*, 213–227. doi: 10.1080/10683160600750264

Hartwig, M., Granhag, P. A., Strömwall, L, & Doering, N. (2010). Impression and information management: On the strategic self-regulation of innocent and guilty suspects. *The Open Criminology Journal, 3*, 10–16.

Harvey, A., Vrij, A., Nahari, G., & Ludwig, K. (2017). Applying the Verifiability Approach to insurance claims settings: Exploring the effect of the information protocol. *Legal and Criminological Psychology, 22*, 47–59.

Hauch, V., Sporer, S. L., Michael, S. W., & Meissner, C. A. (2014). Does training improve the detection of deception? A meta-analysis. *Communication Research* published online May 25, 2014 doi: 10.1177/0093650214534974

Hocking, J. E., & Leathers, D. G. (1980). Nonverbal indicators of deception: A new theoretical perspective. *Communication Monographs, 47*, 119–131.

Horvath, F., Blair, J. P., & Buckley, J. P. (2008). The Behavioral Analysis Interview: Clarifying the practice, theory and understanding of its use and effectiveness. *International Journal of Police Science and Management, 10*, 101–118.

Horvath, F., Jayne, B., & Buckley, J. (1994). Differentiation of truthful and deceptive criminal suspects in behavioral analysis interviews. *Journal of Forensic Sciences, 39*, 793–807.

Houston, P., Floyd, M., & Carnicero, S. (2012). *Spy the lie.* New York: St. Martin's Press.

Inbau, F. E., Reid, J. E., Buckley, J. P., & Jayne, B. C. (2013). *Criminal interrogation and confessions* (5th ed.). Burlington, MA: Jones & Bartlett Learning.

Kassin, S. M. (2005). On the psychology of confessions: Does innocence put innocents at risk? *American Psychologist, 60*, 215–228. doi: 10.1037/0003-066X.60.3.215

Kassin, S. M., Appleby, S. C., & Torkildson-Perillo, J. (2010). Interviewing suspects: Practice, science, and future directions. *Legal and Criminological Psychology* (Special issue "What works in investigative psychology"), *15*, 39–56. doi: 10.1348/135532509X449361

Kraut, R. E. (1978). Verbal and nonverbal cues in the perception of lying. *Journal of Personality and Social Psychology, 36*, 380–391.

Levine, T. R., Kim, R. K., & Hamel, L. M. (2010). People lie for a reason: Three experiments documenting the principle of veracity. *Communication Research Reports, 27*, 271–285. doi: org/10.1080/08824096.2010.496334

Levine, T. R., & McCornack, S. A. (1996). Can behavioral adaptation explain the probing effect? *Human Communication Research, 22*, 604–613.

Mann, S., Vrij, A., & Bull, R. (2004). Detecting true lies: Police officers' ability to detect deceit. *Journal of Applied Psychology, 89*, 137–149. doi: org/10.1037/0021-9010.89.1.137

Meissner, C. A., & Kassin, S. M. (2002). "He's guilty!": Investigator bias in judgments of truth and deception. *Law and Human Behavior, 26*, 469–480. doi: 10.1023/A:1020278620751

Meyer, P. (2010). *Lie spotting: Proven techniques to detect deception.* New York: St. Martin's Press.

Millar, M. G., & Millar, K. U. (1995). Detection of deception in familiar and unfamiliar persons: The effects of information restriction. *Journal of Nonverbal Behavior, 19*, 69–84.

Moston, S. J., Stephenson, G. M., & Williamson, T. M. (1992). The effects of case characteristics on suspect behaviour during police questioning. *British Journal of Criminology, 32*, 23–39.

Münsterberg, H. (1908). *On the witness stand: Essays on psychology and crime.* New York: Doubleday.

Nahari, G., Leal, S., Vrij, A., Warmelink, L., & Vernham, Z. (2014). Did somebody see it? Applying the verifiability approach to insurance claims interviews. *Journal of Investigative Psychology and Offender Profiling, 11*, 237–243. DOI: 10.1002/jip.1417.

Nahari, G., & Vrij, A. (2014). Can I borrow your alibi? The applicability of the verifiability approach to the case of an alibi witness. *Journal of Applied Research in Memory and Cognition, 3*, 89–94. doi: 10.1016/J/JARMAC.2014.04.005

Nahari, G., Vrij, A., & Fisher, R. P. (2012). Does the truth come out in the writing? SCAN as a lie detection tool. *Law & Human Behavior, 36*, 68–76. doi: 10.1007/s10979-011-9264-6

Nahari, G., Vrij, A., & Fisher, R. P. (2014a). Exploiting liars' verbal strategies by examining the verifiability of details. *Legal and Criminological Psychology, 19*, 227–239. doi: 10.1111/j.2044-8333.2012.02069.x

Nahari, G., Vrij, A., & Fisher, R. P. (2014b). The Verifiability Approach: Countermeasures facilitate its ability to discriminate between truths and lies. *Applied Cognitive Psychology, 28*, 122–128. doi: 10.1002/acp.2974

Noller, P. (1985). Video primacy—a further look. *Journal of Nonverbal Behavior, 9*, 28–47.

Ofshe, R. J., & Leo, R. A. (1997). The decision to confess falsely: Rational choice and irrational action. *Denver University Law Review, 74*, 979–1112.

O'Sullivan, M., Frank, M. G., Hurley, C. M., & Tiwana, J. (2009). Police lie detection accuracy: The effect of lie scenario. *Law and Human Behavior, 33*, 542–543.

Park, H. S., Levine, T. R., McCornack, S. A., Morrisson, K., & Ferrara, M. (2002). How people really detect lies. *Communication Monographs, 69*, 144–157.

Reid, J. E., & Arther, R. O. (1953). Behavior symptoms of lie-detector subjects. *Journal of Criminal Law, Criminology and Police Science, 44*, 104–108.

Reinhard, M. A., & Sporer, S. L. (2008). Verbal and nonverbal behaviour as a basis for credibility attribution: The impact of task involvement and cognitive capacity. *Journal of Experimental Social Psychology, 44*, 477–488.

Spence, S. A., Farrow, T. F. D., Herford, A. E., Wilkinson, I. D., Zheng, Y., & Woodruff, P. W. R. (2001). Behavioural and functional anatomical correlates of deception in humans. *Neuroreport: For Rapid Communication of Neuroscience Research, 12*, 2849–2853. doi: 10.1097/00001756-200109170-00019

Sporer, S. L., & Schwandt, B. (2006). Paraverbal indicators of deception: A meta-analytic synthesis. *Applied Cognitive Psychology, 20*, 421–446. doi: 10.1002/acp.1190

Strömwall, L. A., Granhag, P. A., & Hartwig, M. (2004). Practitioners' beliefs about deception. In P. A. Granhag & L. A. Strömwall (Eds.), *Deception detection in forensic contexts* (pp. 229–250). Cambridge: Cambridge University Press.

Strömwall, L. A., Granhag, P. A., & Jonsson, A. C. (2003). Deception among pairs: 'Let's say we had lunch together and hope they will swallow it'. *Psychology, Crime, & Law, 9*, 109–124.

Strömwall, L. A., Hartwig, M., & Granhag, P. A. (2006). To act truthfully: Nonverbal behaviour and strategies during a police interrogation. *Psychology, Crime, & Law, 12*, 207–219. doi: 10.1080/1068316051233 1331328.

Trovillo, P. V. (1939a). A history of lie detection, I. *Journal of Criminal Law and Criminology, 29*, 848–881.

Trovillo, P. V. (1939b). A history of lie detection, II. *Journal of Criminal Law and Criminology*, 30, 104–119.

Vredeveldt, A., van Koppen, P. J., & Granhag, P. A. (2014). The inconsistent suspect: A systematic review of different types of consistency in truth tellers and liars. In R. Bull (Ed.), *Investigative interviewing* (pp. 183–207). New York: Springer Science+Business Media. doi 10.1007/978-1-4614-9642-7_10

Vrij, A. (2008a). *Detecting lies and deceit: Pitfalls and opportunities* (2nd ed.). Chichester, UK: John Wiley and Sons.

Vrij, A. (2008b). Nonverbal dominance versus verbal accuracy in lie detection: A plea to change police practice. *Criminal Justice and Behavior, 35*, 1323–1336.

Vrij, A. (2014a). Interviewing to detect deception. *European Psychologist, 19*, 184–195 doi: 10.1027/1016-9040/a000201

Vrij, A. (2014b). Myths and opportunities in verbal and nonverbal lie detection. In M. St Yves (Ed.), *Investigative interviewing: The essentials* (pp. 226–239). Toronto, Canada: Thomson Reuters.

Vrij, A. (2015). A cognitive approach to lie detection. In P. A. Granhag, A. Vrij, & B. Verschuere (Eds.), *Deception detection: Current challenges and new approaches* (pp. 205–229). Chichester, UK: Wiley.

Vrij, A., Fisher, R., Blank, H. (2017). A cognitive approach to lie detection: A meta-analysis. *Legal and Criminological Psychology, 22*, 1–21. doi: 10.1111/lcrp.12088

Vrij, A., & Ganis, G. (2014). Theories in deception and lie detection. In: D. C. Raskin, C. R. Honts, & J. C. Kircher (Eds.), *Credibility Assessment: Scientific Research and Applications* (pp. 301–374). Oxford, UK: Academic Press.

Vrij, A., & Granhag, P. A. (2007). Interviewing to detect deception. In S. A. Christianson (Ed.), *Offenders' memories of violent crimes* (pp. 279–304). Chichester, UK: John Wiley & Sons, Ltd.

Vrij, A., & Granhag, P. A. (2012). Eliciting cues to deception and truth: What matters are the questions asked. *Journal of Applied Research in Memory and Cognition, 1*, 110–117. doi.org/10.1016/j.jarmac.2012.02.004

Vrij, A., Granhag, P. A., & Porter, S. B. (2010). Pitfalls and opportunities in nonverbal and verbal lie detection. *Psychological Science in the Public Interest, 11*, 89–121. doi: 10.1177/1529100610390861

Vrij, A., Hope, L., & Fisher, R. P. (2014). Eliciting reliable information in investigative interviews. *Policy Insights from Behavioral and Brain Sciences, 1*, 129–136. doi: 10.1177/2372732214548592

Vrij, A., Leal, S., Mann, S., Vernham, Z., & Brankaert, F. (2015). Translating theory into practice: Evaluating a cognitive lie detection training workshop. *Journal of Applied Research in Memory and Cognition, 4*, 110–120. doi: 10.1016/j.jarmac.2015.02.002

Vrij, A., & Mann, S. (2001). Telling and detecting lies in a high-stake situation: The case of a convicted murderer. *Applied Cognitive Psychology, 15*, 187–203. doi: 10.1002/1099-0720(200103/04)15:2<187:AID-ACP696>3.0.CO;2-A

Vrij, A., Mann, S., Fisher, R., Leal, S., Milne, B., & Bull, R. (2008). Increasing cognitive load to facilitate lie detection: The benefit of recalling an event in reverse order. *Law and Human Behavior, 32*, 253–265. doi: 10.1007/s10979-007-9103-y

Vrij, A., Mann, S., Leal, S., & Granhag, P. A. (2010). Getting into the minds of pairs of liars and truth tellers: An examination of their strategies. *The Open Criminology Journal, 3*, 17–22. doi: 10.2174/1874917801003010017

Vrij, A., & Nahari, G. (2016). Verbal lie detection. Manuscript submitted for publication.

Vrij, A., Nahari, G., Isitt, R., & Leal, S. (2016). Using the verifiability lie detection approach in an insurance claim setting. *Journal of Investigative Psychology and Offender Profiling, 13*, 183–197.

Walczyk, J. J., Igou, F. P., Dixon, A. P., & Tcholakian, T. (2013). Advancing lie detection by inducing cognitive load on liars: A review of relevant theories and techniques guided by lessons from polygraph-based approaches. Frontiers in Psychology, 4, 14. doi: 10.3389/fpsyg.2013.00014

Walczyk, J. J., Roper, K. S., Seemann, E., & Humphrey, A. M. (2003). Cognitive mechanisms underlying lying to questions: Response time as a cue to deception. *Applied Cognitive Psychology, 17*, 755–774.

Zuckerman, M., DePaulo, B. M., & Rosenthal, R. (1981). Verbal and nonverbal communication of deception. In L. Berkowitz (Ed.), *Advances in experimental social psychology* (Vol. 14, 1–57). New York: Academic Press.

9

Building a Case

The Role of Empirically Based Interviewing
Techniques in Case Construction

TIMOTHY J. LUKE, MARIA HARTWIG, LAURE BRIMBAL,
AND PÄR ANDERS GRANHAG

In the first published American interrogation manual, Kidd (1940) succinctly wrote, "The test of any police procedure is: Does it work?" (p. vii). It is difficult to disagree with such an intuitive standard. Of course we want procedures that work. However, the simplicity of the question "Does it work?" belies the complexities of how we know whether or the extent to which a given practice works. Moreover, what does it mean for a practice to "work"?

In this chapter, we want to grapple with the issue of what it means for an investigative technique to "work." Although researchers have made substantial progress in developing investigative techniques, particularly in the realm of interviews and interrogations, we believe that research hitherto has viewed these interactions in a decontextualized fashion, neglecting the broader settings in which the techniques play a role. This in turn has led to what we believe to be restricted definitions and measurements of effectiveness.

This chapter is, in part, aimed at providing researchers and practitioners with a suggested lens through which to consider research on investigative interviewing and deception detection, with a particular focus on the question of how to evaluate the effectiveness of various techniques. This lens places special focus on the notion of *case construction*. In brief, case construction refers to the processes involved in the investigation of crime, interpretation of evidence, and prosecution of a defendant. While there has been some discussion of case construction in criminology and sociology of law (e.g., Smith, 1997), to our knowledge, psycho-legal research has almost entirely neglected this notion. Here, we discuss the available literature on interviewing and interrogation techniques using the framework of case construction.

While other disciplines may define case construction differently, we offer a framework that we believe is suitable for thinking about interviews and interrogations. Our case construction framework emphasizes two premises: one descriptive and one prescriptive. Our descriptive premise is straightforward and uncontroversial, and postulates that interviews and interrogations occur as one step in the larger context of a criminal investigation, which ultimately may lead to the prosecution and conviction (or acquittal) of a person. Expressed differently, interviews and interrogations do not occur in a vacuum, but instead as one element of a chain of legal events. Our second premise is prescriptive, and hopefully strikes the reader as equally uncontroversial: A central goal of a criminal process is to exclude innocent suspects from suspicion, or if they are facing trial, acquit them; and conversely, build a solid case against guilty suspects that leads to their conviction in court. Of course, we acknowledge that criminal processes have multiple goals (e.g., uphold due process, protect public safety, etc.). However, here we focus on the epistemic goal of distinguishing between guilty and innocent people. Hence, we argue that the effectiveness of any given interview technique must be viewed in the light of the extent to which it provides information or evidence that can be used to exonerate the innocent and convict the guilty. In other words, an effective interview technique should substantively facilitate the process of case construction—that is, the actual processes in which legal actors are engaged.

We begin with a review of the psychological research literature on deception detection and on interviewing and interrogation. From there, we describe the new wave of applied research on questioning techniques designed to improve deception detection and information collection. We conclude with a discussion of the state of the science of interviewing, especially with respect to its relevance for case construction.

The Strategic Use of Evidence (SUE) technique, a framework for interviewing suspects, will take center stage in our discussion of the relationship between empirically grounded techniques and case construction. As we discuss later, we believe the SUE technique shows particular promise for the purpose of case construction.

RESEARCH ON DECEPTION AND ITS DETECTION

> . . . [W]e must recognize that most defendants have, in effect, two trials. They are first tried by the police . . . . The man on the beat is the first judge. Without any basis in law, he repeatedly acts as judge and jury, prosecution and defense counsel (Kidd, 1940, p. 15–17).

Before a suspect is charged with a crime and prosecuted, the police form an impression that a suspect is guilty. Unless the suspect volunteers an admission of guilt, arriving at this judgment involves assessing the (dis)honesty of a suspect's denial. As such, the detection of deception is an essential component of criminal investigations (although it should be acknowledged that assessing veracity during the investigative phase is of little or no relevance to a prosecutor's case construction). However, the psychological literature on deception detection suggests that humans' ability to detect deceit is highly limited.

More specifically, a metaanalysis of decades of research on human deception detection accuracy indicates that lie catchers, unassisted by technology or specific interviewing techniques, perform only slightly above chance levels of accuracy (54%; Bond & DePaulo, 2006). Accuracy rates are moderated by several variables such as the level of motivation of the sender (i.e., the person lying or telling the truth) and whether the receiver (i.e., the person judging a message) had prior familiarity with the sender, but the effects of these factors are relatively small. Some factors that might intuitively be expected to confer advantages to deception detection (e.g., interacting directly with the sender vs. merely observing the sender) do not significantly improve accuracy. Moreover, there is no more variance in people's ability to detect lies than would be expected by random chance (Bond & DePaulo, 2008). Rather than individual differences in lie catcher ability, variation in accuracy is largely due to individual differences of sender credibility (viz. the likelihood of a sender being judged as honest) and detectability (viz. the extent to which a sender is accurately judged).

Deception detection accuracy seems constrained primarily by the fact there are few reliable cues to deception, and those that are reliable are quite weakly associated with deceit. In a metaanalytic review of the literature on cues to deception, DePaulo and her colleagues (2003) found that the median effect size (d), across all measured cues to deception, was .10—a small effect by most standards. Thus, liars and truth tellers tend to behave so similarly that there is insufficient information to make highly accurate judgments. Even if one were to rely on valid cues (e.g., number of details, contextual embedding, vocal immediacy), accuracy would still be highly limited. In a metaanalytic review relevant to this point, Hartwig and Bond (2011) found that lie catchers' judgments of veracity are generally guided by the handful of cues that are indeed correlated with deception. However, the weakness of the cues places a low upper limit on the achievable accuracy rates. In a second metaanalytic review, Hartwig and Bond (2014) synthesized regression statistics in order to assess the extent to which using multiple cues simultaneously could improve deception detection accuracy. They found that, systematically across the regressions they metaanalyzed, the single strongest cue in any given model explained the lion's share of variance in classification accuracy. Thus, the use of multiple cues—as many interrogation manuals advocate (e.g., Inbau, Reid, Buckley, & Jayne, 2013)—provides little to no benefit to improve deception detection accuracy. In summary, lie catchers seem to do as well as they possibly can; the nature of the task is such that they cannot do better. Detecting deception with high accuracy is, therefore, a virtually impossible challenge, rather than one that is dependent on individual skill or talent, as some researchers have argued in the past (e.g., Ekman & O'Sullivan, 1991).

Although the research literature paints a clear picture of deception detection as an extremely difficult task, it should be noted that the research reviewed here is specifically concerned with detecting deception without the use of technology, specialized questioning techniques, or evidence against which to check a sender's statement. When people detect lies in their everyday lives, they typically use information from third parties or physical evidence to ascertain the truth (Park et al., 2002). Additionally, when lie catchers have information about situational incentives to lie (viz. the conditions under which deception would be beneficial to the sender), they can achieve high accuracy rates (Bond, Howard, Hutchison, & Masip, 2013), presumably because such information is highly diagnostic of people's actual decisions to lie. In the paradigmatic laboratory lie detection study, people are deprived of these useful sources of information. However, there is still good reason to think that people are poor lie catchers outside of the laboratory. Data from a series of diary studies demonstrate the difficulties of detecting deceit in the real world. In these studies, people reported that most of their lies in everyday life go undetected (DePaulo et al., 1996), and greater than 40% of the serious lies (e.g., marital infidelity) people reported went undiscovered (DePaulo, Ansfield, Kirkendol, & Boden, 2004). Thus, even when people are likely to have access to resources of which they are deprived in many lab studies, a substantial amount of deceit is misjudged.

In sum, evaluating whether a person is lying or telling the truth is critically important in the context of a criminal investigation, and the general findings of the psychological literature on deception detection is not encouraging for practice. A suspect's statements are a potentially useful source of evidence in an investigation, but the research literature suggests that investigators are prone to misjudgments of deception and truth.

RESEARCH ON INTERROGATION AND INTERVIEWING

Contemporary American interrogation techniques typically draw a distinction between interviews and interrogations (Inbau et al., 2013; Kassin, 2005). In this framework, interviews of suspects are conducted prior to interrogations and are used to gather information and to form a judgment about whether the suspect is guilty. Interrogations, in contrast, are aimed at eliciting an admission of guilt and a written or recorded confession. Whether an impression of a suspect's guilt (or innocence) is formed during a pre-interrogation interview or other investigative processes, the accuracy of such judgments is of paramount importance for identifying the true perpetrator of a crime (and for eliminating actually innocent persons from the investigation). Given the practical issues plaguing deception detection reviewed reviously, it cannot be assured that investigators make accurate determinations of guilt. In places where confession-oriented techniques are widely used, such as the United States and Canada (see Gudjonsson, 2003; Williamson, Milne, & Savage, 2009), incorrect judgments of guilt at early stages of an investigation can lead to innocent suspects being subjected to potentially coercive interrogation techniques (Kassin, 2005), and these techniques can lead innocent people to confess to crimes they did not commit (Kassin et al., 2010).

There exist numerous interrogation techniques designed to elicit confessions from suspects, but they are united by substantial similarities. For example, two of the most widely popular interrogation techniques, the Reid Technique (Inbau et al., 2013) and the Wicklander-Zulawski Technique (Zulawski & Wicklander, 2000), both advocate the development, through the course of an interrogation, of so-called *themes* that provide explanations, rationalizations, or justifications of the crime in question. John E. Reid & Associates, the company that provides training in the Reid Technique, has published a manual of interrogation themes, organized by the type of crime (Senese, 2008). The development of themes that create the perception that the seriousness of the offense was less severe has been termed *minimization* (Kassin & McNall, 1991). For example, the interrogator may suggest that the crime was a "mistake" or that the victim somehow deserved it. Minimization is a venerable interrogation tactic. The earliest American interrogation manuals recommend minimization (Inbau, 1942; Kidd, 1940), but the practice of developing minimizing themes to facilitate confessions extends at least as far back as the Spanish Inquisition, wherein Grand Inquisitors recommended the use of minimization on suspected heretics (see Sabatini, 1913).

Despite the widespread use and centuries-long history of minimization, it was not until the early 1990s that empirical research on minimization began. There is now a substantial body of experimental research demonstrating the risks of minimization. Minimizing themes have been demonstrated to pragmatically imply that a confession will lead to more lenient sentencing (Kassin & McNall, 1991). This should come as no surprise—if an interrogator suggests that a crime was less morally serious, it would be reasonable for a suspect to assume that confessing to the act will not carry severe consequences. The purpose of minimization is to make confessing a more appealing option to guilty suspects (Jayne, 1986), but it also has the effect of inducing many innocent suspects to confess as well (Russano et al., 2005). When they believe the suspect they are questioning is guilty, interrogators exert more pressure to get a confession (Kassin, Goldstein, & Savitsky, 2003) and more frequently use minimization tactics (Narchet, Meissner, & Russano, 2011). Suspects are motivated to escape the often stressful environment of an interrogation, and they frequently prioritize immediate relief from interrogative pressure over the long-term consequences of confessing (Madon et al., 2012). Minimization tactics diminish the perceived consequences of confessing for all suspects, regardless of guilt, and for that reason, minimization tactics elicit confessions from both innocent and guilty suspects (Horgan, Russano, Meissner, & Evans, 2012; Russano et al., 2005). As such, the diagnostic value of confessions (viz. the extent to which a confession is a valid indication that a suspect is guilty) is greatly reduced by minimization tactics.

Because they extensively incorporate tactics that elicit confessions from innocent people, confession-oriented techniques present significant practical problems. Although confessions are widely prized as highly useful evidence, the methods generally used to obtain them substantially curtail the extent to which they are accurate indications of the suspect's guilt. Intuitively, a criminal confession should be excellent evidence for constructing a case against a suspect. Indeed, even in the face of exculpatory evidence, jurors overwhelmingly perceive defendants who have confessed to be guilty (Kassin & Sukel, 1997). However, given their limited diagnosticity, the substantial evidentiary weight that factfinders ascribe to confessions is miscalibrated.

In the last 40 years, police investigators in the United Kingdom and Scandinavia, as well as several other countries in Europe (see Williamson, Milne, & Savage, 2009), have shifted away from confession-oriented techniques and toward a model of *investigative interviewing*—that is, interviewing approaches that are focused on collecting information from suspects in a nonaccusatory manner, with the objective of obtaining as much information as possible about the crime under investigation. The United Kingdom has implemented an interviewing model known as PEACE (which stands for *P*lanning and preparation, *E*ngage and explain, *A*ccount, *C*losure, *E*valuation), which is drawn from Shepherd's (1986) concept of conversation management and from Fisher and Geiselman's (1992) Cognitive Interview. In contrast to confession-oriented approaches in which interrogators dominate the conversation (see Inbau et al, 2013), the PEACE model and other similar investigative interviewing approaches are intended to be led by the interviewee (Shawyer, Milne, & Bull, 2009). That is, the suspect should be the one doing most of the talking in an investigative interview.

Although research on what happens in suspect interviews is somewhat limited due to the practical difficulties involved in conducting such research, the available data suggest that, at least in the United Kingdom, implementation of investigative interviewing has resulted in the police rarely, if ever, using minimization and other potentially problematic tactics (Baldwin, 1992, 1993). Moreover, it appears that the rate of confessions in the United Kingdom has remained fairly stable following the implementation of investigative interviewing (Soukara et al., 2009). It is difficult to empirically test with real world data, but investigative interviewing procedures seem to provide considerable safeguards against false confessions by removing the more coercive elements from police questioning (Kassin et al., 2010). Laboratory studies on investigative interviewing approaches suggest that they are more effective at gathering information than confession-oriented approaches (e.g., Evans et al., 2013). In a recent metaanalysis comparing accusatorial and investigative interviewing approaches, Meissner and his colleagues (2014) corroborated these overall findings of the research literature. Investigative interviewing techniques tended to elicit just as many (and occasionally more) confessions than accusatorial, confession-oriented techniques. Moreover, the diagnosticity of confessions obtained through investigative interviewing is substantially higher compared with confession-oriented techniques.

Thus, investigative interviewing seems to confer many potential advantages for the purpose of case construction: The outcomes of investigative interviews are likely to be more diagnostic of guilt and innocence, compared with those of confession-oriented approaches. As such, the investigative interviewing approach is highly beneficial for case construction. However, even when useful safeguards are in place against coercing innocence suspects into confessing, there remains considerable difficulty in judging whether suspects are lying or telling the truth. We turn next to specialized techniques purposed to meet this challenge.

DEVELOPMENTS IN INTERVIEWING
TO DECEPTION DETECTION

As the literature on deception reviewed previously indicates, there are serious practical difficulties associated with deception detection. These difficulties are primarily due to the weak diagnostic value of cues to deception. In the past decade, as part of a new wave of research on deception detection, psychologists have striven to mitigate this challenge by designing techniques aimed at eliciting from people more diagnostic cues to deception (Vrij & Granhag, 2012a). That is, researchers have been attempting to develop ways of actively intervening in order to produce indications that people are lying or telling the truth, rather than merely passively observing their behavior.

The Behavior Analysis Interview

The idea of actively provoking behavior for the purpose of detecting deception is not new. The aforementioned Reid Technique includes a questioning approach known as the Behavior Analysis Interview (BAI; Inbau et al., 2013). Although the BAI did not inspire psychologists' recent attempts to develop techniques of eliciting cues to deception, the BAI does predate this new wave of deception detection research by several decades (see Inbau, Reid, & Buckley, 1986). The BAI includes several "behavior-provoking questions," which are intended to elicit responses that distinguish between innocent and guilty denials. Unfortunately, the BAI has been subjected only to limited empirical testing. Jayne, Horvath, and Buckley (1994) conducted a study intended to test the effectiveness of the BAI, but this study is marred by serious methodological flaws (e.g., failing to establish ground truth in the interviews used as stimulus material for judging veracity). In the one methodologically sound test of the BAI to date, Vrij, Mann, and Fisher (2006) experimentally tested the BAI and found that, out of the 16 questions included in the technique, only three questions produced responses that statistically distinguished between liars and truth tellers—but two of those three questions produced differences in the direction opposite of what was predicted (e.g., liars were more helpful and less nervous). The one question that distinguished between liars and truth tellers in the expected direction was the so-called "bait question"—a question in which the interviewer asks whether it is possible that some hypothetical evidence might exist (e.g., "Is there some reason we might find your fingerprints on the murder weapon?"). Since this study published in 2006, we are not aware of any subsequent tests of the diagnostic value of suspect responses to bait questions. However, even if bait questions are effective at improving deception detection, recent research suggests that bait questions may result in serious memory errors, as they may introduce misinformation about the evidence possessed by investigators (Luke, Crozier, & Strange, in press).

It is somewhat unsurprising that the BAI has failed to find empirical support, as its predictions seem to be mere restatements of common sense (Masip, Barba, &

Herrero, 2012; Masip, Herrero, Garrido, & Barba, 2011), and the findings of psychological literature on deception starkly conflict with people's stereotypes and intuitions about deception (Global Deception Research Team, 2006). The BAI's usefulness for case construction is, at best, severely limited, and at worst, it is a counterproductive approach that may lead to incorrect judgments of suspects. The BAI was designed, in part, by experienced practitioners, so it is probable that it is generally consistent with the descriptive premise of our framework of case construction (i.e., the BAI likely fits well into the context of an actual investigation). Although the BAI has not received empirical support, the central underpinning idea of provoking behavior that is diagnostic of deception is a potentially viable one.

There are two broadly successful programs of research that rely on this core idea of eliciting cues to deception, which are reviewed in the following: (1) one, which we will call the *cognitive load approach*, that focuses on magnifying differences between liars and truth tellers based on their differences in cognitive busyness and (2) another, which we will call the *strategic approach*, that focuses on taking advantage of differences in the self-regulatory strategies liars' and truth tellers' respectively use to cope with others scrutinizing their statements. We review both approaches below, but we place substantially greater emphasis on the strategic approach, in order to set the stage for our discussion of how such techniques can be used for case construction.

The Cognitive Load Approach

The *cognitive load approach* is largely derived from Baddeley's (2012) working memory model, which posits that humans have a limited bandwidth of memory and attention that can be used for parallel tasks. Because deception often involves multiple simultaneous cognitive activities (e.g., suppressing the truth, fabricating a story, managing verbal and nonverbal behavior), deception is thought to generally involve greater cognitive load than telling the truth (Sporer, 2016; Zuckerman, DePaulo, & Rosenthal, 1981). To the extent that this is the case, imposing additional cognitive load on liars ought to make the task of deception more difficult, thus making lies more detectable.

Cognitive load can be imposed in a variety of ways, such as having people tell their stories in reverse order (Vrij et al., 2008, 2012) or having them engage in a concurrent task (Jordan, 2016; Patterson, 2009; Vrij et al., 2010). Increasing cognitive load elicits several differences between liars and truth tellers. For example, under load, liars' stories include fewer details and contextual embeddings and more cognitive operations and speech errors (Vrij et al., 2008). Liars' statements under cognitive load are also perceived as less plausible compared with lies told without additional load (Vrij et al., 2012). In short, when liars are subjected to additional cognitive load, the quality of their statements is significantly diminished.

Although the cognitive load approach has been generally successful, some results suggest qualifications to its usefulness. For example, truth tellers with dispositionally low working memory capacity may be adversely affected by cognitive load manipulations, such that their behaviors resemble liars (Lane, Martin, & Mennie, 2014). This effect could lead to people telling the truth being misclassified as deceptive. Additionally, at least one attempt to replicate the basic effect of cognitive load on cues to deception failed (Jordan, 2016). However, overall, the cognitive load approach is a promising program of research that has led to potentially useful interviewing techniques (Vrij et al., 2015) and theoretical insights (Sporer, 2016). To the extent that the cognitive load approach facilitates deception detection, it is potentially useful for assisting in case construction, at least insofar as it can potentially assist investigators in ascertaining the veracity of suspects' statements. Moreover, although these techniques were largely developed in the laboratory, it is likely that cognitive load approaches can be readily incorporated into real-world interviews (Vrij et al., 2015).

The Strategic Approach

The principal development of the *strategic approach* is an interviewing procedure known as the Strategic Use of Evidence (SUE) technique. The SUE technique is built on a theoretical understanding of how suspects cope with the challenge of being interviewed. The specific tactics of the SUE technique are designed to influence the strategies of innocent and guilty suspects. Influencing the strategies of suspects can serve a number of purposes, including establishing a suspect's culpability.

COUNTER-INTERROGATION STRATEGIES

Being interviewed by the police poses a challenge to the credibility of suspects—both innocent and guilty. Innocent and guilty suspects alike are motivated to create the impression that they are innocent of the crime about which they are being questioned. However, the manner in which innocent and guilty suspects pursue their goal of being perceived as innocent varies substantially, especially with respect to the manner in which they handle potentially incriminating information (Granhag & Hartwig, 2008; Hartwig, Granhag, Strömwall, & Doering, 2010). The strategies suspects use to pursue their goals when being questioned are termed *counter-interrogation strategies*.

Generally, innocent suspects perceive that their goals of establishing and maintaining their credibility would be served if the investigators were aware of what occurred and what they know (Granhag & Hartwig, 2008, 2015). For this reason, they typically adopt counter-interrogation strategies that involve being forthcoming with information and telling the truth as it happened (Hartwig, Granhag, & Strömwall, 2007). Thus, innocent suspects' statements are generally consistent with evidence held by the interviewer (Hartwig et al., 2005; Luke et al.,2013; Sorochinski et al., 2014). In the terms of the SUE framework, the extent to which a suspect's statement matches the available evidence is referred to as *statement–evidence (in)consistency*. Innocent statements tend to feature few, if any, statement–evidence inconsistencies.

In some ways, innocent suspects' strategic tendencies could be construed as naïve, but there are basic social psychological principles that explain why they might behave this way. First, people often overestimate the extent to which their internal state is visible to others (Gilovich & Savitsky, 1999; Gilovich, Savitsky, & Medvec, 1998). This illusion of transparency may lead innocent suspects to believe that their innocence will be clear and apparent to investigators. Second, people generally maintain a belief in a just world (Lerner, 1980). This implicit belief that people tend to "get what they deserve and deserve what they get" can lead innocent people into assuming that they will be perceived to be innocent, simply because they are innocent. Kassin (2005) has termed this constellation of perceptions the *phenomenology of innocence.* Under certain circumstances (e.g., when subjected to guilt-presumptive, coercive interrogation tactics), innocent suspects' preference for cooperation and forthcomingness is potentially danger-ous: If they are misclassified as guilty by investigators, innocent suspects' ten-dency to overestimate the extent to which their innocence is obvious could lead them to remain in situations in which they may be subjected to powerful forms of persuasion that can lead to false confessions (Kassin, 2005). However, when inter-viewed in a nonaccusatory style and when interrogators are specifically trained to attend to statement evidence (in)consistencies (Hartwig, Granhag, Strömwall, & Kronkvist, 2006; Luke et al., 2016), interviewers can use forthcoming behavior and consistency with the evidence as a cue to honesty.

In contrast to innocent suspects, guilty suspects typically perceive that it is counterproductive to their goals for the interviewer to know about the suspect's activities in relation to the crime in question (Granhag & Hartwig, 2008, 2015). They tend to adopt strategies that involve keeping their stories short and simple and avoiding the disclosure of potentially incriminating information (Hartwig, Granhag, & Strömwall, 2007). However, guilty suspects also adapt to their percep-tion of the interviewer's knowledge. That is, because they generally do not want to contradict information the interviewer already knows, they will adjust their strat-egy to account for information and evidence they think the interviewer already possesses (Luke, Dawson, Hartwig, & Granhag, 2014; Luke, Hartwig, Shamash, & Granhag, 2016). For this reason, when guilty suspects become aware of evidence held by the investigator, through inference or through disclosure of that evidence by the interrogator, they attempt to adjust their stories to offer benign, nonculpable explanations for that evidence. However, when evidence is withheld from them, guilty suspects tend to provide statements that deviate from their actual activities, and therefore they provide statements that are discrepant with evidence that sug-gests their involvement (Hartwig et al., 2005; Luke et al.,2013; Sorochinski et al., 2014). Thus, the degree to which guilty suspects' statements contain statement–evidence inconsistencies varies as a function of their perception of how much the interviewer knows (Granhag & Hartwig, 2008, 2015). For example, imagine a case in which the police have found the suspect's fingerprints on furniture in a house that was burglarized. If the police were to reveal this evidence to the suspect, he or she may be able to generate a story that innocently explains the existence of the evidence (e.g., having been in the house for an innocent reason). However, if the police withheld the evidence from the suspect, he or she is likely to deny having been in the house—thus creating statement–evidence inconsistencies.

Guilty suspects' strategic tendencies are thought to be grounded in basic self-regulatory strategies of avoiding dangers and approaching objectives that further one's goals (see, e.g., Carver & Scheier, 1981, 1998, 2011; Granhag & Hartwig, 2008, 2015). In the case of an interrogation, a guilty suspect must generally avoid situations in which investigators become aware of information that inculpates the suspect. As such, guilty suspects need to be skilled navigators. First, they need to craft a compelling story that creates an impression of innocence and accounts for the interviewer's knowledge (an approach-oriented activity). Second, they need to avoid disclosing any more potentially incriminating information than they need to in order to maintain their credibility. Third, they need to make sure that their story does not include elements that contradict the knowledge already held by the interviewer (i.e., they need to avoid statement–evidence inconsistencies). Fourth, they need to avoid situations where they are forced to alter their previous statement not to be inconsistent with evidence presented to them (i.e., they need to avoid within-statement inconsistencies). In much the same way that a person attempts to navigate physical terrain from one point to another while avoiding obstacles in the way, a guilty suspect must navigate an interview while avoiding incriminating disclosures, contradicting the interviewer's knowledge, and contradicting one's own previous statement.

QUESTIONING STRUCTURE AND EVIDENCE DISCLOSURE

Equipped with the foregoing understanding of suspect counter-interrogation strategies, the SUE technique comprises a set of techniques designed to take advantage of and influence what strategies suspects tend to adopt. The SUE technique's questioning approach follows a "funnel structure"—in which broad, open-ended questions are asked first, followed by increasingly specific follow-up questions (see Hartwig, Granhag, & Luke, 2014). In order to ensure that guilty suspects cannot easily adapt to the interviewer's knowledge, evidence is generally withheld from the suspect until after questioning. The open-ended questions serve to elicit a free narrative from the suspect. The follow-up questions serve to clarify information or to obtain information that the suspect may have omitted from his or her previous responses. Additionally, if the suspect has provided a statement that is inconsistent with the evidence, the interviewer asks specific follow-up questions to test possible nonculpable alternative explanations of the evidence. For example, if it is known that the suspect's fingerprints were on a gun used in a crime, the interviewer could ask questions about noncriminal activities that could explain the presence of the fingerprints (e.g., "Have you handled any firearms recently?" "Have you ever handled this particular model of gun?"). Asking nonaccusatory, information-gathering questions in this way provides opportunities for innocent suspects to provide truthful, nonculpable explanations for the existence of the interviewer's evidence, and it provides opportunities for guilty suspects to generate statement–evidence inconsistencies, thus revealing their deception.

Following questioning, evidence may be disclosed to the suspect. If a suspect has contradicted the evidence, evidence may be disclosed in order to prompt a change in his or her counter-interrogation strategy. Sometimes, when presented with some of the evidence that is discrepant with their statements, suspects will revise their stories. Repairing the gap between what they previously stated and the evidence as it is disclosed to them will result in within-statement inconsistencies. Research shows that within-statement inconsistencies are very rare for innocent suspects (Granhag, Strömwall, Willén, & Hartwig, 2013). Furthermore, these revised stories sometimes contradict other evidence held by the interviewer, and these further statement–evidence inconsistencies can serve as additional indications of a suspect's deceit. Additionally, disclosures of evidence about some of the suspect's activities can give the suspect the impression that the interviewer is highly knowledgeable. This perception can lead suspects to disclose more information when questioned about other aspects of their activities, and in doing so, suspects may reveal information the interviewer was previously unaware of (Tekin et al, 2015). Thus, strategic evidence disclosure can be used to elicit new information from suspects.

APPLYING THE RESEARCH: PRACTICAL CONSIDERATIONS FOR CASE CONSTRUCTION

Research has provided clear insights about counterproductive practices and the challenges faced by investigators when attempting to distinguish between lies and truths. Practitioners are in need of empirically sound techniques for improving interviewing and interrogation procedures. As reviewed earlier, there have been at least two branches of research that have found fairly robust methods of widening the differences between liars and truth tellers. However, research devoted to developing empirically supported questioning techniques for practitioners has often inadequately addressed the role of such techniques in the broader context of an investigation and subsequent prosecution. To return to Kidd's (1940) standard for police procedures, which opened this chapter, researchers have developed techniques that "work" in some senses of the word—but to what extent do they produce outcomes that are useful as evidence in court?

As discussed, the BAI of the Reid Technique has found virtually no support in the research literature. However, even the proponents of the BAI are cautious about its usefulness as evidence in a case. Although the authors of the Reid Manual assert that the BAI can be used to classify suspects as having generally innocent or guilty responses, they offer this warning:

> For court purposes, it is not recommended that the investigator categorize a suspect's response to behavior-provoking questions as truthful or deceptive at the time each question is asked. This practice may invite a defense attorney to ask the investigator to explain exactly why he classified each response as he did, to explain the research findings supporting this classification, and to comment on the differential diagnosis of the response. (Inbau et al., 2013, p. 169)

Despite this warning, one can easily imagine a defense attorney pressing an investigator as to the basis of a classification made from the overall outcome of a BAI, rather than from the individual behavior-provoking questions. This point aside, it seems clear from that warning that not even Inbau and colleagues (2013) believe that the BAI has much usefulness for the purpose of case construction. The authors of the Reid Manual do not seem to have confidence that testimony about BAI results would withstand close scrutiny. Although we disagree with Inbau et al. (2013) about the usefulness of the BAI for deception detection, we concur with their suggestion that its results are not strong grounds on which to build a case. In our view, even if its predictions about honest and deceptive behavior were correct, the usefulness of the BAI would be curtailed by the equivocal nature of its results. That is, although the BAI has guidelines for interpreting a suspect's behavior, it lacks an objective criterion against which to compare a suspect's statement.

Ideally, interviewing techniques should help satisfy both the descriptive and prescriptive premises of case construction we described earlier: For a technique to be maximally useful for case construction, it should assist an investigator in inferring whether a suspect is innocent or guilty, but it should also produce outcomes that facilitate the legal processes involved in successfully clearing a case. In the SUE technique, the evidence and intelligence collected in the investigation serve as factually-based criteria—something the BAI lacks—and it is because of this that the SUE technique is so potentially useful for case construction.

The SUE Technique and Case Construction

In essence, the SUE technique may contribute to the prosecution's case construction in three different ways. First, interviewing in line with the SUE technique often generates statement–evidence inconsistencies from guilty suspects (Hartwig, Granhag, & Luke, 2014). Second, guilty suspects trying to repair the gap between what they previously said and the evidence as it is disclosed to them will produce within-statement inconsistencies, whereas innocent suspects tend to present statement with zero level of within-statement inconsistency (Granhag & Hartwig, 2015). If the interview is well documented (audio or video), both statement–evidence inconsistencies and within-statement inconsistencies may contribute to the prosecutor's case construction. Broadly speaking, what takes place in court is a "war of the narratives" (Bennet & Feldman, 1981). In essence, it is about which narrative is assessed as the most credible—the one presented by the prosecution or the one presented by the defense. A credible story needs to be consistent with the facts of the case, and it needs to be internally consistent (e.g., Levett et al., 2005). Hence, investigative interviews resulting in statement–evidence inconsistencies and/or within-statement inconsistencies will be powerful weapons in the hands of prosecutors who want to undermine the credibility of the story presented by the defense.

The third way that the outcome of the SUE technique may contribute to the prosecutor's case construction is by eliciting admissions from guilty suspects. In brief, in a recent line of research Tekin and her colleagues (2015) has shown that

(a) strategically playing the evidence speaking to a suspect's guilt can (b) result in statement–evidence inconsistencies (due to the suspect's aversive counter-interrogation strategies), which, in turn, (c) can result in the suspect changing his or her initial, and proven ineffective, strategies to more forthcoming counter-interrogation strategies ("I am better off telling what they already know"), (d) resulting in an increased amount of information previously unknown to the interviewer (admissions). A prosecutor building a story to be presented in court, a story that must cover as many pieces of the evidence in the case as possible (Levett et al, 2005)—is obviously assisted by admissions from the suspect. In summary, the first two outcomes of the SUE technique (different forms of inconsistencies) can be used by the prosecutor to undermine the credibility of the story presented by the defense and the third outcome (admissions) can be used to strengthen the story that he or she needs to construct.

Proponents of confession-oriented techniques frequently make the argument that it is necessary to seek confessions, especially in cases in which evidence is suggestive of a suspect's guilt but not conclusive—and potentially insufficient to secure a conviction (see e.g., Inbau et al., 2013). This is an understandable problem. There are surely cases that depend extensively on circumstantial evidence, and these cases maybe challenging to close. However, given the numerous issues with confession-oriented techniques, in terms of practical outcomes (i.e., false confessions; Kassin et al., 2010), ethics (Hartwig, Luke, & Skerker, 2016), and legality (Williamson, Milne, & Savage, 2009), seeking a confession to close such cases is highly problematic. However, the SUE technique presents a research-based alternative. If interviewers elicit statements from a suspect that are discrepant with circumstantial evidence, the probative value of that circumstantial evidence is effectively increased. For example, imagine a case in which investigators have cell phone tower data that indicate that a suspect's phone was in the area of a homicide at the time the crime occurred. On its own, the usefulness of this evidence is fairly limited for demonstrating a suspect's guilt. However, if the suspect were to make statements that contradict that evidence in the course of an interview (i.e., that he or she has never been to the location in question or was not there at that particular time), the value of the cell phone records for determining and demonstrating that suspect's guilt would be increased. As such, in addition to generating outcomes that are useful for the construction of cases in which there is plentiful evidence, the SUE technique may be highly beneficial to case construction in investigations that rely heavily on circumstantial evidence.

The inferences investigators draw about a suspect based on statement–evidence inconsistency have the advantage of being based on a factual criterion. In the SUE technique, veracity judgments are guided by a relatively unambiguous point of reference: Do the suspect's statements match the facts of a case, as known by the investigators? If they do, there is a high likelihood that the suspect is being truthful. If they do not, there is a high likelihood that the suspect is deceptive, and moreover, the suspect's inconsistencies with the evidence are clear demonstrations of deceit. Deception judgments based on statement–evidence inconsistencies are buttressed by strong empirical support (Granhag & Hartwig, 2015;

Hartwig, Granhag, & Luke, 2014), and they are persuasive evidence to factfinders (see later; Brimbal & Jones, in process).

Although we have confidence in the usefulness of the SUE technique, this is not to say that the outcomes of an interviewing using the SUE technique are always unambiguous. It would be dangerously brash to make such a claim. We would be remiss if we did not present a major caveat to the usefulness of the SUE technique for case construction: The SUE technique's objectivity is necessarily constrained by the quality of the evidence used to guide the questioning. Evidence must be properly collected and correctly interpreted. The myriad practical problems with forensic evidence, therefore, may present serious issues to the implementation of the SUE technique in some circumstances (see National Research Council, 2009). The problems with forensic science are, of course, not only an issue for the SUE technique but for the criminal justice system as a whole. Flaws in one part of the justice system frequently have rippling effects in other parts of the system. Poor evidence does not exist in a vacuum; it can have ramifications on other parts of an investigation and on the prosecution of a defendant (Hasel & Kassin, 2009; Kassin, Dror, & Kukucka, 2013). Because of the SUE technique's dependence on investigative evidence, it is essential that its integrity is maintained.

Research-Based Interviews as Evidence in Court

Confessions have intuitive appeal as evidence in court. However, the movement away from confession-oriented approaches raises the question of whether the questioning of suspects in models such as PEACE or the SUE technique function as effective evidence for the prosecution of a defendant. Understanding how these newly developed techniques can be used and used productively in court is essential to their implementation with practitioners. Although law enforcement may be (and ought to be) concerned with the ethical implications of the techniques they use, their effectiveness is evaluated, in large part, by their successful investigation and clearance of cases. It is not unreasonable to suspect that their motivation is outcome-oriented: to collect sufficient evidence for the prosecution of a case. Depriving investigators and prosecutors of valuable confession evidence is an understandable criticism of research-based interviewing techniques, as they may leave the prosecution with tools that reduce their ability to do their job. Indeed, in our experience speaking with many police investigators, this is a common concern in implementing the interviewing techniques researchers now recommended.

Although we believe this concern to be, to a large extent, unjustified (for reasons detailed later), it is an understandable and important problem to address. Indeed, following the implementation of the Police and Criminal Evidence Act, which outlawed a substantial number of the techniques UK police had used to obtain confessions, there was widespread concern and disorientation about how to conduct questioning of suspects (Baldwin, 1993; Gudjonsson, 2003). Ultimately, these concerns were at least partially ameliorated with the adoption of the PEACE model and associated training (Griffiths & Milne, 2006), though in the United

States there continues to be considerable resistance to the implementation of techniques derived from research and opposed to the venerable confession-oriented techniques (see chapter 8; Buckley, 2012; Vrij & Granhag, 2012b). To date, however, almost no research has been conducted on the usefulness of research-based interview techniques for case construction.

Some research has begun to evaluate the utility of research-based interview techniques in the court room. Brimbal and Jones (in process) conducted two studies investigating the comparative value of using the outcome of a SUE interview and a confession-oriented interrogation. The basic question "do exposed lies convince a jury to the same extent as a confession?" was tested by Brimbal and Jones (in process). In this study, the authors provided participants with the prototypical response of an innocent defendant to a SUE interview (i.e., consistent statement), a guilty defendant to a SUE interview (i.e., inconsistent statement), and a confession. Because the SUE technique is engineered to expose deception (via statement–evidence inconsistencies and within-statement inconsistencies) in guilty suspects, it is particularly well suited for this purpose. Attending to statement–evidence inconsistencies increases deception detection accuracy (Hartwig, Granhag, Strömwall, & Kronkvist, 2006), and as such, this cue could also be an indicator of guilt for jurors.

Given that the SUE technique reliably differentiates between guilty and innocent, the implication of guilt is less dangerous than that of a confession, which is frequently obtained using means that severely curtail their diagnostic value. Furthermore, it is possible that interviews conducted in line with the SUE technique can serve to assist the prosecution in creating a compelling, factually grounded narrative that is comprehensible to jurors or other factfinders. A confession is a potent piece of evidence that has the power to influence people's interpretations of other evidence, often distorting their view of other evidence, including exculpatory evidence (Hasel & Kassin, 2009; Kassin, 2012; Kassin & Sukel, 1997). Factfinders seem to have an inadequate grasp of the coercive environment in which confessions are often obtained, and this leads to inappropriate attributions of guilt on the basis on confession evidence (Kassin, 1997). On the other hand, the SUE technique might be used to appropriately guide factfinders to evaluate the evidence in a case using the suspect's statement, to assist in discerning lies from truths. That is, the SUE technique can potentially assist factfinders in the use of factual reference points to judge the veracity of statements. Thus, the SUE technique provides numerous benefits for case constructions throughout the process of an investigation (i.e., accurately distinguishing innocent and guilty suspects) and prosecution (i.e., providing outcomes that can be used to construct a compelling prosecutorial narrative).

Preliminary findings from these studies are encouraging. Brimbal and Jones (in process) provided support for the idea that exposed lies were no different from confessions in securing convictions. Furthermore, the supporting evidence was found to be more important to mock jurors when the SUE technique was used in the interview process. This study is only the first attempt to explore this topic, but the finding that statement evidence inconsistencies are interpreted as a cue for guilt by mock jurors is encouraging.

The aforementioned research is very specific to the SUE technique. The value of other techniques (e.g., cognitive load) for case construction has not been examined in mock court settings. Yet it is possible to test other techniques, such as those of the cognitive load approach, in the paradigm Brimbal and Jones (in process) used. However, using the results of cognitive load techniques as evidence in court may be problematic for the same reason that the BAI would be problematic evidence: The criterion for judging deception is less clear when using cognitive load techniques.

We do not deny that cognitive load techniques may be useful as part of an investigation. To the extent that such techniques enhance investigators' ability to determine whether a suspect is lying or telling the truth, they will indeed be useful for identifying the culprit in a case and for removing innocent people from suspicion. For reasons already reviewed ealier, it is of paramount importance that investigators arrive at correct impressions of suspects' culpability. However, we are somewhat skeptical of the usefulness of cognitive load techniques for producing compelling evidence that could be used in the construction of a case. This issue remains empirically untested, though, and it ought to be explored in future research.

CONCLUSION

This chapter attempted to develop a lens focused on case construction, though which interviewing and interrogation techniques can be viewed. Researchers have heretofore neglected the role of interviewing techniques for case construction, and we believe practitioners and researchers alike would benefit from consideration of this crucial aspect of the criminal justice process. We have argued that applying the SUE technique during the investigative phase is highly viable for case construction. Hence, we believe that there is a judicial (evidentiary) dimension to the SUE technique, a dimension that many other approaches for detecting deceit lack (Granhag & Hartwig, 2015). Furthermore, to the extent that applied researchers seek to be as helpful to practitioners as they can be, one should bear in mind not only that the techniques developed must accurately discriminate between the innocent and the guilty, but also that interviewing and deception detection must fit in the context of investigative and legal processes.

REFERENCES

Baddeley, A. (2012). Working memory: Theories, models, and controversies. *Annual Review of Psychology, 63*, 1–29.

Baldwin, J. (1992). *Videotaping of police interviews with suspects: An evaluation.* Police Research Series, Paper No 1. London: Home Office.

Baldwin, J. (1993). Police interview techniques: Establishing truth or proof, *British Journal of Criminology, 33*, 325–352.

Bennet, W. L., & Feldman, M. (1981). *Reconstructing Reality in the Courtroom: Justice and Judgment in American Culture.* New Brunswick: Rutgers University Press.

Bond, C. F., Jr., & DePaulo, B.M. (2006). Accuracy of deception judgments. *Personality and Social Psychology Review, 10*, 214–234.

Bond, C.F., Jr., & DePaulo, B.M. (2008). Individual differences in judging deception: Accuracy and bias. *Psychological Bulletin, 134*, 477–492.

Bond Jr, C. F., Howard, A. R., Hutchison, J. L., & Masip, J. (2013). Overlooking the obvious: Incentives to lie. *Basic and Applied Social Psychology, 35*, 212–221.

Brimbal, L., & Jones, A. M. *Perceptions of suspect statements: A comparison of exposed lies and confessions.* [In proces.]

Buckley, J. P. (2012). Detection of deception researchers needs to collaborate with experienced practitioners. *Journal of Applied Research in Memory and Cognition, 1*, 126–127.

Carver, C. S., & Scheier, M. F. (2011). Self-regulation of action and affect. In K. D. Vohs, R. F. Baumeister (Eds.), *Handbook of self-regulation: Research, theory, and applications* (2nd ed., pp. 3–21). New York: Guilford Press.

Carver, C. S., & Scheier, M. F. (1981). *Attention and self-regulation: A control-theory approach to human behavior.* New York: Springer-Verlag.

Carver, C. S., & Scheier, M. F. (1998). *On the self-regulation of behavior.* Cambridge: Cambridge University Press.

DePaulo, B. M., Ansfield, M. E., Kirkendol, S. E., & Boden, J. M. (2004). Serious lies. *Basic and Applied Social Psychology, 26*, 147–167.

DePaulo, B. M., Kashy, D. A., Kirkendol, S. E., Wyer, M. M., & Epstein, J. A. (1996). Lying in everyday life. *Journal of Personality and Social Psychology, 70*, 979–995.

DePaulo, B. M., Lindsay, J. J., Malone, B. E., Muhlenbruck, L., Charlton, K., & Cooper, H. (2003). Cues to deception. *Psychological bulletin, 129*, 74–118.

Ekman, P., & O'Sullivan, M. (1991). Who can catch a liar? *American psychologist, 46*, 913–920.

Evans, J. R., Meissner, C. A., Ross, A. B., Houston, K. A., Russano, M. B., & Horgan, A. J. (2013). Obtaining guilty knowledge in human intelligence interrogations: Comparing accusatorial and information-gathering approaches with a novel experimental paradigm. *Journal of Applied Research in Memory and Cognition, 2*, 83–88.

Fisher, R., & Geiselman, R. E. (1992). *Memory enhancing techniques for investigative interviewing: The cognitive interview.* Springfield, IL: Charles C. Thomas.

Gilovich, T., & Savitsky, K. (1999). The spotlight effect and the illusion of transparency egocentric assessments of how we are seen by others. *Current Directions in Psychological Science, 8*, 165–168.

Gilovich, T., Savitsky, K., & Medvec, V. H. (1998). The illusion of transparency: Biased assessments of others' ability to read one's emotional states. *Journal of Personality and Social Psychology, 75*, 332–346.

Global Deception Research Team. (2006). A world of lies. *Journal of Cross-Cultural Psychology, 37*, 60–74.

Griffiths, A., & Milne, B. (2006). Will it all end in tiers? Police interviews with suspects in Britain. In T. Williamson, *Investigative interviewing: Rights, research, regulation* (167–189). Devon, UK: Willan Publishing.

Granhag, P. A., & Hartwig, M. (2008). A new theoretical perspective on deception detection: On the psychology of instrumental mind-reading. *Psychology, Crime & Law, 14*, 189–200.

Granhag, P.A., & Hartwig, M. (2015). The Strategic Use of Evidence (SUE) technique: A conceptual overview. In P. A. Granhag, A. Vrij, & B. Vershuere (Eds.),

Deception detection: Current challenges and new directions (pp. 231–251). Chichester, UK: Wiley.

Granhag, P. A., Strömwall, L. A., Willén, R. M., & Hartwig, M. (2013). Eliciting cues to deception by tactical disclosure of evidence: The first test of the Evidence Framing Matrix. *Legal and Criminological Psychology, 18*, 341–355.

Gudjonsson, G. (2003). *The Psychology of interrogations and confessions.* Chichester, UK: Wiley.

Hartwig, M., & Bond, C. F. (2014). Lie detection from multiple cues: A meta-analysis. *Applied Cognitive Psychology, 28*, 661–676.

Hartwig, M., & Bond, C.F., Jr. (2011). Why do lie-catchers fail? A lens model meta-analysis of human lie judgments. *Psychological Bulletin, 137*, 643–659.

Hartwig, M., Granhag, P. A., & Luke, T. J. (2014). Strategic use of evidence during investigative interviews: The state of the science. In D. C. Raskin, C. R. Honts, & J. C. Kircher (Eds.), *Credibility assessment: Scientific research and applications* (pp. 1–36). Waltham, MA: Academic Press.

Hartwig, M., Granhag, P.A., & Strömwall, L. A. (2007). Guilty and innocent suspects' strategies during police interrogations. *Psychology, Crime & Law, 13*, 213–227.

Hartwig, M., Granhag, P. A., Strömwall, L. A., & Doering, N. (2010). Impression and information management: On the strategic self-regulation of innocent and guilty suspects. *The Open Criminology Journal, 3*, 10–16.

Hartwig, M., Granhag, P. A., Strömwall, L. A., & Kronkvist, O. (2006). Strategic use of evidence during police interviews: When training to detect deception works. *Law and human behavior, 30*, 603–619.

Hartwig, M., Granhag, P. A., Strömwall, L. A., & Vrij, A. (2005). Detecting deception via strategic disclosure of evidence. *Law and Human Behavior, 29*, 469–484.

Hartwig, M., Luke, T. J., & Skerker, M. (2016). Ethical perspectives on interrogation: An analysis of contemporary techniques. In J. Jacobs & J. Jackson, *Routledge handbook of criminal justice ethics* (pp. 326–347). London, UK: Routledge.

Hasel, L. E., & Kassin, S. M. (2009). On the presumption of evidentiary independence: Can confessions corrupt eyewitness identifications?. *Psychological Science, 20*, 122–126.

Horgan, A. J., Russano, M. B., Meissner, C. A., & Evans, J. R. (2012). Minimization and maximization techniques: Assessing the perceived consequences of confessing and confession diagnosticity. *Psychology, Crime & Law, 18*, 65–78.

Horvath, F., Jayne, B., & Buckley, J. (1994). Differentiation of truthful and deceptive criminal suspects in behavior analysis interviews. *Journal of Forensic Science, 39*, 793–807.

Inbau, F. (1942). *Lie detection and criminal interrogation.* Baltimore: Williams and Wilkins.

Inbau, F. E., Reid, J. E., & Buckley, J. (1986). *Criminal Interrogation and Confessions* (3rd Edition). Baltimore: Williams & Wilkins.

Inbau, F., Reid, J., Buckley, J., & Jayne, B. (2013). *Criminal interrogations and confessions* (5th ed). Burlington, MA: Jones & Bartlett.

Jayne, B. C. (1986). The Psychological Principles of Criminal Interrogation. In F. E. Inbau, J. E. Reid, & J. Buckley (Eds.), *Criminal Interrogation and Confessions,* 3rd edition (pp. 327–347). Baltimore: Williams & Wilkins.

Jordan, S. (2016). *The effect of cognitive load on liars and truth-tellers: Exploring the moderating impact of working memory capacity.* Doctoral dissertation.

Kassin, S. M. (1997). The psychology of confession evidence. *American Psychologist, 52*, 221–233.

Kassin, S. M. (2012). Why confessions trump innocence. *American Psychologist, 67*, 431–445.

Kassin, S. M. (2005). On the psychology of confessions: Does innocence put innocents at risk? *American Psychologist, 60*, 215–228.

Kassin, S. M., Drizin, S. A., Grisso, T., Gudjonsson, G. H., Leo, R. A., & Redlich, A. D. (2010). Police-induced confessions: Risk factors and recommendations. *Law and human behavior, 34*, 3–38.

Kassin, S. M., Dror, I. E., & Kukucka, J. (2013). The forensic confirmation bias: Problems, perspectives, and proposed solutions. *Journal of Applied Research in Memory and Cognition, 2*, 42–52.

Kassin, S. M., Goldstein, C. C., & Savitsky, K. (2003). Behavioral confirmation in the interrogation room: On the dangers of presuming guilt. *Law and human behavior, 27*, 187–203.

Kassin, S. M., & McNall, K. (1991). Police interrogations and confessions: Communicating promises and threats by pragmatic implication. *Law and Human Behavior, 15*, 233–251.

Kassin, S. M., & Sukel, H. (1997). Coerced confessions and the jury: An experimental test of the" harmless error" rule. *Law and Human Behavior, 21*, 27–46.

Kidd, W. R. (1940). *Police Interrogation.* New York: Basuino.

Lane, S., Martin, S., & Mennie, K. (2014). *Working memory capacity and cognitive load influence people's veracity judgments of interviewees.* Paper presented at the 2014, American Psychology-Law Society, New Orleans, LA.

Lerner, M. (1980). *The belief in a just world.* New York: Springer.

Levett, L. M., Danielsen. E. M., Kovera, M., & Culter, B. (2005). In K. Williams & N. Brewer (Eds.), *Psychology and Law: An Empricial Perspective* (pp. 365–406). New York: Guilford.

Luke, T. J., Crozier, W., & Strange, D. (in press). Memory errors in police interviews: Bait questions as a source of misinformation. *Journal of Applied Research on Memory and Cognition.*

Luke, T. J., Dawson, E., Hartwig, M., & Granhag, P. A. (2014). How awareness of possible evidence induces forthcoming counter-interrogation strategies. *Applied Cognitive Psychology, 28*, 876–882.

Luke, T. J., Hartwig, M., Brimbal, L., Chan, G., Jordan, S., Joseph, E., Osborne, J., & Granhag, P. A. (2013). Interviewing to elicit cues to deception: Improving strategic use of evidence with general-to-specific framing of evidence. *Journal of Police and Criminal Psychology, 28*, 54–62.

Luke, T. J., Hartwig, M., Joseph, E., Brimbal, L., Chan, G., Dawson, E., Jordan, S., Granhag, P. A., & Donovan, P. (2016). Training in the Strategic Use of Evidence: Improving deception detection accuracy of American law enforcement officers. *Journal of Police and Criminal Psychology, 31*, 270–278.

Luke, T. J., Hartwig, M., Shamash, B., & Granhag, P. A. (2016). Countermeasures against the Strategic Use of Evidence technique: Effects on suspects' strategies. *Journal of Investigative Psychology and Offender Profiling, 13*, 131–147.

Madon, S., Guyll, M., Scherr, K. C., Greathouse, S., & Wells, G. L. (2012). Temporal discounting: The differential effect of proximal and distal consequences on confession decisions. *Law and human behavior, 36*, 13–20.

Masip, J., Barba, A., & Herrero, C. (2012). Behaviour analysis interview and common sense: A study with novice and experienced officers. *Psychiatry, Psychology and Law, 19*, 21–34.

Masip, J., Herrero, C., Garrido, E., & Barba, A. (2011). Is the behaviour analysis interview just common sense? *Applied Cognitive Psychology, 25*, 593–604.

Meissner, C. A., Redlich, A. D., Michael, S. W., Evans, J. R., Camilletti, C. R., Bhatt, S., & Brandon, S. (2014). Accusatorial and information-gathering interrogation methods and their effects on true and false confessions: A meta-analytic review. *Journal of Experimental Criminology, 10*, 459–486.

Narchet, F. M., Meissner, C. A., & Russano, M. B. (2011). Modeling the influence of investigator bias on the elicitation of true and false confessions. *Law and Human Behavior, 35*, 452–465.

National Research Council Committee on Identifying the Needs of the Forensic Science Community (2009). *Strengthening forensic science in the United States: A path forward.* Washington DC: National Academies Press.

Park, H. S., Levine, T., McCornack, S., Morrison, K., & Ferrara, M. (2002). How people really detect lies. *Communication Monographs, 69*, 144–157.

Patterson, T. D. (2009). *The effect of cognitive load on deception.* Doctoral Dissertation.

Russano, M. B., Meissner, C. A., Narchet, F. M., & Kassin, S. M. (2005). Investigating true and false confessions within a novel experimental paradigm. *Psychological science, 16*, 481–486.

Sabatini, R. (1913). *Torquemada and the Spanish Inquisition: A history.* London: Stanley Paul & Co.

Senese, L. (2008). *Anatomy of interrogation themes.* Chicago: John E. Reid and Associates.

Shawyer, A., Milne, B., & Bull, R. (2009). Investigative interviewing in the UK. In T. Williamson, B. Milne, & S. Savage (Eds.), *International developments in investigative interviewing* (pp. 24–38). London: Routledge.

Shepherd, E. (1986). The conversational core of policing. *Policing, 2*, 294–303.

Smith, D. J. (1997). Case construction and the goals of criminal process. *British Journal of Criminology, 37*, 319.

Sorochinski, M., Hartwig, M., Osborne, J., Wilkins, E., Marsh, J., Kazakov, D., & Granhag, P. A. (2014). Interviewing to detect deception: When to disclose the evidence?. *Journal of Police and Criminal Psychology, 29*, 87–94.

Soukara, S., Bull, R., Vrij, A., Turner, M., & Cherryman, J. (2009). What really happens in police interviews of suspects? Tactics and confessions. *Psychology, Crime & Law, 15*, 493–506.

Sporer, S. L. (2016). Deception and cognitive load: Expanding our horizon with a working memory model. *Frontiers in Psychology, 7*, 1–12.

Tekin, S., Granhag, P. A., Strömwall, L., Mac Giolla, E., Vrij, A., & Hartwig, M. (2015). Interviewing strategically to elicit admissions from guilty suspects. *Law and Human Behavior, 39*, 244–252.

Vrij, A., & Granhag, P. A. (2012a). Eliciting cues to deception and truth: What matters are the questions asked. *Journal of Applied Research in Memory and Cognition, 1*, 110–117.

Vrij, A., & Granhag, P. A. (2012b). The sound of critics: new tunes, old tunes, and resistance to play. *Journal of Applied Research in Memory and Cognition, 1*, 139–143.

Vrij, A., Mann, S., & Fisher, R. P. (2006). An empirical test of the behaviour analysis interview. *Law and human behavior, 30*, 329–345.

Vrij, A., Leal, S., Mann, S., & Fisher, R. (2012). Imposing cognitive load to elicit cues to deceit: Inducing the reverse order technique naturally. *Psychology, Crime & Law, 18,* 579–594.

Vrij, A., Leal, S., Mann, S., Vernham, Z., & Brankaert, F. (2015). Translating theory into practice: Evaluating a cognitive lie detection training workshop. *Journal of Applied Research in Memory and Cognition, 4,* 110–120.

Vrij, A., Mann, S. A., Fisher, R. P., Leal, S., Milne, R., & Bull, R. (2008). Increasing cognitive load to facilitate lie detection: The benefit of recalling an event in reverse order. *Law and Human Behavior, 32,* 253–265.

Vrij, A., Mann, S., Leal, S., & Fisher, R. (2010). 'Look into my eyes': Can an instruction to maintain eye contact facilitate lie detection? *Psychology, Crime & Law, 16,* 327–348.

Williamson, T., Milne, B., & Savage, S. (2009). *International developments in investigative interviewing.* London: Routledge.

Zuckerman, M., DePaulo, B. M., & Rosenthal, R. (1981). Verbal and nonverbal communication of deception. In L. Berkowitz (Ed.), *Advances in experimental social psychology* (Vol. 14, pp. 1–59). San Diego, CA: Academic Press.

Zulawski, D. E., & Wicklander D. E. (2000). *Practical aspects of interview and interrogation,* (2nd ed.). Boca Raton, FL: CRC Press.

10

Detection Deception Using Psychophysiological and Neural Measures

EWOUT H. MEIJER AND BRUNO VERSCHUERE

People perform notoriously poorly when it comes to detecting deception (see chapter 8). Resorting to physiology has therefore been a popular approach to increasing deception detection accuracy. The search for physiological cues to deception goes back over a century, and historically, the use of the polygraph has attracted substantial attention among both legal professionals and academics (see e.g., Lykken, 1998 for an extensive review). More recently, the use of brain imaging for the detection of deception has been widely discussed. This chapter discusses to what extent these—and other—techniques can be used in the legal arena to detect deception.

THE POLYGRAPH AND ITS QUESTIONING FORMATS

The polygraph was first introduced in the 1920's by physiologist and police officer John Larsson from the University of California, Berkley (Larson, 1932). He developed a machine that measured multiple physiological signals—blood pressure, pulse, respiration, and palmar sweating—simultaneously, and applied this machine in over 100 legal cases to evaluate whether the suspect was telling the truth. The polygraphs in use nowadays are not fundamentally different from that developed by Larson in the 1920s. Although the ink and lengthy rolls of paper used to record the physiological signals have been replaced by laptop computers, the machines still record multiple physiological signals, typically cardiovascular measures, respiration, and skin conductance.

Advocates of polygraph testing argue that the physiological recordings can be used to infer deception when combined with a proper questioning format. Thus, rather than inferring deception directly from the physiological responses to a specific question of interest, the responses are contrasted to those evoked by control questions. Several question formats exist, but the format most widely used by law enforcement agencies worldwide is the Control Question Test (CQT; Reid, 1947).

In this type of test, the suspect answers relevant and control questions while physiological reactions are being recorded. The relevant questions refer specifically to the incident under investigation (e.g., "In the night of Nov, 3, did you stab X?"). The physiological responses to these questions are compared with those elicited by the control questions. These control questions are more generic, but also deal with undesirable behavior (e.g., "In the first 25 years of your life, have you ever done anything illegal?").

Importantly, a CQT polygraph test is preceded by a lengthy interview that serves to convince the suspect that the polygraph can determine to an extremely high degree of accuracy whether the suspect is lying or not. This can be achieved by, for example, a rigged lie test using playing cards. During this interview, it is implied that an innocent examinee can confidently and honestly answer "no" to the relevant questions. After all, the polygraph will show that this answer is the truth. In addition, the interview serves to maneuver the examinee into answering "no" to the control questions, for example by suggesting that confessing illegal activities will negatively influence the polygrapher's impression of the examinee (for an example of how this is achieved, see Offe & Offe, 2007). The physiological signals registered by the polygraph covary with emotion (Kreibig, 2010), and the innocent examinee is assumed to show the strongest physiological responses to the control questions, fearing that his/her deceptive answer to this question will get him/her convicted for the crime under investigation. For guilty suspects, on the other hand, the relevant questions will pose the biggest threat, and will therefore elicit the strongest physiological responses.

Although the use of the CQT is widespread (Meijer & van Koppen, 2008), its merits have been debated for decades. At the core of the debate surrounding the CQT is the general assumption that the relevant questions will elicit stronger emotions—and thus larger responses—only in guilty suspects. The emotion-inducing effect is not so much a property of the control question (after all: Who has not done anything illegal in his life?), but rather of the way it is introduced to the suspect in the pretest interview (Offe & Offe, 2007). Whereas proponents have argued that a capable polygraph examiner is able of creating an atmosphere where an innocent suspect indeed perceives the control question as more threatening, critics argue that this assumption has no basis in psychological or psychophysiological research, is not convincing in its inner logic, and means the test is highly unstandardized (Ben-Shakhar, 2002; Fiedler, Schmid, & Stahl, 2002; Iacono, 2008; Lykken, 1998).

CONTROL QUESTION TEST ACCURACY

To what extent the CQT is prone to erroneous outcomes also remains debated. In part, this debate can be traced back to the research methodology. Laboratory studies are popular because deception can be manipulated by, for example, having participants engage in a mock theft ("did you steal the wallet from the secretaries office?"), having participants pick a playing card ("did you pick the ace of spades?"), or having participants lie about their autobiographical information ("is your fist name John"). As such, they offer full control of who is deceptive and who is not. Such studies, however, lack ecological validity; participants do not face severe consequences when failing the test. This is especially problematic because one can easily imagine that the threat of these consequences influences the magnitude of the physiological responses. An innocent suspect may, for example, perceive a relevant question (but also a control question) in a real-life test as much more threatening than a participant in a laboratory study.

The alternative to laboratory studies is to use field data. That is, data from real-life cases. Although such data have been collected under real-life circumstances, they have an important disadvantage; it is difficult to establish with 100% certainty whether the suspect was really deceptive or not—the ground truth. Importantly, this ground truth should be independent of the test outcome. If not, the accuracy will be an overestimation of the real accuracy. Take, for example, a confession as a measure of ground truth. If a deception test determines who will be questioned (those who failed the test) and who will not (those who passed the test), confessions will only be elicited in those who fail the test. False negative errors (i.e., deceptive suspects deemed truth tellers) will be excluded from such a sample, as those who pass the test will not be questioned. False positives (i.e., truthful suspects deemed deceptive) will be excluded, assuming that innocents who fail the test will not (falsely) confess. This way, even a test that performs at chance level will show high accuracy when tested against confessions (Iacono, 1991). Moreover, this problem is not limited to confessions. Dependence between test outcome and ground truth may also be present in other measures of ground truth. Investigative authorities may, for example, invest more resources in crime scene analysis once a suspect fails a test, which increases the probability of finding test-corroborating (physical) evidence.

Keeping the limitations of laboratory and field studies in mind, accuracy estimates of the CQT derived from laboratory studies range from 74% to 82% for guilty examinees, with a 7% to 8% false negative rate (guilty participants erroneously classified as innocent), and 60% to 83% for innocent examinees, with a false positive rate (innocent participants erroneously classified as guilty) varying from 10% to 16%. Estimates derived from field studies range from 84% to 89% for guilty examinees, with 1% to 13% false negatives, and 59% to 75% for innocent examinees with 12% to 23% false positives (Table 10.1). It should be noted that these percentages do not necessarily add up to 100% because of an inconclusive category. This inconclusive outcome occurs when the magnitude of the reactions to the relevant and the control questions are similar, and no conclusion regarding deception is made.

In 2003, the American National Research Council published a report summarizing the literature on the CQT, including its accuracy. The National Research Council did not report accuracy in terms of percentage of correct decisions, but expressed accuracy in terms of the area under the Receiver Operating characteristic Curve (ROC a) that can vary from 0.5 (chance level) to 1 (perfect accuracy).[1] The 37 laboratory studies and 7 field studies that passed the minimum

Table 10.1. OVERVIEW OF THE ACCURACY FIGURES YIELDED BY LABORATORY AND FIELD STUDIES FOR THE CONTROL QUESTION AND CONCEALED INFORMATION POLYGRAPH TEST

	n studies	Guilty Examinee			Innocent Examinee		
		Test outcome correct	Test outcome incorrect	Test outcome inconclusive	Test outcome correct	Test outcome incorrect	Test outcome inconclusive
Laboratory studies employing Control Question Test							
Office of Technology Assessment (1983)	12	74	7	19	60	16	24
Kircher et al. (1988)	14	74	8	18	66	12	22
Ben-Shakhar and Furedy (1990)	9	80	7	13	63	15	22
Honts (2004)	11	82	7	11	83	10	7
Field studies employing Control Question Test							
Office of Technology Assessment (1983)	10	87	11	2	75	19	6
Ben-Shakhar and Furedy (1990)	9	84	13	3	72	23	5
Honts (2004)	4	89	1	10	59	12	29

Laboratory studies employing Concealed Information Test

Ben-Shakhar and Furedy (1990)	10	84	16	94	6
Elaad (1998)	15	81	19	96	4
Lykken (1998)	8	88	12	97	3
MacLaren (2001)	22	76	24	83	17

Field studies employing Concealed Information Test

Elaad (1990)	1	42	58	98	2
Elaad, Ginton and Jungman (1992)	1	76	24	94	6

standards for review showed an ROC a of .85 and .89, respectively. It led the panel to conclude that "specific-incident polygraph tests can discriminate lying from truth telling at rates well above chance, though well below perfection" (National Research Council, 2003, p. 4). This conclusion was highly similar to a U.S. government report that was published 20 years earlier (Office of Technology Assessment, 1983), which concluded that ". . . the polygraph detects deception at a rate better than chance, but with error rates that could be considered significant."

The above allows for a number of conclusions. First, there are a certain number of degrees of freedom when it comes to selecting data on which accuracy estimates are based. Inconclusive outcomes can, for example, be counted as errors or not. Also, with the pros and cons of laboratory and field studies in mind, different authors apply different in- and exclusion criteria for studies on which they base their evaluation of the CQT's accuracy. As a consequence, accuracy estimates between reviews vary substantially. Second, even though the exact accuracy remains unknown, the CQT performs above chance level, meaning its outcome contains diagnostic information about deception. Third, the accuracy figures highlight that the error rate of the CQT can be substantial. Finally, the accuracy estimates listed imply the test is especially prone to false positive outcomes. This is problematic for application in the legal arena, as it is alien to legal doctrine abbreviated in the so-called Blackstone Maxim: "Better that ten guilty persons escape than that one innocent suffer (Blackstone, 1882; see also Volokh, 1997)."

THE CONCEALED INFORMATION TEST

The shortcomings of the CQT were recognized in the late fifties of the previous century, among others by psychologist David Lykken. Lykken developed an alternative question format, which he named the Guilty Knowledge Test (Lykken, 1959, 1960). This test is nowadays commonly referred to as the Concealed Information Test (CIT; Verschuere, Ben-Shakhar, & Meijer, 2011). In contrast to the CQT, the CIT does not measure deception, but attempts to establish whether an examinee possesses relevant crime-related information. In the CIT, questions presented to the examinee (e.g., "the murder weapon was a") are followed by one relevant alternative (e.g., the actual murder weapon: an ice pick) and several neutral (control) alternatives (e.g., a knife, a letter opener, a pair of scissors, a piercer) presented in random order. These neutral alternatives are chosen such that an innocent suspect would not be able to discriminate them from the relevant alternative. In contrast, a suspect who is familiar with the details of the crime would be able to discriminate between the relevant and the neutral control items, and the relevant items will elicit enhanced physiological responses such as increased skin conductance, a decrease in respiration, and changes in heart rate (Meijer, klein Selle, Elber, & Ben-Shakhar, 2014). In sum, crime knowledge is inferred from systematic stronger responding to the correct alternatives.

The CIT countered some of the main criticisms of the CQT, most notably the risk of an innocent suspect failing the test (i.e., false positive outcome). Under the assumption that all alternatives are equally plausible, and an innocent suspect cannot distinguish between the relevant and the neutral control alternatives, the false positive rate follows the laws of probability: A false positive test outcome means that, merely by chance, a pattern of stronger responding to the correct alternatives has occurred. The probability of this happening depends on two factors. The first factor concerns the test's properties; the false positive probability is inversely related to the number of questions and the number of answer alternatives per question. The second factor that determines false positive probability is how one defines "a pattern of stronger responding." When a guilty test outcome requires the suspect to respond maximally to the correct alternatives of all five questions, the probability of this happening by chance is smaller than when one requires a maximal response for only three out of the five correct alternatives. This control over false positive probability has important implications. For one thing, it allows the examiner to set the false positive probability at an arbitrary low level, as prescribed by legal doctrine in many countries. It also allows for calculation of the probability that a guilty test outcome is incorrect. This is essential information if an incriminating test outcome is introduced in court proceedings, as it allows for proper weighing by the judge or jury.

The CIT originally described by Lykken (1959) used only skin conductance responding as the dependent measure. This measure has by far received the most attention in CIT research, and has been shown to be robust in discriminating between guilty and innocent participants (see Table 10.1). Elaad (1998), for example, reviewed 15 mock crime studies and found average detection rates of 81% for guilty examinees and 96% for the innocent. Similar accuracy rates were reported by Ben-Shakhar and Furedy (1990). They reviewed 10 mock crime studies and found detection rates of 84% and 94%, respectively. MacLaren (2001) reported successful detection of 76% of participants with concealed knowledge, and 83% of those without. The two available field studies (Elaad, 1990; Elaad, Ginton, & Jungman, 1992) show equally high detection of innocent suspects (98% and 94%, respectively), but somewhat lower detection accuracy among guilty suspects (42% and 76%, respectively). Metaanalytic research on 80 studies showed very large effects ($d = 1.55$; Meijer et al., 2014). Finally, in its 2003 report, the National Research Council selected 13 studies that passed their minimum standards, yielding an area under the Receiver Operating Characteristic curve of .88. There is evidence to suggest that adding respiratory and cardiovascular signals to skin conductance adds to CIT accuracy (Gamer, Verschuere, Crombez, & Vossel, 2008).

FROM POLYGRAPH TO BRAIN IMAGING

Can brain recordings overcome the shortcomings of the polygraph? In the exploration of the neural signatures of deception, it is indeed often—implicitly or explicitly—assumed that brain measures can overcome the shortcomings of the polygraph (e.g., Bles & Haynes, 2008; Farah et al., 2014; Kozel et al., 2004;

Langleben et al., 2005). One measure of brain activity that has received notable attention in deception research is the P300 waveform. Two groups of researchers (Farwell & Donchin, 1991; Rosenfeld et al., 1991) introduced this measure to detect concealed information. Specifically, these authors used a CIT-like protocol, exchanging measures of the autonomic nervous system for measurement of brain activity as measured with the electroencephalogram. Their starting point was the widely known phenomenon that a deviant stimulus in a series of nondeviants (e.g., a series of tones in which 1 out of 5 has a low pitch) elicits a larger positive brainwave approximately 300 ms after stimulus presentation, the so-called "P300 component" (Donchin, 1981). In a CIT, the correct alternative (e.g., murder weapon) is the equivalent of the low tone only for guilty suspects, and a P300 evoked by the correct alternative indicates knowledge.

In essence the P300-based CIT uses the same question format, but uses P300 rather than skin conductance as the dependent measure. In fact, both P300 and skin conductance have been argued to reflect the same psychological process, namely attention toward a significant stimulus (Nieuwenhuis, de Geus, & Aston-Jones, 2011; klein Selle, Verschuere, Kindt, Meijer, & Ben-Shakhar, 2015; Suchotzki, Verschuere et al., 2016). A recent metaanalysis (Meijer et al., 2014) compared the accuracy between P300 and skin conductance measures for CITs probing mock crime details and autobiographical details. The results showed that the P300 outperformed skin conductance only in the autobiographical tests. The authors attributed this to the use of more salient details—and not to better detection—in the P300-based CIT than in the skin conductance based tests. There was no difference between skin conductance and P300 for the forensically more relevant mock crime tests. Besides skin conductance and P300, functional magnetic imaging (fMRI) has also been used in conjunction with the CIT. (See Gamer, 2011 for a review.) However, only a limited number of studies allowed for a conclusion about accuracy, which Meijer and colleagues (2016) estimated at .94 (Table 10.2). Given the low number of participants and the large number of degrees of freedom when it comes to analyzing fMRI data, it remains to be seen whether this accuracy estimate will stand the test of time.

Table 10.2. OVERVIEW OF THE ACCURACY
OF THE DIFFERENT MEASURES IN THE CIT

Measure	*n*	ROC
SCR	3863	.85
ERP	646	.88
fMRI	134	.94

Adapted from Meijer et al. (2016).
NOTE: CIT, Concealed Information Test, *n*, total number of participants; ROC, area under the ROC curve; SCR, skin conductance response; ERP, event-related brain potentials; fMRI, functional magnetic resonance imaging.

Besides the CIT, the use of fMRI for the detection of deception has also attracted great attention in another form. The rationale behind this form can be illustrated by the case of Ms. X: In 2003, in the United Kingdom, a 42-year-old woman was convicted of a crime against a child in her care. She served her prison term, yet continued to profess her innocence even after she was released. Four years after the conviction, psychiatrist Sean Spence administered a deception test based on fMRI to assess her credibility. Spence and colleagues derived the rationale for the test performed on Ms. X from one of their earlier studies (Spence et al., 2001). In this study, Spence invited 10 participants to the laboratory and presented them with a total of 36 autobiographical statements, such as "made your bed" and "taken a tablet" while the fMRI scanner registered their brain activity. Participants answered with key presses labeled "yes" and "no" based on color coding (e.g., lie in response to green or red). Results revealed that lying—compared with truth telling—was associated with activity in the right ventrolateral prefrontal, left ventrolateral prefrontal, and medial premotor areas. Ventrolateral prefrontal activation had previously been shown associated with response inhibition (Garavan, Ross, & Stein, 1999). This pattern—which has been found in many studies since (for reviews, see Gamer, 2014; Ganis, 2014)—led the authors to conclude that deception constitutes an executive function, including withholding the truth, and response manipulation and monitoring. In other words, truthful responding is the default modus of the brain, and when being deceptive, this truth needs to be inhibited, and the deceptive response needs to be selected and executed.

Ms. X also pressed buttons marked "yes" or "no" in response to statements about the incident (e.g., "You were innocent of the charges"). The test of the 42-year-old woman revealed a pattern of brain activation highly similar to that found in the 2001 study: increased activation in the ventrolateral prefrontal and anterior cingulate cortices when she endorsed the accuser's version of the events. Based on this neuroimaging data, Spence and colleagues concluded that her functional anatomical parameters behaved as if she were innocent (Spence, Kaylor-Hughes, BrookLankappa, & Wilkinson, 2008). The logical reasoning behind this conclusion would be as follows: When endorsing the accusation ("yes, I did it"), her brain activation showed inhibition. This inhibition means the "yes, I did it" is a lie. And if "yes, I did it" is a lie, she is innocent.

The case of Ms. X illustrates that in order to go from a pattern of brain activation to a decision about whether the suspect is innocent or not, a number of logical inferences need to be made. As acknowledged by Spence et al. (2008), such inferences pose logical problems. For instance, the assumption that lying is associated with inhibition came from a study in which participants came to the laboratory and lied about past actions on the spot. For that task, inhibition was required. But the 42-year-old-woman was presented with exemplars of an act she had been denying for years. Would it be possible that she had indeed harmed the child, but years of practice made her (false) denial the default response? While repeated lying has been found to make lying easier, it remains unclear whether such a reversal can indeed take place (Garrett et al., 2016; Hu et al., 2012; Van Bockstaele et al., 2012, 2015; Verschuere et al., 2011). Still, the logical consequences of such a reversal are interesting. If the lie, rather than the truth, becomes the default response, activation in brain regions associated with inhibition now denotes the truth. Consequently, inhibition concurrent with "yes, I did it" now denotes she is guilty. This example serves to point out that there is no unique brain area associated with deception, and errors can be made due to a flawed logic underlying the test. Such errors cannot be remedied by more sophisticated scanners that better image inhibition.

The reader might have noticed that questions presented to Ms. X while in the scanner differ from either the CQT and the CIT explained earlier. This question format—where one answers questions both truthfully and deceptively, was originally developed by John Furedy and his colleagues using skin conductance (e.g., Furedy, Davis, & Gurevich, 1988), and named the Differentiation of Deception paradigm (DoD). In a more recent variant of the DoD paradigm, participants are asked to answer each question twice: once truthfully and once deceptively. This test was labeled the Sheffield Lie Test (e.g., Spence et al., 2001). Because each question is answered both truthfully and deceptively, the DoD paradigm isolates deception to a high degree. The DoD is of utmost interest to academics studying deception, but its applied usage remains to be demonstrated.

COUNTERMEASURES AND FIELD STUDIES

No dependent measure—peripheral or "direct" from the brain—is exclusively related to deception. As a consequence, all physiological and neural measures are sensitive to countermeasures. Countermeasures refer to deliberate attempts by the examinee to alter the physiological responses, and thereby obtain a truthful test outcome. Polygraph measures are relatively easy to elicit, for example by vividly imagining an emotional event (Ben-Shakhar, 2011; Kunzendorf & Sheikh, 1990). More recent research has shown that countermeasures can also be effective against neuroimaging measures. A P300, for example, is elicited by any stimulus that is deviant. Research showed that if the participant attaches meaning to the different neutral control alternative (e.g., by wiggling their toe or by imagining the experimenter slapping them in the face), these neutral options also become significant, and diagnostic accuracy decreased (Rosenfeld et al., 2004). Ganis et al. (2011) demonstrated that comparable countermeasures also worked in an fMRI setting and reduced CIT detection accuracy from 100% to only 33% (see also Uncapher, Boyd-Meredith, Chow, Rissman, & Wagner, 2015). The only test that has been shown relatively robust against countermeasures so far is Rosenfeld's Complex Trial Protocol (Rosenfeld et al., 2013). This test is a variant of the P300-based CIT, but requires more resources from the participant. The participant first acknowledges perceiving the relevant stimulus, and shortly thereafter makes a decision about an unrelated target/nontarget. Interestingly, it is not the measure, but the questioning format that seems robust against countermeasures.

NEUROSCIENCE-BASED DECEPTION DETECTION: BETTER THAN THE POLYGRAPH?

Neuroscience-based lie detection has attracted great attention. Numerous authors posed the question whether such tests are better than the polygraph test. Before a meaningful answer to this question can be formulated, the questioning format needs to be defined. The CQT polygraph test is fundamentally flawed, not because the peripheral physiological measures are poor indices of emotion, but because the relevant and control question differ on many dimensions besides deception. At a superficial level, one can argue that neuroscience-based deception detection is indeed better than the polygraph, simply because it does not employ the flawed CQT questioning format. Just as there is no unique peripheral physiological response associated with deception, there is no unique brain region associated with deception. Decisions are determined by logical inferences: Deception is inferred from inhibition and cognitive control in the DoD, and knowledge is inferred from attentional orienting in the CIT. Logical inferences allow for logical errors, regardless of whether the dependent measures are recorded with a polygraph or with an MRI scanner. The logical inference problems associated with deception research are solved by introducing proper controls in the questioning format, not by new introducing new technology. Moreover, the polygraph and fMRI measures may tap similar psychological mechanisms (klein Selle et al., 2016; Suchotzki, Verschuere et al., 2015). When they do, only limited incremental validity can be expected.

LEGAL STATUS

The distinction between question formats and dependent measures is also relevant for legal discussions about admissibility. Two legal doctrines are relevant here. First, when looking at the four Daubert criteria (testability, error rate, peer review and publication, and general acceptance; Daubert v. Merrell Dow Pharmaceuticals Inc., 1993), it becomes clear the CQT does not meet these criteria (see e.g., Gallai, 1999; Saxe & Ben-Shakhar, 1999). As outlined previously, discussions surrounding the CQT revolve around the question format, and the introduction of measures of brain activity will not fundamentally change this state of affairs. For the CIT and the DOD, the known error rate is the crucial lacking criterion, as no field data is available (Ben-Shakhar & Kremnitzer, 2011; Rosenfeld, Hu, Labkovsky, Meixner, & Winograd, 2013; see also United States v, Semrau, 2012). So far, fMRI and P300 studies have been almost exclusively limited to laboratory studies. Langleben and Moriarty (2013) called for clinical trials of fMRI deception tools. But without an a priori specification of how these trials will deal with independently determining ground truth, such trials are likely to result in a similar discussion that has plagued CQT polygraph testing for decades.

A second relevant act of jurisprudence is the U.S. Supreme Court's decision, United States v. Scheffer (1998). In this case, the court decided that credibility determination is the jury's task, rendering a CQT polygraph test inadmissible (see also Wilson v. Corestaff Services. L.P., 2010). Based on this, several authors have argued that this renders both the CQT and DoD inadmissible, as they detect deception, but not the CIT because it detects recognition (e.g., Rosenfeld et al., 2013; Frederiksen, 2011). But as explained, one could also argue that none of the tests tap deception directly. They can be used to tap emotion in the CQT, and attentional orienting and/or inhibition in the CIT and DoD. From these processes—emotions, orienting, and inhibition—inferences about involvement in a crime can be made. If none of these tests tap deception directly, one can also argue that none of them should a priori be ruled inadmissible on conceptual grounds.

CONCLUSION

Research into the detection of deception using psychophysiology goes back almost a century. Historically, it has been plagued by a lack of theory development, and "research . . . has not progressed over time in the manner of a typical scientific field" (National Research Council, 2003, p. 213). Starting early this century, neuroimaging studies—and especially the fMRI studies—have moved from using the flawed CQT to the more controlled CIT and DoD. They have introduced new theoretical concepts of inhibition and cognitive control, and are thereby partly responsible for the contemporary cognitive approach to deception detection (Blandón-Gitlin, Fenn, Masip, & Yoo, 2014; Vrij, Fisher, Mann, & Leal, 2006). Yet for practical purposes, it has done little to solve problems that have plagued deception research for decades. The biggest challenge is not to find new technology that can accurately detect deception, but to find a question format that isolates deception, and to corroborate laboratory data with methodologically sound field studies.

NOTE

1. ROC curve (a) represents the detection efficiency regardless of any specific cutoff point (for a detailed description of generating ROC curves in CIT experiments, see Lieblich, Kugelmass, & Ben-Shakhar, 1970). The area under the ROC curve ranges between 0 and 1, such that an area of 0.5 means that the two distributions (i.e., the detection score's distributions for guilty and innocent examinees) are indistinguishable (i.e., detecting whether an examinee is deceptive or not will be at chance level). An area of 1 means that there is no overlap between the two distributions and thus a perfect classification is possible.

REFERENCES

Ben-Shakhar, G. (2002). A critical review of the control questions test (CQT). In M. Kleiner (Ed.), *Handbook of polygraph testing* (pp. 103–126). Waltham, MA: Academic Press.

Ben-Shakhar, G. (2011). Countermeasures. In B. Verschuere, G. Ben-Shakhar, & E. Meijer (Eds.), *Memory detection: Theory and application of the Concealed Information Test* (pp. 200–214). Cambridge: Cambridge University Press.

Ben-Shakhar, G., & Furedy, J. J. (1990). *Theories and applications in the detection of deception: A psychophysiological and international perspective*. New York: Springer-Verlag Publishing.

Ben-Shakhar, G., & Kremnitzer, M. (2011). The CIT in the courtroom: Legal aspects. In B. Verschuere, G. Ben-Shakhar, & E. Meijer. *Memory detection: Theory and application of the Concealed Information Test* (pp. 276–290). Cambridge: Cambridge University Press.

Blandón-Gitlin, I., Fenn, E., Masip, J., & Yoo, A. H. (2014). Cognitive-load approaches to detect deception: Searching for cognitive mechanisms. *Trends in cognitive sciences, 18*(9), 441–444.

Blackstone, W. (1882). *Commentaries on the laws of England* (3rd ed.). London: Murray.

Bles, M., & Haynes, J. D. (2008). Detecting concealed information using brain-imaging technology. *Neurocase, 14*, 82–92. doi: 10.1080/13554790801992784

Donchin, E. (1981). Surprise! . . . surprise? *Psychophysiology, 18*, 493–513. doi: 10.1111/j.1469-8986.1981.tb01815.x

Elaad, E. (1990). Detection of guilty knowledge in real-life criminal investigations. *Journal of Applied Psychology, 75*(5), 521–529.

Elaad, E. (1998). The challenge of the Concealed Knowledge Polygraph Test. *Expert Evidence, 6*(3), 161–187.

Elaad, E., Ginton, A., & Jungman, N. (1992). Detection measures in real-life criminal guilty knowledge tests. *Journal of Applied Psychology, 77*(5), 757–767.

Farah, M. J., Hutchinson, B., Phelps, E. A., & Wagner, A. D. (2014). Functional MRI-based lie-detection: Scientific and societal challenges, *Nature Reviews Neuroscience, 15*, 123–131. doi: 10.1038/nrn3665

Farwell, L. A., & Donchin, E. (1991). The truth will out: Interrogative polygraphy ("lie detection") with event-related potentials. *Psychophysiology, 28*, 531–547. doi: 10.1111/j.1469-8986.1991.tb01990.x

Fiedler, K., Schmid, J., & Stahl, T. (2002). What is the current truth about polygraph lie detection? *Basic and Applied Social Psychology, 24*, 313–324.

Frederiksen, S. (2011). Brain fingerprint or lie detector: Does Canada's polygraph jurisprudence apply to emerging forensic neuroscience technologies? *Information & Communications Technology Law, 20*, 115–132. doi: 10.1080/13600834.2011.578930

Furedy, J. J., Davis, C., & Gurevich, M. (1988). Differentiation of deception as a psychological process: A psychophysiological approach. *Psychophysiology, 25*, 683–688. doi: 10.1111/j.1469-8986.1988.tb01908.x

Gallai, D. (1999). Polygraph evidence in federal courts: Should it be admissible? *American Criminal Law Review, 36*, 87–116.

Gamer, M. (2011). Detecting of deception and concealed information using neuro-imaging techniques. In B. Verschuere, G. Ben-Shakhar, & E. Meijer (Eds.), *Memory Detection: Theory and Application of the Concealed Information Test* (pp. 90–113). Cambridge: Cambridge University Press. doi:10.1017/CBO9780511975196.006

Gamer, M. (2014). Mind reading using neuroimaging: Is this the future of deception detection? *European Psychologist, 19*, 172–183. doi: 10.1027/1016-9040/a000193

Gamer, M., Verschuere, B., Crombez, G., & Vossel, G. (2008). Combining physiological measures in the detection of concealed information. *Physiology & Behavior, 95*(3), 333–340.

Ganis, G. (2014) Deception detection using neuroimaging. In P. A. Granhag, A. Vrij, & B. Verschuere (Eds.), *Detecting deception: Current challenges and cognitive approaches.* Chichester, UK: John Wiley & Sons, Ltd.

Ganis, G., Rosenfeld, J. P., Meixner, J., Kievit, R. A., & Schendan, H. E. (2011). Lying in the scanner: Covert countermeasures disrupt deception detection by functional magnetic resonance imaging. *Neuroimage, 55*, 312–319. doi: 10.1016/j.neuroimage.2010.11.025

Garavan, H., Ross, T. J., & Stein, E. A. (1999). Right hemispheric dominance of inhibitory control: An event-related fMRI study. *Proceedings of the National Academy of Sciences of the United States of America, 96*(14), 8301–8306.

Garrett, N., Lazzaro, S. C., Ariely, D., & Sharot, T. (2016). The brain adapts to dishonesty. *Nature Neuroscience, 19*(12), 1727–1732.

Honts, C. R. (2004). The psychophysiological detection of deception. In P. A. Granhag & L. A. Strömwall (Eds.), *The detection of deception in forensic contexts* (pp. 103–126). Cambridge: Cambridge University Press.

Hu, X., Chen, H., & Fu, G. (2012). A repeated lie becomes a truth? The effect of intentional control and training on deception. *Frontiers in Psychology, 3*, 488. doi: 10.3389/fpsyg.2012.00488

Iacono, W. G. (1991). Can we determine the accuracy of polygraph tests? In P. K. Ackles, J. R. Jennings, & M. G. H. Coles (Eds.), *Advances in psychophysiology* (pp. 201–201). Greenwich, CT: JAI Press.

Iacono, W. G. (2008). Effective policing—Understanding how polygraph tests work and are used. *Criminal Justice and Behavior, 35*, 1295–1308.

Kircher, J. C., Horowitz, S. W., & Raskin, D. C. (1988). Meta-analysis of mock crime studies of the Control Question Polygraph Technique. *Law and Human Behavior, 12*, 79–90.

klein Selle, N., Verschuere, B., Kindt, M., Meijer, E. H., & Ben-Shakhar, G. (2016). Orienting versus inhibition in the Concealed Information Test: Different cognitive processes drive different physiological measures. *Psychophysiology, 53*, 579–590. doi: 10.1111/psyp.12583

Kozel, F. A., Ravell, L. J., Lorenbaum, J. P., Shastri, A., Elihai, J. D., Horner, M. D., . . . George, M. S. (2004). A pilot study of functional magnetic resonance imaging brain correlates of deception in healthy young men. *Journal of Neuropsychiatry and Clinical Neuroscience, 16*, 295–305. doi: 10.1176/jnp.16.3.295

Kreibig, S. D. (2010). Autonomic nervous system activity in emotion: A review. *Biological psychology, 84*(3), 394–421.

Kunzendorf, R. G., & Sheikh, A. A. (Eds.). (1990). *The psychophysiology of mental imagery: Theory, research, and application* (Vol. 3). Amityville, NY: Baywood Publishing Co.

Langleben, D. D., Loughhead, J. W., Bilker, W. B., Ruparel, K., Childress, A. R., Busch, S. I., & Gur, R. C. (2005). Telling truth from lie in individual subjects with fast event-related fMRI. *Human Brain Mapping, 26*, 262–272. doi: 10.1002/hbm.20191

Langleben, D. D., & Moriarty, J. C. (2013). Using brain imaging for lie detection: Where science, law, and policy collide. *Psychology, Public Policy, and Law, 19*, 222–234. doi: 10.1037/a0028841

Larson, J. A. (1932). *Lying and Its Detection.* Chicago: University of Chicago Press.

Lieblich, I., Kugelmass, S., & Ben-Shakhar, G. (1970). Efficiency of GSR detection of information as a function of stimulus set size. *Psychophysiology, 6*, 601–608.

Lykken, D. T. (1959). The GSR in the detection of guilt. *Journal of Applied Psychology, 43*, 385–388. doi: 10.1037/h0046060

Lykken, D. T. (1960). The validity of the guilty knowledge technique: The effects of faking. *Journal of Applied Psychology, 44*, 258–262. doi: 10.1037/h0044413

Lykken, D. T. (1998). *A tremor in the blood: Uses and abuses of the lie detector.* Berlin: Plenum Press.

MacLaren, V. V. (2001). A quantitative review of the guilty knowledge test. *Journal of Applied Psychology, 86*(4), 674–683.

Meijer, E. H., klein Selle, N., Elber, L., & Ben-Shakhar, G. (2014). Memory detection with the Concealed Information Test: A meta analysis of skin conductance, respiration, heart rate, and P300 data. *Psychophysiology, 51*, 879–904. doi: 10.1111/psyp.12239

Meijer, E. H., & van Koppen, P. J. (2008). Lie detectors and the law: The use of the polygraph in Europe. In D. Canter, & R. Zukauskiene (Eds.), *Psychology and law: Bridging the gap* (pp. 31–50). Aldershot, UK: Ashgate.

Meijer E. H., Verschuere B., Gamer M., Merckelbach H., & Ben-Shakhar G. (2016). Deception detection with behavioral, autonomic, and neural measures: Conceptual and methodological considerations that warrant modesty. *Psychophysiology, 53*(5), 593–604.

National Research Council. Committee to review the scientific evidence on the Polygraph. Division of Behavioral and Social Sciences and Education. (2003). *The polygraph and lie detection.* Washington, DC: The National Academies Press.

Nieuwenhuis, S., De Geus, E. J., & Aston-Jones, G. (2011). The anatomical and functional relationship between the P3 and autonomic components of the orienting response. *Psychophysiology, 48*, 162–175. doi: 10.1111/j.1469-8986.2010.01057.x

Offe, H., & Offe, S. (2007). The comparison question test: Does it work and if so how? *Law and Human Behavior, 31*, 291–303. doi: 10.1007/s10979-006-9059-3

Office of Technology Assessment. (1983). *Scientific validity of polygraph testing: A research review and evaluation.* Washington, DC: US Government Printing Office.

Reid, J. E. (1947). A revised questioning technique in lie-detection tests. *Journal of Criminal Law and Criminology, 37*, 542–547. doi: 10.2307/1138979

Rosenfeld, J. P., Angell, A., Johnson, M., & Qian, J. H. (1991). An ERP-based, control-question lie detector analog: Algorithms for discriminating effects within individuals' average waveforms. *Psychophysiology, 28*, 319–335. doi: 10.1111/j.1469-8986.1991.tb02202.x

Rosenfeld, J. P., Hu, X., Labkovsky, E., Meixner, J., & Winograd, M. R. (2013). Review of recent studies and issues regarding the P300-based complex trial protocol for detection of concealed information. *International Journal of Psychophysiology, 90*, 118–134. doi: 10.1016/j.ijpsycho.2013.08.012

Rosenfeld, J. P., Soskins, M., Bosh, G., & Rayan, A. (2004). Simple, effective countermeasures to P300-based tests of detection of concealed information. *Psychophysiology, 41*, 205–219. doi: 10.1111/j.1469-8986.2004.00158.x

Saxe, L., & Ben-Shakhar, G. (1999). Admissibility of polygraph tests: The application of scientific standards post-Daubert. *Psychology, Public Policy, and Law, 5*(1), 203.

Spence, S. A., Farrow, T. F., Herford, A. E., Wilkinson, I. D., Zheng, Y., & Woodruff, P. W.(2001). Behavioural and functional anatomical correlates of deception in humans. *NeuroReport, 12*, 2849–2853. doi: 10.1097/00001756-200109170-00019

Spence, S. A., Kaylor-Hughes, C. J., Brook, M. L., Lankappa, S. T., & Wilkinson, I. D. (2008). 'Munchausen's syndrome by proxy' or a 'miscarriage of justice'? An initial application of functional neuroimaging to the question of guilt versus innocence. *European Psychiatry, 23*, 309–314.

Suchotzki, K., Verschuere, B., Peth, J., Crombez, G., & Gamer, M. (2015). Manipulating item proportion and deception reveals crucial dissociation between behavioral, autonomic, and neural indices of concealed information. *Human Brain Mapping, 36*, 427–439. doi: 10.1002/hbm.22637

Uncapher, M. R., Boyd-Meredith, J. T., Chow, T. E., Rissman, J., & Wagner, A. D. (2015). Goal-directed modulation of neural memory patterns: Implications for fMRI-based memory detection. *Journal of Neuroscience, 35*(22), 8531–8545.

Van Bockstaele, B., Verschuere, B., Moens, T., Suchotzki, K., Debey, E., & Spruyt, A.(2012). Learning to lie: Effects of practice on the cognitive cost of lying. *Frontiers in Psychology, 3*, 526. doi: 10.3389/fpsyg.2012.00526

Verschuere, B., Ben-Shakhar, G., & Meijer, E. H. (Eds.). (2011). *Memory detection: Theory and application of the Concealed Information Test.* Cambridge: Cambridge University Press.

Verschuere, B., Spruyt, A., Meijer, E. H., & Otgaar, H. (2011). The ease of lying. *Consciousness and Cognition, 20*, 908–911. doi: 10.1016/j.concog.2010.10.023

Volokh, A. (1997). n Guilty men. *University of Pennsylvania Law Review, 146*, 173–211.

Vrij, A., Fisher, R., Mann, S., & Leal, S. (2006). Detecting deception by manipulating cognitive load. *Trends in Cognitive Sciences, 10*(4), 141–142. doi: 10.1016/j.tics.2006.02.003

PART IV

Malingering in the Courtroom

11

Seven Myths About Feigning

MARKO JELICIC, HARALD MERCKELBACH,
AND IRENA BOŠKOVIĆ

Several years ago, we (the first and second author) were asked to serve as expert witnesses in a court case that involved a man who was accused of murdering his wife and young son. The defendant claimed he had stabbed the victims to death because voices in his head told him to do so. Because the court was not convinced that the man genuinely suffered from command hallucinations, we were asked to evaluate the authenticity of his hallucinations (Merckelbach, Peters, & Jelicic, 2011). After checking his medical records and the police file, we interviewed the defendant and administered a range of tests to him. Because feigners usually do not know what kind of symptoms true patients experience, we specifically asked the defendant whether or not he suffered from atypical and bizarre symptoms (of course we did not tell him that these symptoms were improbable symptoms). Our test battery included two symptom validity tests—instruments specifically designed to measure the validity of symptoms or test performance (Larrabee, 2012). The defendant's medical records showed that, in the years before the violent incident, he had visited his family doctor a number of times because of feeling depressed. And while awaiting his trial in prison, a psychiatrist diagnosed him with an affective disorder. Although he did have a history of mental illness, the interview and his tests results showed that the defendant probably was faking his command hallucinations. For one thing, he endorsed many rare or improbable symptoms such as "the voices in my head are always present" and "I just have to comply with the commands" during the interview, which is indicative of feigning (see Knoll & Resnick, 2008; Resnick, 2007). Furthermore, on both symptom validity tests the defendant had scores comparable to people who were instructed to feign mental illness. After confronting the defendant with our findings, he admitted that he had feigned his command hallucinations in the hope to be found not guilty by reason of insanity (NGRI).

People have different reasons for feigning mental illness. A small percentage of feigners pretend to suffer from a psychiatric disorder out of the unusual desire to be seen as a patient—a condition known as factitious disorder (Feldman, 2004).

Their primary goal is to get attention and sympathy from family, friends, and medical personnel. Factitious disorder is a poorly understood condition, but the research that exists shows that it is a psychiatric disease. For example, Lawlor and Kirakowski (2014) performed a text analysis on Internet communications of an online support group for people with factitious disorder and found that these people exhibit an addiction-like desire to occupy the sick role. Most of them were upset by this, felt guilt, and wanted to be treated. Note that most individuals feigning mental illness do not want to adopt the "sick role," but engage in this type of deceptive behavior for external incentives (Pankratz, 1998; Young, 2014). People with dead-end jobs may pretend to have a disorder to obtain sickness benefits. Individuals who have been involved in a traffic or workplace accident may feign symptoms to receive insurance money. Some people may pretend to have symptoms to be prescribed psychoactive medications. Soldiers may feign mental illness to avoid certain military duties or to receive service-connected disability pensions. And individuals who are standing trial, just like the case described earlier, may pretend to suffer from a mental illness to reduce their criminal responsibility. People who have external reasons for feigning are often labeled *malingerers*. Malingering is a deliberate act of deception, not a disease. Thus, malingering is not diagnosed, but detected. Psychiatric disorders are especially susceptible to feigning, because the diagnosis of such disorders usually relies on subjective symptoms reported by patients (Resnick, 2007). Also, it is good to realize that feigning is not an all-or-nothing phenomenon (Conroy & Kwartner, 2006). Although some individuals may fabricate a complete disorder, others will grossly exaggerate existing psychiatric symptoms.

As pointed out by Ornish (2001), individuals standing trial for a serious offense will do virtually anything to get the lowest punishment possible. Because psychotic disorders such as schizophrenia or schizoaffective disorder may lead to an NGRI verdict, feigning command hallucinations and other psychotic symptoms has some popularity among deceptive defendants (Chesterman, Terbeck & Vaughan, 2008). Posttraumatic stress disorder (PTSD) is often regarded as a mitigating circumstance by judges and juries. Therefore, some defendants—in particular those who have been involved in military operations—pretend to suffer from this trauma-related disorder (Hall & Hall, 2007). Although crime-related amnesia is not always considered a mitigating factor (cf. Tysse, 2005), a number of defendants feign loss of memory for their criminal offenses (Cima et al., 2002). They pretend to suffer from crime-related amnesia because they do not want to talk about shameful offenses such as sexually molesting children. Or they feign memory loss because it suggests that their criminal acts were impulsive, rather than conducted in a premeditated way (premeditated crimes are usually considered more serious than impulsive offenses). Occasionally, defendants will engage in feigning exotic disorders such as dissociative identity disorder or low serotonin syndrome (Ornish, 2001).

In recent years, feigning of mental illness has gained some attention among forensic (neuro)psychologists. At present, leading forensic (neuro)psychology journals regularly publish articles on this topic. Several books on feigning have

appeared (e.g., Kitaeff, 2007; Morel, 2010; Young, 2014), and a number of ded-
icated conferences on this issue have been organized (e.g., the 4th European
Conference on Symptom Validity Assessment, which was held in 2015). Despite
growing interest among mental health professionals, a number of misconceptions about feigning exist. This chapter describes seven myths pertaining to feigning. Most of them have been around in the psychiatric literature for more than a
hundred years and can be traced back to the writings of 19th century German-
speaking psychiatrists.

MYTH ONE: FEIGNING CAN BE EASILY DETECTED USING A CLINICAL INTERVIEW

More than a century ago, German psychiatrists such as Falkenhorst (cited in
Vyleta, 2007) believed that feigners could be detected by observing the way individuals move. Today, some mental health experts still adhere to that idea. Singh,
Avasthi, and Grover (2007), for instance, wrote that: "In a malingerer, illustrators
i.e. gestures that accompany speech are used less frequently; emblems i.e. gestures
that communicate a specific meaning in a specific culture, may be discordant
with spoken language, and manipulators i.e. movements involving self-grooming,
scratching, pulling, rubbing another body part and use of props viz. a pen, are dis-
tinctly prolonged and frequently repeated by the subject" (p. 128). However, such
indicators of feigning lack any empirical support. Feigning can be seen as a case
of deception—it is deliberate falsification of symptom reports—and an extensive
literature shows that non-verbal indicators provide, at best, very weak cues for
detecting deception and most of the time they are not diagnostic at all (DePaulo
et al., 2003).

In a classic study, Rosenhan (1973) had eight normal individuals—Rosenhan
himself, one psychology student, three psychologists, two physicians, and a house-
wife—admitted to psychiatric institutions. All of them claimed hearing voices during the intake procedure. Although they stopped complaining about hallucinations
once admitted to the clinic, all of them were diagnosed with schizophrenia, were
prescribed psychoactive medications, and had to stay in the hospital for a considerable time (9 to 52 days). More recently, Hickling, Blanchard, Mundy, and Galovski
(2002) hired six actors and taught them how to feign PTSD. Subsequently, all six
visited a clinic that specialized in diagnosing PTSD. None of them was labeled as
a feigner. Rosen and Phillips (2004) identified 12 studies in which normal people
instructed to feign a somatic condition were asked to visit a medical doctor. In all
studies, physicians detected feigners at a very low rate, from 0% to 25%.

It should be mentioned here that one special interview technique does have
some value in detecting feigning. This technique was employed in the case presented at the beginning of this chapter. As mentioned before, most feigners do
not know exactly what kind of symptoms genuine patients experience. When
confronted with improbable symptoms (i.e., symptoms that seem to pertain to
a certain disorder but are hardly ever reported by bonafide patients), it is quite
likely that feigners will confirm suffering from such symptoms. There is evidence

that endorsement of many unlikely symptoms is indicative of feigning (Knoll & Resnick, 2008; Resnick, 2007). The rationale behind this interview technique is also applied in a number of instruments designed to detect feigning (see the following).

How to Detect Feigning?

As shown in the case described at the start of this chapter, symptom validity tests may be useful in detecting feigning. One such test is the Structured Inventory of Malingered Symptomatology (SIMS; Smith, 2008; Smith & Burger, 1997). The SIMS is a self-report instrument designed to screen for feigning of psychopathology and/or memory impairment. It consists of 75 items pertaining to feigning in five different areas including psychosis and depression. The idea behind the SIMS is that feigners are unfamiliar with how genuine symptoms manifest themselves. As a result, they tend to endorse atypical and bizarre symptoms that superficially may seem to be related to the condition they are feigning. A typical SIMS item is "There is nothing I can do, besides taking medication, that has any effect on the voices I hear." By and large, the SIMS correctly identifies 95% of instructed feigners and labels 7% honest responders incorrectly as simulators (Van Impelen, Merckelbach, Jelicic, & Merten, 2014). Although these are not perfect statistics, they are substantially better than the detection rates that clinical interviews generate.

Another symptom validity test is the Amsterdam Short-Term Memory test (ASTM; Schmand, de Sterke, & Lindeboom, 1999). This test capitalizes on the fact that most feigners do not know that genuine neurological and psychiatric patients perform well on simple recognition tests. The ASTM consists of 30 items. In each item, the participant is presented with five printed words from the same semantic category (e.g., apple, peach, grape, pear, banana), which she or he has to read aloud and try to remember. Next, the participant is given a simple written addition or subtraction task (e.g., $27 + 15 = ?$), which she or he has to solve mentally. Finally, five words from the same semantic category as before are presented (e.g., apple, grape, melon, peach, kiwi). The participant has to indicate the three words that were also presented in the first series. The maximum score is 90 (30 items × 3 words correct). Scores below 85 points are considered to be indicative of aggravation or feigning of memory disturbances. About 90% of instructed feigners achieve such a low test score, while 7% of honest people will score below the cut off. Again, the detection rate is not perfect, but still better than what can be attained with clinical interviews.

But what if feigners have knowledge of psychopathology or memory disorders? Are they able to defeat tests such as the SIMS or ASTM? It appears that knowledge of mental disorders does not seem to undermine the efficacy of symptom validity tests to a large degree. In one study, mental health experts and laypeople were given the SIMS and asked to imagine that they were feigning psychosis because they were standing trial for a serious offense and wanted to avoid legal responsibility (Jelicic, Van Gaal, & Peters, 2013). Although the experts engaged in less fragrant feigning on the SIMS than people without expertise in psychiatry, most participants (92%) were identified as feigners by this instrument, regardless of their knowledge of psychopathology. The reason for this is probably that instruments like the SIMS confront feigners with a calibration problem: On the one hand, they have to endorse a certain number of symptoms (otherwise they would appear to be healthy people), while on the other, they are afraid to go over the top.

Note that the SIMS and ASTM are not feigning tests, but symptom validity tests. Feigners will often perform in the abnormal range on these tests, but not all individuals with abnormal scores are feigners. Take for instance a nonmotivated patient with a high SIMS score who filled out the instrument in a random fashion. Such a patient is a sloppy respondent, not a feigner. As mentioned before, feigning pertains to exaggerating or fabricating symptoms to obtain a certain incentive. A high score on the SIMS does not reveal the motive for endorsing many symptoms. Because high scores may point to feigning, follow-up examinations (e.g., gathering collateral information) in patients with such scores is recommended. Such a detailed examination should make clear if a patient has something to gain by exaggerating or fabricating symptoms. It should be mentioned here that patients often strive for certain benefits without their therapists knowing this. Van Egmond, Kummeling, and Van Balkom (2005) asked psychiatric outpatients whether or not they expected to gain something from being a patient. A substantial minority (30%–40%) reported that this was indeed the case. They admitted that their patient status may help them to get a new home, sickness benefits, or a resident permit. Thus, it appears that psychiatric outpatients often have a hidden agenda that pertains to other ambitions than just recovering from their symptoms. This agenda may fuel symptom exaggeration and treatment stagnation (van Egmond & Kummeling, 2002). The link between feigning and poor therapeutic success—including lack of cooperation, high dropout rate, and increased healthcare utilization—has now been well documented (e.g., Anestis et al., 2015; Horner et al., 2014) and should in itself be sufficient reason to give high priority to the evaluation of feigning as a diagnostic option.

MYTH TWO: FEIGNING IS RARE

Clinicians who do not use symptom validity tests will often fail to detect feigning of mental illness. As a consequence, they will think that only in rare cases will individuals pretend to have a psychiatric disorder. Just like the first misconception about feigning, this second myth also has old roots. In his monograph *Über Simulation von Geistesstöringen* ("On the simulation of psychopathology," 1903), Carl Gustav Jung wrote that, during his long career, he spoke to thousands of people admitted to a psychiatric institution, and only 11 of them were feigners. German psychiatrist Többen (1935) also opined that feigning was rare. He studied 3.156 files of patients who were admitted to the clinic where he was working, and reported that only two of them were pseudo-patients. And Jung and Többen were not the only ones believing that feigning was rare; many old German psychiatrists thought that feigning of mental illness did not occur (cf. Siemens, 1888). To a large extent, this belief was motivated by the fear of labeling truly sick people as malingerers, a practice that had been all too real in the pre-19th history of psychiatry (Ledebur, 2012). This fear is still with us today, and might explain why, for example, Yates, Nordquist, and Schulz-Ross (1996) found in their evaluation of 227 patients who attended the emergency department of a general hospital that 13% of them were suspected of feigning, while in their medical records this option was completely dropped. The forensic psychologist Lees-Haley has a completely different perspective on this: "If I think you are malingering, my job is to say so just as surely as I'm supposed to say so if I think you are suffering a major depression or have an IQ of 100. Those experts who avoid the term of malingering because it is 'serious'—as if other diagnoses were not serious—are making a specious argument and failing to consider the impact of their statements on the victims of malingerers" (Heilbronner, 2005; p. 358).

Some contemporary authors also think that feigning hardly ever occurs. For example, in an editorial comment on functional complaints in children, neurologist Ramesh (2013) stated that feigning is rare. He backed this conclusion with a reference. The article Ramesh cited describes two cases of children with functional paralysis. Quite surprisingly, the term *feigning* is not mentioned in that article, although a hidden agenda was evidently present in both. Thus, it seems that the idea that feigners are rare is a commonly held belief in medicine not needing any further explanation. This view has been challenged by British psychiatrist Theodore Dalrymple (2012). Writing about people with disability and sickness benefits, he remarked that in 2006, at the height of a period of economic growth in the United Kingdom, there were 2.9 million people in that country who received benefits because they were unable to work due to illness. When the financial crisis broke out, the British government announced that all people receiving such benefits again had to undergo a medical evaluation. Because of this announcement alone, hundred thousands of them gave up their claims. After all people receiving benefits had been reevaluated, it appeared that only one in eight was deemed too ill to work. Dalrymple's example suggests that, at least in the area of disability and sickness benefits, feigning is ubiquitous and costing society lots of money.

A recent criminal case from the Netherlands shows that, whatever its precise prevalence, feigning of mental illness has an enormous impact. In this case, two psychiatrists recruited dozens of potential pseudo-patients (Zweep, 2011). They were trained in how to fake depression or other disorders. Subsequently, they applied for disability and sickness benefits and were all seen by professionals. In about a third of the cases, the pseudo-patients had to talk to a psychiatrist (not the two instigators). With one notable exception, none of the professionals engaged in evaluation of the imposters was able to unmask the pseudo-patients. It took special police teams to identify feigning of psychiatric disorders in the imposters. In one hilarious case, a police observation team noticed how a man claiming major mental illness, incontinence, and severe immobility, jumped in his Mercedes car and drove to the beach for a long and agreeable walk on the boulevard. At the time we wrote this chapter, the court case against the two psychiatrists had just come to an end.[1] One of them was given a 4-year prison sentence; the other received a fine and a 5-year suspension to work as a psychiatrist. The case against the pseudo-patients is still pending. The prosecutor announced that he would demand the imposters pay back 5.6 million Euros for wrongly received benefits. Although one could argue that this case is just an incident, it is in line with research in which large groups of patients were given symptom validity tests. For example, Dandachi-FitzGerald, Ponds, Peters, and Merckelbach (2011) administered the SIMS and ASTM to 183 outpatients of a mental health clinic. They found that 15 (8%) of their patients had abnormal scores on both tests. Although we do not know whether these patients had legal or economic reasons for their abnormal scores, other studies do shed more light on the motive for abnormal scores on symptom validity tests. In a study examining 125 people seeking financial compensation from the Dutch government for interpersonal violence, 23 (18%) of the claimants had dubious SIMS scores (Kunst, Winkel, & Bogaerts, 2011).

As mentioned, some defendants feign crime-related amnesia. Cima, Merckelbach, Hollnack, and Knauer (2003) administered the SIMS to a group of forensic mental health patients who claimed memory loss for their offense. They found that 50% of the patients had very high SIMS scores, that is, scores comparable to students who were asked to feign amnesia. Although this study suggests that—in criminal cases—feigning occurs on a large scale, it is not entirely clear how many defendants pretend to have a disorder. Mittenberg, Patton, Canyock, and Condit (2002) surveyed 144 American neuropsychologists about the base rate of feigning in legal cases. The respondents opined that feigning takes place in about 30% of civil law cases and 20% of criminal law cases. Because skilled feigners might be mistaken for genuine patients, these numbers are probably an underestimation of the problem. As Faust (1995, p. 255) remarked: "Doctor, each time you've been fooled, you don't know, do you?" But even if feigning takes place in just 20% to 30% of all cases, it is clear that pseudo-patients frequently enter the legal arena.

MYTH THREE: PEOPLE ARE UNABLE TO FEIGN SYMPTOMS FOR A PROLONGED PERIOD OF TIME

Conroy and Kwartner (2006) contended that intensive observation is the best way to detect feigning of mental illness. They argued that to maintain a consistent symptom pattern while being observed in a clinic is difficult even for the most adept feigner. The idea that feigning can be detected by in-patient observation is not new. The influential German psychiatrist Richard Von Krafft-Ebing (1885) wrote that feigners differed in one important way from actors: Actors can leave the stage after a few hours, while pseudo-patients must play their role for a much larger period of time. And sooner or later, feigners will be unmasked because they forget to play their role as a patient.

Many case reports show that people are able to convincingly feign a disorder for a prolonged period of time. Take, for example, the case of Welshman Alan Knight (Quinn, 2014). This 47-year old man not only pretended to be paralyzed and suffering from epilepsy, every now and then he would slip into a coma. His wife was part of the conspiracy. She pushed Knight around in his wheelchair. For some time Knight managed to stay out of prison. He had been indicted because he had manipulated a demented neighbor into giving him thousands of pounds. Each time Knight had to appear in court, he had himself admitted to a hospital. The hospital doctors thought he was an exceptional case, but did not suspect feigning. Knight and his wife were caught when a CCTV camera spotted them shopping in a neighboring town: Alan Knight was maneuvering a full shopping cart—not exactly skills that can be observed in a person living in an almost vegetative state. At the moment he was unmasked as a feigner, Knight had played the role of a paralyzed epileptic for 2 years. There are more examples of long-term malingerers. The most famous one is probably Rudolf Hess, the high ranking Nazi official who first was held in captivity in England and later had to stand trial in Nuremberg. From February 1941 through February 1945, Hess claimed episodes of memory loss for vital parts of the recent German history in which he had played such a decisive role. Various psychiatrists interviewed Hess and came to the conclusion that his amnesia was genuine. Then, in February 1945, Hess declared in court that he had simulated his amnesia altogether. In letters to his wife, Hess explained that the role of an amnesic was a strategy so as to not having to share vital information with his interrogators (Douglas-Hamilton, 2010). Cases like Hess and Knight do not square with the idea of Von Krafft-Ebing and many others that feigners can convincingly play their role as a patient for only a limited period of time.

MYTH FOUR: FEIGNERS ARE ILL

If a patient has curious symptoms, the clinician will wonder about the origins of such symptoms. Sometimes symptom validity tests will be administered to such a patient. What does it mean if the patient scores in the abnormal range on such tests? Drob, Meehan, and Waxman (2009; p. 101) argued that, in cases of severe illness, patients will unintentionally show strange responses on symptom validity tests. A phenomenon labeled by the authors as "unconsciously determined distortion." Such a term could have been put forward by antique German psychiatrists. Siemens (1883; p. 42), for example, wrote: "Wie oft kommen den Irrenartz Fälle vor, die wie Simulation aussehen und doch keine sind! Daher is gewiss a priori Krankheit anzunehmen" [How often does a psychiatrist see a case that looks like feigning but is not! One should first think of illness].

One could reason that the SIMS or the ASTM should not be administered to patients who suffer from an acute psychosis, advanced dementia, or a psycho-organic syndrome. But why should these instruments be given to such patients in the first place? There is no doubt about the authenticity of their symptoms. If we exclude those patients, is it conceivable that patients will unconsciously endorse the fake symptoms listed on the SIMS? Or that they unintentionally will exhibit poor performance on the very easy trials of the ASTM? Based on experiments that show that negative expectations may lead to decrements in performance on neuro-psychological tests, Silver (2012) argued that these questions should be answered affirmatively. He pointed out that, if a clinician thinks a patient is severely ill, he will activate negative expectations in the patient's mind, which will then result in abnormal performance on symptom validity tests. There is indeed evidence for a performance-undermining effect of negative expectations, but the effect is rather small (Niesten, Merckelbach, & Dandachi-FitzGerald, 2015). From a scientific point of view, it is unlikely that such a trivial effect will affect a patient's performance in a way that he or she will score in the abnormal range on the SIMS or the ASTM. Note that speculating about "unconsciously determined distortion" may lead to circular reasoning: Because a patient is ill, she or he will score in the abnormal range on a symptom validity test. And because of this abnormal score on a symptom validity test, the patient must be ill. This circularity has been dubbed the *psychopathology-is-superordinate* fallacy, that is, the mistaken belief that abnormal scores on symptom validity tests are both caused by psychopathology *and* prove psychopathology (Merten & Merckelbach, 2013). It is a fallacy because we know that even young children and patients with serious brain damage are able to attain almost perfect scores on instruments such as the ASTM (Blaskewitz, Merten, & Kathmann, 2008; Rienstra, Spaan, & Schmand, 2010).

MYTH FIVE: MENTAL HEALTH PROFESSIONALS SHOULD BE KIND TO FEIGNERS

The idea that mental health professionals should be kind to feigners builds on the notion that feigners are ill. A professional affiliated with a Dutch center specializing in the treatment of medically unexplained symptoms stated: "An individual who feigns is ill. What does one win by saying: you are just a pretender? It will only cause resistance. Which will society ultimately cost more money (Mat, 2008; our translation)." This point of view can also be found in the scientific literature. Drob et al. (2009, p. 105), for example, stated that feigning of symptoms does not occur solely because of the patient, but emerges in the interaction with a suspicious mental health professional. The professional should not be hypervigilant and suspicious, but will have to respond in an empathetic way: "open to hearing his or her pain." Their opinion resembles the adage from antique psychiatrist Siemens that doctors should not act as police officers. This mentality may explain the findings from the study on emergency admissions to an American psychiatric hospital that was already mentioned. In that study, about 10% of the patients feigned psychiatric symptoms to get a bed and free meals, but none of them were reprimanded for their deceptive behavior (Yates et al., 1996).

Suchy, Chelune, Franchow, and Thorgusen (2012) decided to empirically test the effect of providing feigners with confrontational feedback on their poor test performance. They studied a group of patients with suspicious scores on a symptom validity test. Half of them did not receive any information about test performance, the others were confronted with their abnormal scores and were told that honest scores were important for the assessment. Next, all patients were again given psychological tests, including symptom validity tests. The group that was not given any information about their deviant symptom validity test scores continued to exaggerate their complaints. The group that was informed about the abnormal symptom validity test score, however, ceased to exaggerate their symptoms.

Not confronting feigners with their behavior may contribute to symptom escalation, as feigners may come to believe their lies. Pseudo-patients know that exaggerating symptoms conflicts with their self-definition of being an honest person. Because most of them think that they are decent people, they will experience cognitive dissonance. A sympathetic and warm mental health expert will make this dissonance worse, because a feigner will realize even more that he is deceiving the professional and will feel guilt and shame about it. The best way to reduce feelings of dissonance is to engage in self-deception. Just as smokers often tell themselves that their chain-smoking grandfather reached the age of 92, feigners who are under the care of sympathetic professionals will start to believe that, in a way, they do have real complaints (cf. Merckelbach & Merten, 2012). Thus, a sympathetic way of dealing with feigners may add insult to injury, in the sense that it may lead to continued medical consumption by feigners.

MYTH SIX: FEIGNERS ARE PSYCHOPATHS

The belief that feigners have psychopathic or antisocial traits is a special variant of the idea that feigners are ill, but it also alludes to the myth that feigning is rare ("only in psychopaths"). The belief has been advocated by the successive editions of the *Diagnostic and Statistical Manual of Mental Disorders*, up to its fifth edition (DSM-5; American Psychiatric Association, 2013). Thus, the DSM-5 lists the presence of antisocial features in patients among the key indications that warrant heightened suspicion of malingering.

Some high-profile cases seemed to confirm the close link between psychopathy and habitual feigning. A fine example is the story of Vincent Gigante, a mafia boss, who started to walk around the neighborhood dressed in his bathrobe and muttering in himself whenever he had to stand trial. Renowned experts testified that Gigante suffered from psychosis and vascular dementia, and PET scans were shown in court to bolster these claims. However, later, Gigante admitted that he faked his mental illness in order to avoid conviction (Newman, 2003).

Notwithstanding its popularity, empirical support for the psychopathy-feigning link is conspicuously absent. Niesten, Nentjes, Merckelbach, and Bernstein (2015) conducted a thorough literature search by means of *Google Scholar* and identified 19 studies that explored whether psychopathic and antisocial behavior are related to malingering. Of these, 10 found an association—albeit a relatively weak one—8 did not find a relation, and 1 study produced conflicting results. Niesten, Nentjes, et al. (2015) found even less evidence for the idea that high levels of psychopathy or antisociality are associated with a greater proficiency in malingering. Rather, their empirical data show that feigning symptoms is to a large extent context dependent. The authors compared 12 prisoners and 70 forensic patients in a treatment facility with each other and found that, while levels of psychopathy were similar in both groups, 3 (25%) of the prisoners against 1 (1%) of the forensic patients engaged in feigning. This is not surprising when one considers that prisoners might have more motives to feign symptoms. Thus, for prisoners but less so for forensic inpatients it may make sense to fabricate symptoms so as to be transformed to a psychiatric ward or to obtain psychotropic medication.

As pointed out by Niesten, Nentjes, et al. (2015; see also Van Impelen et al., 2016), a strong belief in the psychopathy-feigning link is not without practical consequences. It favors a highly selective use of symptom validity tests: They may be overemployed when psychopathy or antisocial features are present and under-employed in the absence of these features. Ultimately, this practice may lead to underestimating the scale on which feigning occurs.

MYTH SEVEN: FEIGNERS ARE NOT FAKING GOOD

According to the bipolarity hypothesis (Greene, 2000), faking bad (fabricating or aggravating symptoms) and faking good (hiding symptoms) are two mutually exclusive categories. That is, people who feign are not expected to also engage in faking good. There is no solid evidence for this widespread idea. Thus, in the Niesten, Nentjes, et al. (2015) study cited, the prisoners sample engaged in both feigning symptoms and faking good.

The temporal patterns of faking bad and good testify as to the situational rather than characterological origins of feigning. Thus, during the pretrial phase, defen-dants may feign mental illness and cognitive impairments in an attempt to reduce their criminal responsibility. Once convicted, these same individuals may engage in faking good—downplaying their genuine symptoms—so as to acquire privi-leges, including parole. Likewise, plaintiffs involved in civil litigation may feign certain symptoms (e.g., circumscribed amnesia or PTSD) but at the same time emphasize their virtues and deny any substance abuse problems, so as to pres-ent to the triers of fact as a decent and healthy person (Merckelbach, Smeets, & Jelicic, 2009). The dynamics of faking bad and good have been understudied, and one reason for this is the mistaken belief that they never occur together and that when they occur, this is related to a low base-rate personality feature such a psychopathy.

CONCLUSION

In contrast to what many mental health professionals believe, this chapter has shown that: (1) Clinical interviews cannot be used to detect feigning of psychopa-thology and cognitive impairments; (2) pretending to have a disorder is ubiqui-tous in forensic and general psychiatry: (3) people are able to feign for a prolonged period of time; (4) feigners are not ill; (5) mental health professionals should not be kind to feigners; (6) there is no exclusive feigning–psychopathy link; and (7) feigning and faking good may occur together.

There are many myths pertaining to psychology. Some years ago, Lilienfeld, Lynn, Ruscio, and Beyerstein (2009) debunked 50 of them. The misconceptions portrayed by Lilienfeld and colleagues are erroneous ideas about psychological concepts held by the general population. Because the myths discussed in this chapter are held by mental health experts, they may be more harmful than wrong-ful ideas held by laypeople. Assume that a defendant has decided to feign a serious psychiatric disorder to avoid criminal responsibility. If this person is evaluated by a mental health expert who solely relies on clinical interviews to rule out the pos-sibility of feigning, there is a substantial chance that the defendant may fool the expert and will be diagnosed with psychopathology. This defendant may receive an NGRI verdict and end up in a psychiatric facility instead of prison.

The authors recommend the use of symptom validity tests in all forensic mental health evaluations. Such tests should be used in all evaluations because even defendants with a history of mental illness may aggravate their symptoms. Although symptom validity tests are not perfect, they are much better in detecting feigning than clinical interviews. Because individuals with genuine psychopathol-ogy occasionally score in the abnormal range on a symptom validity test, labeling someone as a feigner can only be done when there is converging evidence for feigning. In the case described at the beginning of this chapter, there was substan-tial reason to believe that the defendant was feigning his command hallucinations. He endorsed many improbable psychotic symptoms and had abnormal scores on two symptom validity tests. Later, the defendant admitted that he, indeed, had feigned his command hallucinations.

The authors do not want to suggest that the work of all antique German schol-ars should be thrown in the garbage bin. For example, many ideas about memory put forward by Ebbinghaus in his opus magnum *Über das Gedächtnis* ("On mem-ory"; 1885) are still correct. And much of what Münsterberg wrote about legal psychology in his classic book *On the witness stand* (1908) has withstood the test of time. However, the ideas of old German authors about feigning have proved to be myths and should be dismissed forever.

NOTE

1. Dutch court cases ECLI: NL: RBROT: 2016: 5917 and ECLI: NL: RBROT: 2016: 5919.

REFERENCES

American Psychiatric Association. (2013). *Diagnostic and statistical manual of mental disorders* (5th ed.). Arlington, VA: American Psychiatric Publishing.

Anestis, J. C., Finn, J. A., Gottfried, E., Arbisi, P. A., & Joiner, T. E. (2015). Reading the road signs: The utility of the MMPI-2 Restructured Form Validity Scales in predicting premature termination. *Assessment, 22*, 279–288.

Blaskewitz, N., Merten, T., & Kathmann, N. (2008). Performance of children on symp-tom validity tests: TOMM, MSVT, and FIT. *Archives of Clinical Neuropsychology, 23*, 379–391.

Chesterman, L. P., Terbeck, S., & Vaughan, F. (2008). Malingered psychosis. *Journal of Forensic Psychiatry & Psychology, 19*, 275–300.

Cima, M., Merckelbach, H., Hollnack, S., & Knauer, E. (2003). Characteristics of psychiatric prison inmates who claim amnesia. *Personality and Individual Differences, 35*, 373–380.

Cima, M., Merckelbach, H., Nijman, H., Knauer, E., & Hollnack, S. (2002). I can't remember Your Honor: Offenders who claim amnesia. *German Journal of Psychiatry, 5*, 24–34.

Conroy, M. A., & Kwartner, P. P. (2006). Malingering. *Applied Psychology in Criminal Justice, 2*, 29–51.

Dalrymple, T. (2012). Malingerers. *British Medical Journal, 344*, 78.

Dandachi-FitzGerald, B., Ponds, R. W., Peters, M. J., & Merckelbach, H. (2011). Cognitive underperformance and symptom over-reporting in a mixed psychiatric sample. *The Clinical Neuropsychologist, 25*, 812–828.

DePaulo, B. M., Lindsay, J. J., Malone, B. E., Muhlenbruck, L., Charlton, K., & Cooper, H. (2003). Cues to deception. *Psychological Bulletin, 129*, 74–118.

Douglas-Hamilton, J. (2010). *The truth about Rudolf Hess*. Edinburgh: Mainstream Publishing.

Drob, S. L., Meehan, K. B., & Waxman, S. E. (2009). Clinical and conceptual problems in the attribution of malingering in forensic evaluations. *Journal of the American Academy of Psychiatry and the Law, 37*, 98–106.

Ebbinghaus, H. (1885). *Über das Gedächtnis: Untersuchungen zur experimentellen Psychologie* [On memory: Studies in experimental psychology]. Leipzig: Verlag von Duncker & Humblot.

Faust, D. (1995). The detection of deception. *Neurological Clinics, 13*, 255–265.

Feldman, M. (2004). *Playing sick? Untangling the web of Munchausen syndrome, Munchausen by proxy, malingering & factitious disorder*. Philadelphia: Brunner-Routledge.

Greene, R. L. (2000). *The MMPI-2/MMPI: An interpretive manual*. Boston: Allyn & Bacon.

Hall, R. C. W., & Hall, R. C. W. (2007). Detection of malingered PTSD: An overview of clinical, psychometric, and physiological assessment. *Journal of Forensic Sciences, 52*, 717–725.

Heilbronner, R. L. (2005). *Forensic neuropsychology casebook*. New York: Guilford Press.

Hickling, E. J., Blanchard, E. B., Mundy, E., & Galovski, T. E. (2002). Detection of malingered MVA related posttraumatic stress disorder: An investigation of the ability to detect professional actors by experienced clinicians, psychological tests and psychophysiological assessment. *Journal of Forensic Psychology Practice, 2*, 33–53.

Horner, M. D., VanKirk, K. K., Dismuke, C. E., Turner, T. H., & Muzzy, W. (2014). Inadequate effort on neuropsychological evaluation is associated with increased healthcare utilization. *The Clinical Neuropsychologist, 28*, 703–713.

Jelicic, M., Van Gaal, M., & Peters, M. J. V. (2013). Expert knowledge doesn't help: Detecting feigned psychosis in people with psychiatric expertise using the Structured Inventory of Malingered Symptomatology (SIMS). *Journal of Experimental Psychopathology, 4*, 38–45.

Jung, C. G. (1903). Über Simulation von Geistesstörungen [On the simulation of psychopathology]. *Journal für Psychologie und Neurologie, Journal of Psychology and Neurology, 5*, 181–2012.

Kitaeff, J. (2007). *Malingering, lies, and junk science in the courtroom*. Amherst, NY: Cambria.

Knoll, J. L., & Resnick, P. J. (2008). Insanity defense evaluations: Basic procedure and best practices. *Psychiatric Times, 25*, 35–41.

Kunst, M., Winkel, F. W., & Bogaerts, S. (2011). Recalled peritraumatic reactions, self-reported PTSD, and the impact of malingering and fantasy proneness in victims of interpersonal violence who have applied for state compensation. *Journal of Interpersonal Violence, 26*, 2186–2210.

Larrabee, G. J. (2012). Performance validity and symptom validity in neuropsychological assessment. *Journal of the International Society of Neuropsychology, 18*, 625–630.

Lawlor, A., & Kirakowski, J. (2014). When the lie is the truth: Grounded theory analysis of an online support group for factitious disorder. *Psychiatry Research, 218*, 209–218.

Ledebur, S. (2012). On the epistemology of exclusion diagnosis: ignorance, discourse and investigation techniques in the simulation of mental illnesses. In M. Wernli (Ed.), *Knowledge and non-knowledge in the clinic: Dynamics of psychiatry around 1900* (pp. 17–50). Bielefeld, Germany: Transcript Verlag.

Lilienfeld, S. O., Lynn, S. J., Ruscio, J., & Beyerstein, B. L. (2009). *50 great myths of popular psychology: Shattering widespread misconceptions about human behavior.* Chichester, UK: Wiley-Blackwell.

Mat, J. (2008, February 17). Vage klachten [Vague symptoms]. *NRC Handelsblad.* Retrieved from http://www.nrc.nl.

Merckelbach, H., & Merten, T. (2012). A note on cognitive dissonance and malingering. *The Clinical Neuropsychologist, 26*, 1217–1229.

Merckelbach, H., Peters, M. J. V., & Jelicic, M. (2011). Een verdachte die stemmen hoort. Over geveinsde bevelshallucinaties [A suspect who hears voices: About feigned command hallucinations]. *Nederlands Tijdschrift voor Geneeskunde [Netherlands Journal of Medicine], 155*, A3238.

Merckelbach, H., Smeets, T., & Jelicic, M. (2009). Experimental simulation: Type of malingering scenario makes a difference. *Journal of Forensic Psychiatry & Psychology, 20*, 378–386.

Merten, T., & Merckelbach, H. (2013). Symptom validity testing in somatoform and dissociative disorders: A critical review. *Psychological Injury and Law, 6*, 122–137.

Mittenberg, W., Patton, C., Canyock, E. M., & Condit, D. C. (2002). Base rates of malingering and symptom exaggeration. *Journal of Clinical and Experimental Neuropsychology, 24*, 1094–1102.

Morel, K. R. (2010). *Differential diagnosis of malingering versus post-traumatic stress disorder: Scientific rationale and objective scientific methods.* New York: Nova.

Münsterberg, H. (1908). *On the witness stand: Essays on psychology and crime.* New York: Doubleday, Page & Company.

Newman, A. (2003, April 18). Gigante says he was crazy . . . like a fox. *New York Times.* Retrieved from http://www.nytimes.com.

Niesten, I. J. M., Merckelbach, H., & Dandachi-FitzGerald, B. (2015). Diagnosis threats: Zo bedreigend zijn ze niet [Not very threatening]. *Tijdschrift voor Neuropsychologie [Journal of Neuropsychology], 10*, 1–14.

Niesten, I. J. M., Nentjes, L., Merckelbach, H., & Bernstein, D. P. (2015). Antisocial features and "faking bad": A critical note. *International Journal of Law and Psychiatry, 41*, 34–42.

Ornish, S. A. (2001). A blizzard of lies: Bogus psychiatric defenses. *American Journal of Forensic Psychiatry, 22*, 19–30.

Pankratz, L. (1998). *Patients who deceive: Assessment and management of risk in providing health care and financial benefits.* Springfield, IL: Charles C. Thomas.

Quinn, B. (2014, January 22). Man in £ 40.000 scam who faked disability is caught on shopping trip. *The Guardian.* Retrieved from http://www.theguardian.com

Ramesh, V. (2013). Functional neurological disorders in children and young people. *Developmental Medicine and Child Neurology, 55,* 3-4.

Resnick, P. J. (2007). My favorite tips for detecting malingering and violence risk. *Psychiatric Clinics of North America, 30,* 227-232.

Rienstra, A., Spaan, P. E. J., & Schmand, B. (2010). Validation of symptom validity tests using a "child-model" of adult cognitive impairments. *Archives of Clinical Neuropsychology, 25,* 371-382.

Rosen, G. M., & Phillips, W. R. (2004). A cautionary lesson from simulated patients. *Journal of the American Academy of Psychiatry and the Law, 32,* 132-133.

Rosenhan, D. L. (1973). On being sane in insane places. *Science, 179,* 250-258.

Schmand, B., de Sterke, S., & Lindeboom, J. (1999). *Amsterdamse Korte-Termijn Geheugen test [Amsterdam Short-Term Memory test].* Amsterdam: Pearson.

Siemens, F. (1883). Zur Frage der Simulation der Seelenstörungen. *Archiv für Psychiatrie und Nervenkrankheiten* [On the simulation of mental disorders]. *Archive of Psychiatry and Nervous Diseases, 14,* 40-86.

Silver, J. M. (2012). Effort, exaggeration and malingering after concussion. *Journal of Neurology, Neurosurgery & Psychiatry, 83,* 836-841.

Singh, J., Avasthi, A., & Grover, S. (2007). Malingering of psychiatric disorders: A review. *German Journal of Psychiatry, 10,* 126-137.

Smith, G. P. (2008). Brief screening measures for the detection of feigned psychopathology. In R. Rogers (Ed.), *Clinical assessment of malingering and deception* (3rd ed.). (pp. 323-339). New York: Guilford.

Smith, G. P., & Burger, G. K. (1997). Detection of malingering: Validation of the Structured Inventory of Malingered Symptomatology (SIMS). *Journal of the American Academy of Psychiatry and the Law, 25,* 180-183.

Suchy, Y., Chelune, G., Franchow, E. I., & Thorgusen, S. R. (2012). Confronting patients about insufficient effort: The impact on subsequent symptom validity and memory performance. *The Clinical Neuropsychologist, 26,* 1296-1311.

Többen. H. (1935). Ein Beitrag zur Simulation von Geisterstörungen [An article on the simulation of mental disorders]. *German Journal of Comprehensive Forensic Medicine, 25,* 212-222.

Tysse, J. E. (2005). Note: Right to an "imperfect" trial—amnesia, malingering, and competency to stand trial. *William Mitchell Law Review, 32,* 353-387.

Van Egmond, J., & Kummeling, I. (2002). A blind spot for secondary gain affecting therapy outcomes. *European Psychiatry, 17,* 46-54.

Van Egmond, J., Kummeling, I., & Van Balkom, T. (2005). Secondary gain as hidden motive for getting psychiatric treatment. *European Psychiatry, 20,* 416-421.

Van Impelen, A., Merckelbach, H., Jelicic, M., & Merten, T. (2014). The Structured Inventory of Malingered Symptomatology (SIMS): A systematic review and meta-analysis. *The Clinical Neuropsychologist, 28,* 1336-1365.

Van Impelen, A., Merckelbach, H., Niesten, I. J. M., Jelicic, M., Huhnt, B., & à Campo, J. (2016). Biased symptom reporting and antisocial behavior in forensic samples: A weak link. *Psychiatry, Psychology and Law* (in press).

Von Krafft-Ebing, R. (1885). *Lehrbuch der Gerichtlichen Psychopathologie, 2. Auflage* [Textbook of Forensic Psychopathology]. Stuttgart: Enke.

Vyleta, D.M. (2007). *Crime, Jews, and news: Vienna 1895-1914*. New York: Berghahn.

Yates, B. D., Nordquist, C. R., & Schultz-Ross, R. A. (1996). Feigned psychiatric symptoms in the emergency room. *Psychiatric Services, 47*, 998–1000.

Young, G. (2014). *Malingering, feigning, and response bias in psychiatric/psychological injury: Implications for practice and court*. Dordrecht: Springer.

Zweep, L. (2011). *Knelpunten in de opsporing van fraude met pgb's en WAO/WIA-uitkeringen* [Problems in the detection of false claims of disability benefits]. Den Bosch, The Netherlands: Stafbureau BPO/Openbaar Ministerie.

12

False Symptom Claims and Symptom Validity Assessment

THOMAS MERTEN

In the legal arena, claims of cognitive symptoms are not rare at all, reaching from reported nonspecific memory and attention problems to intellectual disability, full-blown autobiographical memory loss (an inability to recall autobiographical memories before the onset of amnesia), or crime-related amnesia (a focal amnesia limited to events associated with a crime the person in question has allegedly committed). The potential consequences of such claims—if they are found to be genuine—are immense and reach from multimillion dollar awards to the exclusion from criminal responsibility, or even suspension of the death penalty in some states of the United States (McCaffrey, Williams, Fisher, & Laing, 1997). They depend upon the legal system and the exact legal question and may differ considerably from country to country.

To determine the nature and severity of cognitive symptoms is the core of clinical neuropsychology, dealing more generally with the question of brain–behavior relationships. Consequently, a qualified neuropsychological assessment is the method of choice in forensic cases when cognitive impairment is claimed. The basic problem of interpreting test profiles lies in the fact that test performance highly depends upon the motivation of the person in question to employ the best of his or her abilities on the tests. With high incentives for the claimant to present him- or herself as impaired (so called secondary gain; see later for further details), the validity of test performance cannot be taken at face value. Neuropsychological test performance (and questionnaires answers alike) can be easily manipulated without prior knowledge. Many neuropsychologists continue to rely on their clinical intuition and are uncorrectably convinced of their ability to distinguish between test profiles of genuine patients and those of feigners, although empirical research has long shown that there is no such ability (e.g., Heaton, Smith, Lehman, & Vogt, 1978).

In this respect, valuable lessons can be learned from lie detection research (e.g., Hartwig & Bond, 2011; Vrij, 2008), but psychiatrists and clinical psychologists appear to be very reluctant to accept the limitations of subjective judgments and continue to rely heavily on their intuition in determining the truthfulness of symptom claims. Neither historical cases of successfully deceiving experts nor the growing number of fraud cases published in the media appear to be able to shake clinicians' self-confidence in their abilities. One of the most prominent cases of malingered auto-biographical memory loss was that of Rudolf Hess, the deputy of Adolf Hitler who feigned amnesia during the Nuremberg trials and convinced the psychiatric experts of the truthfulness of his claim (Gilbert, 1947). Later on, when the intended tactical advantages were not obtained through feigned amnesia, he gave up, confessed that his claim had been false, and later even admitted that he had enjoyed deceiving the experts and was proud of his achievement. It is more than revealing that reportedly there was only one person, and not a psychiatric expert but a military commandant, who told Hess to his face that he was a fraud (Douglas-Hamilton, 2016).

This makes legal determinations about the authenticity of symptom claims very vulnerable to biased judgment from experts. This bias continues to be prevalent in neuropsychologists with a strong reliance on their clinical impression, which is difficult to overcome even when they do forensic work (Dandachi-FitzGerald, Ponds, & Merten, 2013).

Symptom validity assessment (SVA) was developed to tackle this problem. With a growing involvement of neuropsychologists in medicolegal determinations in contexts where cognitive functioning or cognitive impairment was relevant to the legal question, a powerful approach of distinguishing between genuine and non-genuine cognitive symptom presentations was developed and refined, beginning in the late 1980s. In contrast to impression-based clinical judgment (with an expected low base-rate of nongenuine symptom presentations; cf. Reuben, Mitchell, Howlett, Crimlisk, & Grünewald, 2005), the newly developed symptom validity tests (SVTs) allowed for a data-driven and evidence-based approach with the primary goal of arriving at sound and reliable determinations about the validity of test profiles, determinations that are largely independent of the clinician's subjective impression.

With the introduction of SVTs, on a larger scale, in medicolegal contexts, it may be said that a new era of malingering assessment and malingering research began, with a wealth of empirical studies and major theoretical and conceptual contributions, which have boosted our knowledge base about nongenuine symptom claims. Up until today, neuropsychologists are the major contributors to research activities with keywords like malingering or feigning sustained at a high level (cf. Berry & Nelson, 2010; Sweet & Guidotti-Breting, 2013). In the following text, a review of major aspects of psychological SVA is given, with some case vignettes to illustrate in particular the power of forced-choice testing.

DEFINITIONS AND CONCEPTUAL ISSUES

The term *symptom validity* describes "the accuracy or truthfulness of the examinee's behavioral presentation (signs), self-reported symptoms (including their cause and course), or performance on neuropsychological measures" (Bush et al., 2005, p. 420). The process that leads to determinations about symptom validity is called symptom validation or symptom validity assessment. The two most common forms of response bias in forensic psychological assessment are overreporting (in free symptom report and/or standardized symptom questionnaires) and underperformance (in psychological testing). Standardized SVTs traditionally comprise both self-report validity measures and cognitive SVTs, more recently dubbed *performance validity tests* (PVTs; Larrabee, 2012).

Distorted symptom presentation can originate from different sources, with feigning being only one of them, describing deliberate symptom fabrication or gross exaggeration.

Feigning includes both malingering and factitious disorder. The term *malingering* contains, in contrast to feigning, a specification about the motivational basis of distorted symptom presentation that, by definition, has to be external, outside the patient role and medical treatment (also called secondary gain). The Diagnostic and Statistical Manual of Mental Disorders (DSM-IV, American Psychiatric Association 1995, p. 701) describes malingering as " . . . the intentional production of false or grossly exaggerated physical or psychological symptoms, motivated by external incentives . . . " Also, false imputations are conceptually included in the concept of malingering. A false imputation is "the attribution of actual symptoms to a cause consciously recognized by the individual as having no relationship to the symptoms" (Resnick, West, & Payne, 2008, pp. 111–112). For example, a plaintiff suffering with chronic headaches may falsely maintain that it first occurred after a whiplash injury and claim financial compensation for it.

In contrast, factitious disorders are not primarily motivated by external incentives. Although phenomenologically they may not be distinguishable from malingering, the motivation for feigned symptom presentation is assumed to be linked to the sick role and to medical treatment. The authors of DSM-5 (American Psychiatric Association, 2013) inappropriately subsume factitious disorder under *Somatic Symptom and Related Disorder* and describe identified deceptive behavior as central for the diagnosis. In fact, factitious disorder may relate to the mental and cognitive sphere and largely exclude physical symptom presentation (for a recent summary review, see Bass & Halligan, 2014).

The prevailing view today is that the methods known as SVA represent the diagnostic approach used by the expert to differentiate between credible and noncredible, between authentic and nonauthentic symptom presentations, rather than that they directly detect absence or presence of malingering. Nonauthentic symptom presentation can stem from different sources than malingering, such as factitious disorder, anger, a hostile attitude toward the examination or the examiner, indifference, or negativism. Consequently, positive results in symptom validity assessment do not directly indicate malingering, but malingering is only one possible explanation for noncooperative behavior, and SVTs should not be called malingering tests (Merten & Merckelbach, 2013a). Depending on the results of SVA, different degrees of certainty as to a distorted symptom presentation can be established (Slick, Sherman, & Iverson, 1999), but an ultimate diagnosis of malingering, factitious disorder, or uncooperativeness in the presence of another genuine mental or physical disease largely rests on a clinical decision-making process.

Table 12.1. THE DIFFERENTIAL DIAGNOSIS BETWEEN THREE FORMS
OF NONAUTHENTIC SYMPTOM PRESENTATION LARGELY RESTS ON SUBJECTIVE
JUDGMENT ABOUT THE INTENTION AND MOTIVATION FOR SYMPTOM DISTORTION

Diagnostic Category	Distorted Symptom Presentation	Incentives for Distorted Symptom Presentation	Examples of Incentives
Malingering	Intentional, deliberate, controlled (conscious)	Cognizant, self-reflected (conscious); external incentive, secondary gain	Sick leave, financial compensation, escape from legal responsibility
Factitious disorder	Intentional, deliberate, controlled (conscious)	Nonreflective, unaware (unconscious); internal incentive, primary gain	Medical treatment, incl. surgery, sick role
Somatoform, dissociative, and conversion disorder	Unintentional, involuntary, uncontrolled (unconscious)	Nonreflective, unaware (unconscious); internal incentive, primary gain; secondary gain may also be present	Conflict management, stress reduction

This is because clinical judgement about nonauthentic symptoms often refers to unobservable, purely internal mental states, in particular the patient's awareness of the nature of the claimed symptoms and his or her underlying motivation (Eisendrath, 1995; cf. Table 12.1). A further difficulty in the decision-making process stems from the fact (which appears to be commonly accepted today) that the three major diagnostic categories where the diagnostician is confronted with distorted, nongenuine symptom report and symptom presentation are not at all mutually exclusive. Thus, a patient with a genuine and severe factitious disorder, which, per se, is characterized by nongenuine symptom presentation, may fight a court battle to gain financial compensation from an insurance company, falsely imputing part of his or her alleged symptomatology to a motor vehicle accident.

METHODS OF SYMPTOM VALIDITY ASSESSMENT

The Franco-Swiss neuropsychologist André Rey was the first to translate concerns about the validity of test profiles into a set of tests presumably measuring cognitive performance (speed, visual retention, verbal memory), but, in fact, yielding information about the interpretability of other performance test scores (Rey, 1941, 1958). He took a rather modern, not at all simplistic, stance when he warned not to base far-reaching diagnostic decisions solely on the results of a single test, but to include information from multiple sources, such as the individual constellation of the case, personality, and motivation (Rey, 1958; cf. Frederick, 2002, for a sound historical appraisal of Rey's contribution to SVA). Although his tests, like the Fifteen-Item Test or the Dot Counting Test, suffer from limited classification accuracy, which was improved only with more refined test approaches

(Hartman, 2002), they continue to enjoy high popularity among test users (cf. Martin, Schroeder, & Odland, 2015, for the most recent survey on SVA practices) (Figure 12.1). However, from today's perspective and with a wealth of data about sensitivity and specificity of different SVTs, it may be said that limiting symptom validity test use to an instrument like the Fifteen-Item Test is not better than using no SVT at all (cf. Blaskewitz, in press, for a comprehensive critical appraisal).

With the introduction of forced-choice testing in the 1980s for identifying attempts to mislead the examiner as to the presence of severe cognitive impairment (Pankratz, 1983), a new, powerful tool was made available. (Incidentally, a first proposal of this technique stemmed from Loewer and Ulrich, 1971, but it was published in a German-language textbook so it had no detectable wider repercussion on diagnostic practice and test development.) The testing principle consists in presenting a series of dichotomous choices to the examinee; if he or she does not know the correct answer (e.g., remembering a memory test item), guessing is required. With a response accuracy of 50% by mere guessing (which would be compatible with a total loss of function), the binomial distribution can be applied to check if the response pattern is compatible with claimed functional deficit (Table 12.2). The presence of a response pattern *below the threshold for pure guessing* then signals that the person intentionally chose false responses to demonstrate impairment. Most researchers in the field of SVA agree that such response patterns below chance are the best and most powerful criterion for identifying deliberate attempts to feign cognitive symptoms. The hidden paradox behind

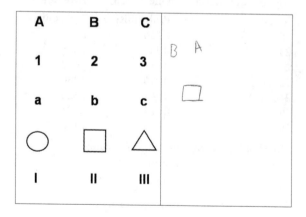

Figure 12.1 The Fifteen-Item Test, although known to produce a high number of false-negative results, continues to be used on a wide scale. It may be useful as one component of a more comprehensive set of SVTs, and it may even be a good choice in cases of blatant symptom exaggeration (extreme, noncredible underperformance). The test is presented as a difficult memory task. A display of 15 items (*left side*) is presented for 10 seconds to the patient. On the right side, the immediate reproduction performance of a 54-year old Turkish claimant with a pseudodementia-like profile of severe cognitive impairment is presented. She claimed disability benefits for chronic severe depression, which was not detectable on the level of clinical presentation.

forced-choice SVTs consists of the fact that, in order to score below chance on a forced-choice test, the patient must have the cognitive capacity of a person who scores above chance. In the extreme, a person who scores zero in a forced-choice test must know all correct answers (or almost all of them), else, such an extremely improbable response pattern cannot be explained. Consequently, Iverson (2003; p. 169) proposed the following standard formulation for reporting below-chance performance in a forced-choice testing: "The patient scored below chance on a (. . .) forced-choice procedure, indicating that she knew the correct answer and *deliberately* chose the incorrect answer. This performance invalidates the entire set of neuropsychological test results" (italics added).

This response format occupies a special place in the toolbox of forensic neuro-psychologists because its results may allow the expert to arrive at a definite decision as to the intentionality of false symptom presentation. Within the criteria for malingered neurocognitive dysfunction, below-chance response patterns are the key criterion for concluding intentional symptom distortion (Slick, Sherman & Iverson, 1999), *the* red-flag for deliberate feigning, or as "tantamount to confession of malingering" (Larrabee, 2004). With the application of the binomial

Table 12.2. CUMULATIVE PROBABILITIES FOR A 50-ITEM TEST LIKE THE TEST OF MEMORY MALINGERING, WITH A 50% CHANCE LEVEL FOR PURE GUESSING

Number of Correct Responses	One-Tailed Probability	Two-Tailed Probability
25	0.556	1
24	0.444	0.888
23	0.336	0.672
22	0.240	0.480
21	0.161	0.322
20	0.101	0.203
19	0.059	0.120

Threshold for below-chance performance, one-tailed hypothesis testing

18	0.032	0.065

Threshold for below-chance performance, two-tailed hypothesis testing

17	0.016	0.033
16	0.008	0.016
15	0.003	0.006
14	0.001	0.002

The same table was applied to the 50-item Grimm's Fairy Tale Test (see Table 12.6). Exact probabilities can easily be retrieved for any number of items and differing chance levels.

distribution, the forensic expert has to decide beforehand whether one- or two-tailed significance testing is appropriate, depending on specific a priori hypotheses. In cases where other pieces of information from within the evaluation or from collateral sources (behavioral presentation, numerous inconsistencies, implausible history, etc.) are strongly suggestive of feigning, one-tailed hypothesis testing of below-threshold response patterns will be appropriate (Frederick & Speed, 2007, for a detailed discussion).

Hiscock and Hiscock (1989) were the first to construct a standardized test consisting of strings of digits that are presented for some seconds. After a short waiting interval, the target has to be recognized, choosing between two alternatives. This Digit Recognition Test served as a model for a number of SVTs, some of them using similar strings of digits, others pictures or words presented to the test subject. Their common feature is that they are seemingly measuring cognitive performance while, in fact, the cognitive load to fulfil the task is so low that low test results usually signal a reduced motivation to perform to the best of one's abilities rather than cognitive impairment. Table 12.3 lists a number of standardized SVTs, most of them resorting either to alternative choices or adapted test formats (such as 3-in-5 for the Amsterdam or 1-in-5 for the One-in-Five Test).

TAILOR-MADE FORCED-CHOICE TESTS IN CRIMINAL FORENSIC ASSESSMENT

The first SVTs were tailor-made to model individual symptom claims (such as reported sensory loss, general memory impairment, or crime-related amnesia); in that sense, these approaches can be called "single-case experiments in the differential diagnosis of intentional symptom distortion" (Merten & Merckelbach, 2013b, p. 20). Soon after Pankratz's (1983) work to test the authenticity of cognitive impairment through forced-choice response formats, the method was used in the context of criminal forensic referral questions. Thus, Brandt, Rubinsky, and Lassen (1985) described the case of a 64-year old man charged with the murder of his wife, who claimed total amnesia for the event. In a verbal memory test with force-choice format, he scored below chance, showing the falseness of his amnesia claim. Frederick, Carter, and Powel (1995) refined the testing principle in the forensic arena, showing that tailor-made memory questions can help to dismantle claims of amnesia. With Denney (1996), the problem was centered on claimed crime-related amnesia. He published three case vignettes of below-chance responding by the culprits. In these cases, the pool of questions was limited to information from the crime scene that was only available to the perpetrator himself. Another more recent case report was published by Denney (2009). The defendant, a 52-year-old man, was charged with a variety of offenses, including use of firearms in drug trafficking and child molestation. He claimed psychosis and autobiographical amnesia, which also included knowledge about the alleged crimes and the subsequent investigations. Again, below-chance results in a 35-item forced-choice test indicated that his amnesia claim was false and intentionally used to give the appearance of mental incompetency.

Table 12.3. Selected Standardized Cognitive Symptom Validity Tests (Performance Validity Tests)

Symptom Validity Test, Authors	Test Material, Number of Items	Major Test Characteristics
Amsterdam Short-Term Memory Test (ASTM), Schmand & Lindeboom (2005)	Sets of five semantically associated words, 30 items	Computerized test; multiple-choice test format (3-in-5); more difficult to be identified as an effort test and more resistant to coaching Should not be used in patients with clinically obvious symptoms (elevated risk of false positives)
Coin-in-the Hand Test, Kapur (1994)*	A coin, 10 items	Forced-choice procedure, employable for bedside use; easy and fast; no cost Easy to be identified as SVT. Should only be applied in cases of blatant symptom presentation
Computerized Assessment of Response Bias (CARB), Allen, Conder, Green, & Cox (1997)*	Strings of digits, 111 items	Computerized test; forced-choice test format; can easily be employed in patients with low degrees of language proficiency May be easy to be identified as an effort test and easy to coach
Dot Counting Test (DCT), Rey (1941)	Index cards with dots, 12 items	Analysis of the ratio of counting ungrouped vs. grouped dot displays Early test with low classification accuracy
Fifteen-Item Test (FIT), Rey (1958)	Single display of 15 letters, numbers, and symbols, 15 items	Easy and fast, no cost. Easy to be identified as an effort test Early test with low classification accuracy
One-in-Five Test, Gubbay (n.d.), Tydecks, Merten, & Gubbay (2006)	Displays of 4 digits each, 36 items	Adaptation of former digit recognition tests, with 80% correct responses by pure chance Easy to be identified as SVT Should only be applied in cases of blatant symptom presentation, such as questionable claims of dementia

Test	Stimuli	Description
Medical Symptom Validity Test (MSVT), Green (2004)*	Pairs of words, 20 items	Modification of the Word Memory Test, with fewer items and higher associative strength between the pairs of words; developed to reduce false-positive classifications in patients with genuine dementia Secondary analysis over a set of subtests to distinguish between profiles of genuine severe cognitive impairment and profile of feigned memory impairment
Non-Verbal Symptom Validity Test (NV-MSVT), Green (2008)*	Colored images of pairs of objects, 20 items	Extension of the testing principle of the Word Memory Test and the Medical Symptom Validity Test, developed to reduce false-positive classifications in patients with genuine dementia Secondary analysis over a set of subtests to distinguish between profiles of genuine severe cognitive impairment and profile of feigned memory impairment
Recognition Memory Test, (Warrington, 1984; Millis, 1992)*	Faces and words, 50 items each	Adaptation of an existing memory test with forced-choice response format to assess symptom validity
Test of Memory Malingering (TOMM), Tombaugh (1996)*	Line drawings of common objects, 3 trials, 50 items each	One of the best investigated SVTs with a broad empirical data base, language-free test; can easily be employed in illiterate and foreign-language patients; high face validity
Victoria Symptom Validity Test (VSVT), Slick, Hopp, Strauss, and Thompson (1997)*	Strings of five digits, 48 items	Computer-administered forced-choice SVT One of a couple of tests using the basic principle of Hiscock and Hiscock's (1989) Digit Recognition Test
Word Memory Test (WMT), Green (2003)*	Pairs of words, 40 items	Computerized test, multilingual test versions, very broad data base from numerous studies and diverse diagnostic and cultural contexts. Paper-pencil test version available for special contexts Secondary analysis over a set of subtests to distinguish between profiles of genuine severe cognitive impairment and profile of feigned memory impairment

NOTE: * Tests (at least partially) based on the forced-choice approach. SVT = symptom validity test.

Table 12.4. Forced-Choice Test Procedure to Evaluate the Potential
Authenticity of Claimed Crime-Related Amnesia. Selection of Items from
an Experimental Study (Mock Crime Study)

Item	Answer 1*	Answer 2*
What was the color of the strongbox?	White	*Green*
What was placed on the table in front of the victim?	*A chocolate*	A sandwich
Was the door open or closed when you went into the room?	Open	*Closed*
What sort of glasses were on the table in front of the victim?	Reading glasses	*Sun glasses*
What object was placed on top of the strongbox?	*A camera*	A puncher

*Correct responses are printed in italics.
Courtesy of Dr. Peter Giger, Bern, Switzerland.

Numerous experimental studies have proved the potential of tailor-made SVTs in the criminal forensic arena (e.g., Jelicic, Merckelbach, & van Bergen, 2004; Shaw, Vrij, Mann, Leal, & Hillman, 2014; van Oorsouw & Merckelbach, 2006; cf. Giger, Merten, & Merckelbach, 2012; Jelicic & Merckelbach, 2007 for reviews about crime-related amnesia). The forced-choice method has even found its way into popular TV drama (*Cracker—Mad Woman in the Attic*, directed by Jimmy McGovern, Great Britain 1993). However, such tailor-made, single-case experimental designs appear to have little impact on real-life crime-related forensic assessment.

For illustration, Table 12.4 shows a tailor-made forced-choice test from an experiment performed in Switzerland (Giger, Merten, Merckelbach, & Oswald, 2010). The participants of the study had to commit a mock crime. They were instructed to enter a room in order to steal some allegedly secret information. However, they inadvertently found another person sitting in the room (it was, in fact, a shop window dummy). Participants were further instructed to hit the person with great force, etc. Later on, in the process of criminal investigation, they should try to convincingly feign crime-related amnesia in an attempt to avoid criminal responsibility. The table lists some items of the guilty knowledge SVT, which was part of a more comprehensive psychological evaluation.

CASE VIGNETTE: CLAIMED AUTOBIOGRAPHICAL AMNESIA AND ACALCULIA

In a civil forensic evaluation, a 21-year old man of Turkish origin, a second-generation migrant, claimed, among other things, complete retrograde autobiographical memory loss. Two years ago he had suffered severe brain injury in a motor vehicle accident, with cerebral haemorrhage, subarachnoid bleeding, and peritraumatic cerebral ischemia. Severe posttraumatic functional deficits were well documented, with a prolonged treatment in rehabilitation centers. Premorbid adjustment and educational achievement were poor; the possibility of preexisting mild intellectual disability could not be excluded on the basis of documented evidence (cf. Harvey, 2002, for a discussion of difficulties in assessing patients with dual diagnosis of intellectual disability and traumatic brain injury).

Symptom claim and symptom presentation during the evaluation appeared doubtful. Thus, the asserted autobiographical memory loss was falsified by numerous "giveaways" of memory content when the patient was involved in a discussion about topics apparently unrelated to the amnesia claim itself. (In the context of what was called hysteria in the past, the terms *giveaway* or *giveaway sign* were used to designate lapses into normal function, in contradiction to claimed functional loss, under certain circumstances such as when the patient believed he was not observed.) At the beginning of the test session, he was asked to solve some arithmetic problems. Invariably, he gave responses that were near misses, always missing the correct answers by the factor 1 (e.g., $6 + 5 = 10$; $10 - 2 = 7$). Incidentally, such a pattern of Ganser-like near misses in arithmetic, in mental status and some other tasks is a red flag for feigning, giving information that the person has deliberately given false answers (Rogers, Harrell, & Liff, 1993; cf. Chafetz, Abrahams, & Kohlmaier, 2007, for a more recent discussion). With this noncredible demonstration of severe acalculia, an ideal target for forced-choice SVA for investigating the authenticity of the symptom claim was offered by the claimant: 40 items of arithmetic problems were given to him, with an alternative choice option (Table 12.5).

He scored 29 false and 11 correct in the test. Binomial distribution shows a probability of 3 per 1,000 (0.3%) for a person with complete functional loss (genuine total acalculia) to score only 11 or less out of 40 with a 50% chance

Table 12.5. THE FIRST TEN ITEMS (OF A TOTAL OF 40) OF A TAILOR-MADE FORCED-CHOICE TEST, IN A CASE OF DEMONSTRATED COMPLETE ACALCULIA

Arithmetic Problem	Alternative Solutions		Chosen Response	
$3 + 3$	6	7	7	false
4×4	15	16	15	false
$7 + 8$	15	14	15	
$13 - 7$	7	6	7	false
$15 : 3$	4	5	5	
5×5	24	25	24	false
$6 + 17$	24	23	24	false
$17 + 18$	35	36	36	false
7×9	64	63	64	false
$63 - 17$	46	47	46	

performance. The below-chance response pattern confirmed the hypothesis that he, in fact, knew the correct answers but chose to give false responses. At the very end of the evaluation, the claimant was cautiously confronted with having exaggerated his symptoms and encouraged to give up his excessive symptom claim, without losing face. Surprisingly enough, he followed the suggestion of the examiner and, on a fresh trial, was able to solve all the arithmetic problems that he had previously demonstrated to be unable to solve. Although the claimant had undoubtedly suffered traumatic brain damage with probable long-term consequences, the forensic report could not rely on an invalid test profile to estimate the severity of the cognitive impairment.

CASE VIGNETTE: CLAIMED COMPLETE AUTOBIOGRAPHICAL AND SEMANTIC MEMORY LOSS

Merten and Merckelbach (2013b) described the case of a young man, aged 20, who attended a party with peers. In the middle of the night, he went out into the open and returned after a few minutes with a minor skin scratch on his forehead. He told his friends in a somewhat confused way that he had met a group of strangers outside. Then, all of a sudden, he asked them who they, his friends, were, and who he himself was. He claimed neither to remember his own name nor to recognize his parents upon their arrival. From then on, he claimed to have lost all knowledge about himself, his biography, other people, and all the knowledge he had acquired during schooling and professional training. After careful exclusion of brain damage, the treatment diagnosis was dissociative amnesia, and the behavioral therapist spent a lot of time and effort to reestablish semantic memory content. However, what seemed to have gone unnoticed by then, was that he had subscribed to two attractive insurance schemes that would allow him to live without financial problems for the rest of his life.

In the forensic psychological assessment, his cognitive test performance was completely normal; in particular, he performed well on all memory measures. As for autobiographical and semantic memory, he showed an astonishingly detailed source memory for all items; so he often commented spontaneously where he had presumably relearned information about his past life and the meaning of objects, names of animals and plants, etc. He also scored relatively high in a semantic memory test (Schmidtke & Vollmer-Schmolck, 1999). There was only one subtest relating to the knowledge of fairy tales where he failed almost completely. Given the depth of representation of such knowledge acquired early in life, this result, per se, would raise doubt about the veracity of his semantic knowledge loss. It was also identified as an ideal target for a tailor-made SVT because items could be constructed with ease.

Some examples from the 50-item single-case experimental forced-choice test constructed ad hoc are given in Table 12.6. He scored 18 correct, which is a below-chance performance, signaling with high confidence ($p > 95\%$) that he deliberately chose false responses in order to convince the examiner of the presence of his symptoms. In combination with other sources of information (history, analysis of

Table 12.6. Grimm's Fairy Tale Test: Single-Case Experimental Design in a Case of Claimed Complete Autobiographical and Severe Semantic Memory Loss in a Young Adult of German Origin

Test Item	Alternative 1*	Alternative 2*
Sleeping Beauty slept for . . .	One year	*A hundred years*
She pricked her finger on a . . .	*Weaving loom*	Spindle of a spinning wheel
What was it Little Red Riding Hood took to her grandmother?	*A bottle of wine*	A bottle of juice
Who helped the prince and Cinderella become a couple?	Pigeons	*Mice*
Hänsel and Gretel lost their way in the forest. What was the house built from that they found after a while?	*Emeralds and rubies*	Gingerbread
A guy succeeded in making a very sad princess laugh. He carried . . .	A golden goose	*A magic flute*
There was a princess who could not sleep. What was the cause of it?	A pea under the mattress	*A pearl under the mattress*
Who helped another princess get back her golden ball which had fallen into a well?	*The Lion King*	The Frog Prince

*The responses chosen by the claimant are printed in italics.

plausibility and consistency, evident secondary gain), a malingered neurocognitive disorder was diagnosed with the highest degree of certainty.

FURTHER DEVELOPMENTS AND BEYOND FORCE-CHOICE TESTING

While response patterns below chance continue to be the most powerful indicator of feigned cognitive impairment, their sensitivity is clearly limited; moreover, the procedure can easily be detected even by naïve examinees and it can easily be coached. Given the low objective difficulty of recognition tests with alternative response format, other criteria for diagnosing possible or probable negative response bias were introduced, in particular empirical cutoffs. For example, it is relatively rare for patients with genuine sequelae of brain injury or brain disease to score more than five errors in the second and third trial of the Test of Memory Malingering, as long as the level of cognitive impairment does not reach the level of dementia (e.g., Merten, Bossink, & Schmand, 2007; Teichner & Wagner, 2004). Today, all standardized forced-choice tests rely on empirically established cutoffs.

Also, response patterns at the level of pure chance responding are compatible with a total loss of the function in question, but they would contradict partial functional loss. Table 12.7 lists different degrees of confidence that can be derived from different response patterns in forced-choice testing. As can be seen, clinical decision making is a crucial part of the final interpretation of SVT results. As a consequence, a sound clinical qualification of the expert appears indispensable for a thorough interpretation of deviant test scores if false classifications are to be avoided. This final recourse to a clinical decision-making process may currently be identified as the greatest challenges to SVA (cf. Dandachi-FitzGerald, Merckelbach, & Ponds, 2015). In this vein, Cripe (2002, p. 98) maintained that:

> Reported symptoms and the correlation with a particular disorder requires that the doctor have a thorough knowledge and experience with the disorder in question. . . . The greatest insurance against being deceived by a counterfeit in the diagnostic process is knowing what the genuine looks like.

In the context of the diagnostic criteria for malingered neurocognitive dysfunction (Slick et al., 1999), this final recourse to clinical expertise is formulated as criterion D: "Behaviors. . . [meeting previously defined criteria] . . . are not fully accounted for by Psychiatric, Neurological, or Developmental Factors" (p. 554).

Another important development was the growing interest in what was called embedded validity indicators. These are scores or indices derived from neuropsychological tests. According to Greve and Bianchini (2009), they offer several advantages, such as:

1. An enhancement of the sensitivity of the entire battery of SVTs without requiring extra administration time
2. The provision of direct information about the validity of performance on specific tests
3. Their reduced susceptibility to coaching
4. A potential to evaluate performance validity in the absence of specialized techniques, including the potential for a retrospective evaluation of data sets when no PVTs were employed

Today, embedded indicators are also subsumed under the terms *cognitive SVT* or *PVT*. A more detailed account of embedded validity indicators derived from instruments like the Wechsler intelligence and memory tests, the Wisconsin Card Sorting Test, Raven's Standard Progressive Matrices, the Rey Auditory Verbal Learning Test, the Complex Figure Test and Recognition Trial, etc., can be found in Boone (2007). While embedded measures continue to enjoy great popularity both among test users and researchers, it has to be noted that their classification accuracy usually does not reach that of stand-alone tests, and they may, in fact, be particularly vulnerable to yield false-positive scores in bona-fide patient populations with genuine cognitive impairment (cf. Merten et al., 2007, for a more detailed discussion of this problem). The reason for unacceptably high false-positive rates

Table 12.7. DIFFERENT DEGREES OF CONFIDENCE AS TO THE DIAGNOSIS OF FEIGNING
IN FORCED-CHOICE AND MULTIPLE-CHOICE TESTS

Response Pattern	Certainty Of Diagnosis	Further Procedure/ Recommendation
Response pattern significantly below the threshold of pure guessing (below-chance response pattern)	Definite negative response bias. Highest degree of diagnostic certainty about feigned cognitive impairment.	The remaining risk for a false-positive result is low ($p < 5\%$). With convergent lines of evidence (other test results, inconsistencies and implausibility from other sources of information, etc.) using a multimethod assessment strategy, this remaining risk can usually be reduced to (practically) zero.
Response pattern within the limits of chance responding	Possible negative response bias. The response pattern is compatible with a total functional loss in the modality in question, such as (for the realm of memory) amnestic syndrome or moderate to severe dementia.	A careful analysis of other sources of information (well documented history, medical data, clinical presentation, test profile, activities of daily living) has to be performed to ascertain the presence or absence of a genuine severe neurocognitive disorder (e.g., severe dementia, amnestic syndrome).
Response pattern significantly above chance, but below an empirically established cutoff	Possible negative response bias. The response pattern can be compatible with the presence of genuine cognitive deficits sufficiently severe to interfere significantly with the demand characteristics of the task.	A careful analysis of all available information is necessary to determine the presence or absence of a genuine neurocognitive disorder that may or may not explain failure in one or several symptom validity tests (correct-positive or false-positive classification). This analysis has to be presented in an explicit, strictly logical, evidence-based and convincing way.

in genuine patient populations lies in the fact that neuropsychological tests from which embedded measures are derived were specifically constructed to measure cognitive impairment, and low test scores, often combined with low scores on embedded measures, are expected in patients with true cognitive deficits. This has also been shown in a recent study by Loring et al. (2016) for patients with early Alzheimers's disease and amnestic mild cognitive impairment.

Also, specially developed questionnaire measures play an important role as self-report symptom validity tests, reaching far beyond the traditional measures of the so-called "*F* family" of the MMPI, MMPI-2, or MMPI-RF (e.g., Bolinger,

Reese, Suhr, & Larrabee, 2014; Rogers, Sewell, Martin, & Vitacco, 2003). In particular, the Fake Bad Scale or Symptom Validity Scale (Lees-Haley, English, & Glenn, 1991) and the Response Bias Scale (Gervais, Ben-Porath, Wygant, & Green, 2007) have reached great popularity. The latter scale was specially constructed for forensic neuropsychological or disability assessment settings. Besides several stand-alone questionnaire measures developed to assess distorted symptom reporting (e.g., Widows & Smith, 2005), structured interviews such as the Structured Interview of Reported Symptoms (Rogers, Sewell, & Gillard, 2010) and the Miller Forensic Assessment of Symptoms Test (Miller, 2001) were developed to identify feigning in claimants with psychiatric symptom presentation.

Available base-rate estimates of malingering, feigning, and negative response bias in forensic examinations are diverse, and refer to multiple referral and cultural backgrounds, diagnostic groups, and claimed symptomatology. The basic results of a landmark survey performed by Mittenberg, Patton, Canyock, and Condit (2002) have been confirmed through numerous studies: it is a sizeable, nonnegligible proportion of claimants in forensic neuropsychological examinations who feign, exaggerate, or distort their symptom presentation up to a degree that the examiner will not be able to rely on their test profiles to arrive at valid inferences about cognitive abilities and/or nature and severity of cognitive impairment. In some contexts, the prevalence of claimants with significantly distorted symptom presentation may reach or even exceed the 50% level (e.g., Chafetz, et al., 2007; Schmand et al., 1998; Sullivan, May, & Galbally, 2007). Thus, Ardolf, Denney, and Houston (2007) examined 105 criminal offenders and found a high number of participants with probably and definitely malingered neurocognitive dysfunction (54.3%), applying the criteria of Slick et al. (1999). There is broad evidence today that in forensic psychological contexts, exaggerated symptom presentation and feigning have a higher impact on neuropsychological test scores than the effects of brain injury and other adverse conditions known to influence cognitive functioning (e.g., Green, Rohling, Lees-Haley, & Allen, 2001; Iverson, 2005; Stevens, Friedel, Mehren, & Merten, 2008).

It is beyond the scope of this chapter to give a more complete, comprehensive account of methodological and conceptual developments in the field of psychological SVA, but the reader can resort to a number of textbooks and editorial works summarizing the most important aspects (e.g., Boone, 2007, 2013; Larrabee, 2005, 2007; Morgan & Sweet, 2009; Rogers, 2008; Young, 2014; both Carone & Bush, 2013, and Reynolds & Horton, 2012, with special emphasis on traumatic brain injury; Morel, 2010, on posttraumatic stress disorder; and Chafetz, 2015, on intellectual disability issues). The results of surveys on current symptom validity test use and other important issues of diagnostic practice where possible feigning is an issue were published by Martin et al. (2015) for North American neuropsychologists, and Dandachi-FitzGerald et al. (2013) for a number of European countries. An account on European developments that have long been lagging behind American standards was given by Merten, Dandachi-FitzGerald, Hall, Schmand, Santamaría, & González-Ordi (2013).

CONCLUSION

Malingering research and symptom validity assessment can be considered as a success story of forensic neuropsychology, with no other subdiscipline of medical or psychological sciences contributing more to methodological and conceptual progress in this field. Response validity and test effort in forensic evaluations cannot be taken at face value. The purely clinical judgment of experts as to response validity has repeatedly been shown to be unreliable. Today, most forensic neuropsychology experts would agree that neuropsychological testing has to be understood as incomplete if not adequately checked for possible distortions (e.g., Bush et al., 2005; Heilbronner et al., 2009). With the state of the art currently reached, SVA renders diagnostic decision making regarding the validity of individual test profiles and possible response bias more reliable than any other method known to date. Positive results of SVA indicate that a claimant's test profile is probably uninterpretable, but it does not inform the examiner about the cause of this failure. As SVT failure may occur in cooperative patients with authentic neurocognitive or mental impairment (false-positive results), a careful analysis of consistency and plausibility is indispensable, imposing high demands on the expert's clinical qualification. The determination of feigning and malingering requires the expert to draw inferences about the degree of intentionality of distorted symptom presentation and the underlying motivation. In this respect, below-chance response patterns in forced-choice tests, either standardized or tailor-made, are of prime importance in that they signal deliberate attempts to deceit the examiner. The special place of SVTs as a fully evidence-based approach of forensic experts was underlined by Chafetz (2015, p. 20) when he wrote: "It is difficult if not impossible to determine if someone is malingering without full assessment of symptom and performance validity."

However, it has to be kept in mind that uncooperativeness in forensic exams with resulting uninterpretable test profiles may also result from other sources than feigning, such as anger, boredom, or nonconformity. Moreover, invalid test profiles that may also occur in the context of a genuine mental disorder should never be misclassified as feigning, but the presence of a mental disorder does not exclude deliberate symptom distortion in an attempt to achieve a significant secondary gain.

REFERENCES

Allen, L. M., Conder, R. L., Green, P., & Cox, D. R. (1997). *CARB '97 manual for the computerized assessment of response bias.* Durham, NC: CogniSyst.

American Psychiatric Association. (1995). *Diagnostic and statistical manual of mental disorders* (4th ed). International version with ICD-10 codes. Washington, DC: Author.

American Psychiatric Association. (2013). *Diagnostic and statistical manual of mental disorders* (5th ed). Washington, DC: Author.

Ardolf, B. R., Denney, R. L., & Houston, C. M. (2007). Base rates of negative response bias and malingered neurocognitive dysfunction among criminal defendants referred for neuropsychological evaluation. *The Clinical Neuropsychologist, 21,* 899–916.

Bass, C., & Halligan, P. (2014). Factitious disorders and malingering: Challenges for clinical assessment and management. *Lancet*, *383*, 1422–1432.

Berry, D. T. R., & Nelson, N. W. (2010). DSM-5 and malingering: A modest proposal. *Psychological Injury and Law*, *3*, 295–303.

Blaskewitz, N. (in press). Rey Fifteen-Item Test (FIT), auch: Rey Memory Test (RMT). In D. Schellig, D. Heinemann, B. Schächtele, & W. Sturm (Eds.), *Handbuch neuropsychologischer Testverfahren, Band 2* [Handbook of neuropsychological tests, 2nd volume]. Göttingen, Germany: Hogrefe.

Bolinger, E., Reese, C., Suhr, J., & Larrabee, G. J. (2014). Susceptibility of the MMPI-2-RF Neurological Complaints and Cognitive Complaints scales to over-reporting in simulated head injury. *Archives of Clinical Neuropsychology*, *29*, 7–15.

Boone, K. B. (Ed.) (2007). *Assessment of feigned cognitive impairment: A neuropsychological perspective.* New York: Guilford.

Boone, K. B. (2013). *Clinical practice of forensic neuropsychology: An evidence-based approach.* New York: Guilford.

Brandt, J., Rubinsky, E., & Lassen, G. (1985). Uncovering malingered amnesia. *Annals of the New York Academy of Sciences*, *444*, 502–503.

Bush, S. S., Ruff, R. M., Tröster, A. I., Barth, J. T., Koffler, S. P., Pliskin, N. H., Reynolds, C. R., & Silver, C. H. (2005), Symptom validity assessment: Practice issues and medical necessity. Official position of the National Academy of Neuropsychology. *Archives of Clinical Neuropsychology*, *20*, 419–426.

Carone, D. A., & Bush, S. S. (Eds.) (2013). *Mild traumatic brain injury: Symptom validity assessment and malingering,* New York: Springer.

Chafetz, M. (2015). *Intellectual disability. Civil and criminal forensic issues.* New York: Oxford University Press.

Chafetz, M. D., Abrahams, J. P., & Kohlmaier, J. (2007). Malingering on the Social Security Disability Consultative Exam: A new rating scale. *Archives of Clinical Neuropsychology*, *22*, 1–14.

Cripe, L. I. (2002). Malady vs. malingering: A tricky endeavor. In N. D. Zasler & M. F. Martelli (Eds.), *Functional medical disorders: State of the art reviews in physical medicine and rehabilitation* (pp. 95–112). New York: Hanley and Belfus.

Dandachi-FitzGerald, B., Merckelbach, H., & Ponds, R. (June, 2015). *Prediction of SVT performance & professional communication of SVT failure.* Paper read at the Fourth European Symposium on Symptom Validity Assessment. Maastricht, NL.

Dandachi-FitzGerald, B., Ponds, R. W. H. M., & Merten, T. (2013). Symptom validity and neuropsychological assessment: A survey of practices and beliefs of neuropsychologists in six European countries. *Archives of Clinical Neuropsychology*, *28*, 771–783.

Denney, R. L. (1996). Symptom validity testing of remote memory in a criminal forensic setting. *Archives of Clinical Neuropsychology*, *11*, 589–603.

Denney. R. L. (2009). Evaluating competency to stand trial and sanity in the face of marked amnesia and claimed psychosis. In J. E. Morgan & J. J. Sweet (Eds.), *Neuropsychology of malingering casebook* (pp. 413–427). Hove, UK: Psychology Press.

Douglas-Hamilton, J. (2016). *The truth about Rudolf Hess.* Barnsley, UK: Frontline Books.

Eisendrath, S. J. (1995). Psychiatric aspects of chronic pain. *Neurology*, *45*, S26–S34.

Frederick, R. I. (2002). A review of Rey's strategies for detecting malingered neuropsychological impairment. *Journal of Forensic Neuropsychology*, *2*, 1–25.

Frederick, R. I., Carter, M., & Powel, J. (1995). Adapting symptom validity testing to evaluate suspicious complaints of amnesia in medicolegal evaluations. *Bulletin of the American Academy of Psychiatry and the Law, 23,* 231–237.

Frederick, R. I., & Speed, F. M. (2007). On the interpretation of below-chance responding in forced-choice tests. *Assessment, 14,* 3–11.

Gervais, R. O., Ben-Porath, Y. S., Wygant, D. B., & Green, P. (2007). Development and validation of a Response Bias Scale (RBS) for the MMPI-2. *Assessment, 14,* 196–208.

Giger, P., Merten, T., & Merckelbach, H. (2012). Tatbezogene Amnesien—authentisch oder vorgetäuscht? [Crime-related amnesia: Real or feigned?] *Fortschritte der Neurologie und Psychiatrie, 80,* 368–381.

Giger, P., Merten, T., Merckelbach, H., & Oswald, M. (2010). Detection of feigned crime-related amnesia: A multi-method approach. *Journal of Forensic Psychology Practice, 10,* 140–163.

Gilbert, G. M. (1947). *Nuremberg diary.* New York: Farrar, Straus and Co.

Green, P. (2003). *Green's Word Memory Test.* User's Manual. Edmonton, Canada: Green's Publishing.

Green, P. (2004). *Green's Medical Symptom Validity Test (MSVT) for Microsoft Windows.* User's Manual. Edmonton, Canada: Green's Publishing.

Green, P. (2008). *Green's Non-Verbal Medical Symptom Validity Test (NV-MSVT) for Microsoft Windows.* User's Manual 1.0. Edmonton, Canada: Green's Publishing.

Green, P., Rohling, M. L., Lees-Haley, P. R., & Allen, L. M. (2001). Effort has a greater effect on test scores than severe brain injury in compensation claimants. *Brain Injury, 15,* 1045–1060.

Greve, K. W., & Bianchini, K. J. (2009). Schmerz und Beschwerdenvalidierung [Pain and symptom validity assessment]. In T. Merten & H. Dettenborn (Eds.), *Diagnostik der Beschwerdenvalidität* [Symptom validity assessment] (pp. 193–229). Berlin: Deutscher Psychologen Verlag.

Gubbay, J. (n.d.). *Guidelines for 1-In-5 Test.* Unpublished Manuscript. Sydney, Australia.

Hartman, D. E. (2002). The unexamined lie is a lie worth fibbing. Neuropsychological malingering and the Word Memory Test. *Archives of Clinical Neuropsychology, 17,* 709–714.

Hartwig, M., & Bond, C. F. (2011). Why do lie-catchers fail? A lens model meta-analysis of human lie judgments. *Psychological Bulletin, 137,* 643–659.

Harvey, M. (2002). Neuropsychological assessment of individuals with dual diagnosis. *The NADD Bulletin, 5,* 22–26.

Heaton, R. K., Smith, H. H., Lehman, R. A. W., & Vogt, A. T. (1978). Prospects for faking believable deficits on neuropsychological testing. *Journal of Consulting and Clinical Psychology, 46,* 892–900.

Heilbronner, R. L., Sweet, J. J., Morgan, J. E., Larrabee, G. J., Millis, S. R., & Conference Participants (2009). American Academy of Clinical Neuropsychology consensus conference statement on the neuropsychological assessment of effort, response bias, and malingering. *The Clinical Neuropsychologist, 23,* 1093–1129.

Hiscock, M., & Hiscock, D. (1989). Refining the forced-choice method for the detection of malingering. *Journal of Clinical and Experimental Neuropsychology, 11,* 967–974.

Iverson, G. L. (2003). Detecting malingering in civil forensic evaluations. In: A. M. Horton & L. C. Hartlage (Eds.), *Handbook of forensic neuropsychology* (pp. 137–177). New York: Springer.

Iverson, G. L. (2005). Outcome from mild traumatic brain injury. *Current Opinion in Psychiatry, 18,* 301–317.

Jelicic, M., & Merckelbach, H. (2007). Evaluating the authenticity of crime-related amnesia. In S. A. Christianson (Ed.), *Offenders' memories of violent crimes* (pp. 215–233). Chichester, UK: Wiley.

Jelicic, M., Merckelbach, H., & van Bergen, S. (2004). Symptom validity testing of feigned amnesia for a mock crime. *Archives of Clinical Neuropsychology, 19,* 525–531.

Kapur, N. (1994). The Coin-in-the-Hand Test: A new "bedside" test for the detection of malingering in patients with suspected memory disorder. *Journal of Neurology, Neurosurgery and Psychiatry, 57,* 385–386.

Larrabee, G. J. (2004). Differential diagnosis of mild head injury. In J. H. Ricker (Ed.), *Differential diagnosis in adult neuropsychological assessment* (pp. 243–275). New York: Springer.

Larrabee, G. J. (Ed.) (2005). *Forensic neuropsychology: A scientific approach.* New York: Oxford University Press.

Larrabee, G. J. (Ed.) (2007). *Assessment of malingered neuropsychological deficits.* Oxford: Oxford University Press.

Larrabee, G. J. (2012). Performance validity and symptom validity in neuropsychological assessment. *Journal of the International Neuropsychological Society, 18,* 625–631.

Lees-Haley, P. R., English, L. T., & Glenn, W. J. (1991). A Fake Bad Scale on the MMPI-2 for personal injury claimants. *Psychological Reports, 68,* 208–210.

Loring, D. W., Goldstein, F. C., Chen, C., Drane, D. L., Lah, J. J., Zhao, L, & Larrabee, G. J. (2016). False-positive error rates for Reliable Digit Span and Auditory Verbal Learning Test performance validity measures in amnestic mild cognitive impairment and early Alzheimer disease. *Archives of Clinical Neuropsychology, 31,* 313–331.

Loewer, H. D., & Ulrich, K. (1971). Eine Alternativ-Wahl-Form des Benton-Testes zur besseren Erfassung von Aggravation und Simulation [A forced-choice version of the Visual Retention Test for improved assessment of malingering]. In E. Duhm (Ed.), *Praxis der klinischen Psychologie,* Band 2 [The practice of clinical psychology, volume 2] (pp. 63–75). Göttingen, Germany: Hogrefe.

Martin, P. K., Schroeder, R. W., & Odland, A. P. (2015). Neuropsychologists' validity testing beliefs and practices: A survey on North American professionals. *The Clinical Neuropsychologist, 29,* 741–776.

McCaffrey, R. J., Williams, A. D., Fisher, J. M., & Laing, L. C. (1997). *The practice of forensic neuropsychology: Meeting challenges in the courtroom.* New York: Plenum Press.

Merten, T., Bossink, L., & Schmand, B. (2007). On the limits of effort testing: Symptom validity tests and severity of neurocognitive symptoms in nonlitigant patients. *Journal of Clinical and Experimental Neuropsychology, 29,* 308–318.

Merten, T., Dandachi-FitzGerald, B., Hall, V., Schmand, B.A., Santamaría, P., & González-Ordi, H. (2013). Symptom validity assessment in European countries: Development and state of the art. *Clínica y Salud, 24,* 129–138.

Merten, T., & Merckelbach, H. (2013a). Symptom validity testing in somatoform and dissociative disorders: A critical review. *Psychological Injury and Law, 6,* 122–137.

Merten, T., & Merckelbach, H. (2013b). Forced-choice tests as single-case experiments in the differential diagnosis of intentional symptom distortion. *Journal of Experimental Psychopathology, 4,* 20–37.

Miller, H. A. (2001). *Miller-Forensic Assessment of Symptoms Test*. Professional manual. Odessa, FL: Psychological Assessment Resources.

Millis, S. R. (1992). The Recognition Memory Test in the detection of malingered and exaggerated memory deficits. *The Clinical Neuropsychologist, 6*, 406–414.

Mittenberg, W., Patton, C., Canyock, E. M., & Condit, D. C. (2002). Base rates of malingering and symptom exaggeration. *Journal of Clinical and Experimental Neuropsychology, 24*, 1094–1102.

Morel, K. R. (2010). *Differential diagnosis of malingering versus posttraumatic stress disorder: Scientific rationale and objective scientific methods*. New York: Novinka Books.

Morgan, J. E., & Sweet, J. J. (Eds.) (2009). *Neuropsychology of malingering casebook*. Hove, UK: Psychology Press.

Pankratz, L. (1983). A new technique for the assessment and modification of feigned memory deficit. *Perceptual and Motor Skills, 57*, 367–372

Resnick, P. J., West, S., & Payne, J. W. (2008). Malingering of posttraumatic stress disorder. In R. Rogers (Ed.), *Clinical assessment of malingering and deception* (3rd ed., pp. 109–127). New York: Guilford.

Reuben, M., Mitchell, A. J., Howlett, S. J., Crimlisk, H. L., & Grünewald, R. A. (2005). Functional symptoms in neurology: Questions and answers. *Journal of Neurology, Neurosurgery, and Psychiatry, 76*, 307–314.

Rey, A. (1941). L'examen psychologique dans les cas d'encéphalopathie traumatique [The psychological examination in cases of traumatic encephalopathy]. *Archives de Psychologie, 28*, 286–340.

Rey, A. (1958). L'examen clinique en psychologie [The clinical examination in psychology]. Paris: Presses Universitaires de France.

Reynolds, C. R., & Horton, A. M. (Eds.). (2012). *Detection of malingering during head injury litigation* (2nd ed.). New York: Springer.

Rogers, R. (Ed.) (2008*). Clinical assessment of malingering and deception* (3rd ed.). New York: Guilford.

Rogers, R., Harrell, E. H., & Liff, C. D. (1993). Feigning neuropsychological impairment: A critical review of methodological and clinical considerations. *Clinical Psychology Review, 13*, 255–275.

Rogers, R., Sewell, K. W., & Gillard, N. D. (2010). *Structured Interview of Reported Symptoms* (2nd ed., SIRS-2). Professional Manual. Lutz, FL: Psychological Assessment Resources.

Rogers, R., Sewell, K. W., Martin, M. A., & Vitacco, M. J. (2003). Detection of feigned mental disorders: A meta-analysis of the MMPI-2 and malingering. *Assessment, 10*, 160–177.

Schmand, B., & Lindeboom, J. (2005). *Amsterdam Short-Term Memory Test— Amsterdamer Kurzzeitgedächtnistest*. Manual—Handanweisung. Leiden, NL: PITS.

Schmand, B., Lindeboom, J., Schagen, Heijt, R., Koene, T., & Hamburger, H. L. S. (1998). Cognitive complaints in patients after whiplash injury: The impact of malingering. *Journal of Neurology, Neurosurgery, and Psychiatry, 64*, 339–343.

Schmidtke, K., & Vollmer-Schmolck, H. (1999). Autobiographisches Altgedächtnisinterview und semantisches Altgedächtnisinventar [Autobiographical memory interview and the semantic memory test]. *Zeitschrift für Neuropsychologie, 10*, 13–23.

Shaw, D. J., Vrij, A., Mann, S., Leal, S., & Hillman, J. (2014). The guilty adjustment: Response trends on the symptom validity test. *Legal and Criminological Psychology*, *19*, 240–254.

Slick, D., Hopp G., Strauss E., & Thompson, G. B. (1997). *Victoria Symptom Validity Test version 1.0 professional manual*. Odessa, FL: Psychological Assessment Resources.

Slick, D. J., Sherman E. M., & Iverson, G. L. (1999). Diagnostic criteria for malingered neurocognitive dysfunction: Proposed standards for clinical practice and research. *The Clinical Neuropsychologist*, *13*, 545–561.

Stevens, A., Friedel, E., Mehren, G., & Merten, T. (2008). Malingering and uncooperativeness in psychiatric and psychological assessment: Prevalence and effects in a German sample of claimants. *Psychiatry Research*, *157*, 191–200.

Sullivan, B. K., May, K., & Galbally, L. (2007). Symptom exaggeration by college adults in attention-deficit hyperactivity disorder and learning disorder assessments. *Applied Neuropsychology*, *14*, 189–207.

Sweet, J. J., & Guidotti Breting, L. M. (2013). Symptom validity test research: Status and clinical implications. *Journal of Experimental Psychopathology*, *4*, 6–19.

Teichner, G., & Wagner, M. T. (2004). The Test of Memory Malingering (TOMM): Normative data from cognitively intact, cognitively impaired, and elderly patients with dementia. *Archives of Clinical Neuropsychology*, *19*, 455–464.

Tombaugh, T. N. (1996). *Test of Memory Malingering (TOMM)*. North Tonawanda, NY: Multi-Health Systems.

Tydecks, S., Merten, T., & Gubbay, J. (2006). The Word Memory Test and the One-in-Five-Test in an analogue study with Russian-speaking participants. *International Journal of Forensic Psychology*, *1* (3), 29–37.

van Oorsouw, K., & Merckelbach, H. (2006). Simulating amnesia and memories of a mock crime. *Psychology, Crime & Law*, *12*, 261–271.

Vrij, A. (2008). *Detecting lies and deceit: Pitfalls and opportunities* (2nd ed.). Chichester, UK: Wiley.

Warrington, E. K. (1984). *Recognition memory test*. Manual. Berkshire, UK: NFER-Nelson.

Widows, M. R., & Smith, G. P. (2005). *SIMS—Structured inventory of malingered symptomatology*. Professional Manual. Lutz, FL: Psychological Assessment Resources.

Young, G. (2014). *Malingering, feigning, and response bias in psychiatric/psychological injury: Implications for practice and court*. Dordrecht, NL: Springer.

Index

Note: Page numbers followed by 'f' and 't' refers to figures and tables